ABSOLUTE POWER

Arcturus Publishing Limited
26/27 Bickels Yard
151–153 Bermondsey Street
London SE1 3HA

Published in association with
foulsham
W. Foulsham & Co. Ltd,
The Publishing House, Bennetts Close, Cippenham,
Slough, Berkshire SL1 5AP, England

ISBN-13: 978-0-572-03229-6
ISBN-10: 0-572-03229-3

This edition printed in 2006

British Library Cataloguing-in-Publication Data: a catalogue record for this book is available from the British Library

Cover image: Ivan the Terrible © Corbis UK
Illustrations by Barrington Barber

Printed in Finland

ABSOLUTE POWER

The Real Lives of Europe's Most Infamous Rulers

C.S. Denton

Acknowledgements

In the two long years this book was both a job and an obsession, many people offered me their advice and support. First I would like to thank the staff at the Alderman Library at the University of Virginia. Without their assistance and the resources there, my research simply wouldn't have made it very far. Also I thank Bruce Gordon, webmaster of 'Regnal Chronologies' (http://www.hostkingdom.net/regindex.html), and Mariusz Pazdziora's 'Sovereigns, Kingdoms and Royal Landmarks of Europe' (http://homepage.mac.com/crowns/) for providing invaluable resources of information on dates and burial sites.

Then there are my friends who provided both moral support and editorial insights: Michelle Branco, Matt Michaels, Lauren Martella, Keith Barber, Brad and Jennifer Medas, Sarah Rose-Jensen, Andre Bennett, Michael Rash, Sarah Warden, Suzanne Grub and Nathan Shumate.

Contents

ROME . . . 1
Tarquin 'The Proud' . . . 2
Tiberius . . . 8
Caligula . . . 24
Nero . . . 40
Domitian . . . 54
Commodus . . . 60
Caracalla . . . 66
Elagabalus . . . 69
IBERIA . . . 75
Egica . . . 76
Abdallah Ibn Muhammad . . . 79
Muhammad III . . . 82
Pedro IV 'The Ceremonious' . . . 85
Pedro I 'The Cruel' . . . 89
Juana 'The Mad' . . . 95
Sebastian . . . 108
Don Carlos . . . 114
Afonso VI . . . 119
Carlos II . . . 122
Philip V . . . 129
Fernando VI . . . 135
Maria I . . . 138
FRANCE . . . 143
Fredegund . . . 144
Charles VI . . . 150
Catherine de' Medici . . . 156
Henri III . . . 173
Louis XVI . . . 177
Napoleon . . . 195
THE BRITISH ISLES . . . 225
Maelgwyn (Maglocunus, Malgo) 'The Tall' . . . 226
Ethelred II 'The Unready' . . . 228
Macbeth . . . 232
William II 'Rufus' . . . 234
Stephen . . . 237
John . . . 241
Edward II . . . 252
Robert III . . . 258
Richard II . . . 261
Henry VI . . . 267
Richard III . . . 277

Henry VIII 286
'Bloody' Mary I 302
George III 319
SCANDINAVIA 333
Erik 'Bloodaxe' 334
Harald IV 'Gilchrist' 337
Christian II 341
Erik XIV 347
Christian VII 352
GERMANY AND AUSTRIA 365
Wenceslas (Wenzel or Václav) 'The Drunkard' 366
Rudolf II 370
Friedrich Wilhelm I 375
Ferdinand 383
Ludwig II 387
ITALY 399
Giovanna I 400
Cesare Borgia 406
Lucrezia Borgia 421
Cosimo III 434
Gian Gastone 441
HUNGARY AND THE BALKANS 448
Vlad III 'The Impaler' 449
Elizabeth Bathory 457
Gabor Bathory 465
Alexander Obrenovic V 468
THE BYZANTINE AND OTTOMAN EMPIRES 472
Phokas 473
Justinian II 477
Irene 485
Constantine VIII 492
Mustafa I 496
Murad IV 500
Ibrahim 503
Abdul Aziz 508
RUSSIA 514
Sviatopolk 'The Accursed' 515
Ivan IV 'The Terrible' 518
Fyodor I 'The Sanctified Tsar' 529
Peter I 'The Great' 532
Anna 544
Peter III 550
Paul 560
Nicholas II 568
Index . . . . .

Introduction

Throughout the history of Europe, all monarchs who had any real degree of power have lived with that strange dichotomy of simultaneously being human and more than human. Absolute kingship was perhaps the most unique condition into which any human being could have been born. Imagine a life with seemingly no limits on your freedom or your wealth, where honest friends are hard to find but flattering sycophants are everywhere, where you are raised from birth to believe that you embody the voice of God and the nation, and day to day live with the knowledge that anyone could turn into a traitor and at any time take your crown and your life. Under this strange life and its all too dangerous pressures, it is possible that being conditioned to rule as king, queen, or emperor was itself a cause of mental illness and all monarchs were, in their own ways, mad. After all, even the 'good' monarchs had their dark sides. Queen Elizabeth I of England nearly strangled one of her ladies-in-waiting, whose only crime was marrying without her explicit permission. Constantine the Great, celebrated for being the first Christian Emperor of Rome, ordered the execution of his own son and, later, his wife. Isabel and Fernando of Spain, besides being connected with the infamous Spanish Inquisition, exiled thousands of Jews from the country, and rebuked the Pope himself when he gave some of the expatriates refuge in papal lands. But what about the monarchs whose lives are detailed in this book?

The monarchs mentioned above were not only successful rulers, but also talented figureheads. They knew what their societies expected from them and met those demands brilliantly, making themselves into legendary figures in their own time. Today we tend to look at such a monarch as a dictator of sorts, but occupying the top of the political hierarchy was only one aspect of the role. As strange as it may seem to us in this democratic age, the core duty of a monarch was to serve as a representative of the people, a sacred duty passed directly from the hand of God. For example, in the peasant villages of Russia, the Tsar was often called in *Batiushka*, literally 'the Father of the Russian people', up until the twentieth century.

What unites all the figures in this book is that they had badly disappointed the high, semi-divine hopes placed on them and, because of that, they have been judged by history as a bizarre curiosity, a living catastrophe, or both. A few, such as George III, might have been well-remembered or unremarkable if not for some mental illness or psychological nightmare that transformed them into novelties. Some, like Louis XVI, were unfairly written off as tyrannical or depraved villains by propaganda, and then there were some, like Caligula, who might have rightfully earned their reputations, exaggerated as they were. Finally, there are the ones celebrated as great men and denounced as monsters in equal proportion, sometimes in the same breath, like Peter the Great or Henry VIII. All were carried away, or even overwhelmed, by their exalted status . A few were driven completely mad by it.

The great age of the European monarchs came to a halt in the opening decades of the twentieth century with the 'Great War'. If the Second World War was the bloody birth of the modern world, the First World War brought with it the dying convulsions of the old. During the course of the war, the last great dynasties of Europe – the Hohenzollerns of Germany, the Romanovs of Russia, and the Habsburgs of Austria–Hungary – were swept away while the empires of the Ottomans, the Russians, the Germans and the Austrians were dismantled, leaving in their ruins what was quite literally a new world order.

There are, of course, still kings, queens, princesses, and princes in Europe; not only in Great Britain, but also in Norway, Spain, Denmark, the Netherlands, Belgium and Sweden, not counting smaller principalities. Yet very few monarchies today serve much more than a ceremonial role (although the Prince of the small

European state of Liechtenstein recently, as of this writing, assumed considerable political power). In our time, when monarchies seem little more than tourist curiosities and democracy is taken for granted, it is easy to look at the old great monarchs as living lives out of a fantasy book, completely detached from our world and our ancestors, and it is easier to forget that for nearly two thousand years monarchy was almost the only form of government acceptable, if not imaginable, across Europe and the world. Compared to that record, democracy in Europe – and elsewhere – seems like only a sudden fad.

As extravagant as the personalities of rulers such as Catherine de' Medici or Ivan the Terrible may seem, they are far from unreal, but have sprung from the condition of being born or raised to a position from where they were expected to steer the fates of entire nations. These people, either through their own actions or through circumstances beyond even their control, were all condemned by the history books. In our era it is hard to imagine what it would be like to have been a prince, a king, or an emperor during the apex of monarchy, but something of our own selves can be seen in these otherwise legendary figures. Although history would have us look at them as gods, monsters or both, in the final analysis they were simply people, after all.

Chad Denton
Virginia
December 30, 2003

For Cynthia Kelley

and

Theresa Kennedy

ROME

TARQUIN 'THE PROUD'

Reign: *534–510 BC*

Even 219 years after the legendary founding of Rome by Romulus and his entourage of thugs and outcasts, the city still had much to endure before its glory days would come around. In the sixth century BC, the city that would crown an empire spreading from the Atlantic Ocean to the Caspian Sea was itself under the boot of the Etruscan people. Only bits and pieces about the long extinct Etruscan civilization are known, because once Rome found itself in power, the vindictive Roman people would demand nothing less than the complete obliteration of even the memory of their former conquerors.

If one can trust the legends (and no one does), Rome had seven kings from its founding to the establishment of the Republic. The last of these kings came from the Tarquins, a family of wealthy Etruscans who came to power in a Rome which was a far cry from the thriving metropolis it would become. Through the Tarquins, the Etruscan people contributed much to Rome's development, furnishing the emerging city with paved streets, stone houses, a sewage system, an alphabet (itself derived from the Greeks), and the other traits of a healthy young civilization. Even with all the perks from this relationship, the Romans despised the ostentatious culture of the Etruscans that contrasted so jarringly with their own austere ways. It was not unlike the love/hate-but-take relationship the Romans would develop with the similarly extravagant Greeks over the centuries.

Our subject, Lucius Tarquin the Proud, would not only be the last Etruscan to rule Rome, but also the last king of Rome (unless one counts the Roman Emperors, but the Romans themselves would have taken issue with that). It is difficult to get a firm grasp on Lucius's character, assuming he actually existed, since he was so ensnared by Roman patriotic legends he might as well be a one-dimensional fictional villain: cartoonishly cruel and stupid. Secretly, so the stories go, Lucius loathed his uncle, father-in-law and predecessor Servius, a king cherished by the people for his generosity, and it never did occur to him that murdering the popular Servius and seizing his throne would earn him little love from the populace.

Perhaps, though, the blame is not entirely Lucius's, and he was indeed only a pawn in a larger game, as the first-century AD Roman historian Livy suggests. The aristocrats in the Senate of Rome did anything but approve of Servius's generous concessions of land and wartime booty to the plebeians, the poorer citizens of Rome, and Lucius volunteered to be the Senate's advocate against the king. Livy writes that Lucius was also egged on by Servius's daughter, his mistress Tullia, an ambitious woman who, like all ambitious women in Roman historical records, was absolutely irredeemable. The little inconvenient fact that Tullia was already married, to Lucius's brother, and that Lucius himself was married to Tullia's sister had not kept them from furthering their love affair. Before too long, the freshly poisoned corpses of their respective spouses paved Lucius's and Tullia's path to marriage.

When the time was ripe for a coup, Lucius, with the comfort of being backed by a band of well-armed mercenaries, crowned himself the new king. When Servius got wind of Lucius's sudden declaration, he confronted his presumptuous nephew in front of the meeting place of the Senate. According to the legend, Lucius then grabbed the elderly Servius and hurled him down into the streets where his mercenaries murdered the elderly monarch. With pure dramatic flair, Livy finishes his account of the murder with Tullia driving a carriage over her own father's still warm body.

Although the new regime had a fiendishly theatrical start, it came out of the gate stumbling. The plebeians hated Lucius because he was the one responsible for the death of their beloved benefactor, which was to be expected, but the Senate also hated him because he did not bother allowing them the traditional courtesy of 'approving' his assumption of power. What did it matter that it would have been a completely empty gesture? Lucius's response to this overwhelming resentment should come as no surprise: he had as many of his critics permanently silenced as possible. Even the senators who were once his supporters during Servius's reign were not immune. Not only did Lucius have many of them executed on trumped-up charges of treason, he refused to allow anyone new to be enrolled into the Senate to replace them.

Although his temper seems to have been dangerously impulsive, Lucius is also credited in the legends with occasional flashes of cleverness. At war with a neighboring tribe, the Galbi, Livy claims that Lucius staged a violent argument with his youngest son Sextus at a camp within full sight of the enemy. Afterwards Sextus pretended to sneak out of Rome and went crying to the Galbi chieftains, claiming to be willing to defect to his father's enemies for the sake of revenge.

Sextus rose to prominence as a general for the enemy, even leading them on devastating raids against Roman territory, but after receiving a secret sign from his father, Sextus used the trust and fame he had gained to assassinate the enemy leaders or turn them against each other.

Lucius's intelligence or lack thereof is also the topic of a well-known anecdote. The Sybil, a Roman oracle, came one morning to Tarquin, offering nine books containing prophetic wisdom for a high price. Unwilling, but not unable, to pay, the king rudely turned her away. Days later the Sybil came back again, this time with six books. When the king asked what had happened to the other three books, the Sybil curtly replied, 'I burned them'. She offered the remaining books to him, but for the same price as before. Now more than a little irked, he still refused. The Sibyl eventually returned again, claiming she had burnt three more of the books and the price for them was unchanged from before. This time, even 'the Proud' relented, although one version of the tale says he did so only under the advice of Tullia.

A clue that this legend was only a fabrication is that Lucius Tarquin did not get any wiser regarding his family's future. He had no warning, otherworldly or otherwise, that the Roman people would eventually rise up against him, drive him and his family out of the city and establish a new form of government, the Republic. What was the straw that finally broke even the Romans' stoic backs? The whole truth is buried deeply under one of the most well-known Roman legends, the patriotic tragedy of Lucretia.

Lucretia was a virtuous woman in the old Roman fashion, mostly meaning that she was utterly obedient to her husband, Lucius Collatinus, a nephew of Tarquin's. One day Collatinus made a hefty bet with his cousin, the aforementioned prince Sextus, that Lucretia was more trustworthy than Sextus's own wife and to prove it the two men would come home to their spouses while they were supposed to be away from Rome. That evening, Sextus rushed home to find his wife being a bit too friendly with some men at a party she was hosting without his permission. Lucretia, on the other hand, was as dutiful as ever, sitting at home patiently waiting for the return of her husband. Humiliated and now lacking a substantial amount of money, Sextus attempted to seduce Lucretia in order to discredit her and get back at Sextus. When she would not relent to his charisma, Sextus flew into a rage and raped her. Lucretia soon after gathered together her husband and father, in tears explained what had been done to her, then stabbed herself through the heart with a knife. In the eyes of the Romans who would proudly repeat this fable through the generations, Lucretia's suicide was not merely a tragedy, but an act of selfless heroism, a sacrifice for the sake of the Roman ideal of honor. Taking advantage of the outrage caused by Lucretia's rape and suicide, Lucius Junius Brutus, the son of the brother the king had killed in order to marry Tullia, encouraged the Senate and the people to rise up against the Tarquins. Brutus had long been sick of the Tarquins and had protected himself from suspicion by pretending to be an idiot, thus earning himself the scornful name of 'Brutus'. Now at last, with the help of Collatinus, he could abandon his charade and strike down his father's killer. Lucius Tarquin happened to be away from Rome at the time of Brutus' insurrection, and though he sped back as swiftly as possible, it was far too late. Lucius Tarquin and his family (with the exception of Brutus and Collatinus, of course) were forced into exile. Most of the Tarquins went to Etruria, the Etruscan country from which their own ancestors had come to rule Rome long ago. Sextus, however, ended up in the hands of the Galbi he had once betrayed. Needless to say, those hands were not kind ones.

Although stories claim that Lucius made a few doomed attempts to reclaim Rome, perhaps he and his clan were relieved in the end to be rid of the responsibility of dealing with those troublesome Romans. In the meantime the Republic the Romans had created to replace their monarchy would last from 509 to 32 BC (although it would not always remain free from tyrants of its own), ending officially when one man, Octavian Caesar, would be christened

Augustus and declared *princeps*, or 'first among equals', by a humbled Senate. Even after all those centuries, the Roman hatred for Lucius Tarquin, whether or not he was ever flesh and blood, was still so fresh that Augustus was careful to avoid having the Latin word for king, *rex*, applied to him. Such tact notwithstanding, that was essentially what Augustus and his successors were: the new kings of Rome.

Further Reading

Cassius Dio (trans. Earnest Carey), *History of Rome*: Book II (Harvard University Press, 1924)

Dyer, Thomas Henry *The History of the Kings of Rome* (Kennikat Press, 1971)

Franzero, Charles Marie *The Life and Times of Tarquin the Etruscan* (A. Redman, 1960)

Livy *Ab Urbe Condita*: Book I (Harvard University Press, 1967)

TIBERIUS

Reign: *September 18, AD 14–March 16, AD 37*
Born: *November 16, 42 BC*
Died: *March 16, AD 37*
Buried: *Mausoleum of Augustus*

If Tiberius had nothing else, he had the benefit of birth. Through both of his parents, Livia Drusilla and the elder Tiberius, he was linked by blood to the aristocratic Claudian family, a hot-blooded clan that spawned some renowned and notorious figures throughout the long years of the Republic. It was probably the pride that came with this blue blood that drove Tiberius's parents to get into so much trouble during his earliest years. Although the elder Tiberius did support Julius Caesar during the civil wars that ultimately dealt a death blow to the Roman Republic, he later changed his mind for an unknown

reason and threw his lot in with Caesar's killers. After that turned out to be a dead end, he was blacklisted by the 'Second Triumvirate'[1], which included Julius Caesar's grandnephew and heir, Octavian, the future Emperor Augustus. With their two-year-old son Tiberius, the small family barely escaped Rome with their lives and had to hide out from Octavian's soldiers while waiting for a chance to sail away from Italy. According to the Roman biographer Suetonius, writing over a century later, the couple were almost given away by the younger Tiberius's crying.

After displaying more poor judgment in working for Octavian's rivals, Sextus Pompilius and Mark Antony, the elder Tiberius, along with other expatriates, was given the chance to return to Italy by Octavian, by now eager for peace, without having to worry about his neck. In a twist proving reality actually is stranger than fiction, Livia and the elder Tiberius divorced, whereupon Livia married Octavian, the very man from whose troops they had fled in fear of their lives. By this date Octavian had been given the quasi-religious title 'Augustus', meaning 'exalted one', by the Senate . He also had the reins of power so firmly in his grasp that he is recognized as the first Roman emperor. The gossip of the day claimed that lust played a major role in Augustus' decision to marry Livia and, in fact, the two probably did have an affair while Livia was still the elder Tiberius' wife, but there were also practical enough reasons for this union. Augustus won the link to the old Roman nobility he needed, since despite being the sole heir of the famous Julius Caesar he was burdened by a rather humble background (his family was the closest thing the Romans had to middle class and Augustus was sometimes slandered for having a banker for a grandfather). Livia, for her part, gained the best security available in all of Rome. Whether or not she or Augustus had any qualms about her being pregnant with another

[1] The Second Triumvirate was never an official political office, but it is often termed as such.

child, Drusus, by the elder Tiberius, even as they went about the marriage ritual, is something that is unfortunately overlooked by the history books.

The young Tiberius and his new brother Drusus were both raised in Augustus's household as though they were his own sons (and perhaps Drusus actually was Augustus's child, conceived during his affair with Livia, as one persisting rumor went). Once both boys came of age, they were encouraged to carve out grand careers of their own in the Roman armies; for quite a few noble Romans, the battlefield was to young adults what the university is today. Tiberius was only seventeen years old when he went off on his first military campaign, but he started playing an important role before too long. Despite what most would expect, Tiberius did not rise in the ranks so quickly simply because he was the Emperor's stepson, although the connection certainly did not hurt. Even Tiberius's most relentless critics agree he possessed a good deal of authentic military talent, which became clear when he fought successfully against the Parthians[2], a people who had been a thorn in Rome's side since a disastrous campaign against them in 53 BC.

When dealing with political matters later in life, Tiberius could be just as successful thanks to the fact that he was honest and pragmatic, if more than a bit cautious and tight-fisted. Despite his love of money, however, Tiberius could be fair enough to the average man. When writing to a provincial governor who imposed heavy taxes on his province, Tiberius admonished him by stating a good shepherd should shear his flock, not skin it. Never a political creature even as emperor, Tiberius did not seem to want to gather too much wealth or attention. Even though a man's public life and political career were, as today, inextricably linked, Tiberius never bothered to cultivate a public image to accentuate his political standing. He rarely went to the Circus Maximus or any large functions and

[2] The Parthian Empire spanned modern day Iran and Iraq.

although he did as a young man host a few gladiatorial shows in honor of his father and grandfather, these shows were paid for by Augustus and Livia.

Now Livia was most likely not the warmest of mothers. Even so, she was not the cold-blooded villainess who paved her son's path to the throne through schemes and murders portrayed in Robert Graves' *I, Claudius* novels or the BBC television series based on them. Nevertheless, Livia betrayed motherly ambitions for her son when she had a hand in forcing him to divorce his beloved pregnant wife, Vispania Agrippa. Around that time, Augustus had decided or realized that he needed a designated heir for the position he had carved out for himself and so he adopted Gaius and Lucius, his two grandsons, as his sons and heirs. After Tiberius's divorce to Vispania had been carried through in 12 BC, he was made to marry Julia, the mother of Gaius and Lucius, his stepsister and Augustus's spoiled daughter, and a woman he disliked intensely. Livia did not waste tears about her son's feelings on the matter; after all, why would he complain, when such a marriage would place him firmly in the running for the imperial office, along with his two stepsons?

For Tiberius, the prospect of such power did nothing to ease the blow of the divorce. Since an early age Tiberius had been married to Vispania and they loved each other passionately, not a common thing in a class where marriage was just another potent political tool. Days after the divorce was finalized, Tiberius caught sight of Vispania at a bath-house and silently followed her around the city with tear-stained eyes. After that embarrassing incident, Augustus and Livia saw to it personally that their paths would never cross again and arranged for Vispania to marry a senator. Three years later, the only other person Tiberius may have sincerely loved, his brother Drusus, died during a military campaign in Germany. If Tiberius had lived a charmed life thus far, it now came to an end.

A year after his brother's death, Tiberius gave up his political career (by this point he had been twice elected Consul, a senior post in Roman government) to retire in the prime of his life to the island of Rhodes. The tragedies of the past few years and the smoldering resentment he must have felt toward his mother and stepfather inspired this drastic move, but the excuse he gave was that he did not want to look like a rival to Lucius and Gaius, who were still Augustus's heirs and just beginning their own careers. There was also the ugly matter of Julia. She and Tiberius put up with each other well enough to conceive a child, but after it died suddenly things went sour and Tiberius refused to sleep with Julia again. This was not a long-term problem for Julia who had been inviting half of Rome to take his place in her bed while Tiberius gladly turned his back. Julia had a habit of taking lovers, a pastime well known to everyone in Rome who mattered, except her father. One story claims that Julia, when asked by a friend how she avoided getting pregnant from all her lovers, quipped that she only 'took passengers when the freight is full', meaning she slept with other men only when she was pregnant. With all the slander floating around his wife's name, Tiberius was quite eager to get out of Rome. When Augustus tried to dissuade him, Tiberius protested by starving himself for four days.

Once Tiberius had made it to Rhodes, Augustus pronounced to the world that Tiberius had betrayed his sacred duties to the family and the State. Tiberius could not have cared less. Picking out a country estate for himself and taking up the study of Greek philosophy and poetry, Tiberius finally put those meddlesome parents and sultry wife of his behind him. He also picked up a fascination with astrology and hired a personal astrologer, a Greek named Thrasyllus, who would stay Tiberius's advisor for the rest of his life.

It was not long, back in Rome, before Augustus finally discovered what all of Rome knew: his daughter Julia was a notorious – and celebrated – nymphomaniac. Augustus, a firm backer of morality in what he saw as an increasingly decadent Rome, was made to look like a hypocrite who could not keep his own house in order. Furthermore, Julia was not just a political embarrassment for Augustus, but also

a personal outrage. After Augustus heard that a friend of Julia's who had participated in her orgies hanged herself after the scandal came out, Augustus hissed, 'I would rather have been her father'. For her extensive catalogue of sins, Julia was banished to a tiny island off the Italian coast for five years, her only visitors being those who had the personal approval of Augustus himself: essentially, no one but old women, eunuchs, and children. Even when she was finally allowed back to the mainland, Augustus refused ever to see her again and had her every step watched and carefully reported. Augustus, meanwhile, let Tiberius divorce Julia, but resented Tiberius for not putting a stop to Julia's night-time escapades. Indeed, Augustus might have blamed Tiberius for treating her so badly that she went 'insane'. At any rate, Tiberius was told flatly that, stepson or no, he would not be setting foot on a Roman street any time in the near future.

Months passed before Augustus finally allowed Tiberius back to the capital, but even in the cosmopolitan environment of Rome he continued his hermit-like ways and whiled away his days quietly in a private villa (although it is likely that a still-furious Augustus had barred him from any public office). While Tiberius languished, Augustus's family problems had reached a climactic point. Lucius and Gaius died within a few months of each other while campaigning with the Roman army (the Roman historian Tacitus hinted a century later that they may have died through 'their stepmother Livia's treachery'). Augustus may have considered instating Gaius's and Lucius's younger brother Agrippa Postumus as his heir, only to end up banishing him, like his mother. Tacitus once again blames Livia for Augustus's actions, arguing it was because of her growing influence on an increasingly senile Augustus. Suetonius, meanwhile, implies that Agrippa was not entirely sane or at least had a very nasty personality. Most likely Suetonius was closer to the mark, but Tacitus' theory does make for more interesting reading.

Around AD 12, Augustus, with over forty years of imperial rule behind him, was beginning to decline mentally and physically. With Augustus's immediate family decimated, Tiberius's place as Augustus's successor was assured. There were rumors that in his last days Augustus tried making amends with his banished grandson and wanted to make preparations for his return to Rome. No one was sure even then if Augustus really would forgive Agrippa, much less if he was going to be proclaimed the imperial heir. In the event, it did not matter: after Augustus finally surrendered his ghost and before all of Rome knew of his death, a centurion stabbed Agrippa to death on his island prison. Even the most avid historians of the period are unclear on who actually gave the order for Agrippa's death. It might have been an order from Augustus just before his death, or from Livia acting in her husband's name, with or without the knowledge of Tiberius. Whoever was responsible, the result was the same: Tiberius's hold on the imperial office was now absolute. As far as Tiberius was concerned, however, he would have been much better off without it. He compared being Emperor of Rome to 'holding a wolf by its ears', which turned out to be a keen prediction on his part.

Tiberius's natural miserliness and humility did not change when he became emperor, so he started out as more or less the antithesis of what one today would expect an emperor of the Roman Empire to be like. He refused to be voted the title of 'Augustus' by the Senate and might have even briefly considered dividing imperial power between himself and two other men. Nor did he seem terribly to mind public criticism, at least at the beginning. When the Senate pointed out one fervent critic of his, expecting their emperor to persecute him, Tiberius calmly replied, 'If so-and-so criticizes me I shall take to render an account of my acts and words; if he persists, our enmity will be mutual.' Whenever he invited the consuls to a banquet, he treated them as though they were his equals, rising to meet them and personally escorting them out of his home after the 'good nights' were said. He despised all forms of flattery, refused to allow any statues and buildings to be built in his honor without his

permission, and scorned the honors that were heaped prodigiously on his lap. When the Senate asked to name the month of his birth after him (just as they had done with Augustus, giving us our 'August'), Tiberius grumpily asked, 'What will you do, then, if there are thirteen Caesars?' Tiberius summed up his opinion of this obedient Roman Senate with one pithy phrase: 'Men fit to be slaves!' Perhaps it is not too far-fetched to think that this son of Caesar's and Augustus's enemy secretly harbored republican sympathies in his heart all his life.

Now that her only living son was raised to the purple, Livia became a cross on Tiberius's back, expecting him to give her as much influence as she had wielded during Augustus's time. In the middle of a heated argument over political matters, she even went so far as to pull out old letters written to her by Augustus years before that talked about Tiberius as though he were a spoiled child. Although he resisted Livia's domineering at every possible turn, it became the punchline of countless jokes that Livia rightfully saw herself as the one directly responsible for Tiberius's place as emperor. As the historian Dio Cassius claimed, 'Still others proposed that Tiberius should be named after her, so that, just as the Greeks were called by their father's name, he should be called by that of his mother.' When Livia, then well into her eighties, finally reached her deathbed in AD 29, Tiberius, who had already established his permanent residence at Capri (partially because, perhaps, of his festering hatred for Livia), declined to visit her. He also completely threw out her will and refused to allow her deification, as Augustus had been, arguing that it was her own wish, rather than the will of the people.

Tiberius's adoption as heir did not come without its price, for he was required to adopt his young nephew Germanicus as his son and next in line to become emperor. Germanicus was already immensely popular among both the Roman soldiers and the public for his good humor, dashing appearance and chivalrous personality, all of which Tiberius lacked in abundance. Even though Germanicus averted a military rebellion against Tiberius and showed nothing but the humblest loyalty, Tiberius was understandably nervous about the possibility that Germanicus might have enough support to seize the Empire for himself. So when Germanicus mysteriously died while visiting Egypt, all eyes looked in Tiberius's direction. Gnaeus Piso, Tiberius's personal friend and governor of Syria, was widely suspected to be Tiberius's agent in the 'murder' of Germanicus, for the good reason that Piso heartily disliked Germanicus, so much so he and his wife Plancina threw a party the night they heard he was dead.

Piso and Plancina were put on trial, not only for killing Germanicus, but for killing him through the forbidden art of witchcraft. Piso probably expected his old friend Tiberius to bail him out or at least keep the enraged Roman mobs from his throat. He also hoped that Plancina, who was friendly with Livia (still alive at the time of the trial), would be able to do something to help their cause. Unfortunately, even the great Augustus's widow could do nothing about the simple fact that Rome demanded a scapegoat and throwing Piso to the wolves was more than convenient. As with all show trials throughout history, the case against the accused in Piso and Placina's trial was less than convincing, relying mainly on 'evidence' that Piso and his wife dabbled in sorcery. Even with his friend's life and reputation on the line, Tiberius acted in the trial with professional impartiality, declining to speak decisively for or against his friend, while out on the streets a crowd waited to tear Piso to shreds on the off chance he was found innocent. Livia did agree to help protect Plancina, but only if she was willing to leave her husband to his fate, to which she consented. Before the verdict was announced, Piso was given the choice of cutting his wrists or disgracing his family with a guilty verdict. Like any good Roman, he picked the former option.

If the Romans' attitude toward their new ruler had been cool, Tiberius's refusal to do anything one way or another about the Piso affair, and a lingering suspicion that Tiberius really did mastermind

the murder of Germanicus now made it ice cold. Germanicus's widow, Agrippina, made it her personal mission to make sure Tiberius never forgot about his involvement in the alleged murder of her husband. Nor did she have to work hard to make sure her opinion, that her husband was a martyr of Tiberius's evil, was shared across Rome. In the highest circles, she told her friends over banquets that Tiberius had schemed to exterminate the bloodline of Augustus in favor of his own from the very beginning. Once she even stormed up to Tiberius as he prayed to the Divine Augustus, calling him a hypocrite for praying to the very man whose descendants he was busy exterminating. Turning to Agrippina, Tiberius frostily suggested that she was actually much more upset about losing her chance of becoming empress than she was over Germanicus's death.

Soon Tiberius, painfully conscious of the waves of contempt riding over him, became more and more dependent on the advice of his right-hand man Sejanus, prefect of the Praetorian Guard. Sejanus had the sort of no-nonsense personality Tiberius approved of, so he rapidly found himself in the Emperor's favor. Encouraged by Tiberius's growing paranoia in the wake of Piso's trial, Sejanus began to try to consolidate greater personal power, possibly with his eye fixed on the imperial office itself.

To that end, Sejanus had already begun an affair with Tiberius's niece and daughter-in-law, Livilla. With or without her help, he may have poisoned Tiberius's son and Livilla's husband Drusus in order to remove a potential rival and leave him a widow who would one day give him access to the Julio-Claudian family. Drusus, although popular, was a dissolute drunk (something he may have inherited from his father who was known for his love of drink as well), so it was assumed by everyone that his death was only natural. Tiberius reacted to the demise of his only son with his usual stoicism, at least in the public eye, refusing to allow the customary mourning period to go on longer than usual. Drusus and Livilla did have one son who survived past childhood, Gemellus Tiberius, but later it was believed, especially by Tiberius, that he was actually the son of Sejanus.

Encouraged by his success in removing Drusus from the board, although thwarted by Tiberius in his aim of marrying Livilla, Sejanus now turned his attentions to Tiberius's immediate heirs, the sons of Germanicus: Nero[3] and the younger Drusus. He continued to encourage the growing conflict between Agrippina and Tiberius by carefully playing both sides, placing Agrippina and her sons in greater political danger while justifying Tiberius's increasing isolation and paranoia. In this respect, Sejanus's plans worked too well: when he eventually fell from grace, one of the weapons used against him was his association, however loose it may have been, with Agrippina and her faction.

Just a year after Drusus's death, Sejanus began to orchestrate a vicious persecution of any friends and sympathizers of Agrippina, but carefully making it seem as though Tiberius, driven to the brink of insanity by fear, was entirely behind it. Things were made so tense that once, when Tiberius had invited Agrippina to dinner, she feigned illness and refused to eat anything, even an apple that Tiberius offered her with his own hand. Tiberius was enraged by Agrippina's lack of trust, although he seems to have feared being poisoned by Agrippina as well.

As his terror of Agrippina's faction and a disloyal populace shaped his domestic policy and forced his boot down on dissenters, Tiberius began to acquire the reputation of a tyrant. Treason trials, almost always ending in the accused's degradation and death, had become a common occurrence. Tiberius's early leniency was forgotten as he became systematic in punishing his critics and stories began to flow about his enthusiasm for physical punishments. A unique form of torture, where the victim drinks until his bladder is about to burst and a rope is tied extremely tightly around the victim's genitalia so that he would not be able to urinate, was said to have been invented

[3] Not to be confused with the Emperor Nero.

by Tiberius. Once when a tortured and broken prisoner begged Tiberius to have him killed, he answered, 'I have not yet become your friend'. Another anecdote claims that after a prisoner died unexpectedly in custody, before he could be put to the rack, Tiberius cried out with bitter disappointment, 'He got away!'

Tiberius's sadism, sorely exaggerated or not, was rooted in a deeply pathological insecurity about his own safety. It comes as no surprise that Tiberius never returned to Rome after leaving for the island of Capri in AD 26. With this, and the politically powerful Livia's death, Sejanus was at last free to pursue his ambitions with little restraint. Agrippina and her family were banished or imprisoned on grounds of treason. With the willing aid of Drusus, Cain to Nero's Abel, Sejanus was able to drive Nero to suicide.

Living on Capri, Tiberius allegedly dived into a lifestyle of absolute decadence. In fact, Tacitus, who admittedly had a grudge against Tiberius even though he was long dead by his own time, argues that Tiberius's main reason for leaving for Capri was so that he could finally let his appetites loose without worrying about any bad publicity. Although the stories of Tiberius's sexual exploits were without a doubt heavily embellished, some are chilling enough to be somewhat convincing. His villa was said to have held special rooms filled with pornographic literature and art as well as special 'how-to' manuals. A portrait, worth about a million sesterces, of the mythological heroine Atlanta performing oral sex on Meleager was hung in his bedroom. In the gardens and woods around his villa at Capri, young girls dressed like nymphs and boys costumed as the god Pan would dance, play music, and make love for his amusement. When he swam, boys he called his 'minnows' would swim around him, licking and biting at his 'bait'.

Providing the Emperor with such entertainment cannot have been a pleasant task, since he was by then an old man with a body covered with festering sores and body hair. His villa was nicknamed 'the old goat's garden' by the Roman wags[4] and one young woman committed suicide rather than be subjected to Tiberius's 'games' again. Unfortunately, if one happened to catch the Emperor's eye, one did not have much of a choice beyond death or submission: two brothers, who dared to complain after being raped by Tiberius at a religious ceremony, had their legs broken. It should be borne in mind, however, that these are the sort of stories one might expect of an unpopular ruler who sequesters himself away from his people.

During Tiberius's endless vacation, Sejanus had reached the pinnacle of his power. Statues honoring him were placed around the cities of the Empire and the Senate declared his birthday a national holiday. Within two years, however, Sejanus would be thrown down from power and brutally killed on Tiberius's orders. What finally caused Tiberius to turn against the man who had been his chief henchman for so many years is uncertain, since a lack of historical sources for the period between Sejanus's triumphant rise and his abrupt fall makes it obscure.

Certainly, even a man as clever as Sejanus could not do everything to protect himself from Tiberius's pathologically suspicious eyes, nor should we think that Tiberius was completely blind to his subordinate's ambition, especially after he showed an interest in marrying into the imperial family. It is also very likely that, given Tiberius's nature, he would not long tolerate someone with Sejanus's popularity amongst the Roman people. One very dramatic explanation is handed to us in the story that Antonia, Livilla's mother, wrote a letter denouncing Sejanus, accusing him of the murder of Drusus and putting forward evidence that he was plotting to kill Germanicus's youngest son, Gaius 'Caligula'.

Whatever led to it, Tiberius formulated a complex plan to remove Sejanus without igniting a civil war. The plot began when

[4] It was a clever pun on the name of the island, which meant 'goat,' and a joke on Tiberius's hairy body.

Tiberius appointed Sejanus Consul, and even gave him a title, 'Sharer of my Cares', that implied Tiberius considered Sejanus to be a co-ruler, even though he soon began favoring Caligula and giving hints that he was thinking about making Caligula his heir. Next Tiberius reported to the Senate that he was very ill and planning to return to Rome, all the while having conflicting reports spread, in which Sejanus was either praised or condemned. This strange and contradictory behavior kept Sejanus on his toes, leaving him uncertain as to whether or not he should act or remain watchful.

When the public adoration of Sejanus began to reach an ebb, Tiberius acted for himself. Sejanus came to the Senate with high hopes, to hear a reading of a letter from Tiberius, probably expecting to hear himself declared heir. Instead he found that the letter in fact denounced him for a series of relatively minor offenses, then ended suddenly with a request that Sejanus be immediately arrested. As though suddenly awakened to the change in the Emperor's heart, the senators began to rise up one by one and, now feeling free to state their own past grievances against Sejanus, began their own denunciations. They then unanimously ordered that Sejanus be imprisoned. As he was led out of the Curia in chains, the same crowds that had not long before idolized him now pelted him with trash and excrement. Seeing for certain that the Roman people no longer cared one way or the other about Sejanus, the Senate ordered that he and his young children be executed. A letter from Sejanus's wife, who killed herself after the deaths of her children, supposedly described Sejanus's affair with Livilla and the murder of the elder Drusus. As for Livilla herself, her mother Antonia was said to have personally starved her to death for her crime. After Sejanus's execution, the Romans – citizens and soldiers – rioted and anyone judged guilty by the court of the mob for having sympathy for Sejanus was butchered on the spot.

The fall of Sejanus may have saved Tiberius's reputation for a while at least, but it did nothing for the surviving family of Germanicus. Agrippina, who had been exiled to an island for years, was beaten so badly by a guard that she lost an eye. In time she starved herself out of grief, despite efforts to force feed her. Tiberius had the Senate name her birthday a day of ill omen and published a letter saying Agrippina was lucky that he did not have her strangled and her corpse thrown on the streets. The Senate praised Tiberius for his inspirational clemency.

The younger Drusus, still a prisoner in Rome, was starved at Tiberius's own command. The official version in Tiberius's own memoirs[5] went that the death of Drusus was in retaliation for his involvement in the death of his brother. The Roman public was not naïve and once again they turned on Tiberius, centering their hopes around Germanicus' sole surviving son Caligula, who had been adopted by Tiberius and now lived with him at Capri. However, even Tiberius' adoption of Caligula could not erase the belief that Tiberius had been out to destroy Germanicus and his family from the very beginning.

Tiberius ended up naming both Caligula and his grandson Gemellus as heirs to the imperial office, although he still harbored suspicions about Gemellus's legitimacy and speculated that Caligula would probably kill Gemellus at some point (he was right). In naming Caligula as heir, Tiberius may have simply wanted to placate the Romans whose fond memories of Germanicus never faded, but instead brightened. It has been speculated that Tiberius was well aware of Caligula's incapacity to rule and chose him either to make his own reign look better by comparison (the same was said about Augustus adopting Tiberius) or just out of pure spite. Either way, one account goes that Tiberius had this to say about his young heir: 'I am nursing a viper in Rome's bosom'.

[5] Ancient sources describe and quote from an autobiography written by Tiberius, but unfortunately it appears that no copy has survived.

Once Tiberius was dead, Caligula was almost immediately proclaimed Emperor to widespread popular acclaim. When the reports of Tiberius's death turned out to have been exaggerated, one legend has it that the current prefect of the Praetorian Guard, Macro, smothered Tiberius with his pillow. While this story was most likely just that, Tiberius, a man in whom great hopes had apparently been placed, and who never wanted to spend one minute as Rome's most powerful man, died despised by his own people. No wonder the Roman writer Pliny the Elder called him *tristissimus homo*, the saddest man.

When word of his death reached Rome the city erupted into weeks of unrestrained celebration. The tyrant who had usurped power from the Divine Augustus'S rightful heirs was dead, and now the son of the beloved hero and martyr Germanicus would usher in a new golden age for the Roman people. On Tiberius's death Rome believed that it had seen the worst of tyranny: it was about to receive a harsh lesson in reality.

Further Reading

Dio Cassius (trans. Earnest Carey), *History of Rome*: Books LVIII–LIX (Harvard University Press, 1924)

Grant, Michael *The Roman Emperors: A Biographical Guide to the Rulers of Imperial Rome 31 BC – AD 476* (Weidenfield & Nicolson, 1985)

Shooter, David *Tiberius Caesar* (Routledge, 1992)

Suetonius (trans. J.C. Rolfe) *The Twelve Caesars*: Augustus, Tiberius (Harvard University Press, 1998)

Tacitus (trans. A.J. Church and W.J. Brodribb), *Annals*: Books I-II (Modern Library, 2003)

Wiedemann, Thomas *The Julio-Claudian Emperors: AD 14–70* (Bristol Classical Press, 1989)

CALIGULA

Reign: *March 17, AD 37–January 24, AD 41*
Born: *August 31, AD 12*
Died: *January 24, AD 41 (assassination)*
Buried: *Mausoleum of Augustus*

Gaius, better known to history by his childhood nickname 'Caligula', is, with the possible exception of his nephew Nero, perhaps the most notorious of all the Roman Emperors. In a way, he might have very well been the first 'true' Emperor of Rome. Although his predecessors, Augustus and Tiberius, were not shy about wielding the powers handed to them on a silver platter by the people and the Senate of Rome, they still kept up a charade as modest statesmen and shied away from pointing out to the Romans the elephant that was now in the room: a near-hereditary, absolutist monarchy. Caligula, on the other hand,

would come closer to matching the modern image of a Roman Emperor: utterly debauched and happily despotic. Raised at a time when the Republic was history and the imperial office was reality, Caligula smashed with glee the delicate lie spun by Augustus that the Romans were still a free people. Yet in the end, Caligula overestimated the Romans' willingness to put up with a young god-king.

Caligula's father was Germanicus, the Emperor Tiberius's nephew, adopted son and designated heir. In the eyes of the Roman people Germanicus was nothing less than a hero who could have very well walked right out of the old Roman legends of patriotic heroism. Caligula's mother was Agrippina, a granddaughter of Augustus, who also basked brightly in the public spotlight. Through his paternal grandmother Antonia he was descended from Mark Antony, that ill-fated lover of Cleopatra and doomed enemy of Augustus. Apart from arguably Antony, the only blotch in his immediate biological family's history was with his grandmother Julia, who was banished by her father Augustus for an unlucky career of sexual escapades, and his aunt, also named Julia, who shared a similar fate.

Through his great-grandfather the Emperor Augustus he may have inherited epilepsy, which Suetonius calls *morbus vexatus*, 'the falling sickness', a disease that inflicted his famous ancestor Julius Caesar. Suetonius also explains that Caligula suffered from severe insomnia, being able to sleep only three hours a night at the most, and from recurring periods of extreme physical and mental exhaustion. What may have actually caused Caligula all this torment is uncertain, but ancient writers are quite clear in saying Caligula was definitely not a healthy or robust man.

Whatever biological reasons for his assumed insanity there might have been, we can see more apparent psychological causes for traumas in Caligula's dangerous and strange youth. His earliest memories would have been of fantastic military parades and crowds of citizens flowing down narrow streets for just a glimpse of his beloved father, already at the apex of his nearly legendary military career. Young Caligula was never for a second spared the glories or the hardships of his father's life. At the age of just two, Caligula was with his parents in the wilds of Germany where Germanicus was leading a campaign to tame the German tribes.

From all indications, Caligula's life at the soldiers' camp was actually a happy one, if odd and chaotic. The harshly trained, tough-as-nails soldiers of the Roman legions actually adopted Caligula as a mascot and Agrippina started to dress him in a small soldier's uniform, complete with a tiny version of the soldiers' boots. It was this small footwear that inspired the soldiers to give Gaius the name that would stay with him throughout history, 'Caligula', which in Latin means 'little boots', a nickname that Caligula in fact detested throughout his life. (To appreciate the irony of this nickname, just imagine Joseph Stalin having the nickname 'Buttons'.) The soldiers cherished their 'Little Boots' so much that, when their particular regiment began to mutiny against Germanicus, the thought that Agrippina would have to flee the camp with a sobbing Caligula in her arms might have helped persuade some of the troops into backing down.

With luck, diplomacy, and a few drastic measures, including a threat to kill himself right in front of his men, Germanicus was eventually able to restore some sense of loyalty to his legions and lead them onward to more successful battles against the Germans. Although Germany would forever defy complete conquest by Roman swords, it was for the time being subdued and Germanicus at Tiberius's request returned to Rome with his family to celebrate a triumph. Caligula rode with his siblings in his father's chariot before a great throng of people revering Germanicus and his family like gods. He was only five years old then.

Still riding high on his successes, Germanicus was given authority over the easternmost provinces of the empire, although the Emperor Tiberius asked his friend Gnaeus Piso, the governor of Syria, to keep notes on Germanicus's activities. Tiberius was always as cautious as Germanicus was energetic. If not for Tiberius's orders

to the contrary, Germanicus may have campaigned even longer in Germany. Understandably Tiberius was also very weary of Germanicus's immense popularity with the public and the military, sso it comes as no surprise that it had not been Tiberius' desire to adopt Germanicus as his heir, but a decision forced on him by his predecessor Augustus.

If Tiberius really was using Piso as a check against Germanicus's influence, he could have chosen a better agent. Piso and his wife Plancina were the natural nemeses of Germanicus and Agrippina: the former were as hated as the latter were beloved. From the start, Piso and Plancina began spreading gossip and criticism about Germanicus and Agrippina within their own social circles and among the army. Eventually the festering tension between Germanicus and Piso hit a climax when Germanicus and his family journeyed to Egypt. With Germanicus away, Piso felt free to veto many of Germanicus's acts in the regional government. When he returned to Syria, Germanicus was less than happy with Piso's arrogant breach of authority. Germanicus publicly rebuked Piso and may have considered taking legal action against him, but then suddenly he became bedridden with an illness. Around Germanicus's home, various relics suggesting sorcery including some mummified human remains were allegedly found while Germanicus himself told Agrippina that Piso had poisoned him. After over a week of agony in his bed with Agrippina by his side, he died at the age of thirty-three. Agrippina was utterly devastated, as were the citizens of Rome. It almost seems that the only people who did not at all mourn Germanicus were Piso and Plancina, who instead decided to throw a party to celebrate the demise of their enemy.

Innocent or not, all Romans wanted nothing less than Piso's lifeless head. Dragged before the Emperor and the Senate on trial, Piso had almost no solid evidence brought against him, but still everyone knew the outcome as well as they knew whether or not the sun would rise the next day. When Tiberius did not even seem to consider coming to his friend's aid, Piso killed himself before the trial's conclusion to save his family from his guilt.

Things were about to become even worse for Agrippina and her family. Agrippina refused to let Tiberius off the hook for Germanicus's death and spread the word that Tiberius had engineered it as part of his plan to destroy their family in favor of his own. It was no secret that she believed her eldest son Nero should be put in line to become the next emperor, not Tiberius's own son, Drusus. Fear and ambition were subjects the young Caligula was thoroughly familiar with.

Tiberius's prefect of the Praetorian Guard and right-hand man, Sejanus, who may have hoped one day to become emperor himself, gladly threw fuel on the conflict between Agrippina and Tiberius. To keep himself busy, Sejanus had begun a persecution of Agrippina's friends, allies and family. When this hatred of Agrippina and other factors drove Tiberius to move to the island of Capri, Sejanus was finally free to rid himself of the family of Germanicus, who obstructed his path to ultimate power. Luckily Caligula was still an adolescent and thus out of Sejanus's line of fire, at least for the time being.

Unfortunately, the same could not be said of Caligula's older brothers, Nero and Drusus. Nero's every word was reported by Sejanus's agents and his slightest angry comment about recent politics was interpreted as treason. Even Drusus, who despised his brother, fed the informers with lies and rumors against Nero. Eventually Nero was banished to an island where he was driven to suicide and soon afterwards Agrippina was likewise banished. Caligula was sent to live with Tiberius's mother, Livia, who was by that time in her eighties and approaching her deathbed. After Livia's death and some time living with his grandmother Antonia, Caligula was moved to Tiberius's villa at Capri. Tiberius may have done so to start making Caligula his heir and even perhaps to protect him from Sejanus, but it must still have been a terrifying prospect for Caligula,

who was just entering adulthood, to spend every day and night with the man in whose name his family was being massacred.

Sejanus finally fell from grace with a resounding thud, perhaps thanks in part to the efforts of Antonia who feared that Caligula would be the next to die for Sejanus's ambitions. The fall and execution of Sejanus still did not save Agrippina and Drusus. Drusus, who was kept in a prison in Rome, was starved to the point where he ate the stuffing of his own mattress in an effort to keep alive. In utter despair, Agrippina starved herself to death.

While his mother and brother perished, Caligula resided peacefully at their murderer's residence in Capri. Tiberius and his agents meticulously watched and listened for the slightest suggestion of treason on Caligula's part, which meant Caligula could not dare show any sign of grief or anger at the horrific treatment his mother and brother endured. Under these nightmarish circumstances, which could not have failed to leave an imprint on his mind, Caligula learned absolute secrecy. So perfectly did Caligula play the part that it was once said about him, 'Never was there a better slave or a worse master'.

Not only did Caligula endure the ordeal of staging apathy at his family's dismemberment, but he also witnessed, and perhaps participated in, the aged Emperor's less than modest lifestyle. Exactly what Caligula was exposed to, if anything, can never be known, but accounts hint that by this point Caligula was no stranger to depravity. Suetonius writes that at the ripe age of seventeen he had already made love to his favorite sister Drusilla, who received his more than brotherly attentions with open arms.

In AD 35, at the age of twenty-three, Caligula was at Tiberius' insistence engaged to Junia, the daughter of a consul on good terms with Tiberius. Almost nothing is known about her or how the couple got along, because Junia died from a difficult childbirth less than a year later, with the child following her. Once more, death had touched the young Caligula's life.

Finally, a year after Junia died, Tiberius the 'old goat' himself went to the grave. According to a barely credited legend, the current Praetorian prefect Macro, seeing that Tiberius was still alive, if just barely, fixed the reaper's botched job and smothered the Emperor with a pillow to put Caligula in his debt. This story came from the fact that Macro was already distrusted by Tiberius for his blatant shows of loyalty toward Caligula. These little displays of devotion went as far as Macro encouraging his own wife Ennia to sleep with the future Emperor.

In his will, Tiberius asked that both Caligula and his grandson, Gemellus, be instated as co-emperors. The Senate and Caligula had other ideas and declared that Tiberius was not of sound mind when he composed his will. No one cared, but Caligula at least honored the bequests Tiberius arranged in his will. The Romans had their own reasons to ignore Gemellus, besides lingering hatred for the tyrant Tiberius. He was barely a teenager and many, even Tiberius, doubted his legitimacy (his mother was believed to have had a long-standing affair with Sejanus). In spite of Caligula's own sound reasons to loathe the man, Tiberius was given a good funeral, despite the cries of 'Tiberius to the Tiber![6]' from the Roman mob. Caligula even generously adopted Gemellus as his son and designated him as heir to the Empire. He also vowed he would not seek retribution against the people who had informed against his mother and brothers and, in order to make good on his word, Caligula burned in public the papers that implicated them. All the same, Suetonius alleges that Caligula spent the night before this bonfire making secret copies which he used later to persecute the informers to the death.

The Romans never forgot their grand champion Germanicus and so the 24-year-old Caligula's ascension was good cause for optimism across Rome. Lovingly the populace talked about Caligula as their 'baby', 'chick' and 'star'. After taking a pilgrimage to the

[6] In early Roman custom, the bodies of criminals were dragged on hooks through the streets of Rome and thrown into the Tiber River.

island where his mother died, Caligula gathered his mother's ashes with those of Drusus and had them taken to the Mausoleum of Augustus. This show of familial mourning was commemorated later on with an expensive parade. Thousands of sacrifices were then made in honor of Caligula and his family while expensive games were thrown: Tiberius had rarely allowed them, both on financial grounds, and out of concern about their effect on the populace's morality. Within just one year, the 2,700,000 or so sesterces that Tiberius with all his penny pinching had left behind were gone. The fact that Caligula from the very beginning of his reign dispersed massive amounts of money to the people and the army, and had to have at least one spectacular event a day, whether it was a play, a chariot race, or a gladiatorial show, explains the treasury's vanishing act.

With the Roman economy at his fingertips, Caligula's fascination with entertainment evolved into an obsession. He may have had sexual relations with male actors, although such accusations of 'buggery'[7] were a favorite weapon in the arsenal of Roman historians against unpopular and 'effeminate' rulers. Annoyed whenever people did not come to the events he held, Caligula had all periods of mourning and lawsuits postponed on days when certain shows were thrown so that no one would have an excuse not to attend.

Just barely into his reign, Caligula had a nasty disagreement with his grandmother Antonia, the same woman who may have saved his life. Annoyed at Antonia's constant butting-in on his legal and political decisions, Caligula is said to have answered her unwanted advice with, 'Remember that I have the right to do anything to anybody'. Antonia killed herself not long afterwards, perhaps having been driven to it by Caligula. Whether or not her suicide was a direct result of his harassment, Caligula refused to attend her funeral

[7] Male homosexual intercourse was accepted in Rome for the most part, but the idea of a Roman of noble birth letting himself be penetrated by anyone, especially a man of lower class, a slave, or a freedman was disgusting to the Roman mindset.

personally, but rather watched her funeral pyre at a distance from the comfort of his palace.

This was just a prelude to what was about to come. Soon after Antonia's death, Caligula fell ill for two months. All of Rome held its breath, afraid that Caligula would be taken away as abruptly as Germanicus. Prayers and sacrifices were offered for Caligula's recovery and one man named Publius even pledged his life to the gods in exchange for Caligula's. Modern scholars have debated over the exact nature of Caligula's illness and theories have ranged from a nervous breakdown to a serious attack of epilepsy to a form of schizophrenia. Whatever it was, it seems Caligula may have gone mad after he 'recovered'. His first order of business, Suetonius tells us, was having Publius thrown off a cliff, simply so the poor man could fulfill the promise he had made to the gods. After all, Caligula simply could not allow anyone to commit perjury, especially not on his behalf.

Gemellus was later charged with treason, just for being suspected of privately wishing the illness would finish off Caligula. When Gemellus took some medicine for a sore throat, Caligula then accused him of trying to take some kind of protective medicine against poison, which would have been an insulting and even treasonous insinuation about Caligula's intentions, and exclaimed, 'What! An antidote against Caesar?' To prove beyond a doubt that no such medicine existed, Gemellus was butchered by a centurion sent by Caligula.

Even if the illness did not leave him technically mad, Caligula began to embrace the lifestyle afforded by the imperial office with great enthusiasm. It is claimed he bathed in perfumed oils, ate on golden dishes, and dressed only in the finest silks. He also still enjoyed throwing money down upon the populace, although one account has it that he at least once mixed heavy pieces of iron with the gold, killing some of the people crowded down on the ground. Caligula's personal motto became, 'One ought to be frugal or Caesar'.

This kind of a life did not come cheaply, so Caligula had to

arrange certain alternative avenues of income. He reinstated the treason trials that had once been a fact of life under Tiberius, and which he himself swore at the beginning of his reign never to have, simply to be able to confiscate the wealthy estates of the accused. When one man who was executed turned out to have been much poorer than thought, Caligula sadly noted, 'He died in vain'. He even held an auction where he sold off most of the heirlooms kept by the imperial family, including items that had been owned by Augustus and Mark Antony. No one was now left to restrain him. Antonia was long dead and both Macro and his wife were eventually driven to suicide.

Bound with this need for extravagance there was a maniacally vain mind. Two consuls were discharged from office because they forgot it was their Emperor's birthday. It became a capital offense to look down from a high place on Caligula because of his incipient baldness (an affliction that long cursed his ancestors, despite their name being derived from *caesaries*, which means 'a head of hair') and it was risky to mention 'goats' in conversation, since Caligula was sensitive about another undesirable family trait: his overabundance of body hair. During a gladiatorial show, another story goes, Caligula noticed one man named Aesius who was famous across the city for his powerful body and handsome appearance. Without warning, Caligula ordered the man to be thrown into an arena and forced to fight. When Aesius held his own, even against the trained fighters, Caligula had him chained up, dressed in rags, paraded through the streets for all the women of Rome to see, and then executed.

The many others who happened to taste Caligula's wrath whether they deserved it or not fared little better than poor Aesius. Like Tiberius, Caligula was said to have invented his own unique brand of torture, where the victim is cut with countless small wounds. Caligula urged his executioners on with this by shouting, 'Let him feel that he is dying'. One report has it that when a man whose son was scheduled to die excused himself from attending the execution on account of illness, Caligula graciously provided a litter to convey the father to the site of his son's execution. Worse than actual death was the terror Caligula could instill in all those around him. Once at a dinner party, Caligula unexpectedly erupted in laughter. A consul sitting near him asked politely what the joke was and if he could share it. Still laughing, Caligula replied, 'Isn't it obvious? With one nod of my head I could have your throat cut whenever I please!'

This does not mean that Caligula did not participate in more acceptable ways to amuse himself. He particularly took special pride in his oratorical skills, a lauded talent in Graeco-Roman culture. Domitius, an old enemy of Agrippina and a man renowned for his speaking talents, was brought before the Senate on a charge of treason like so many others. Caligula erupted into the Curia, the Senate meeting place, with a long, elaborate speech condemning Domitius and demanding his death. When Caligula had finished, Domitius did not even say one sentence in his own defense but got down on his knees and exclaimed that he had no hope of survival at all now that such a brilliant and passionate speech had been made against him. His ego now sufficiently flattered, Caligula gave up his grudge against Domitius and released him from all charges. When a friend later asked Caligula why he bothered bringing Domitius to trial in the first place, he replied, 'It would not have been right for me to keep such a speech to myself.'

Besides himself, the one true love of Caligula's life was his own sister Drusilla. He supposedly slept with her most of his adult life, and in fact may have also counted Drusilla's husband Marcus Lepidus among his lovers. However, Caligula's love for Drusilla was far more than physical. In all official oaths, the names of Caligula, Drusilla and their other sisters had to be invoked. When Drusilla died from a sudden illness, Caligula became absolutely grief-stricken. During the customary mourning period, bathing, laughing or dining with one's family all became capital offenses for all Roman citizens. Drusilla

would later at Caligula's insistence become the first woman deified by the Senate.

Despite the tales about Drusilla, Caligula did try frequently to find love outside his own family. He had a second wife, Livia Orestilla, and in wooing her Caligula found no obstacle in the fact that she was already married. He simply sent a letter to her husband, saying, 'Do not have sex with my wife', and declared the next day that he had taken a new bride in the same way as Romulus, who led the legendary rape of the Sabine women, and Augustus, whom rumor said forced his wife Livia's divorce to her first husband. Only a few days later, though, Caligula tired of Livia and divorced her. His third marriage was to Lollia Paulia, who was also already married and also found herself suddenly snatched away by Caligula. Again, they were divorced after a short period, but this time he also ordered her never again to have sex with another man.

Caligula at last found true love in Milonia Caesonia, an older woman with children from another marriage and a reputation among the Roman elite for being a bit loose, yet the fickle Emperor may actually have loved her. He certainly showed it when he proudly displayed her nude in front of friends and the legions. How she managed to appease him so much and for so long will never be known, but being the wife of someone who was a cynical libertine at best or an unpredictable madman at worst surely was not the most enviable of positions. Suetonius writes that Caligula seriously threatened to torture Milonia one day to make her confess how she made him love her so deeply. Even with such awkward domestic moments, it seems that their marriage was happy, if bizarre. They even conceived a little girl, named Drusilla after Caligula's late, cherished sister.

While the elder Drusilla was made a goddess because of her brother's love, Caligula's other sisters, Agrippina and Livilla, soon fell out of favor. They, along with the late Drusilla's husband Lepidus, engineered a conspiracy against the life of their brother.

When the plot was exposed, Lepidus was put to death while the sisters were banished to small, distant islands. Exactly why they initiated the conspiracy to begin with is a mystery, especially since they were all among Caligula's closest loved ones. Perhaps his insanity had become too much even for them.

The most startling proof for this alleged madness cited by historians comes from his short-lived military career. Caligula's first objective was to fulfill his father's dream of conquering Germany, which led him to go on a venture that in the end was less than satisfactory. He ordered his German bodyguards to pretend they were the enemy at one point, he fought no battles, he captured only a few harmless hostages and one night with his friends he cut branches from trees and made them into 'victory crowns'. After the 'hardships' of this campaign he took a vacation in Gaul where he held the aforementioned auction and had some of the province's wealthiest citizens executed for the sake of lining his pockets with their fat fortunes.

Even after all this, Caligula was not finished and decided to accomplish what even Julius Caesar had failed to achieve: the conquest of Britain. Caligula organized his troops along the coast of Gaul and went to cross the English Channel. Suddenly, before he reached British shores, he turned around and came back to Gaul. The legions were probably a tad dismayed to find the Emperor now ordering them to use their helmets to gather seashells from along the beaches. To commemorate this peculiar victory, Caligula had a lighthouse constructed to imitate the one built by Alexander the Great at Alexandria. These shells, along with a handful of Celts who surrendered to the Roman army on sight, were all Caligula had to show for his 'invasion' of Britain. These were not exactly the foundations for an immortal military reputation, but he must have felt they were more than enough. He still planned excitedly to celebrate a triumph at Rome and display both shells and captives to a loving populace. When Caligula returned to Rome and instead found that not even the slightest

spark of celebration had been ignited for him, he was furious and threatened to have all of the ungrateful senators put to the sword. The small fact that before he left he forbade the Senate to hold a triumph for him did not matter.

Caligula's megalomania finally reached a crescendo when he reached the sensible conclusion that being Emperor was not enough: it was only logical that he was also a god. After all, his ancestor Julius Caesar had been made a god, as had his great-grandfather Augustus and his own sister Drusilla. Why should he have to wait until after he was dead and not be a god during his lifetime, like the Egyptian pharaohs had been? Caligula soon formed his own cult, complete with rituals and priests, and had the heads from the statues of certain gods knocked off and replaced with his own sacred visage. He even considered doing the same to the statue of Zeus at Olympia, one of the seven wonders of the world. The Romans themselves would probably not have felt touched by the divine when they saw the Emperor appearing in public dressed as Jupiter, Apollo, Hercules or even Venus or Juno.

In spite of his own upstart godhood, Caligula managed to hold rather healthy relationships with the other Roman deities. He felt confident in inviting the moon goddess Diana to come down from the heavens to sleep with him. Although Caligula did have serious disagreements with Jupiter (legend has it that once Caligula said to a statue of Jupiter, 'Raise me up to Olympus or I'll cast you down to Hell'), the two eventually became friends and Caligula even had his bedroom connected to Jupiter's temple so that the Emperor could be more accessible to the great god. Once Caligula casually asked his friend, the actor Apelles, who was more powerful, himself or Jupiter. When Apelles hesitated, Caligula had him severely beaten and then complimented Apelles on the emotion in his groans of pain and pleas for mercy. The Jews almost rebelled over Caligula's pretensions to godhood and his careless demand that they place images of him in the Temple). They probably would have actually risen against Rome if not for some quick diplomacy on the part of Caligula's friend Herod Agrippa, the King of Judea, .

In spite of all these accounts, was Caligula truly driven insane by either his youth or his illness? Given the gossipy nature of most Roman historians and Caligula's massive unpopularity, it is an open question. Caligula might just have had a sense of humor so wicked the Romans could not get in on the joke. Certainly the allegations that Caligula literally turned the imperial palace into a brothel and made his favorite racehorse a consul seem more the acts of a jovial hedonist than an outright madman. Contemporaries also accused Caligula of being an atheist in the modern sense, refusing to believe in the existence of any god and, worse, being quite honest about it. In light of this information, his self-proclaimed divinity looks more like absurdist theatre, centuries before its time. There was at least one instance that suggested Caligula did not take his own godhood seriously. When he learned from an official that a Gallic farmer said openly that the Emperor being a god was frankly just a bunch of bullshit, he did not have the man punished. On the contrary, Caligula found it hilarious.

Mad or not, people soon had their fill of their former hero. One day, when Caligula was walking unguarded down a narrow alley between a stadium and his palace, a group of assassins took him by surprise and stabbed him to death. Several of the killers then rushed over to the palace, murdered Caesonia, and also seized little Drusilla by her feet to bash her skull open against a wall. About the brutal murders, Dio Cassius writes simply, 'Thus Gaius . . . learned by actual experience that he was not a god.' In the end, Caligula did not go entirely unmourned. As soon as they were recalled to Rome, his living sisters, despite having once participated in a conspiracy for his life, saw to it that he received a decent funeral.

After the slaughter of Caligula and his family, Rome still held its breath. A rumor went around that this was all simply another of Caligula's sadistic jokes. The Praetorian Guard found Caligula's uncle Claudius, who had been consul under Caligula's reign but for

years was ignored by his own family for his physical infirmities, possibly all stemming from cerebral palsy, hiding behind a curtain in the imperial palace. Claudius was scared out of his mind and convinced that all of Rome was rioting against the government. Rather than stabbing him through the heart, Claudius was surprised to find them hailing him as the new emperor. Although Claudius was not the wise, benevolent old man depicted in Robert Graves's novels or the BBC series they inspired, his reign was still a much needed reprieve before Rome would find itself ruled by another ostentatious tyrant of the same family.

Further Reading

Barrett, Anthony *Caligula* (Yale University Press, 1990) (for the argument that Caligula was not insane)

Dio Cassius (trans. Earnest Carey), *History of Rome*: Book LIX (Harvard University Press, 1924)

Ferrill, Arther *Caligula* (Thames & Hudson, 1991) (for a more traditional look at Caligula)

Grant, Michael *The Roman Emperors: A Biographical Guide to the Rulers of Imperial Rome 31 BC–AD 476* (Weidenfeld & Nicolson, 1985)

Suetonius (trans. J.C. Rolfe), *The Twelve Caesars*: Tiberius, Caligula (Harvard University Press, 1998)

Wiedemann, Thomas *The Julio-Claudian Emperors: AD 14–70* (Bristol Classical Press, 1989)

NERO

Reign: *October 13, AD 54–June 9, AD 68*
Born: *December 15, AD 37*
Died: *June 9, AD 68 (suicide)*
Buried: *Formerly near the Church of Santa Maria del Popolo in Rome*[8]

When Nero springs to mind, we see a fat, balding, black-haired man dressed lavishly and sometimes cradling a lyre or an anachronistic fiddle with a short, plump arm. Instead Suetonius writes that Nero had light blonde hair, blue eyes, and was somewhat athletic, although apparently he did have spindly legs, a fat neck, and a tendency to be overweight, but we seem to be

[8] According to legend, the first construction of the church in 1099 was over Nero's grave on the slope of the Pincian hill, but Pope Paschal II ordered that the remains be removed and thrown into the Tiber.

accurate in thinking he had an appetite for luxury. For one thing, Suetonius adds in his not so flattering description that Nero never wore the same garment twice.

Nero's refusal to commit to a wardrobe matched his attitude toward hobbies and occupations. Nero was a true Renaissance man: all at once he was an actor, a wrestler, an architect, a musician, a charioteer, a poet, an orator and a historian. Despite the opprobrium heaped on him by historians, both of Roman times and ours, it is easy to get the feeling that maybe Nero really did have the talent to match at least some of his ambitions. Unfortunately, destiny picked him out for the one occupation at which he proved an utter failure: Emperor of Rome.

His mother Agrippina was the daughter of the war hero Germanicus, and the elder Agrippina, regarded as a martyr of the tyrannical Emperor Tiberius. Through the elder Agrippina's parents Nero was descended from both Augustus, the first Emperor of Rome, and Augustus's still revered enemy, Mark Antony. Nero's mother, the younger Agrippina, did not have the reputation to match her lineage. Her brother was Caligula, a suspected madman who was made emperor, and rumor had it she and her sisters had a relationship with him that was less than appropriate for siblings. Her standing worsened when she married her uncle and next emperor, Claudius, with all Rome disapproving of the incestual match. During her uncle-husband's reign, she became even more hated for trying to exercise formidable political influence and, unlike Augustus's powerful wife, Livia, being quite brazen about it. What people at the time thought of her is shown through a story that she had one of her ex-rivals for the marriage of Claudius killed and ordered that the unlucky girl's head be brought to her as proof.

In the public eye, Nero's father Domitius was no better. He was accused by historians of crimes varying from treason to incest. One account even claims that he once drove his chariot over a young boy out of spite. When Nero was born, Domitius reportedly said,

'Nothing that was not abominable and a public bane could be born of Agrippina and myself', although of course this sort of tale reeks of hindsight. Instead it seems Nero's mother at least put some stock in him from the very beginning. According to legend, Agrippina made a bracelet for Nero, using the cast-off skin of a snake found near his bed, meant to be a good luck charm.

Nero's loathed father died when he was still very young and Nero was doomed to experience, at least for a while, the loss of his mother as well. Agrippina had participated in a conspiracy with her sisters and brother-in-law against Caligula, motivated perhaps by a genuine desire to put an end to her brother's tyranny, yet after Caligula's assassination Agrippina and her sisters would see to his remains, which suggests that they still cared for him despite everything. She and her sisters were spared from death, but were banished indefinitely to small islands. The estate Nero inherited from his father was confiscated by the State and he was forced to live with his paternal aunt Lepida until such time as his mother might return, always assuming she would do so. The experience could not have been pleasant for Nero, especially if he knew that his grandmother, the elder Agrippina, was also banished to an island, beaten so badly she lost an eye, and eventually in utter depression starved herself to death.

When Caligula finally met his end at the hands of his own Praetorian Guard, and his uncle Claudius was raised to the purple, Agrippina was recalled to the mainland and Nero was given back his inheritance. Agrippina ended up in a marriage with her sister-in-law's ex-husband (the same sister-in-law who happened to take care of Nero during Agrippina's banishment), Gaius Crispus. The actual reasons for this marriage remain obscure, but it is not impossible that Agrippina just wanted a new husband and thought a growing boy like Nero should have a surrogate father. There is also the chance that Agrippina was providing protection for herself through Crispus, an influential and wealthy senator, from Messalina, Claudius's young wife, who wanted to guarantee her and Claudius's son Britannicus a

chance at the succession. One story claims that Messalina did indeed send assassins after Nero, but that they were scared off by his snake bracelet, which they somehow mistook for the real thing.

Messalina ended up dashing her son's opportunities herself by having an affair with an ambitious young man named Gaius Silius, who probably had in mind a plan to boot Claudius out of the imperial office and take it for himself. Whatever his true motives, Silius and Messalina married in an extravagant ceremony, despite the nasty problem of Messalina already being married to the most powerful man in the known world. Silius pledged to adopt Britannicus, then the designated imperial heir, as his son. With the considerable political support both Messalina and Silius held between them, it would have been easy for them to have risen against Claudius with a decent chance for victory, but instead inaction sealed their fates. Claudius's men quickly arrested the treasonous lovers during their own wedding feast. Silius was killed while Messalina's enemies (and she had developed more than a few) in Claudius's court made sure she was executed before she could plead with her old husband for mercy. Messalina was only twenty-two years old. With her own husband now dead (possibly from natural causes, not poison, as the ancient sources would have it), Agrippina happily joined in the competition to be Messalina's replacement.

There are many reasons why Claudius might want to marry Agrippina, but Nero himself may have been one of them. Britannicus suffered from epilepsy (a disease that ran in the family) and Claudius's love for him was tainted by his mother's incredible betrayal – not to mention that her lifestyle, if a quarter of the gossip repeated in the histories are true, cast doubt on his legitimacy – so as the next emperor he became unappealing. Nero, on the other hand, was already well liked by the public and showed some youthful promise in Claudius's eyes. So Agrippina eventually won; not only did Claudius marry her, despite society frowning on him for marrying his brother's daughter, but he also adopted Nero as his son and heir. Ironically, this decision, done to cement the dynasty, would instead destroy it.

With his future role in mind, Agrippina only wanted the best for her son, so she hired the Stoic philosopher Seneca as his private tutor. Seneca held the situation with Nero to be exactly like Aristotle's teaching of Alexander the Great, only now there would be an emperor of Rome raised by Stoic principles. Unfortunately, even at an early age, Nero showed a preference for art and chariot races over politics and philosophy. The later historian Dio Cassius summed it up: 'He was not fond of business in any case.' This would prove to be something that would not improve with time.

Agrippina's concern for her son's future was not limited to arranging his education but extended to getting rid of Britannicus's sympathizers. She forced Nero to testify against Britannicus's grandmother – and the aunt that once tended to him – Lepida. The accusation was that Lepida was using witchcraft to try to kill Agrippina. The penalty for witchcraft, even for members of the imperial family, was always death. Agrippina effortlessly won the case.

At some point, Claudius began once again to favor Britannicus and showed signs of becoming quite irritated with Agrippina. Unless she wanted to end up like Messalina, Agrippina had to act quickly and drastically. With some help from Claudius's food-taster, one evening Agrippina poisoned a small portion of Claudius's dinner, cooked mushrooms, his favorite meal. The help of Claudius's doctor and the professional poison-maker Locusta was needed to finish Claudius off after the deadly mushrooms proved somewhat insufficient and only gave Claudius severe indigestion. Once he became Emperor, Nero would jokingly call mushrooms 'the food of the gods' since the Senate deified Claudius not long after his fatal poisoning.

Once Claudius was dead and gone, the ascension of Nero was a done deal. He was only seventeen years old when he was declared Emperor so, after years of an elderly and absent-minded emperor, this young, charismatic prince must have seemed a blessing. Nero

put at ease any anxieties the people held with his amiability and liberal political actions. He promised to put an end to the closed-door trials that had been so common during the reigns of his predecessors (it was a promise meant to be broken) and vowed to reassert the rights of the Senate in the increasingly autocratic government, among other things. The only real slip-up during Nero's ascension was when he read a speech written by Seneca praising the quick, able mind of Claudius. The crowd, knowing their late Emperor well, erupted with laughter. In his cruel satire *The Pumpkinification of Claudius*, where the deceased Emperor is met with unconcealed disgust by the gods of Olympus, Seneca compared Nero to a rising sun, bringing peace and glory to Rome. It would not be too long before Seneca would eat those bitter-tasting words.

Although Nero was now officially in charge, it was really his mother, along with Seneca and the prefect of the Praetorian Guard, Burrus, who took the helm. While the grown-ups dealt with the affairs of the State, Nero was let loose to lead a riotous but artistic lifestyle. He composed poetry and drove chariots in races in the day, but at night he would lead a gang of thugs around the city to mug people on the streets, break into houses and harass women. Art and violence were the forces that drove Nero, which was strangely appropriate for an Emperor of Rome.

In spite of his nocturnal habits, Nero was not exactly the stuff of a bloodthirsty tyrant. Even Suetonius, who is anything but friendly to Nero's memory, writes that while signing a death warrant Nero exclaimed, 'I wish I had never learned how to write!' Nero's squeamishness for violence of the excessively bloody kind extended to the gladiatorial shows, a popular pastime in Rome at the time and one greatly enjoyed by his predecessor Claudius, who, despite his benevolent image, seems to have been fascinated with the sight of men dying horrifically. Contrary to the popular belief that Nero often enjoyed fights to the death in the Colosseum, he never liked bloody combat, even after his reign became more disreputable. In any case, construction on the Colosseum did not even begin until several decades after Nero's death. But Nero's distaste for blood and violence did nothing to stop him from committing one of the most notorious crimes of antiquity: the murder of his own mother.

It is hard to tell what finally drove Nero to it, but he was not alone in wanting Agrippina in a tomb. Seneca and Burrus almost certainly agreed to the murder, if not encouraged it, since a power struggle between the two men and Agrippina had started not long after Nero's reign began. Also the real relationship between Nero and his mother was shrouded by persistent and biting rumors of incest, reported as fact by most Roman historians. One story the historians share, and it was probably rumored at the time, is that Nero once spent hours with his mother in a closed litter and telltale stains on their clothing could be seen afterwards. These rumors – and the very real, stifling mother-son relationship that inspired them – were too much for the boy who began to feel he alone deserved to wield the absolute power that was his birthright.

Already the relationship between Nero and his mother had seen better days. Nero, who had been forced to marry his stepsister Octavia, began not only to have an open affair with a slave-girl named Acte, but wanted to marry a woman named Poppaea whom Agrippina hated. Also there was the strange death of Britannicus, the symptoms of which, brought to us in detail by ancient historians, suggest a fatal epileptic fit. At the time, everyone in Rome, even Agrippina, believed that Nero had poisoned his stepbrother in order to get rid of a rival. It was even more suspicious that this death occurred after Agrippina, in a fury at Nero, had threatened to have him deposed in favor of Britannicus.

Such was the background to the events of the evening when Agrippina sailed across the Bay of Naples to visit her son at his residence in Baiae for a feast. Despite whatever quarrels they were having, Nero was the doting son to his mother the entire evening and cordially led her back to her ship himself. Agrippina did not

suspect in the least that this night was intended to be her last. The ship that was to carry her back across the bay had a roof weighed down with lead and some of the sailors on board were given orders to finish the job if necessary. During the trip, the roof collapsed as planned, killing Agrippina's personal bodyguard and throwing the woman and her attendant into the water. Using their oars, the sailors beat the attendant to death, but only managed to wound Agrippina's shoulder. Even with the injury, Agrippina managed to get to shore and seek help.

Horrified at the news that his mother had actually survived, Nero called upon a sailor named Anicetus to finish the deed. When Anicetus agreed to the Emperor's command, Nero grinned and shouted, 'Today you have given me my empire!' Anicetus and a squad of soldiers were sent to the villa where Agrippina was seen to have fled, arresting anyone that tried to hinder them. As the men approached her, their intentions plain, Agrippina made one final request: 'Strike here', she said, pointing toward the womb that once carried Nero. Her killers politely obliged her.

After Agrippina's murder, Nero was free to divorce Octavia and marry his beloved Poppaea. Octavia was banished to an island where she either killed herself or was murdered by guards bribed by Poppaea, who proved to have an instinct for survival that matched that of her late mother-in-law. In the meantime, Nero's taste for shows and performances grew even greater, now that no-one discouraged it. After one of his performances, his guards proudly proclaimed, 'By yourself, O Caesar, we swear no one surpasses you'. Not even his old advisors, Seneca and Burrus, were around to keep him in check anymore. Burrus died of cancer while Seneca soon resigned, most likely in disgust.

Following their departure, Nero's reign – the beginning of which was hailed by even his sharpest critics as a 'golden age' for Rome – began to slide downhill. In Britain, a Celtic queen named Boudicca (Boadicea) led a bloody and initially successful revolution against the

Roman occupation established under Claudius. Although her revolt was eventually defeated, it was a close-run thing, and not without great cost to the conquerors. Another catastrophe, much closer to home, was the fire of 64. Many Roman historians blame the fire on Nero, even though Nero was away at Antium at the time and, after the fire had run its course, initiated new laws and civic designs meant to help prevent future infernos. The legends had it that Nero stood safely in a tower, watching the destruction with delight and singing a song of his own composition about the sack of Troy. He was also accused of starting the fire so he would have an excuse to build a new city in Rome's place named Neropolis, based on his careful designs.

To many, the fire was an omen that the gods were angry with Rome. To satisfy them, and to dispel rumors of his involvement that were already brewing, Nero began the persecution of a then obscure sect named the Christians, whom Suetonius refers to as 'a class of men given to a new and mischievous superstition'. Although it is impossible that the persecution was as extensive and systematic as later legends claim, persecution of Christians began in earnest during Nero's reign and probably at his own personal insistence. If Nero really did hope to shift the blame for the fire onto the early Christians in the popular imagination, though, he failed miserably.

Nero's standing took another turn for the worse when Poppaea, then pregnant, died, reportedly after Nero kicked her in the abdomen when she yelled at him for coming home late from a chariot race. After her death, intentional or not, a grief-stricken Nero discovered a boy named Sporus who bore a remarkable likeness to her. Nero had the boy castrated, married him in a mock ceremony, and flaunted him around Rome after dressing him up in the traditional clothing of a noblewoman.

Another interesting chapter in Nero's sexual career was a game he played where he, dressed up like a tiger or some sort of animal, would be locked in a cage, as men and women outside the cage were tied to stakes. When the 'animal' was let out, he would chase after and

pounce on his 'prey'. The Romans did not take Nero's bedroom romps kindly, and historians accused Nero of allowing himself to be buggered. The average Roman had no real issue with homosexual sex, just so long as the high-class Roman man always took the dominant role. Whether or not Nero actually disregarded this norm of Roman sexual morality is something that can only be guessed at. Similar accusations were brought against Caligula, another unpopular emperor who also indulged in 'effeminate' hobbies.

Nero's exuberant spending did little more to endear himself to his people. During his reign, he entertained the architect in him with many projects including a massive gold statue that represented him as a sun-god, but the most ambitious project he undertook was the 'Golden House', which is best left for Suetonius to describe:

> Its vestibule was large enough to contain a colossal statue of the emperor a hundred and twenty feet [forty metres] high; and it was so extensive that it had a triple colonnade a mile long. There was a pond too, like a sea, surrounded with buildings to represent cities, besides tracts of country, varied by tilled fields, vineyards, pastures, and woods, with great numbers of wild and domestic animals. In the rest of the house all parts were overlaid with gold and adorned with gems and mother-of pearl. There were dining rooms with fretted ceilings of ivory, whose panels could turn and shower down flowers and were fitted with pipes for sprinkling the guests with perfumes. The main banquet hall was circular and constantly revolved day and night, like the heavens. He had baths supplied with sea water and sulfur water. When the edifice was finished in this style and he dedicated it, he deigned to say nothing more in the way of approval than that he was at last beginning to be housed like a human being.

The cost of providing such toys to the Emperor strained the

economy and skimmed the army's paychecks, inviting conspiracies to begin against his life. The most devastating to Nero was the conspiracy begun by the senator Gnaeus Piso and Seneca. The involvement in the plot of Seneca's nephew Lucan, who hated Nero for banishing him because of some pro-republican lines in one of his poems, convinced Nero that his once valued tutor and advisor was behind it. When the plot was completely exposed to Nero by a conspirator who backed out, Piso killed himself before he could be arrested. Seneca, surrounded by his family, friends, and pupils, opened his veins as well. In order to hunt down the remaining conspirators, Nero brought back the closed-door trials he once swore never to use.

Gossip declared that Claudius's sole surviving daughter Antonia was involved in the plot against Nero's life or, at the least, gave it her blessing. Whether or not this was true, Nero, now seeking a new wife and a son to continue the dynasty, proposed to her, despite all the ugly and very active rumors. Antonia believed Nero was responsible for the deaths of both of her siblings and she may have suspected, as did most of Rome, that his mother killed her father, so no one could blame Antonia for turning him down. Nero would live up to her image of him by ordering her execution afterwards. Later on he married a woman named Statilia, the widow of a man put to death for his involvement in Seneca's conspiracy. The unfortunate woman must have realized she did not have much of a choice in the matter.

Although the murder of Antonia did little good for Nero's ever-worsening reputation, he finally crossed the line when he left for a grand tour of Greece and appointed a Greek freedman named Helius to run the State in his absence. As discontent came to a head in Rome, Nero had the time of his life in Greece. This was the country of the artists, actors, and philosophers he admired; a country that rejoiced in the bohemian lifestyle, rather than scorned it as unmanly as Rome did. Nero was quite fond of saying, 'The Greeks are the only ones who have an ear for music and so they alone are

worthy of my efforts', so he spared nothing in showering them with his humble works. Nero's concerts, for which he prepared his voice by lying down with lead weights on his chest, lasted for hours, with the Emperor refusing any breaks, even to wipe the sweat from his face, outside of an occasional drink of water to clear his throat. The audience was held up to his grueling expectations, not being allowed to leave the show until it was finished. Roman historians are fond of mentioning that infants were born during his performance while people faked dying to be carried out of the theatre. In Greece Nero also joined the races and athletic events where he would always be declared the winner (he returned to Rome with 1,808 victories). At the least, he had the courtesy to dedicate all of his victories to the people of Rome.

These same people were not flattered and, while Nero played in Greece, were preparing to reject him as their Emperor. The humiliation of being lorded over by a former slave – and a Greek at that – was already straining the camel's back. The straw was when Nero decided to commemorate his Greek adventure by exempting Greece from the regular provincial taxation and providing the country a certain degree of autonomy. It was hard to imagine a bigger insult to the Roman people and the Senate, but it is easy to imagine what came next.

The first serious sign of trouble came from Gaul when a general, Vindex, revolted against the Emperor. He was joined by the governor of northern Spain, Galba, an elderly but still dynamic nobleman. At first, Nero responded to this rebellion with apathy, going about his business and trusting the army to do the dirty work for him. Vindex was eventually beaten and driven to suicide, but the rebellion stumbled on without its head. Another general Vergineus turned against the Emperor while Galba, although briefly considering suicide as well once he heard Vindex was dead, continued putting pressure on Rome through the aid of the Praetorian prefect Nymphidius, who had secretly joined forces with Galba.

One night Nymphidius sent away Nero's bodyguards, officers and servants while the Emperor slept. When Nero awoke, he was horrified to find himself almost completely alone. Realizing in a panic that he was in grave danger, he searched for two things: the old serpent bracelet his mother gave him, which he had tossed aside after her death, and a vial of poison he always kept in case he needed a quick death. He failed to find either.

With Sporus and a number of remaining advisors, Nero fled to the house of his freedman Phäon. We can only imagine Nero's shock and horror when at Phäon's house he learned what had been happening in the night: the Senate had declared Galba Emperor and had listed Nero as a public enemy, condemned to be executed in the 'old style'. Nero had to ask what this meant, which he must have immediately regretted doing, since he was then told it entailed being stripped naked, marched through the streets of Rome with one's head and hands bound, and then beaten to death.

Before he went about the business of arranging his own death, Nero had only one request to his friends: not to let anyone desecrate his body. His last words before setting his suicide in motion were allegedly: 'What an artist dies here!' If only he knew that none of his works would survive in their entirety to our day, but his reputation as a tyrant and an enemy of the 'true faith' would echo through the epochs. Unable to work up the guts to do the deed himself, he asked his slave Epaphroditus to help cut his throat. As he was on the point of death, a centurion sent to capture him arrived and grabbed him by the neck, trying to stop the blood. 'So this is your loyalty,' Nero whispered with cynical amusement as the breath left his body. His first true love, the slave Acte, tended to his burial. It was noted with some satisfaction by Suetonius that the day of his death happened to be the anniversary of his mother's murder.

The Julio-Claudian dynasty, the first imperial dynasty of Rome, died with Nero. Its fall was followed by the 'Year of the Four Emperors', where three men – Galba, Otho, and Vitellius – grappled

for the imperial office, meeting abrupt and violent ends in turn, before it was finally claimed by the general Vespasian, a man who had ironically been loyal to Nero up until the end.

Meanwhile Nero, the artist-emperor, has been remade over and over again into a monster, held to be the embodiment of everything that was corrupt and evil in the Roman Empire. Yet his tomb was decorated with flowers for a long time after his death and men later claiming to be the Emperor Nero would appear for years, gaining widespread support among the people. For all his terrible crimes, Nero was in all likelihood a talented but reckless young man who allowed his power to go to his head, like so many rulers who were to come.

Further Reading

Barrett, Antony *Agrippina: Sex, Money, and Power in the early Empire* (Yale University Press, 1996)

Dio Cassius (trans. Earnest Carey), *History of Rome:* Book LIX (Harvard University Press, 1924)

Grant, Michael *The Roman Emperors: A Biographical Guide to the Rulers of Imperial Rome 31 BC–AD 476* (Weidenfeld & Nicolson, 1985)

Holland, Richard *Nero: The Man Behind The Myth* (Sutton, 2000)

Suetonius (trans. J.C. Rolfe), *The Twelve Caesars: Claudius, Nero* (Harvard University Press, 1998)

Wiedemann, Thomas *The Julio-Claudian Emperors: AD 14–70* (Bristol Classical Press, 1989)

DOMITIAN

Reign: *September AD 81–September 18, AD 96*
Born: *October 24, AD 51*
Died: *September 18, AD 96 (assassination)*

The second century Roman historian Suetonius wrote that the Emperor Domitian had little time for any literature except the personal memoirs and letters of the unpopular, hermit-like Emperor Tiberius, even though two remembered poets, Statius and Martial, both wrote for his court. Domitian had even tried his own hand at writing poems (which both Suetonius and Dio Cassius sniff at, saying they were merely 'feigned' works) and wrote and published a self-help book titled *On The Care of Hair*. But Domitian actually did feel a kindred spirit with Tiberius and not without reason. Both were misanthropic leaders who stayed away from a Rome they secretly despised: Tiberius at the island of Capri, and Domitian at his palace in Alba. They were scrupulous bureaucrats, especially taking satisfaction in their capacity as guardians of public morality, and were both forced into an early rivalry with a relative infinitely more popular than themselves. Most of all,

Tiberius and Domitian were universally despised emperors and had more than a healthy share of enemies. Unfortunately, with Domitian, his enemies had the opportunity and heart to act.

After the collapse of the Julio-Claudian dynasty with the denouncement and death of Nero, anarchy followed in the year 69, the 'Year of the Four Emperors'. The man who was the primary force behind Nero's demise, Galba, was killed by the Praetorian Guard a few months after his accension, his body and face grotesquely mutilated. His place was taken by Otho, the ex-husband of Nero's second wife, Poppaea. He lasted five months until he chose to kill himself rather than face down his rivals. The next emperor, Vitellius, was made immortal by his decision to gorge himself on an expensive banquet before he marched against Vespasisn, his rival for the throne. When a defeated Vitellius was led through the streets of Rome to his death at Vespasian's command, the jeering populace showered garbage and exrement on a man already better known as a glutton than a ruler.

The ultimate victor Vespasian had come from a well-connected if obscure family, the Flavii, and at one time was so poor he had to work as a mule-seller. Despite such a humble past, he was unscrupulous enough to be a successful politician but not so much that he was unpopular, thanks to his excellent if cynical grasp on human nature. His eldest son and successor Titus was generally deemed a living saint. Even skeptical historians like Tacitus and Dio Cassius find little fault with him, although Cassius admits that one of the reasons his reign may have been so popular was that it was so short, lasting only about three years. Nevertheless, one story, reflecting the Romans' tender feelings toward him, has it that Titus died while tending personally to people dying of a plague.

His younger brother Domitian, long ignored by his father, hastened to be declared Emperor while Titus was still dying and the story was quickly spread that he himself arranged for Titus to be finished off. The Senate spent their time after Titus' death having him deified and placing a heap of postmortem honors on him, rather than having Domitian officially anointed, postponing this ceremony until the following day. This was not to be the beginning of a happy relationship between Emperor and Senate.

Instead Domitian tried to get along with the Roman people, an attempt which even his detractors (and he had many) say was successful. Frequently he donated his private money to public causes, held grand gladiatorial shows and other contests for the populace's enjoyment and, although it was then customary for all wealthy Romans to place the Emperor in their will, he would not accept anything from those with children.

If the population had reasons to like him, his own court had reasons to fear him. Both Suetonius and Cassius mention how terrified his own court was of him due to his dark sense of humor and penchant for bizarre practical jokes. Cassius gives us one anecdote concerning a banquet the Emperor held after a war against Dacia (modern day Romania). It is so strange it is believable:

> He prepared a room that was pitch black on every side, ceiling, walls and floor, and had made ready bare couches of the same color resting on the uncovered floor; then he invited in his guests alone at night without their attendants. And first he set beside each of them a slab shaped like a gravestone, bearing the guest's name and also a small lamp, such as hang in tombs. Next comely naked boys, likewise painted black, entered like phantoms, and after encircling the guests in an awe-inspiring dance took up their stations at their feet. After this all the things that are commonly offered at the sacrifices to departed spirits were likewise set before the guests, all of them black and in dishes of a similar color. Consequently, every single one of the guests feared and trembled and was kept in constant expectation of having his throat cut the next moment, the more so as on the part of everybody but Domitian there was dead silence, as if they were already in the realms of the dead, and the Emperor himself conversed only upon topics related to death and slaughter.

> Finally he dismissed them; but he had first removed their slaves, who had stood in the vestibule, and now gave his guests in charge of other slaves, whom they did not know, to be conveyed either in carriages or litters, by this procedure he filled them with far greater fear. And scarcely had each guest reached his home and was beginning to get his breath again, as one might say, when word was brought him that a messenger from the Emperor had come. While they were accordingly expecting to perish this time in any case, one person brought in the slab, which was of silver, and then others in turn brought in various articles, including the dishes that had been set before them at the dinner, which were constructed of very costly material; and last of all came that particular boy who had been each guest's familiar spirit, now washed and adorned. Thus, after having passed the entire night in terror, they received the gifts.

When Domitian was deadly serious, he would treat his intended victim as though they were close friends, treating him to a magnificent banquet and flattering him with praises. Only the next day the person would be terrified to discover that the Emperor had just signed his death warrant. His sadism was apparently not limited to people: it was said that Domitian enjoyed pinning down flies and ripping off their wings. Small wonder then, when he finally did meet his end, it was at the hands not of a popular uprising or an anonymous assassin, but of his closest friends and courtesans, who feared being unexpectedly pinned down some day as well.

One of those who had reason enough to fear him, yet devoutly loved him, was his wife Domitia Longina. Domitian had married Domitia at the age of eighteen during the fateful months just before his father rose to power. Vespasian originally wanted Domitian to marry Julia, Domitian's niece, but he refused, perhaps inspired by the painful experience of his role model Tiberius over his arranged marriage with another Julia. When Domitia had an affair with an actor named Paris, Domitian had Paris killed and divorced his wife, moving on to sleep with the same niece he once refused to marry. Yet Domitia and Domitian still loved each other in spite of everything. The two soon remarried, although Domitian continued his affair with Julia. It ended only when Julia died, supposedly of an abortion she was forced to have by Domitian.

Like many politicians before and after him, such an irregular life did not prevent Domitian from being quite moralistic and pious. He had a reputation for disapproving of men who were too intimate with other men, something that allegedly drove the general Antoninus Saturninus, a known homosexual, to rebellion out of fear that Domitian would persecute him. For most of his life, Domitian was a devoted follower of the goddess Minerva, going so far as having a private altar to her in his bedroom. He also paid close attention to the ancient rites and responsibilities of the Vestal Virgins. When the senior Vestal Cornelia was accused of breaking her sacred vow of chastity (and also committing incest, since the Vestal Virgins were considered in a very literal way to be the daughters of the entire community), she was punished according to the ancient method, being buried alive, while her lover was hung from a cross and beaten to death. On another occasion, when Domitian learned that one of his courtesans had built a tomb for his dead son from materials meant for a planned temple of Jupiter, he had the tomb torn apart and the remains of the boy inside thrown into the ocean.

Humility did not figure largely in his religious beliefs, devout as they may have been. He insisted that he be called 'lord' or even 'god', but this might have just been his own special way to gall the Senate he loathed. Tiberius would not have approved yet, just like his role model, paranoia took hold of Domitian as his reign progressed. When he realized that one of his secretaries, Epaphroditus, was the same man who helped Nero kill himself, he had him put to death to serve as some kind of an example. Domitian also arranged for the porticoes of his palace at Alba to be remodeled with a translucent stone so that he

could always see behind him. It must have come as a terrible disappointment when Domitian had a dream in which Minerva herself told him that she would no longer be able to protect him.

Even a deity would be hard pressed to save a man whose most trusted confidants had already set it in their hearts to kill him. Some sources indicate that most of the conspirators were among the staff, courtiers, and freedmen of Domitian. The man to actually carry out the deed was Stephanus, a servant of one of Domitian's nieces. Ironically, the pretext Stephanus used to get to see the Emperor in his private chambers was to confess to being aware of a conspiracy against him. Domitian put up a valiant struggle against the knife-wielding Stephanus, but it was in vain once the younger, stronger man overpowered him. One tradition has it that his body was taken up by his childhood nurse who mixed his ashes with those of his niece Julia. Another says that his corpse was ripped to shreds by an angry crowd and Domitia herself sewed the body together again so that a statue could be made of it as an act of final wifely devotion.

Domitian was succeeded by Nerva, an old and harmless senator who defied all expectations by ushering in a golden age for the Empire that would surpass even the great Augustus's reign. This age would be deemed the *pax Romana*, the Roman peace, by posterity, a time when the Roman Empire would reach its greatest – and final – peak.

Further Reading

Cassius Dio, *History of Rome:* Book LXVII trans. Earnest Carey, (Harvard University Press, 1924)

Grant, Michael *The Roman Emperors: A Biographical Guide to the Rulers of Imperial Rome 31 BC–AD 476* (Weidenfeld & Nicolson, 1985)

Jones, Brian W. *The Emperor Domitian* (Routledge, 1992)

Suetonius *The Twelve Caesars:* Galba, Otho, Vespasian, Titus, Diocletian (Harvard University Press, 1998)

COMMODUS

Reign: *March 17, AD 180–December 31, AD 192*
Born: *August 31, AD 161*
Died: *December 31, AD 192 (assassination)*
Buried: *Mausoleum of Hadrian*

For nearly a century after the death of Domitian, the last emperor of the Flavian dynasty, the office of emperor became one based on the merit of personal ability rather than the merit of birth. This was because the emperors following Domitian did not bow to nepotism and hand the empire over to anyone in their family. It also happened that this period of time was the most prosperous for the Roman Empire.

This fortunate trend came to an end with Marcus Aurelius, the famed philosopher-emperor, whose works *The Meditations* are still read to this day. Aurelius and his wife, Faustina, had fourteen children, among whom were Commodus and his twin brother. Commodus's brother died at the

age of four, leaving Commodus as the only living biological male heir to Marcus Aurelius. This, sadly, would prove to be a very bad development.

At only the age of five, Commodus was declared Caesar, which essentially was the title for the heir designate at the time. Aurelius did his best to raise Commodus for his role, but Commodus always hated studying, preferring athletics and war games to books and lectures. Dio Cassius makes at least one comment about Commodus's 'great simplicity'. It seems that, in one of those cruel twists of fate that mark history more than we think, one of the wisest and most philosophical of men ever to rule the Roman Empire was left with the ancient equivalent of a frat boy as his one and only heir.

When Commodus reached the age of seventeen, Aurelius made him co-emperor, hoping perhaps that a kind of 'imperial internship' would teach the boy a thing or two about ruling. Unfortunately for Rome, Aurelius died only two years later of an illness while he and Commodus were in Germany fighting on a campaign. Commodus was proclaimed the new Emperor on the field, at the age of nineteen, while his father's corpse was still cooling. The army, who put their faith in Commodus's love of physical combat, was less than pleased when Commodus made a hasty peace treaty with the hostile German tribes and quickly made his way back to Rome.

Commodus really preferred to do his fighting in the arena, where the chaos was controlled, applause and cheers drowned out the groans of the dying, and proper precautions could be taken to ensure that imperial blood would not be spilled. Although Commodus also dabbled in chariot racing, his passion was for gladiatorial combat, particularly fighting animals. Leopards, hippopotamuses, elephants, and bears were shipped in to Italy from across Africa and Europe to be skillfully slaughtered by the Emperor. He would usually not fight people in public, at least not to the death (their death, that is), but when he fought in private, Dio Cassius claims, he would mutilate his opponent's face, swiping away their noses and ears, as he fought.

While Commodus was indulging in all this, the State's needs were met – and exploited – by Perennis, the prefect of the Praetorian Guard. Unfortunately, Perennis fell out of favor with the Emperor and came to be accused of treason, thanks to the machinations of an ambitious freedman named Cleander. Perennis and his family were killed in a coup after which Cleander, who turned out to be even more corrupt than Perennis ever was, took his place.

It was only when he was faced with the threat of death that Commodus was motivated to exercise his authority, although perhaps not in the best way. One night a would-be assassin attempted to stab Commodus while shouting, 'The Senate sends you this!' Commodus was saved from an ugly death only by the quickness of his bodyguards. Tradition holds that the real mastermind behind the attack was not the Senate, although the attack certainly might have had their blessing, but Commodus's sister Lucilla, either with or without the support of her husband Claudius Pompeianus. It does seem likely Pompeianus was involved, even if not completely, since he had been an influential advisor under Marcus Aurelius and might have been made heir if not for Commodus's inconvenient existence. But no matter who the true engineer of the plot was, Lucilla and her husband were both arrested and immediately put to death.

Even though the Senate was not explicitly guilty of the crime, many of their numbers suffered from Commodus's consequent paranoia, since Commodus was never on good terms with the Senate. The public loved Commodus for his generosity and his widely publicized feats of strength, but the Senate frankly found him embarrassing. The wrath Commodus unleashed upon the stuffy senatorial classes in return, even if we make room for the usual exaggerations, must have been incredible. After listing a number of victims, Dio Cassius continues:

> I should render my narrative very tedious were I to give a detailed report of all the persons put to death by Commodus,

> of all those whom he made away with as the result of false accusations or unjustified suspicions or because of their conspicuous wealth, distinguished family, unusual learning, or some other point of excellence.

Eventually Cleander, who rose to power in the midst of this bloodshed and spent much of his career getting rich from the selling of political offices to the highest bidder, would meet a bloody end himself. A famine hit Rome and a mob of citizens took to the streets, demanding Cleander's head. Commodus was oblivious to all this until he was warned by Marcia, his favorite mistress, a woman famed for encouraging clemency toward Christians and who was possibly a Christian herself. Although the mob was still friendly to the young, dashing, and muscular Emperor, Commodus was terrified enough of the people's wrath that he let Cleander be torn apart by the mob and ordered the execution of Cleander's only son.

As often happens, a plague soon followed the famine and wrought havoc on Rome and the provinces. Commodus's only reaction, despite all the naysayers, was to declare the years of his reign a 'Golden Age', but his megalomania was not satisfied with just that. Commodus began to circulate stories that he was an incarnation of the demigod Hercules, and one of the images that survives of him shows him wearing the skin of the Nymean lion and holding the club traditionally associated with Hercules. He also started envisioning himself as a new Romulus founding a new city and thought it best to rename Rome as Colonia Lucia Aelia Nova Commodiana. The months were also to be renamed, each after one of Commodus's many names and titles: Amazonius[9], Invictus (Unconquered), Felix (Happy), Pius[10], Lucius, Aelius, Aurelius, Commodus, Augustus,

[9] Commodus was a fan of the myth of the Amazons and referred to Marcia as his 'Amazon'.

[10] From former emperor Antoninus Pius, Commodus's adoptive grandfather, and founder of the Antonine dynasty.

Herculeus, Romanus, and Exsuperatorius (He Who Surpasses). The day the Senate grudgingly voted all this into law was named Commodiana. Dio Cassius[11] shares Commodus's typical greeting to the Senate:

> 'The Emperor Caesar Lucius Aelius Aurelius Commodus Augustus Pius Felix Sermaticus Germanicus Maximus Britannicus, Pacifier of the Whole Earth, Invincible, the Roman Hercules, Pontifex Maximus, Holder of the Tribunician Authority for the eighteenth time, Imperator for the eighth time, Consul for the seventh time, Father of his Country, to consuls, praetors, tribunes and the fortunate Commodian senate, greeting.'

On another occasion, Cassius shares one personal anecdote where Commodus, after killing an ostrich in the arena, walked up to Cassius and his fellow senators with a grin and the bird's head, indicating none too subtly that he might one day do the same to them. Cassius writes that he kept himself from laughing at the sheer absurdity of it all by chewing laurel leaves taken from the garland he was wearing.

A plot was inevitably hatched against Commodus with Cleander's successor, Laetus, and his servant Eclectus as the prime conspirators. Marcia may have also been involved to the point that she poisoned Commodus herself, but if we look at the fact that the traditions cannot agree if she put the poison in his wine or his beef, there is some doubt. Whoever administered the poison found that it only made him vomit; years of hedonism had given Commodus an iron stomach. The conspirators then sent in a wrestler named Narcissus to strangle him during his bath. After Narcissus carried out his assignment, the Senate immediately made one of their own, Pertinax, Emperor.

[11] Although, like almost all Roman historians, Dio Cassius can be relied on to exaggerate and distort, we might be able to trust him somewhat, since he was alive as a senator during Commodus's reign.

Commodus's reign has been marked by the eighteenth century historian Edward Gibbon as the beginning of the fall of the Roman Empire. It has been hypothesized that if the imperial office remained reserved for a certain 'best man' chosen by the Emperor himself, history would have been drastically altered. However, even if Commodus was solely responsible for giving the Roman Empire its turn of bad luck, he would nonetheless be deified by the Emperor Severus, giving Commodus the divinity he so yearned for in life.

Further Reading

Cassius Dio (trans. Earnest Carey), *History of Rome*: Book LXXIII (Harvard University Press, 1924)

Grant, Michael *The Antonines: The Roman Empire in Transition* (Routledge, 1994)

Grant, Michael *The Roman Emperors: A Biographical Guide to the Rulers of Imperial Rome 31 BC–AD 476* (Weidenfeld & Nicholson, 1985)

Hekster, Oliver *Commodus: An Emperor at the Crossroads* (Gieben, 2002)

Herodian (trans. C.R. Whittaker), *Book I* (Cambridge University Press, 1969–1970)

Gibbon, Edward (ed. David Womerlsey) *The Decline and Fall of the Roman Empire* (Penguin Books, 1995)

CARACALLA

Reign: *February 4,* AD *211–April 8,* AD *217*
Born: *April 4,* AD *188*
Died: *April 8,* AD *217*
Buried: *Mausoleum of Hadrian*

Caracalla, so nicknamed after the Gallic style of cloak he wore, was the eldest son of the Emperor Severus and Julia Domna. Julia was the daughter of the high priest of the Syrian sun-god Elagabal, a fact that would influence her great-nephew and future emperor Elagabalus. The character of Severus, one of the more renowned Roman Emperors, is summed up by a remark he made on his deathbed to the urn made to carry his ashes: 'You will hold he whom the world could not'. Sadly, his son and heir would not live up to his lofty standards.

As a teenager, Caracalla was married to Plautilla, the daughter of the Praetorian prefect Plautianus. Caracalla hated this wife intensely, but there were two people he hated even more: his brother Geta, who was made co-emperor with Caracalla and their father, and Plautianus

himself. At the time Plautianus was the most powerful man in Rome, and perhaps for that reason alone he earned the resentment of both Caracalla and Geta, although Caracalla's intense distaste for his daughter certainly did not help in-law relations. Together, the two brothers convinced their father that Plautianus was a threat and he was executed. Apparently for completeness' sake, Caracalla's wife and her brother were then both exiled and later murdered.

After his father's death, Caracalla was still co-emperor with Geta at the age of twenty-two. Geta was only a little less than a year younger. The first year of their reign was spent in a power struggle that Caracalla eventually won at the cost of his brother's life: an event was said to have taken place before his mother's very eyes. Geta's death was followed by a horrific purge that took 20,000 lives, including people Caracalla once counted as friends and advisors. Even his childhood tutor, whom he was known to have called 'father', was not spared.

Although he was named at birth after Marcus Aurelius, the philosopher-emperor, Caracalla happily played the role of soldier-emperor. He dressed, ate and lived no better than an average soldier, but Dio Cassius accuses him of still having too much of a taste for luxury. Caracalla also increased the pay of all the soldiers, a gesture that would become a financial burden on all future emperors, since only a handful would have the guts to tell their armies to expect less money.

Caracalla took as his role model Alexander the Great, whom he tried to emulate and honor in every way possible. He kept one phalanx of soldiers composed entirely of men from Macedonia, Alexander's native country, called 'Alexander's phalanx', and raised one soldier through the ranks up to being senator simply because he could mount a horse well, was Macedonian, and his father's name happened to be Philip[12]. Yet somehow this love of Alexander the

[12] Philip was the name of Alexander's father.

Great did not make Caracalla hesitate to strike viciously at Alexandria, the cosmopolitan Egyptian city founded by his idol, when its citizens rose up against Rome. Alexandria was looted to the last building, countless citizens were massacred and walls were built across the city to keep them from traveling freely.

Although he had the time and energy to crush his idol's city, Caracalla spent most of his time working against Parthia, the Roman Empire's ancient rival in the Middle East. Political unrest had emerged there (in an irony probably not lost on Caracalla, because of a dispute between two royal brothers) and Caracalla wanted to press the advantage, but he would not live to finish the campaign. While marching with his troops through Syria, his mother's homeland, an assassin hired by a man named Macrinus ambushed Caracalla while he was answering nature's call and murdered him. Macrinus managed to get himself raised to the purple shortly thereafter. Caracalla might have been happy to know that even in death he had emulated his legendary idol. After all, Alexander 'the Great' had also died unexpectedly while on a campaign in the East. However, Alexander's death, which was due to illness, was far more dignified than poor Caracalla's.

Further Reading

Cassius Dio (trans. Earnest Carey), *History of Rome:* Book LXXVII–LXXVIII (Harvard University Press, 1924)

Grant, Michael *The Roman Emperors: A Biographical Guide to the Rulers of Imperial Rome 31 BC–AD 476* (Weidenfeld & Nicolson, 1985)

Herodian, (trans. C.R. Whittaker), *History* Book IV (Cambridge University Press, 1969–1970)

Gibbon, Edward (ed. David Womerlsey) *The Decline and Fall of the Roman Empire* (Penguin Books, 1995)

ELAGABALUS

Reign: *June 8,* AD *218–March 11,* AD *222*
Born: AD *204 (203?)*
Died: *March 11,* AD *222 (assassination)*

After the death of her son the Emperor Caracalla, Julia Domna, who played more than an advisory role in Caracalla's government, was banished to Antioch. Her sister, Julia Maesa, unmindful of the lessons her sister learned about the dangers of Roman politics, began to promote her two grandsons Avius and Alexianus among the Roman legions stationed in Syria and orchestrated a revolt against Caracalla's killer and successor Macrinus. She claimed that Avius, who would take the name Elagabalus in honor of his god, was fathered on her daughter Julia Soaemais by Caracalla. The legions, many of whom still honored their great soldier-emperor's memory, were willing to believe it. The fact that many of the soldiers had already converted to the local religion of the Syrian sun-god, of which Elagabalus had inherited the position of high priest from his great-grandfather, added substance to Julia Maesa's arguments. Before long, Macrinus and his son were overthrown and killed, and the fourteen-year-old Syrian boy-priest was brought to Rome to be declared Emperor.

If the soldiers really believed that he was the son of the testosterone-fueled Caracalla, they were quickly dissuaded. Elagabalus greeted his new people in bizarre style wearing red silk, pearls and makeup. His first marriage to a Roman noblewoman named Cornelia, which was arranged by his mother, ended as quickly as it began, leaving Elagabalus to pursue a series of open affairs with men. One of these men, a charioteer named Hierocles, was so loved by Elagabalus that he made him an advisor and even considered naming him heir. Hierocles, however, was an abusive lover, and Dio Cassius alleges that Elagabalus once arrived at a State function sporting a black eye from an argument with Hierocles the day before. Nonetheless, domestic abuse did nothing to harm the Emperor's devotion to the athlete.

There was also a rumor that Elagabalus had tried to have a group of doctors operate on him in order to give him a vagina, a surgical procedure, unfortunately for the Emperor, almost two millennia before its time. Another story claims that Elagabalus once received word of a young athlete named Zoticus, who was rumored to have been very well endowed. Elagabalus sent for him and when he discovered that Zoticus's reputation was indeed justified, he gladly gave him a lofty position in his court. Afraid of being displaced by the not-so-little upstart, Heirocles slipped Zoticus a drug that would prevent him achieving an erection. After several failed attempts at arousal that night, Elagabalus angrily drove Zoticus out of the palace. In the long run, Zoticus, not Heirocles, would be the lucky one.

It seems, though, that Heirocles and Zoticus were far from the only men who caught the Emperor's fickle eye. When Elagabalus discovered a stallion who pleased him enough, he would treat him almost as well as he did Heirocles, whether or not he was an athlete, a craftsman, or an actor, leading the historian Herodian to contemptuously write, 'The Emperor was driven to such extremes of lunacy that he took men from the stage and the public theatres and put them in charge of the most important imperial business.'

His sexual preferences did not hinder Elagabalus from trying again to forge his own dynasty. He attempted another marriage, this time to a Vestal Virgin named Aquilia, an act that appalled Rome to the core. Elagabalus excused himself by saying he was merely trying for holy offspring. Failing that, Aquilia was divorced too, but Elagabalus would remarry her after the failure of his third marriage to Annia Faustina, a descendant of Marcus Aurelius. Meanwhile he continued moving through male lovers, making them advisors and even giving them offices in the government.

The army that once proclaimed him now hated him for this and Elagabalus had no choice but to dismiss many of his beaus from their posts. Even Julia Maesa, who held an important place in the State throughout his reign, started to loudly and clearly denounce him. To avoid sharing Elagabalus's fate when Rome finally grew tired of their new emperor, she now began to promote her other grandson, Alexianus, who was renamed Alexander and made heir designate. Elagabalus still had the unwavering support of his mother, but the walls were closing in fast. Alexander, who lived the sort of quiet Stoic lifestyle Rome always approved of, already showed himself vastly more popular with the army than Elagabalus now did.

When a desperate Elagabalus attempted to arrange the murder of Alexander, his grandmother became enraged and encouraged the soldiers to hunt down and kill him and his mother. Once they found Elagabalus hiding with his mother, both of them were stabbed to death on the spot. Their bodies were then decapitated and dragged through the streets of Rome with hooks. Elagabalus's body, according to an ancient custom pertaining to criminals, was then thrown into the Tiber, while his mother's body was left to be thoroughly desecrated by the masses. Elagabalus was not much older than eighteen when he was cast down from the imperial office and butchered. Many of his lovers, including Heirocles, ended up mutilated and tortured by rioters and soldiers. In our day, a boy like Elagabalus just might have been appreciated for his 'camp value', if nothing else. Sadly for Elagabalus, ancient Rome was never known for its sense of camp.

Further Reading

Cassius Dio (trans. Earnest Carey), *History of Rome*: Book LXXVII–LXXVIII, (Harvard University Press, 1924)

Gibbon, Edward *The Decline and Fall of the Roman Empire* (Penguin Books, 1995)

Grant, Michael *The Roman Emperors: A Biographical Guide to the Rulers of Imperial Rome 31 BC–AD 476* (Weidenfeld & Nicholson, 1985)

Herodian (trans. C.R. Whittaker), *History*, Book V (Cambridge University Press, 1969–1970)

ROMAN RULERS IN FILM AND LITERATURE

Undoubtedly the most well-known historical novels about the Julio-Claudian dynasty, if not any Roman rulers, are Robert Graves's two-part pseudo-autobiography *I, Claudius* and *Claudius the God*. Based on the colorful accounts of Tacitus, Suetonius, and other Roman historians, the novels were given the narration of Emperor Claudius himself and followed the bizarre and tragic history of the Julio-Claudian dynasty up until about Claudius's death. A popular BBC series, *I, Claudius*, was based on the novels.

Another historical novel and pseudo-autobiography concerning Julio-Claudians from this book is Allan Massie's *Tiberius: The Memoirs of the Emperor*.

Tiberius's notorious heir Caligula has notably been the subject of a play by Albert Camus and a novel by Gore Vidal. The former was made into a film in Hungary in 1996, the latter inspired a 1979 film (with a screenplay written by Vidal himself, although after all was said and done he refused to be credited) starring Malcom McDowell and Peter O'Toole. This film had a reputation worthy of its subject: the production was funded by *Penthouse*, banned by authorities in Italy several days after its premiere, and almost received an X rating that would have doomed it to solely the porn market in the United States (it got by with a Mature Audiences rating).

The novel *Quo Vadis?*, written by Henryk Sienkiewicz, focuses on a Roman general, Marcus Vinicius, who falls in love with a Christian slave named Lygia at the time of the Christian persecutions during Nero's reign. Nero and his wife Poppaea play prominent roles. *Quo Vadis?* has had a few film incarnations, including a Polish version made recently in 2001, but the most famous is Mervyn LeRoy's 1952 production, with Peter Ustinov as Nero. Also basing its plot on the fire in Rome and the resulting anti-Christian attacks is Cecil B. DeMille's movie *The Sign of the Cross*, based on a play of the same name. Both films did much to paint our image of Nero and perpetuate the story that Nero set the fire of AD 64. Paul Meier's novel *The Flames of Rome*, which takes Nero as its center, concludes with the fire, but the story begins with Nero's rise to power.

As the title of David Corson's novel *Domitia and Domitian* makes clear, the book explores the lifelong relationship between the Emperor and his love, while giving a sympathetic image of Domitian.

The Emperor Commodus appears as the villain in the films *The Fall of the Roman Empire* in 1964 and *Gladiator* in 2000.

Elagabalus is the focus of two novels, *Family Favorites* by Alfred Duggan and *The Mad Priest of Rome: A Historical Novel or Fictional Document* by J.H. Prince.

IBERIA

EGICA

Reign: *687–702*
Died: *702*

Egica, one of the Visigothic kings of Iberia, was the son-in-law of his predecessor Erwig, who for reasons unknown chose him as his successor over his own biological sons[13]. Despite Erwig forcing him to take a vow on his deathbed to protect the rights of the people as well as ensure the safety of Erwig's family, Egica summoned a council of bishops and pressured them to release him from the latter oath, claiming that it was impossible to see to the well-being of Erwig's family without

[13] Royal succession in Visigothic Iberia was for the most part non-dynastic, so it was perfectly legal and customary for Erwig to bypass his sons.

violating his pledge to the people because crimes committed by Erwig's sons demanded nothing less than justice. That was the claim, anyway. The bishops wrangled themselves out of the mess by not saying anything definite except that the interest of the State was more crucial than the interest of a single family, royal or not, but insisted that for the sake of propriety both oaths must be followed as well as possible. Egica was persistent, though, so at a later gathering he coerced the bishops into placing Erwig's widow Liuvigoto in a convent for the rest of her life, in order to forestall any support she could muster for her disenfranchised sons.

However, Egica's worst crimes were not perpetuated against a single family, but against an entire race. Relentless persecution of the Jews was nothing new to the Spanish Visigoths: laws banning Jewish customs and religious rites and treating practicing Jews as second-class citizens had been prominent in the Visigothic law codes well before Egica. The very wording of the laws themselves reveals the anti-Semitism that was so deeply rooted in the Visigothic theological mind: 'The blessed apostle Paul said, "To the pure all things are pure", but nothing is pure to those who are defiled because they are unbelievers and, for this reason, the execrable life of the Jews and the vileness of their horrible belief, which is more foul than any other detestable error, must be destroyed and cast out.' This sentence began a code simply forbidding the Jews to refuse to eat pork. Under Erwig, the penalty for practicing a kosher diet was a hundred lashes and a scalping. It was King Erwig and not his heir who reconfirmed these anti-Semitic laws, to combat 'the perfidy and cunning of the Jewish heresy', but it was King Egica who brought the persecution of the Jews in Iberia to a new pinnacle.

On November 9, 694, Egica called the Sixteenth Council of Toledo where it was decreed, among other things, that a Christian may not trade with a Jew unless they could prove in front of witnesses that the Jew had converted by eating pork and reciting both the Apostles' Creed and the Lord's Prayer. The penalty for trading with a Jew, if one was a commoner, was a hundred lashes and a fine determined by the royal court (if one was an aristocrat, the only punishment was a predetermined fine). Later that year, Egica called another Council, concerned about rumors that a widespread Jewish conspiracy was forming in Iberia with both native and foreign Jews scheming to overthrow not only the throne, but the Church in Iberia itself. Perhaps even Egica did not take this 'Jewish conspiracy' seriously, but that did not stop the Council on Egica's command from forcibly depriving all Jews of their private property, commanding that their families be sold into slavery where they would be forbidden to observe their religion, and that all their children under seven be given up to be raised by Christian families. The extent to which this law was enforced can only be guessed, but it is unlikely that it was ignored.

In gratitude for this atrocity, the Church issued a decree protecting Egica's family after his death (ironic considering Egica's attempts on his predecessor's family) and encouraged prayers toward the safety of the royal family to be held every day of every year (except on Good Friday, when mass is not held). Egica died peacefully eight years later, not knowing that the centuries-long Visigothic rule of Iberia was destined to end within less than a generation at the hands of the holy warriors of Islam.

Further Reading

King, P.D. *Law and Society in the Visigothic Kingdom* (Cambridge University Press, 1972)

Thompson, E.A. *The Goths in Spain* (Oxford University Press, 1969)

ABDALLAH IBN MUHAMMAD

Reign: *888–912*
Died: *October 15, 912*
Buried: *Alcazar, Cordoba*

Forty-five years after the Muslims swept across most of Iberia, creating the emirate of al-Andalus, the Umayyad dynasty came to power through a man named 'Abd al-Rahman. The Umayyads were already a very distinguished family: not only did a branch once lead the Islamic Caliphate, but they could also proudly claim descent from the tribe of the Prophet Muhammad himself, the Quraysh.

The fifth emir to rule al-Andalus after 'Abd al-Rahman was the elder brother of Abdallah, al-Mundhir. Al-Mundhir was past his prime when he ascended to the throne on his father's death, but still the mood towards him was highly optimistic. Throughout his life he led a series of highly successful military campaigns against the Christian kingdoms in northern Iberia and the squabbling factions within al-Andalus itself. Sadly the story of what he may have accomplished with the power of the emirate in his hands will have to be a work of fiction, since al-Mundhir died a few years after establishing his emirate: not in glorious battle, but from mundane health problems. Power then passed on to Abdallah's hands. More than one contemporary found al-Mundhir's death too convenient and accused Abdallah of poisoning his own brother. If Abdallah had any passion in him for governing, these accusations might have had more weight. As it was, Abdallah was a neurotic recluse who cared only for two things: hunting and his faith. Government was very much the last thing on his mind.

The love and admiration of his own family was also not a primary concern. Two of his brothers were executed at his command while he ordered his son al-Mutarrif to murder his own brother, which he readily did. This show of devotion to his father did not, however, save al-Mutarrif from being accused of treason a few years later and being killed as well. Abdallah also had several more members of his own family arrested, for the crime of walking across a bridge that the emir himself wanted to use that day on the way to the hunt, blocking his progress.

Besides the hunt, the only thing that Abdallah left the palace for was the mosque. Even then Abdallah refused to abandon his hermitic tendencies unless absolutely necessary, keeping the path between his palace and the mosque covered and barred from the public.

Abdallah's endless apathy toward the machinery of the State had ugly results. Almost from the very beginning, his reign was marked by devastating rebellions as the emirate created by Abd al-Rahman fell apart, and local lords cemented their own authority over their own regions. Seville, the second largest city in al-Andalus, fell under the control of Ibrahim ben al-Hajjaj, a nobleman who wore his hostility to the emirs on his sleeve. It might come as a surprise that Abdallah died a natural death: that he died as ruler mostly in name only is less surprising.

Further Reading

Kennedy, Hugh *Muslim Spain and Portugal* (Longman, 1996)

Watt, W. Montgomery *A History of Islamic Spain* (Edinburgh University Press, 1965)

MUHAMMAD III

Reign: *April 1302–March 1309*
Died: *1314*

In the spring of 1302, Muhammad II, emir of Granada (at the time the last remaining outpost of Muslim power in Iberia), must have been in high spirits. Only recently had he concluded a treaty with Granada's enemy, the Christian kingdom of León-Castile, restoring some territory lost to Granada. His reign had been marked by complex and taxing wars with enemies from both Christian Iberia and Islamic North Africa, but finally he had reached a period of peace, something rare for an emirate in as precarious a position as Granada. So it was perhaps with an optimistic eye toward the future that Muhammad II went to visit his eldest son, also named Muhammad, that April. During the visit, the elder Muhammad was served a cake baked by his son's servants. Only a few days later, he was dead from a sudden illness and the son was declared Emir Muhammad III. There could be worse ways to become a king, but not many.

It did not help that from all accounts the new emir was not emotionally stable, to the point that today he might be diagnosed as mildly schizophrenic. Muhammad III had an unpredictable temperament and a streak of sadism, shown in his willingness to execute not only people arrested on a whim, but also those who showed compassion to his prisoners. A guard who shared a piece of bread with several starving prisoners was killed as soon as the emir heard of his good deed. Even with these brutal fits of temper, Muhammad was nonetheless a devout patron of the arts and an avid scholar. A chronicler of the time writes that Muhammad's eyesight faded from reading too many books by candlelight.

Muhammad referred to himself one day as a 'fool' before his entire court. Besides his low self-esteem, Muhammad was probably well aware that the true power in the State had fallen into the hands of his vizier, Ibn al-Hakim, who made no secret of his influence and used his political clout mostly for his own ends. Al-Hakim issued decrees of his own from a palace where he lived better than the emir himself. This cannot have gone down well with either the populace or the nobles at court, since it was common knowledge that al-Hakim had started his political career as nothing more than a secretary.

Inevitably, the vizier stepped on too many toes, made too many false moves, and a coup gained steam. Al-Hakim was stabbed to death before the eyes of Muhammad, who was, politically if not mentally, helpless to do anything to save his own vizier's life. The great al-Hakim's body was finally thrown to the tender mercies of an enraged mob. Taking advantage of the discontent, Muhammad's brother Nasr was able to seize the throne for himself. The fact that Nasr just let Muhammad live out his days quietly in retirement (albeit a retirement enjoyed under armed guards) says much about what a non-entity Muhammad III had become.

Further Reading

Harvey, L.P. *Islamic Spain: 1250-1500* (University of Chicago Press, 1990)

Kennedy, Hugh *Muslim Spain and Portugal* (Longman, 1996)

O'Callaghan, Joseph F. *A History of Medieval Spain* (Cornell University Press, 1975)

PEDRO IV 'THE CEREMONIOUS'

Reign: *January 1336–January 5, 1387*
Born: *September 15, 1319*
Died: *January 5, 1387*
Buried: *Monastery of Poblet, Taragona*

Five centuries before the phrase was invented, Pedro IV of Aragon was a prime candidate for a diagnosis of the Napoleon complex. He was born premature and, because of that, remained quite short and frail throughout his life. Trying desperately to compensate, he developed an appetite for showy excessiveness, earning him the epithet 'Ceremonious', but in time he would become even more notorious for his endless political intrigues and dreams of conquest. By always wearing a dagger on his belt and adopting as his own the motto, 'Thus will we have it and nothing else ought to be done', Pedro spent a lifetime trying to leave no doubts as to his power and lack of qualms about using it.

When he inherited the throne from his father Alfonso IV at the age of just sixteen, he had already set the tone for his reign by placing the crown on his own head, rather than letting himself be crowned by an archbishop as was traditional. By that point Pedro had already learned the truth of the adage, 'Uneasy is the head that wears the crown'. Fear that his stepmother Leonor was scheming to kill him before Alfonso's death probably led him to take an abrupt vacation in France for a while. Whether or not Leonor actually was interested in seeing Pedro fresh in his grave, one of Pedro's first acts as king was ordering her imprisonment. Some time later, she was quietly put to death.

This lack of clemency was to become a feature of Pedro's reign. A rebellion, led by Pedro's own brother Jaime, was fueled by Pedro's decision to declare his daughter, Constanza, heir to the throne if he had no sons. This was not to credit Constanza or the ability of the female sex to rule as monarchs, but to spite Jaime, the original heir presumptive. Relations between the two siblings had gone sour when Pedro suspected Jaime of supporting his brother-in-law, King Jaime III of Majorca, in a recent conflict that ended with Pedro seizing Majorca for himself.

If Pedro had wanted to rouse Jaime to action, his plan worked too well. With the aid of two of Queen Leonor's sons and an array of disgruntled nobles, Jaime forged a 'Union' against Pedro's regime. The king was seething when he was forced to concede to the demands of the Union, so it is not too hard to imagine his delight when, not long after peace was made, Jaime died mysteriously – or perhaps not so mysteriously to Pedro, who might have had his brother poisoned. Another of Pedro's brothers, Fernando, quickly took up the Union cause, but an upswing in loyalty to Pedro and an outbreak of the plague worked to turn the tables on the Union. Pedro personally ripped apart one of the Union's documents with his trusty knife, cutting his hand in the process, leaving him to remark that only the shedding of royal blood could wash away the ink of the impudent declarations of the Union. A few of the captured rebels had molten lead poured down their throats in punishment while Fernando was later stabbed to death before Pedro's grim, emotionless eyes.

Despite these savage tendencies, Pedro tended to be a more enlightened despot than many of his regal peers. He wrote his own poetry; sponsored the writings of encyclopedias, maps and histories, and founded the University of Lérida. But like so many other ambitious medieval kings, Pedro found himself butting heads with a Catholic Church jealous of its own privileges and prerogatives. Legend has it that he had one bishop who had excommunicated him suspended from the top of a high tower, to encourage him to rescind his decision. Pedro also demanded to have his say over ecclesiastical appointments and, when irritated by the Pope's lack of respect for his kingship, would burn copies of papal bulls in public squares.

He treated nations little better than he did the Vatican. Despite disapproval from several powerful rivals and the Pope, Pedro tried to lay claim to the kingdom of Sicily. While a Mediterranian expedition did pave Aragon's way to a greater hold on the island and netted Pedro the titles of Duke of Athens and Neopatras, these were little more than honorifics. Nor was he ever quite able to quell the unrest in Aragon-controlled Sardinia, despite his best efforts. His worst blunder of all was supporting Enrique (Henry), Count of Trastámara, against his half-brother, Pedro I 'the Cruel' of Castile. The resulting war, which dragged in England and France, succeeded only in crippling the Aragonese economy. Although Count Enrique did eventually become King Enrique II, he conveniently forgot his wartime promise to cede over one-sixth of his lands to Aragon upon winning the throne.

By the end of his reign, Pedro witnessed the failure of almost all of his ambitions. Although he did eventually father the male heir he desperately needed, the Infante Juan, this son became a witless pawn of King Charles V of France, who deeply resented Pedro's backing of the English during the Hundred Years' War. The kingdom was pushed to the edge of bankruptcy by the unending wars with Castile. The Mediterranean empire which Pedro envisioned amounted to little more than a pleasant dream. Nonetheless, Pedro did have one thing to be proud of: he had managed to remain on his throne for a half century, which is more than can be said for his peer and rival, Pedro I of Castile, as we shall see.

Further Reading

O'Callaghan, Joseph F. *A History of Medieval Spain* (Cornell University Press, 1975)

Pedro IV (trans. Mary Hillgarth) *The Chronicle of San Juan de la Peña: A Fourteenth-Century Official History of the Crown of Aragon* (Pontifical Institute of Medieval Studies, 1980)

PEDRO I 'THE CRUEL'

Born: *August 30, 1334*
Died: *March 22, 1369*
Reign: *March 28, 1350–1366 (deposed);*
April 3, 1367 (restored)–March 22, 1369 (killed in battle)
Buried: *Cathedral of Seville*

The future Pedro I was the only surviving son of King Alfonso XI of Castile and Maria of Portugal, but as far as his father was concerned, Pedro might as well have been miscarried. Just before Pedro's birth, Alfonso had fallen in love with a noblewoman named Leonor de Guzman and, queen or no queen, they began to live together like husband and wife, leaving Maria to waste away in solitude. While Maria suffered in silence, Alfonso and Leonor had ten children together. Alfonso showered the sons of his unsanctioned romance with titles and lands, making the eldest, Enrique, Count of Trastámara and his twin Fadrique Grand Master of Santiago. Pedro in the meantime had to fight to receive the slightest acknowledgement from his father, much less two of the most prestigious titles in the kingdom.

With her sons benefiting from their father's unconditional love and her family benefiting from her influence, Leonor could be forgiven for believing her position to be firmly secured. But Leonor and her sons had made one powerful enemy, Alfonso's chief advisor, João Afonso de Albuquerque, a Portuguese nobleman who had for much of his life pledged himself to King Alfonso's service. Within one day of her devoted lover's death, Leonor and her sons were arrested at Albuquerque's personal order, on behalf of the new king, Pedro I.

Leonor was transferred to the Castle of Talavera in Toledo where she was killed on Alberquerque's orders. We do not know Enrique and Fadrique's immediate reactions, but one account states that another of Leonor's sons, Tello, requested an audience with King Pedro once he heard the news. The young king asked Tello if he knew about his mother's recent execution and what his feelings on the matter were. Tello calmly replied, 'I have no father or mother other than Your Grace'. Hoping Tello's brothers would follow his example, Pedro staged a public reconciliation with all his half-brothers, while freeing them from captivity and restoring their lands. Albuquerque, who rightfully distrusted his late master's bastards, was less than pleased at this show of clemency, authentic or not.

Although Pedro was king in name, he was still only a teenager and the government rested in the hands of the vindicated queen-mother Maria and of Albuquerque. The first order of business was to arrange a suitable and profitable marriage for their young king. Unanimously it was agreed that the best candidate by far was Blanche de Bourbon, a niece of King Jean (John) II of France. Blanche was not only a princess who would bring with her a useful political alliance for Castile, but also a woman famed at the time for her beauty and piety. Unfortunately, there was one slight complication. According to the gossip of the day, King Pedro had already married.

The alleged bride was a young, pretty Castilian of high birth named Maria de Padilla. Whether or not she was actually married to the king is one of those secrets that were so well kept that no one today knows for certain. Nevertheless, even after he and Blanche were named man and wife in the eyes of God, Pedro lived like Maria's husband instead, ironically taking his cue from the father who abandoned him and his mother. He only consented even to visit Blanche at the insistence of Maria, who apparently had some sympathy for her rival, but even then his visits never lasted longer than several days. In the end, Pedro tired of having to perform this chore and exiled Blanche from court, after which she found herself living like a prisoner, rather than a queen.

The day when Pedro would finally begin to assert his independence was dawning. His mother Maria was pressured, most likely by Pedro himself, into leaving indefinitely for her homeland Portugal. Albuquerque's influence began to wane and soon he too asked to return home. Pedro did not miss him. On his own at last, Pedro started to acquire a reputation that painted his reign as either oppressive, just, or some sort of combination of both.

One of the more flattering legends about him relates that, one night while traveling in Seville, Pedro got into an argument with a stranger. Harsh words led to drawn swords and Pedro ended up killing the man, a murder that was witnessed by one person. When the witness related the incident to the authorities, they were later embarrassed to discover that the testimony proved that the murderer was the king. Although they considered simply ignoring the whole affair and silencing the witness permanently, the king surprised them by agreeing to submit to his punishment, at least in a way that was convenient for him. Customary law demanded that a killer be beheaded and his head placed at the scene of the crime. Pedro ordered that a bust of his head be made and placed on the street as a less grisly substitute. The bust in question was restored in the seventeenth century and put on display at the Calle del Candilejo in Seville.

In his love life, however, Pedro proved himself anything but just. While his neglect of Blanche went on, he had a falling out with Maria de Padilla. Quite what passed between the two of them is uncertain, but this apparently was more than a simple lover's spat, as not only was Maria forced to retire to a convent, but Pedro wrote to the Pope asking him to give her the position of Mother Superior. In Maria's place, Pedro set out to seduce Juana de Castro, whom he managed to convince that he was free to marry. It is unknown what he said to ease her and her family's concerns that she and the king were embarking on bigamy. One possibility is that Pedro's marriage to Blanche was invalid because he had already been married to Maria de Padilla, who even now was being given up to God. Or perhaps he simply sweet-talked Juana into trusting him, since he was, after all, her king. Either way, Juana would soon have reason enough to repent getting involved with Pedro. His ill feelings toward Maria would not last and, only one day after being married to Juana, Pedro took Maria out of the convent and back into the bedroom. By the age of twenty-one, King Pedro I may have been involved in three marriages.

It was not long until the king's messy romantic history would catch up with him in a very real way. Albuquerque would at last return to Castile to incite a rebellion against his late liege lord's son. Joining with him were Enrique, Fadrique and Tello, who had few qualms with siding with their mother's killer. The rebellion was also backed by the powerful Castro family, infuriated by the king's callous treatment of Juana. At the same time, the citizens of Toledo revolted on behalf of Blanche, who had taken refuge at a local cathedral out of fear that the Padilla family wanted to have her killed. After weeks of bitter fighting, the rebellion succeeded when Pedro's own mother surrendered his last important castle to the rebels while he was away seeing to Maria de Padilla's safety. With nowhere left to run, Pedro was thrown into a prison by the rebels, while Queen Maria and his half-brothers took the State into their hands (Albuquerque had suddenly died from illness). However, the public must have still harbored support for their rightful monarch, because things fell apart for the usurpers almost immediately. Not only was the new regime vastly unpopular among the aristocrats and the commoners, but the king managed a daring escape.

Raising an army of loyalists while on the run, Pedro took power again, driving Enrique out of the country and forcing the other treasonous brothers to submit to his authority. In the city of Toro, Pedro personally oversaw the executions of countless dissenters. A few noblemen came to King Pedro there, repentant and pleading for mercy with the queen-mother as their representative. Accounts state that Pedro had these men massacred right before the queen's very eyes. As their blood splashed on her dress, Maria, screaming curses at her son, was dragged away by Pedro's guards to a prison. Because he could not punish his mother outside of keeping her locked up, Pedro put to death her favorite courtesan and lover, Martin Telho, to spite her.

Although he officially made peace with the rest of his treasonous family, Pedro would not be denied his revenge. He could not forget the betrayals he had endured and would not rest in peace again until someone was held accountable. Fadrique would have to be that someone. On the pretext of binding old wounds, Pedro invited Fadrique to his palace for an informal peace conference. After playing the role of the perfect host and good brother, Pedro led Fadrique to the courtyard, where Pedro's men ambushed him and beat him to death. Right after this, Pedro went to his dining hall and calmly sat down to dinner, only a short distance away from where his half-brother had just been murdered.

The twin Enrique, on the other hand, was not to be so easily eliminated. He remained safely at the court of Pedro IV 'the Ceremonious' of Aragon, whom Enrique had convinced to take up his cause. Never missing an opportunity for conquest, Pedro of Aragon agreed to support Enrique's cause in exchange for a small portion of Castile's lands should Enrique ever gain the throne. Unfortunately, the prize would not be worth the effort. King Pedro

I always remained one step ahead, and eventually Aragon was bankrupted by the endless wars. Aragon did win the war eventually in 1366, but only with the aid of French mercenaries led by Bertrand du Guesclin. Pedro was driven out of the country and Enrique was crowned King Enrique II of Castile, but conveniently overlooked his promise to Pedro IV of Aragon.

Enrique II was not to stay comfortable on the throne for too long. During the spring of the next year, Pedro returned with an English army led by Edward, the Prince of Wales, known as 'the Black Prince' for the black armour he habitually wore, a man with a fearsome martial reputation from the Hundred Years' War. Pedro and Edward forced Enrique and his followers to flee at the battle of Nájera. Two years passed with Pedro enjoying his retrieved throne until Enrique and du Guesclin would return yet again. This time, Pedro's enemies made sure to finish the job. When Pedro was cornered at his castle in Montiel, he and his half-brother Enrique wrestled with each other, and Enrique stabbed Pedro to death with a dagger.

Hated by his contemporaries and shaped into a villain by tradition, Pedro found some redemption during the reign of Ferdinand and Isabella (Fernando and Isabel), a time when feudalism had begun to give way to centralized absolutism. Rather than being known as 'the Cruel', he would, to fit the times, come to be known as 'the Justiciar' and would be perceived not as a blood-thirsty despot, but as a defender of the people's rights against a corrupt nobility.

Further Reading

Estow, Clara *Pedro 'the Cruel' of Castile* (E.J. Brill, 1995)

O'Callaghan, Joseph F. *A History of Medieval Spain* (Cornell University Press, 1975)

Storer, Edward *Peter the Cruel, the Life of the Notorious Don Pedro of Castile* (John Lane, 1911)

JUANA 'THE MAD'

Reign: *January 22, 1516–March 29, 1555*
Born: *November 6, 1479*
Died: *April 12, 1555*
Buried: *The Royal Chapel, Granada*

In 1555, in the castle of Tordesillas, a woman in her seventies had been kept in harsh captivity for decades. On her body, so worn down with age, neglect and bad health that she could barely move from her bed, was an ancient black dress all but reduced to rags. She had often told her priest that she was haunted with visions of demons, most particularly of a spectral cat that had devoured the soul of her mother, ravaged the body of her father, and would at any moment destroy her too. Sometimes, gripped by delusions, she would accuse her female attendants of urinating in the holy water and spitting on her cross and rosaries. Then one day her servants forced her into a bath that was too hot, scalding her lower back with second-degree burns. Soon the blisters, which no one bothered to take care of, festered and the woman suddenly came down with a terrible fever. Finally, gangrene began to set in over the burns. No one besides her priest, physicians, and servants saw her during this illness. She died in the morning of March 29, 1555, her last recorded words, 'Christ crucified, help me!'

For nearly four decades, the woman had been queen of Castile, Naples, and Sicily. She was the daughter of Queen Isabella (Isabel) of Castile and King Ferdinand (Fernando) of Aragon, two of the most renowned monarchs in history, famous for their conquest of Granada, sponsorship of Columbus' voyages and introduction of the Inquisition into Spain. Her son became Charles V of the Holy Roman Empire, a man who made his own mark on history and ruled much of western and central Europe. But none of these facts did her any good. She died alone, in great pain, and in no better shape than a peasant.

Yet her life began with a good deal of promise. Juana was a bright, shy girl who was well educated under humanist scholars, became fluent in Latin and had a natural gift for music. However, chroniclers noticed that, even as an adolescent, she had a tendency to dislike human company and showed signs of depression. Her maternal grandmother, Isabel of Portugal, suffered from a mental illness so profound that eventually she lost all sense of self and, like her granddaughter, was destined to spend her last years confined in a castle. It is likely that Juana had inherited something of Isabel's illness, although this would not have been apparent during the early years of her life.

Being the third child and second daughter of Isabel and Fernando, it was not right away expected that she would be anything more than a good chip on the marriage market. In 1496, Juana fulfilled that expectation by becoming engaged to marry Philip Habsburg, heir apparent to the Duke of Austria and Holy Roman Emperor, Maximilian I, who also stood to inherit the Low Countries from his mother. Such an alliance, Isabella and Ferdinand reasoned, would have been the perfect slap in the face to Spain's enemy, France, because not only would it drastically improve Spain's standing in the European arena, but it would also literally place the French between a rock and a hard place.

The proposed marriage did not seem so bad to Juana either. Philip was eighteen at the time – only two years older than Juana herself. Word had it that he was the most handsome prince in Europe (a reputation that stayed with him beyond death, leaving him with the epitaph 'the Handsome') and he had already written Juana a long love letter in Latin (or probably had someone write it for him, since for good reason Philip is not known as 'the Educated'). As part of the pact agreed between her parents and Maximilian, Juana was to sail to meet Philip in Flanders for the marriage and remain there in his household, something that made Juana uneasy, to say the least, but she was raised from a very early age to not only expect but look forward to marriage as a pleasant Christian duty.

Juana, having grown up in the stifling, moralistic atmosphere of the Spanish court, was satisfyingly overwhelmed by the free spirit she found at Flanders. Any anxieties and fears she might have still harbored despite herself were washed away when she first saw her intended at the Hôtel de Berthout. Philip, a very attractive and athletic young man, did indeed live up to his reputation, and Juana was inevitably smitten with this prince who exceeded all her expectations. He must have been suitably impressed with his dark-haired bride, because once formal introductions were done he ordered the nearest priest to marry them on the spot. Afterwards, the royal teenagers made love the instant they could sneak away. With the next day came the formal church ceremony and a lavish celebration. To Juana, it must have felt like a fairy-tale ending.

It was not too long before the cracks began to appear in the storybook façade. Money sent for the maintenance of Juana's household by her parents fell into Philip's hands and never touched Juana's. Many of Juana's Spanish servants were dismissed and replaced by natives, robbing her of even the slightest connection to her homeland. Even worse in Juana's eyes was Philip's constant infidelity. At the time, it was not unusual, but rather expected, that a man of noble birth would have his mistresses and occasional visits to the brothels. Even in such a culture, however, Philip's womanizing was legendary. A contemporary noted, 'Nothing seemed better to him than women's pretty faces'. His insatiable sexual appetite, especially for blonde virgins, was the talk of the court, but he never seemed to neglect his duties as a royal husband nor did Juana force him to sleep on the couch, so to speak. She would have six children by him, the first three born within the first few years of the marriage.

Rumors of Juana's bad treatment made it as far as Spain, so Isabella sent a priest, Prior Martienzo, to Flanders to interview Juana. The prior found Juana unresponsive, 'so cowed she could not hold up her head', and annoyed with his presence. Most unnerving to him was Juana's apathy toward her Catholic faith, especially in light of the fact that Juana's mother was a woman renowned for her devotion to God. When the prior told Juana that her mother would not be happy to hear that she had been neglecting her spiritual duties, Juana replied sternly that she had already kissed her mother's hands 'for telling me how to run my life'.

Even as Juana's dreams of marital bliss crumbled into dust, events that would give her a destiny greater than that of a princely brood mare were unfolding. Her older brother Juan, whom Isabella and Ferdinand prayed would one day inherit a united Spain, died in 1497. In the same year that Juana's first child Eleanor was born, her older sister Isabel died after giving birth to a son, Miguel. Sickly from the start, Miguel did not have to wait long to follow his mother to the grave. Juana and Philip were now left as Isabella and Ferdinand's heirs. With the Low Countries already his, Austria and the Holy Roman Empire bound to be passed down to him, and his wife the heir to Castile, Naples, Sicily, and possibly Aragon as well, Philip had become overnight the most important man in western Europe. Ferdinand and Isabella knew their first priority was to make sure their son-in-law would not ignore the interests of Spain and their daughter was fully aware of her future responsibilities. Unfortunately, France was already one step ahead. Isabella and Ferdinand were horrified to find that Philip and Juana were scheduled to visit King Louis XII of France and, worse, Philip had promised to wed his infant son Charles to Louis' daughter, Claude. The best Ferdinand and Isabella could do was get Philip to promise to come to Spain after the French visit.

As Philip played cards and tennis with Louis, who filled Philip's head with anti-Spanish rhetoric, Juana, 'cowed' as she may have been, did not forget her pride or her heritage. When Juana met Queen Anne of France, it took a sharp push on the arm from a nearby duchess to make her bow. Afterwards at Mass, Juana was told none too subtly that it was customary to make a contribution to the collection plate in the name of one's host. Instead, Juana loudly proclaimed that she would put down a few coins in her own name. Hearing this impudence, Queen Anne stormed out of the church in a huff. Juana waited in the church for some time before she herself left, just long enough to make sure no one thought that she was trying to catch up with the queen.

Juana was relieved when she and Philip finally reached Spain: a first-hand account says she quite literally leapt into her father's arms for an embrace. Her husband was not as warmly welcomed. Decked in the most stylish and current French fashion, he was set down to an interrogation before the two monarchs, dressed as always in modest black. It must have been the most awkward meeting between a man and his in-laws in the history of Western civilization. Unsurprisingly, the results of this landmark meeting were most unsatisfactory to

Isabel and Fernando. Isabel came to the realization she expected but dreaded: it would be in her own and Spain's best interests to separate Juana from her vapid, Francophile husband and try to prepare her alone for her role as queen regnant.

Taking advantage of the fact that Juana was once again pregnant, Isabella insisted that she should not travel back to Flanders on account of her condition. Philip, who had already determined that he loathed the scorching Spanish weather and the frigid locals (and was afraid that his in-laws were plotting to poison him), left without Juana, with Isabella's blessing, claiming that he had pressing business back home. Apparently this business was not quite as urgent as he claimed, since Philip somehow found the spare time to take a year-long tour of Europe.

As Philip was seeing to his 'business', Juana pined away for her dashing prince at the castle of La Mota near Medina del Campo, eating little and talking less, waiting without end for any word from Philip to arrive. He finally sent a letter to her in the winter of that year, insisting that she soon return to Flanders. His intention was to ensure his control over his tether to the Castilian throne. She saw it as a reaffirmation of their love.

Suspecting that her mother would do something to detain her, Juana prepared to leave Spain immediately. Alarmed, Isabella sent the Bishop Fonseca to tell Juana to wait until she and Ferdinand could meet with her before she left. When Fonseca finally reached La Mota, Juana already had everything ready and was leaving the castle just as he arrived, but invoking Queen Isabella's authority he ordered her to stop. An argument erupted between the Infanta and the bishop, ending with Juana screaming death threats from the battlements. Fonseca then did the only thing he could: in Isabella's name he ordered that the gate of the castle be shut and Juana kept from leaving indefinitely.

It is at this point that Juana earned the epitaph 'la Loca', 'the mad'. When the guards and servants proved indifferent to her pleas, commands, and threats, Juana suffered a complete breakdown. In the freezing night, she stood between the inner gate and the outer gate of the castle, refusing to move for anyone or to speak. By the next day, the weather got the best of her and she retreated to a hut just outside the castle grounds, but still refused to acknowledge anyone or seek better shelter. Eventually, Queen Isabella herself was asked to come to La Mota to speak to her daughter.

Isabella, who had once fought through dynastic turbulence and civil war to reach the throne of her father, now found herself facing her own daughter and heir, crouched under a table and spitting obscenities at her. In a letter, Isabella seemed to have lost any maternal feelings she might have had when she wrote about the incident, 'She spoke to me very resentfully words of such disrespect and so far from what a daughter ought to say to a mother, that if it were not for the state in which she was, I would not have suffered it in any way.' Even with her lack of regard for what her daughter's 'state' actually was, Isabella must have been able to conjure up the right words at the right moment, because after that long night she managed to coax Juana into the castle and convince her to at least wait until the spring to travel back to Flanders.

Nevertheless, something in Juana snapped and even back in Flanders she could not maintain the empty illusion of happiness. Anxious about her own black hair and dark complexion in the face of the native blonde women Philip preferred, Juana one afternoon walked in on a blonde mistress of Philip reading a love letter from him. When Juana ordered the girl to give her the letter, the woman instead ripped the paper to pieces and swallowed them one by one. Juana abruptly grabbed a pair of scissors, attacked the stunned woman, sheared off all her hair, and slashed her in the face.

When word got to Philip, he took his wrath out on Juana personally, possibly even to the point of beating her. From then on, Philip and his servants referred to Juana as 'the terror' and often kept her under lock and key, sometimes even with a guard standing outside.

But the worst punishment Philip could and did inflict was denying his wife his body. One report claimed that once, after a heated argument about Juana's servants, Philip went to bed in a separate room under Juana's without a word. All night, Juana knelt at the floor, first banging against it with a rock and then hacking away at it with a knife, crying out, 'Are you there? Are you there? Are you there?'

In the winter of the year 1504, Queen Isabella died. Her will stated that Juana (and by extension Philip) would inherit the throne of Castile, but only if she returned to Spain and, with Juana's 'condition' at La Mota in mind, was proven mentally capable. Otherwise, Ferdinand would become regent of Castile until his death or until Juana's eldest son Charles came of age. Isabel's body was still fresh in her tomb when Ferdinand called a *cortes*, or national council, and had his daughter declared unfit to rule, with the reports that had come in from Flanders as evidence of her insanity. Legally Castile was now under Ferdinand's control, just as he wanted.

Although it was mainly through his own agents that rumors of Juana's madness had spread to Spain, Philip was prepared to wage war against his father-in-law for rights to the Castilian throne. Philip and Juana made plans to sail to Aragon in 1506, but there is some evidence that Juana quite violently opposed Philip's plans to usurp her own father. Philip saw fit to keep Juana under heavy guard at all times and forbade her contact with any Spaniards. Ferdinand, in the end, finally relented under Philip's threat of military force and they agreed a compromise on June 27. This agreement made Philip King of Castile, but left Ferdinand considerable holdings in the Spanish Empire.

All this time, Juana had little or no idea of her father's treachery. While horseriding after she and Philip had reached Spain, Juana suddenly urged her horse to gallop away, probably with the intention of reaching her father who was nearby. She was stopped by Philip's men who surrounded her as she barricaded herself in a small hut. Later, out of fear that Philip would imprison her again, she refused to enter a town they stopped at, preferring instead to spend the night riding around languidly on a mule.

After Philip and Juana reached the city of Burgos, Philip did not feel well after spending the entire afternoon hunting and riding. Overnight his condition steadily worsened. On September 25, 1506, after a week where Juana never left his bedside, he died. Philip's death was probably from smallpox, although some were sure that he was poisoned by Ferdinand. Any hatred and fear Juana felt toward Philip dissipated now that he was gone forever and her absolute love for him was resurrected. After Philip breathed his last, it took three hours to convince Juana to leave his corpse.

While the infamous stories of Juana's necrophilia are completely unfounded, Juana's reaction to her husband's death was anything but restrained. Like Queen Victoria nearly four centuries later, Juana would dress only in black for the rest of her life in a state of unending mourning. Although she was now the unchallenged Queen of Castile with Philip dead and Ferdinand away in Italy furthering his own schemes, she refused to sign any documents or make any commands save those pertaining to her husband's remains. A short time after Philip's funeral in Burgos, his coffin was dug up on the orders of Juana, who had decided to personally transport Philip to Granada to be reburied at the Royal Chapel. Followed by her attendants, a small group of monks chanting the Office of the Dead, and Philip's body which was moved in a cart pulled by four black horses, Juana made her macabre trek across the Spanish countryside. The funeral party stopped at the monastery at Miraflores and Juana had Philip's coffin opened, out of fear that his body might have secretly been taken away to Austria at his father's orders. Everyone was asked to try to see if the corpse resembled Philip's, even though it was already in an advanced state of decay.

The next stop was the town of Torquemada. The reason for the rest was that Juana was ready to give birth to the last of her children by Philip, Catalina. The father was in the meantime placed at a local church where Juana held a nightly midnight vigil over the body. She forbade any women to enter the church, much less come near what was left of Philip. Eventually, after nearly four months, the small group was forced out of Torquemada by an outbreak of the plague. During the next leg of the journey the group was surprised by a storm, but Juana refused to seek shelter at a nearby convent, not even entrusting Philip to the nuns. Soon Juana ended up at a farmhouse in a small village, where she was content to stay, at least until Ferdinand returned to Spain.

When he did so, he sought Juana out and held his daughter in a tearful embrace, gently persuading her to take up residence at the castle of Tordesillas while he took up the business of government on her behalf. She did not know that Tordesillas would be her last destination or that her father had designs on her kingdom. Once Ferdinand left her at Tordesillas, Juana found herself once again under restraint. Philip was to be buried at the convent of Santa Clara, within full sight of Juana's chambers, but only rarely would she be allowed to visit. After Juana endured a few years of 'unofficial' imprisonment at Tordesillas, an observer wrote, 'Because her life was of such a kind, because her clothing was so pitiful and unbecoming her dignity, and because she had been so greatly reduced by her way of living, there seemed little hope that she would survive many days.' Juana was at the time of the writing just into her thirties. Contrary to what was written, she would survive in this wretched state for another forty-five years. In the meantime, her father had married the young princess of Navarre and niece of King Louis XII, Germaine de Foix, in hopes of fathering an heir to Spain who would replace both Juana and her children.

To further this goal, Germaine made an aphrodisiac concocted by boiling bull's testicles in a herbal mixture for her husband. Apparently, he had an unexpected reaction to it, because instead of being sexually invigorated he came down with a fever and nausea. A few days later, on January 22, 1516, Ferdinand died. Because Aragon followed the Salic Law, which forbade royal inheritance by a woman, the kingdom was passed on to Charles, but Juana did stand to inherit Sicily, Sardinia, Naples, and other holdings in the Mediterranean. Juana did not know about any of that, though, even when a riot broke out in Tordesillas in her name. She had not even been told that her father had died.

Juana's son, Charles, was then summoned to Spain to claim his grandparents' kingdoms and rule them as the first king of a unified Spain since 711. When someone announced to Juana that her son 'the king' was coming to visit, she replied, 'I alone am Queen. My son Charles is nothing more than a prince.' Charles finally saw Juana face to face for the first time in twelve years and was greeted with a weary, perhaps bitter smile from his mother. Although the *cortes*, who saw Charles only as a foreigner (and rightfully so), would let Charles rule in only Juana's name, Charles became the one invested with true authority over Spain.

Even with her son in charge, Juana's treatment worsened. Her guard at the castle increased to 300 men and her home became more and more like a jail. Possibly at Charles's personal order, she was kept deliberately in the dark over current events, but the worst crime Charles committed against his mother was when he ordered that Catalina, who had stayed with her mother the entire time, be taken away from Tordesillas and brought to court. When Juana awoke to find Catalina missing, she refused to eat for two days and wandered around the castle's corridors crying out for her missing daughter. Even Charles could not escape his guilt, because soon he delivered Catalina back to Tordesillas personally, blaming the whole incident on his advisors. Juana sometimes protested against her harsh treatment with hunger strikes, but this only resulted in her being force fed and beaten. There was at least one occasion when she made an effort to escape. One day she went to a window and urged some passers-by to break in and slaughter all of her captors, but then a guard dragged her away.

Yet Juana would be given one more chance. When her son Charles was named the Holy Roman Emperor, all of Spain flew into an uproar. The nobles believed that Charles would neglect Spanish interests in favor of those of the Austrian Habsburgs (and they were right) while funneling gold from the New World back east. Loyalists to Charles tried to get Juana to sign a document supporting her son's reign, but she flatly refused. Eventually the rebel army seized Tordesillas and liberated Juana, who urged them to 'take revenge on the evil-doers'. Juana was put back in power and even called a *cortes*. Unfortunately, the long, dark years of confinement and mistreatment had taken their toll on the queen's mind. Overwhelmed by the demands of the rebels and annoyed by the quacks and priests who were sent every day to 'cure' her of her madness, she would not make any decisions and was unable to eat or sleep. The rebel cause was vanquished in April of 1521 and Charles reassumed power. The first loyalist soldier to find Juana saw her standing peacefully in the courtyard in the midst of a battle, 'little understanding or caring what was going on'. She was led gently but firmly back to her lifelong prison, now deprived even of the company of Catalina, who had been sent off to marry King João of Portugal.

Juana's descent was now complete. Her clothing was in bad shape, her eating and sleeping patterns were erratic at best and it was reported that once, when Catalina was still with her and privately hearing Christmas Mass, Juana rushed into the chapel and 'screamed that the altar and everything on it must be taken away'. Even though she was the daughter of the two most celebrated monarchs in Spanish history and the mother of two Holy Roman Emperors and queens of Portugal, France, Hungary, and Denmark, she was all but forgotten, remembered only through the legends of insanity and necrophilia.

Although it has been plausibly argued that perhaps Juana was not in the strictest sense 'mad' but the victim of her husband, father, and son, it seems almost certain that she suffered from some form of clinical depression. While she may have had good control over her senses even in her worst times, she must have endured some disorder, perhaps passed on from a mentally ill grandmother on her mother's side, that led her into periods of uncontrollable rage, emotional instability, and crippling self-doubt.

In a very real sense, Juana was not denied her revenge in the long run. Her genetic legacy, amplified by the practice of frequent inbreeding between both the Spanish and Austrian branches of the Habsburg family, echoed through many of her and Philip's descendants. Her own son Charles, eaten away by depression, would step away from his crowns to retire to a monastery. Not long after Juana's death, Charles' grandson, Prince Carlos, proved to be uncontrollably violent. Eventually he was imprisoned and possibly poisoned at his father's command. In 1700, the line of Spanish Habsburgs would end with King Carlos II, a tragically malformed person who was descended seven times over from Juana. Much later, in 1889, Rudolf, direct heir to the Austrian Habsburgs, shot his mistress and then himself. Here perhaps was the fulfillment of Juana's sad legacy.

Further Reading

Charol, Michael *The Mad Queen of Spain* (G. Allen & Unwin, 1938)

Green, Vivian *The Madness of Kings: Personal Trauma and the Fate of Nations* (Sutton, 1993)

Lynch, John *Spain Under the Habsburgs* (Oxford University Press, 1964)

Miller, Townsend *The Castles and the Crown* (Victor Gollancz, 1963)

SEBASTIAN

Reign: *June 6, 1557–August 4, 1578*
Born: *January 19, 1554*
Died: *August 4, 1578 (killed in battle)*
Buried: *Jeronimos Monastery, Lisbon*

King João (John) III of Portugal was not the best ruler, especially following his father and grandfather, who had established monopolies on the spice trade, Brazil and goods from as far as Japan, and had brought about an end to feudal anarchy in Portugal. Instead João brought corruption to both Church and State, the Inquisition and widespread poverty. By the end of João's time, the colonial empire established in part by Prince Henrique (Henry) the Navigator had seen much better days, as had the dynasty of Aviz that had ruled the nation for centuries. What Portugal needed was a wise and cautious ruler. What it got instead was a pale, sickly three-year old boy, but this was only the start of Portugal's worries.

This boy, Sebastian, was through his mother Juana descended from

the Habsburg family. From them he inherited the infamous 'Habsburg jaw', although it did not plague him as badly as it did his grandfather Emperor Charles V[14], and perhaps something of the mental illness that possessed his great-grandmother, Queen Juana the Mad. Throughout his life, even when he seemed to have recovered from his childhood illnesses, his skin remained unusually pale, a sign that some Portuguese took to mean that their king was sexually impotent.

Sebastian's father, who was heir apparent to the throne, died before Sebastian was born. His mother Juana returned to her homeland Spain at the first opportunity, understandably because the proudly independent Portuguese distrusted and hated their expansionist neighbors. Their loathing was channeled toward Sebastian's grandmother Catalina, who was made regent at King João's death and Sebastian's accession. It was hard enough being a female ruler in those days, but being also a hated foreigner who belonged to a country the Portuguese knew was seeking to absorb them made it unbearable. Only Sebastian and his elderly uncle Henrique, a cardinal and thus technically barred from a royal inheritance, stood between King Philip II of Spain and his own hereditary claim to the Portuguese crown. Rumors flew that Catalina, who was Philip's aunt, was there to make sure that it would happen.

Without too much effort Henrique, whose spiritual devotions did not stop him from playing at Caesar, was easily able to seize power from Catalina, who had no choice but move back to Spain. Now in sole charge of Sebastian's upbringing, Henrique put two Jesuits, the brothers Luiz and Martini Conçalves, in charge of the young king's education. The seeds for Sebastian's later fanaticism had been planted.

In 1568, while still just a teenager, Sebastian was declared of age

[14] Charles' deformity, which caused his lower jaw to extend out further than his upper and made it very difficult to close his mouth, is said to have led a Spanish peasant to say to him: 'Your Majesty, shut your mouth! The flies in this country are very impudent.'

and allowed to assume theoretical power as king. Early on he had a mad zeal to go on a Crusade against the Islamic nations in North Africa that concerned even his Jesuit tutors, while most people agreed (behind his back, of course) that their king was not a terribly bright young man. The bureaucratic corruption that erupted in his father's reign only festered, ignored by the king and not helped by his officials, who were generally corrupt, inept or both. Although the House of Aviz was on the brink of extinction and King Philip of Spain was on the brink of the Portuguese kingship, Sebastian refused to discuss the prospect of a marriage, preferring instead to spend his adolescent energies on honing his military skills for his glorious Crusade. One chronicler wrote that the reason for this was because the king seemed to suffer from a curious terror of the opposite sex.

By the age of sixteen, Sebastian realized that the best way to begin his career as a warrior of Christ would be to launch an invasion of Morocco. The Portuguese already had a foothold in the country, but the fortresses there were constantly besieged and reliant on supplies shipped overseas, having so little land to themselves that farming for the entire population at the fortresses was difficult. If Portugal could take Morocco, Sebastian dreamed, a new Christian empire – Portuguese in nature, of course – could be firmly established on the African continent. Sebastian convinced himself that the damage done to Christendom by the loss of Constantinople to the Ottoman Turks a century earlier would be rendered a small setback once Christian armies, led by no one but himself, overwhelmed Africa. In those days many believed that Judgment Day could only occur once every soul on the planet had been converted to Christianity, by the sword or otherwise. Only an ambition so grandiose and apocalyptic could have driven Sebastian to the lengths of lunacy he gladly took.

Even the Jesuits cautiously advised against all-out war with Morocco, but the 21-year-old Sebastian sailed there secretly with just a little over 1,000 poorly trained men. When the shocked

Portuguese heard of this, prayers were offered in every church in the cities and in the countryside. It is quite telling that these prayers were mostly not for victory, but only for the king's survival and safe return. Joining the exhausted and battle-weary garrisons in the Portuguese fortresses at Tangier and Ceuta, Sebastian fought an army of Moroccans who outnumbered his own small force. The battle was a stalemate at best, but nonetheless Sebastian was delighted by the results and took it as a clear sign that God would favor a second and far more ambitious expedition.

Sebastian became even more convinced of his purpose and guaranteed success when Mulai Muhammad lost control of the Morrocan caliphate of Fez to his uncle 'Abd el-Malek and begged Portugal to help restore him to his throne. Although Sebastian balked at the very idea of coming to the aid of an infidel, he could not deny that the request did provide him with a convenient excuse to invade Morocco. Even someone as devoted to the Christian cause as Sebastian could not be bothered to pass up such a welcoming opportunity, hypocritical as it might have been.

Against the wishes of his uncle Henrique and much of the court, Sebastian set out again on July 29, 1578, this time clearly for the purpose of a total invasion. The procession was an impressive sight: hundreds of monks and musicians marched alongside the troops, filling the air with songs and prayers; portable, private chapels were carried for the king and all the important noblemen; and prostitutes and wives, some of whom even had their children with them, accompanied their clients and husbands. King Sebastian himself was dressed in a magnificent and exquisitely detailed suit of armor, which can be seen today at the Royal Armory of Madrid, and carried the sword of Afonso Henriques, founder of Portugal. But this extravagant show was only that. Not only were rations all but exhausted in only a few days, Sebastian's glorious Christian army was only a quarter the size of 'Abd el-Malek's. The two armies were destined to meet at El-Kzar on August 4, one of the hottest days of that year.

This battle, usually known in European history as the Battle of the Three Kings, was a disaster almost from the beginning. The best chance the Portuguese had was with the death of 'Abd el-Malek, who happened to be mortally ill at the time of the battle. His demise would have most likely given the army an excuse to simply go home and the ethnic tension in Morocco between the indigenous Berbers and the Arabs would have erupted, leading to a crisis that would have been quite advantageous to the Portuguese. While 'Abd el-Malek, who heroically still fought despite a crippling illness, did succumb to death in the middle of the battle, his physicians and advisors managed to keep his demise secret. Meanwhile Mulai had also died: he drowned in a river.

From the beginning of the fight, Sebastian courageously joined in the fray, oblivious to the disasters his death would entail. For all of his grand schemes and holy fervor, the war Sebastian initiated ended only with a Day of Judgment for himself and Portugal. Once the dust cleared and the Moroccans were victorious, the king's body was seen stripped naked and slung over the back of a horse. The Portuguese civilians that had accompanied the doomed Crusade were captured *en masse* and held for ransom. When word of what happened reached Portugal, the populace was flooded with despair. Their young saint-king would eventually return to his nation, but only as a corpse.

Henrique, then a 64-year-old man, became king. He tried to sire an heir by requesting a release from his vow of celibacy from the Pope to marry a thirteen-year-old bride, but the request was not granted. Although Sebastian's cousin Antônio, as well as a few others, was still a prospective heir, Philip II had the best claim through his maternal grandfather, who was the Portuguese king Manuel I. Not only that, Antônio had joined Sebastian's expedition and was still a helpless prisoner in Morocco. In 1581 at Tomár, a satisfied Philip was crowned the King of Portugal. The Spanish Habsburgs would keep Portugal in their grip for the next sixty years.

Even more interesting than Sebastian's disastrous career in life,

though, is his career in death. Three years after Philip II of Spain became Philip I of Portugal, a mystic in Albuquerque claimed that the identity of the body recovered by the Moroccans was mistaken and he was the true Sebastian. The fact that he was only twenty, while Sebastian was twenty-four when he was killed, did not dissuade the government that he was a threat. He was forced to become an oarsman in Philip II's 'Invincible Armada' against Elizabeth I of England and apparently drowned when the armada was defeated.

Less than a year later a monk named Mateus Álvares was proclaimed the long lost Sebastian by a village mob. When officials were sent to make an arrest, the mob refused to hand him over, then stole the crown from a statue of the Virgin Mary at a local cathedral and placed it on his head. Even with the love of 'the people' behind him, it was not too long before Mateus was arrested and executed.

In 1595 a pastry chef, supported by Philip II's illegitimate niece Ana and Ana's confessor, Miguel dos Santos, was the next psuedo-Sebastian. He did not have long to cultivate popular support before he and the confessor were executed and Ana was thrown into prison.

The last serious imposter was Marco Tullio Cattizzone, an adventurer who emerged in Venice in 1598. Backed by local Portuguese expatriates, he went to Florence to drum up further support, but there he was arrested by authorities and sent to Spain where he was tortured and executed. Even after it became too late for anyone to plausibly claim to be Sebastian, he lived on in people's minds and was revered as both a patriotic hero and a religious martyr in a cult called 'Sebastianism' that actually lasted up until the dawn of the twentieth century.

Further Reading

Bovill, E.W. *The Battle of Alcazar* (Batchworth Press, 1952)
Nowell, Charles *A History of Portugal* (Van Nostram, 1952)

DON CARLOS

Born: *July 12, 1545*
Died: *July 24, 1568*
Buried: *El Escorial, Madrid*

Carlos, first-born son of King Philip II of Spain and Maria of Portugal (who died giving birth to Carlos), died long before he could inherit his father's throne. In any normal situation the death of a royal heir would be greeted with both personal sorrow and political anxiety. With Don Carlos, however, there is good reason to believe that the news of this boy's death brought a breath of relief from all concerned, especially his own father.

By the time Carlos was born, the Habsburg family, then in control of Austria, the Holy Roman Empire, the Low Countries and Spain, had taken on an inevitably disastrous policy of keeping marriage a family matter. Instead of the expected eight, Carlos had only four great-grandparents, two of whom were siblings. Cursed by his genetics, Carlos showed obvious signs of physical and mental deformities from birth. He was frail, slightly hunchbacked, and had one shoulder that was higher than the other. As a child he did not learn how to talk until he was around the age of four and even then, up through his teen years, he slurred his 'r's and 'l's and stammered badly.

More noticeable were his emotional handicaps, one observer making the understatement: 'He is angry more often than a young man should be.' His youthful games involved torturing animals, especially burning rabbits alive and blinding horses. He also enjoyed spending his afternoons watching disobedient servants and women whipped in his presence. Even the clergy were not immune from his vicious and unpredictable temper. Once he threatened a cardinal in public with a knife because he had refused to let Carlos watch a play that the cardinal thought would put bad morals in the boy's head.

Even as heir apparent to the Spanish throne, he would roam the streets of Madrid with his drinking buddies, robbing houses and beating up passers-by. He idolized his grandfather Emperor Charles V, mostly for his military prowess, and fantasized about channeling his own violent energies into the glory of war. A story goes that, motivated by his military fantasies, he asked that a pair of specialized boots be made for him, large enough to hide small pistols: but the king intervened and ordered that the Infante's request be disregarded, so the shoemaker came back to Carlos with a pair of normal boots. Much more furious than disappointed, Carlos commanded the shoemaker to eat the boots he had made instead.

Carlos's 'condition' actually went downhill after an accident that occurred on April 19, 1562. Rushing down a flight of stairs to meet a servant's daughter with whom he was infatuated, he tripped, stumbled down the stairway, and severely injured his head. Surgeons and quacks were called in to perform various procedures on the prince, but they seemed only to worsen his condition. When it appeared almost certain that Carlos would die from his injury, Philip made one last desperate effort. He ordered that the mummified corpse of a famous monk, Fra Diego, who had been dead for a century, be placed next to Carlos in his bed for a night. The miracle cure actually seemed to work, even with the expected hygienic complications involved in sharing a bed with an ancient human corpse. Within a couple of months, Carlos was well enough to leave his bed and, in gratitude to the postmortem services performed by the monk, King Philip petitioned the Pope to make Fra Diego a saint. Despite the hopeful signs, however, Carlos was not really cured at all. Since the injury, his temper grew even more extreme.

Although one ambassador wrote that '[Don Carlos] is usually so mad and furious that everyone here pities the lot of the woman who will have to live with him,' the issue of his marriage became a pressing one. Carlos was nearly married to a woman his age, the French princess Elizabeth de Valois, but King Philip ended up marrying her himself after his own unhappy marriage to Queen 'Bloody' Mary of England ended with Mary's death. Another strong prospect was Carlos's Austrian cousin, Anna, but there were rumors around the Spanish court that the young prince was impotent, even though he did have his mistresses. Still, an ambassador did have this to write about one of Carlos's little romantic rendezvous: '[Carlos] went into the bedroom with little dignity and much arrogance the entire night.'

The gossip about his sex life did not seem to trouble Carlos, since he desperately sought to explore another avenue for proving his manhood: combat. The Protestants of the Netherlands were rebelling against the harsh Catholic regime of Philip II and Carlos's only ambition was to lead the charge to silence the pesky *vox populi*. Being the only direct living heir to the throne, Carlos's blood was too important to risk spilling, so the Netherlands issue became a tense one between him and his father. He spoke openly and frequently of ignoring his father's wishes and going to war on his own. When the

Duke of Alva ended up being sent to the Netherlands instead, Carlos threatened Alva with a sword until Alva wrestled him to the ground and knocked the sword away.

One day in the winter of 1567, Carlos wrote to his illegitimate uncle Juan, asking for his support in a plot against his father. Carlos always admired and trusted his uncle, but that trust was sorely misplaced. Rather than reply, Juan immediately went to the king with the treasonous letter in hand. Then Carlos's confessor came forward, claiming that Carlos had told him that he secretly hated his father and often fantasized about killing him. When Philip, who had been in his remote palace at El Escorial, returned to Madrid, Carlos panicked, but Philip did and said nothing until January 18, 1568. That day, the king, leading a small squad of armed men, entered the prince's apartments. They were shocked to discover that the Infante had tried to set up a device that would let him open or lock his door from his bed, but at that pivotal moment the contraption failed. Terrified out of his mind, Carlos asked, 'Does Your Majesty wish to kill me?' With his typical coolness Philip replied, 'What I wish is only for your own good.' Carlos begged Philip's men to kill him and, when they only looked down at him from behind stern poker faces, he tried to do the job himself until he was restrained by force. In a strange coincidence, Carlos was sent to imprisonment at Arèvalo Castle, where his insane ancestor, Isabel of Portugal, had spent her final days.

Although he maintained an aloof façade, Philip was deeply troubled by his son's madness. His entire court, never a place noted for frivolity to begin with, spent the days in quiet mourning, as though they were all stuck at a never-ending funeral. An ambassador at court bluntly wrote, 'they speak of the prince as if he were dead.' Carlos's stepmother, Elizabeth, who had always been close to the prince despite his harsh personality, and his aunt Juana[15] pleaded on

[15] Not to be confused with her mother, Queen Juana the Mad.

his behalf, but Philip turned a cold shoulder to both of them.

In confinement, Carlos's physical health and mental stability worsened by the day. Fearing that he was being poisoned, he went on hunger strikes, leading his guards to force-feed him. One day, he came down with a fever and was unable to swallow anything without vomiting. When he finally died on July 24, the rumor spread that his own father had him slowly poisoned through his food. Abroad, a story was circulated that the real reason Philip had Carlos imprisoned and then killed was because Carlos had become sympathetic to the Protestant cause, if he had not in fact converted. At home in Spain there was no disillusion about the Infante Carlos, as a statement from a contemporary of his makes clear: 'His mental state and his habits were entirely disordered . . . all of us who knew him thank God for his death.'

Further Reading

Green, Vivian *The Madness of Kings: Personal Trauma and the Fate of Nations* (Sutton, 1993)

Greirson, Edward *The Fatal Inheritance: Philip II and the Spanish Netherlands* (Victor Gollancz, 1962)

Woodward, Geoffrey *Philip II* (Longman, 1992)

AFONSO VI

Reign: *November 11, 1656–September 12, 1667 (abdicated)*
Born: *August 21, 1643*
Died: *September 12, 1683*
Buried: *Church of Santa Maria, Lisbon*

At the age of three, Afonso, the heir of King João IV the Liberator, the king who somewhat reluctantly freed Portugal from the humiliation of being a province of Spain, came down with a severe illness that left his right arm and leg paralyzed. His brain was also affected: throughout his life Afonso showed signs of mild mental retardation, as well as suffering periods of uncontrollable anger.

As his mother, Luisa de Guzman, handled affairs of the State, Afonso spent his time hanging around aristocratic thugs and attending most undignified events like cock fights. When he came of age in 1662, the reins of power were snatched away by the Count of Castelo Melhor, a man who was a competent enough ruler yet hopelessly corrupt. Nevertheless, it was under his guidance that Portugal continued to prosper and Spain was finally forced to recognize the harsh reality of Portuguese independence.

Taming Spain might be easy, but finding a bride for the emotionally and physically crippled king was a far more daunting task for Melhor. Even though marriage among royals was still mainly a matter of politics, few monarchs apparently were willing to saddle their daughters with a crippled, unstable husband, much less for the sake of an alliance with Portugal, a land that had only just become an independent nation in its own right. At last, in 1666, Melhor found the perfect candidate after many dead ends: Maria of Savoy. Melhor was expecting a silent, obedient ornament to make Afonso look more acceptable by comparison and provide an heir for the royal family. Not long after the wedding night, however, Maria fell deeply in love with Pedro, Afonso's brother, heir presumptive and Melhor's political archenemy.

Unwilling to cope with her repulsive husband any longer, Maria asked the Pope for an annulment on grounds of her husband's alleged impotence. She received it and began to back Pedro's forceful bid for the crown. While the Portuguese *cortes* was reluctant to depose Afonso, dreading the precedent it would set, they did make Pedro regent on September 23, 1667. Pedro used this new authority to order Melhor's arrest, but he escaped to Britain where he would remain until Afonso's death.

In time Pedro and Maria pressured Afonso into abdicating and he was exiled to the island of Terceira for a while, but was later placed in the town of Sintra where he was given a little bit more liberty, even though there was a failed plot to restore him in 1673. His madness worsened in his later years, however, and reports held that one minute he would be calm and normal and the next violent and wild.

He died in 1683, followed a few months later by his ex-wife, who had ended up in a second marriage with her royal lover Pedro.

Further Reading

D'Auvergne, Edmund Basil *The Bride of Two Kings, A Forgotten Tragedy of the Portuguese Court* (D. Appleton and Co., 1911)

Nowell, Charles *A History of Portugal* (Van Nostram, 1952)

CARLOS II

Reign: *October 14, 1665–November 1, 1700*
Born: *November 6, 1661*
Died: *November 1, 1700*
Buried: *El Escorial, Madrid*

The motto of the Habsburg family of Austria, which grew to become one of the most persistently powerful families in all of Europe, was 'You, happy Austria, marry, while others wage war'. Through constant intermarriage between the two main sides of the family, the Austrian and the Spanish, the Habsburgs had maintained, consolidated, and expanded their power. In an age where genetics was not yet a glimmer in George Mendel's eye, the Habsburgs never suspected, even once it was too late, that their policy of inter-familial marriage would prove as dire and fatal as any policy of warfare. The story of the Spanish Habsburgs ends with this king, Carlos II the Bewitched, the tragic end to generations of inbreeding. The genetic lines of Carlos were so closely tied that seven out of eight of his great-grandparents were directly descended from Juana the Mad and Philip I.

Carlos's father, King Philip IV, had married twice and fathered fifteen legitimate children, only four of whom survived infancy, as well as seemingly countless bastard children. But not only was Philip burdened with an insatiable sexual appetite, but also an unhealthy and pathological fear of God that forced him to confess his many amorous adventures in his lengthy letters to a Sister Maria de Agreda. Philip believed that the deaths of his legitimate children, the robustness of his bastards, and the poor state of the Spanish Empire were all part of God's punishment for his unbridled lusts. In actuality, the latter was more a result of decades of spending Spanish funds on the needs of the Austrian Habsburgs as well as rampant mismanagement from the top down.

When Philip's first wife, Isabella, and their only surviving son, Baltazar Carlos, both died by 1646, Philip married his niece Mariana, who had originally been betrothed to Baltazar. While he was in his mid-forties, she was barely a teenager. Their first son, Felipe Prospero, answered the couple's prayers but died from epilepsy after five years of fragile life. Directly after Felipe Prospero's death, Philip wrote to Maria de Agreda, 'I assure you that what has most exhausted me, much more than the loss, is to see clearly that I have vexed God and that he sent this punishment to castigate my sins.' So Philip must have been relieved when, on November 11, 1661, Mariana gave birth to what appeared to be a relatively healthy baby boy except for an abnormally large head. Philip now had cause to believe that God had at last forgiven him. Sadly, Carlos II would prove cursed by another higher power: nature.

The accounts of Carlos II that we have from various sources for throughout much of his life were unanimous in their descriptions:

> He has a melancholic and faintly surprised look . . . He cannot stand upright when walking, unless he leans against a wall, a table, or somebody else. He is weak in body as in mind. Now and then he gives signs of intelligence, memory and a certain liveliness, but not at present; usually he shows himself slow and indifferent, torpid and indolent, and seems to be stupefied . . .

A British ambassador in the Spanish court wrote when Carlos was thirty-five: 'His constitution is so very weak and broken much beyond his age . . . He has a ravenous stomach, and swallows all he eats whole, for his nether jaw stands so much out that his two rows of teeth cannot meet; to compensate he has a prodigious wide throat, so that a gizzard or a liver of a hen passes down whole, and his weak stomach not being able to digest it, he voids it in the same manner.'

Into adulthood Carlos was plagued by rickets and prone to 'fits' that may have been epileptic. The trouble he had in walking and his overlarge head were probably caused by acromegaly, a hereditary bone disease. The fact that contemporary writers often observed him to be melancholic hints that he suffered from chronic depression, certainly believable in view of his ancestry. There is proof too that his father passed on congenital syphilis since Philip showed symptoms of the disease in his final days. To top all this off, Carlos' mental deficiencies were magnified by the neglect shown toward his education, or lack thereof. For instance, he was not taught how to read or write until past his childhood.

Even though he was the last hope for a dying dynasty and the Spanish Empire itself, no one argued that Carlos was fit to rule. His mother Mariana assumed the regency despite opposition from Carlos's popular bastard half-brother, Juan. Now Juan did have a genuine desire to rid the Spanish Empire of the deeply rooted corruption and ineptitude that riddled the government and, to that end, he wrestled with Mariana in a tug-of-war for Carlos's cooperation. From the start Juan clearly had the advantage since Carlos absolutely idolized his half-brother. While Juan was away in Sicily, he was sent a letter from Carlos ordering him to return to Madrid in order to help him 'rid me of the Queen my mother'. Carlos even refused to sign a document that would have extended Mariana's regency indefinitely. Unfortunately, this little act of defiance was not to last too long. After his mother spoke to him for two hours in private in her chamber, Carlos was spotted running out of the room crying.

Mariana may have beaten down Carlos, but Juan, who had the support of the nobility, would not so easily be reduced to tears. Eventually Juan succeeded in having Mariana's chief minister, the despised Fernando Valenzuela, exiled from the country. Mariana herself was sent away from court while Juan tried to teach Carlos the complexities of politics – or at least how to write legibly. Unfortunately, Juan was not given long to do his work. His chances for lasting reform and his popularity among the people were both hurt by famine, plague and a humiliating war with the French. Just as his hold over the State was crumbling, Juan died after a two-month illness. Afterwards Mariana returned to court and effortlessly resumed her regency.

With Carlos's pitiful and nearly semi-autonomous existence in mind, the great powers of Europe circled the Spanish Empire like vultures. The physical and mental infirmity of one man, as well as the lack of a healthy heir that came without foreign strings attached, was enough to place an empire it had taken generations to build in jeopardy. The only hope of salvation lay in Carlos's ability to marry and bear healthy sons. With this slim hope in mind, Carlos was married to Marie Louise, the niece of King Louis XIV of France, a happy, extroverted girl who was smothered under the dreary atmosphere of the Spanish court. To give an idea as to what kind of culture shock awaited the girl, one of the first 'entertainments' she witnessed in Spain was an *auto de fé*, which involved the royal couple sitting masked in the summer heat listening to an hours-long sermon and then seeing heretics being judged and punished, with a select few burned at the stake[16].

Not from a lack of trying, Carlos and Marie kept failing to conceive a child as the years went by. A French ambassador, claiming to have spoken to Marie, wrote to Louis XIV that the queen believed 'she was not a virgin any longer, but, as far as she could figure things, she would never have children'. All evidence says that either Carlos suffered from premature ejaculation or perhaps that, with Marie having been raised secluded from any and all bawdy talk and Carlos a badly-taught invalid, the two lovers really did not know exactly what to do with themselves in the bedroom.

Thanks to the etiquette of the day, tongues chattered disapprovingly about the fact that Marie dared to make a hobby out of horseback riding alone. Also the court hated her for preferring the company of her French-speaking attendants, while the populace resented her because of widespread distrust of France and her continued failure to produce an heir. Everyone believed that Louis XIV was secretly sending her abortives and that she was having affairs with courtesans and servants before Carlos's very eyes. The loathing of her spread so much that Marie ate every meal in terror of poison. Then suddenly, on February 12, 1689, Marie got sick and died only three days later.

Mariana had always hated Marie and wanted to follow tradition by keeping the matter of Carlos's marriage within the family in the first place (and, if the very worst can be suspected, even arranged Marie's death), but she would find another enemy in the second wife selected for Carlos, Maria Anna of Neuburg. Maria had come from

[16] Contrary to what the reader might think, this custom was not entirely unmerciful. Heretics who repented were strangled to death before being burned.

an aristocratic but poor German family and took advantage of her new position as the Queen of Spain by stripping her husband's palaces of works of art and other valuables and sending them back home as charity for her needy family. With Maria, Mariana found a formidable opponent, but she did not live long enough to truly butt heads with her. The queen mother ended up dying of breast cancer in 1696.

Maria exercised control over her husband and the court by often spreading false reports of being pregnant, but soon enough everyone knew that Maria would be no more likely to bear a child for Carlos than his first wife. Finally, the general consensus became that the fault did not lie with the women, but with Carlos, who had to be impotent not by nature, but through witchcraft. A bizarre tragi-comedy followed as the highest priests in Spain sought to rescue their king from the curse. Theories were discussed that the king must have had a potion put in his food and drink when he was about fourteen years old. One priest, Father Arguelles, tried to get the truth about the king's supernatural affliction from the Devil himself, speaking through a group of possessed nuns. Another time a mad woman came to the palace late one night, claiming that she and two other women had kept the real king, who was kidnapped and shrunk down to the size of an insect, in a box and replaced him with a doppelgänger. Men's careers flourished and died over the raging debate over what sinister invisible source was sapping their king's potency in the bedroom.

The European nations were not so confident in the priests' ability to exorcise Carlos of the curse and continued to argue how best to carve up the Spanish Empire after Carlos's demise. A series of treaties, mostly made without Carlos's consent and at the insistence of William of Orange, divided Spain and its holdings in the Netherlands, the Philippines, the Indies and Italy between the enemies of France. As Carlos felt the cocktail of illnesses and deficiencies within his body threatening to finally claim his life after thirty-nine unexpected years, he made the first decisive act in his reign since his doomed attempt to overthrow his mother: he wrote a will in defiance of the powers that be and left the throne of Spain to his cousin Philip of Anjou, grandson to Louis XIV. Carlos's death in 1700 ended up sparking the War of the Spanish Succession, one of the most bitter conflicts in the history of Europe.

When Carlos's body was examined as custom demanded they found that his heart was the size of a nut, his kidneys were filled with water, not blood, and his liver had three large stones. In a rare moment of self-awareness, Carlos once rightfully said of himself, 'Many people tell me that I am bewitched and I well believe it; such are the things I experience and suffer.'

Further Reading

Davies, Reginald Trevor *Spain in Decline, 1621-1700* (St. Martin's Press, 1961)

Green, Vivian *The Madness of Kings: Personal Trauma and the Fate of Nations* (Sutton, 1993)

Langdon-Davies, John *Carlos: The King Who Wouldn't Die* (Englewood Cliffs, 1963)

Lynch, John *Spain Under the Habsburgs* (Oxford University Press, 1964)

PHILIP V

Reign: *November 1, 1700–January 10, 1724 (abdicated);*
September 6, 1724 (returned)–July 9, 1746
Born: *December 19, 1683*
Died: *July 9, 1746*
Buried: *Church of San Ildefonso, Madrid*

Early in life, while he was still the Duke of Anjou, the future King of Spain and founder of the Spanish Bourbon dynasty that reigns to this day was described as having 'a hesitant character, an exaggerated lack of confidence in himself, and . . . slow of speech'. Time would show that this was not the description of a typical shy young man, but the symptoms of a manic depressive illness that would only get worse with age. Yet, despite his madness and the strong disadvantage of being a foreigner on a throne, Philip would rule for nearly five decades, despite his own wishes to the contrary.

After the living deity of deformities King Carlos II died, the Spanish throne was left without an heir: at least, without one who was not a foreigner. Carlos had stated in his will that he wished to leave Spain and its possessions to the Duke of Anjou, grandson to the French king Louis XIV and a strong claimant to the throne. Unfortunately, William III of England (also known as William of Orange), who hated the thought of throwing France a meaty bone like Spain, and the Habsburgs of Austria, who up until Carlos's death had a family branch ruling the country, both warred savagely against the idea, wanting instead to see the Spanish Empire divided between France's rivals with Spain remaining private Habsburg property.

As for Philip, after arriving in Spain to claim his throne, he would have happily handed it over. His first recorded words once he reached Madrid were: 'I can't stand Spain.' Spanish food, customs, and even their style of coaches were all hard for him to bear. He even felt uncomfortable in a palace built according to Spanish architecture. Philip never bothered to master the Spanish language throughout his reign, conducting all his paperwork in French. He was also at first unable to get over his chronic shyness, even when he had to tend to his royal duties. Philip listened to all meetings of the royal council not in person, but hidden behind a curtain.

In September of 1701, Louis XIV pressured his grandson into marrying Maria Luisa of Savoy. Their marriage got off to a poor start during their honeymoon when Maria refused to sleep with Philip because the servants had served her a Spanish meal instead of French cuisine. Despite this and other daily sources of tension, the two did genuinely come to love each other. Contrary to the fashion of the day, Philip always stayed faithful to her, scorning all mistresses and prostitutes, and she was equally devoted. In one letter to her husband, Maria wrote, 'Farewell, my dearest king. I do not doubt when the campaigns are over you will find nothing else to occupy you, but will come back to your own little wife who loves you a hundred times more than she loves herself.' It is possible, though, that the royal couple were a little too devoted. Observers, ministers and friends often complained about their passion for sex.

The campaigns Maria mentioned in her letter were part of the War of the Spanish Succession that began in May, 1702. Spurred on by William III, Britain, the Low Countries, and Austria all declared war on Spain and France in order to depose Philip in favor of a Habsburg heir. The king himself fought in these wars with what may have been quite literally manic energy. As he said, 'All are risking their lives for me; reason enough that mine should not be counted of any greater importance than theirs.' In his zeal to appease his Spanish supporters, and against the wishes of his overbearing grandfather, Philip renounced any and all claim to the French throne. It would turn out to be an act he regretted.

While Philip was away on the battlefield, Marie ruled in his stead. Despite the usual misogynistic disapproval, Marie presided over meetings of the royal council and arranged her own public appearances to rally popular support. Although many in the court were uneasy about this free and lively Italian, the people came to adore her. She became particularly loudly cheered on when she sold her jewelry for the war effort.

Unfortunately, even the fervor shown by both Philip and Marie was not enough to ensure victory and Spain was forced to submit to the humiliating Treaty of Utrecht, signed in April of 1712. Although Philip kept his throne, Spain's possessions were divided up between Britain, Austria, and Savoy, which had joined the war against Spain in spite of Marie's marriage to Philip. All of Spain's lands in Italy were lost, as were the Spanish Netherlands. If Philip was riding high during the war, the Treaty of Utrecht knocked him down and he fell into a state of extreme depression. Then, just when it seemed things could not get worse, the knife was twisted by a tragedy closer to home. Not long after the war ended, Marie came down with tuberculosis and died on February 14, 1714, much to the horror and despair of her husband.

Because Philip was expected to establish a firm dynasty for Spain and because he found he could not endure long without a bride, he married Elizabeth Farnese of Parma only a year later. Elizabeth found a king with an unquenchable appetite for sex and affection, but mixed with a religious devotion that bordered on the obsessive. The king meanwhile found a perfect replacement for Marie: a pretty, vibrant woman intelligent enough to serve as his advisor and spokeswoman. This role was more important than ever now. Unhinged by the failures of the War of the Spanish Succession and the death of Marie, Philip began to suffer from chronic depression, bringing with it bulimia, extreme feelings of worthlessness, difficulty in concentrating, hypochondria, and suicidal urges. Philip spent days at a time locked in his bedroom, much to the frustration of his ministers. He often became convinced that he was about to die and even quickly scribbled down a will appointing Elizabeth and his chief advisor Alberoni to head a regency in the event of his death. His belief in the fragility of his mortality became so extreme that he once thought that rays from the sun had struck his shoulder and penetrated his organs.

He was not quite a complete invalid and still dutifully maintained his favorite hobbies: hunting, fishing, and book collecting. Unfortunately, what little remained of Philip's self-confidence was shattered beyond repair when France invaded Spain in response to Spanish aggression in Italy. By 1724, Philip quietly declared: 'Nobody wants me. I will retire.'

The seventeen-year-old Infante Luis was made king on February 9 after his father, who made good on his statement, put down his crown. Yet the exchange of power between father and son was more illusionary than anything else. Philip and Elizabeth still virtually controlled the government from their 'retirement' palace in Valladolid. Meanwhile Luis and his French bride Louise Elizabeth did anything but inspire confidence. Luis would today seem like a sporting buffoon, while Louise Elizabeth scandalized the Spanish court through her open flirtations with any man available and her obstinate refusal to wear underwear beneath her gaudy dresses. So shocking was Louise Elizabeth's behavior that Luis once had her locked up for a day

in her apartments. Spain was spared the prospect of this less than glamorous royal couple when Luis died later that year. Philip wanted to replace him with his brother Fernando, but since the Infante was only eleven, Philip reluctantly resumed the throne by September 6.

Aside from a brief upswing that coincided with his plans to restore his claim to the French throne during the seemingly mortal illness of the new French king Louis XV (unfortunately for Philip, the young king made a sudden recovery), Philip's condition steadily worsened. He began to keep himself in bed for days, feeling physically paralyzed by his depression and anxiety. Paranoia also set in: obsessed with the idea that someone could poison him through his clothing, he began to wear only shirts that were tried on by Elizabeth. Once, overwhelmed by the hallucinations that were becoming too frequent, he believed he was dead. Another time he thought he had turned into a frog.

Also about this time Philip began to adopt a schedule foreign ambassadors and royal ministers found very cumbersome. An average day for Philip began around 4 p.m., when he would awaken and attend 'morning' Mass. Around midnight, he would conduct state business and meet with ambassadors and officials. At 2 a.m., he had his supper and would finally go to bed at dawn. This eccentric schedule took its toll on Elizabeth, who remained by Philip's side until the very end. Touching as this devotion was, it also gave rise to rumors that she was influencing her mad husband in all matters political but, despite what their contemporaries believed, she was anything but Philip's puppetmaster in these bad times. The couple argued loudly and at times their arguments even took a violent tone.

Over time Philip's physical state became a reflection of his disordered mind. He refused to cut his toenails and kept a long dirty beard. His hair was always unwashed and uncut, clumsily hidden under a filthy wig. Foreign dignitaries had meetings with the king while he was dressed in his nightclothes with his legs and feet bare. Sometimes he would urinate or defecate in his own bed. The agoraphobic king started to refuse to ever leave his palace, but he did not let that get in the way of his love of fishing. He simply had a large bowl filled with water and fish and did his fishing from that.

Philip did make a few more attempts to abdicate, but all were thwarted by Elizabeth who tried her best to keep all pen and paper from her husband's reach. One day, though, while the queen was away Philip found some paper, hastily scribbled out a declaration of abdication, and gave it to a trusted servant who immediately rushed off to the royal council. Just as the council was preparing to have the note read, a nobleman dispatched by Elizabeth grabbed the paper and immediately ripped it to shreds.

Although he was without a doubt in a dire state, Philip's luck took a turn for the better towards the end of his life. Most of the Italian territories lost to Spain by the Treaty of Utrecht were eventually restored to Spain's possession, with the exception of Milan. Philip and Elizabeth's desire to secure a legacy for their son Carlos was fulfilled when Philip was able to confer all the Italian titles on him by April 1739. Still, Philip never fully recovered from his condition. In this tragic mental state, he died on July 9 of that year, leaving the throne to his surviving son from his first marriage, Fernando, who was not much better off than he was.

Further Reading

Bergamini, John D. *The Spanish Bourbons: The History of a Tenacious Dynasty* (Putnam, 1974)

Green, Vivian *The Madness of Kings: Personal Trauma and the Fate of Nations* (Sutton, 1993)

Kamen, Henry Arthur Francis *Philip V: The King Who Reigned Twice* (Yale University Press, 2001)

Lynch, John *Bourbon Spain, 1700-1808* (Cambridge University Press, 1989)

FERNANDO VI

Reign: *July 9, 1746–August 10, 1759*
Born: *September 23, 1713*
Died: *August 10, 1759*
Buried: *Church of Salesian Nuns, Madrid*

Fernando inherited not only the throne of Spain from his father Philip V, but also much of his mental illness. Like Philip, Fernando was plagued by periods of depression and low self-esteem, which were no less turbulent than those his father suffered even though Fernando reigned in more peaceful and prosperous times.

Although it took a war that lasted over a decade to keep Philip on the throne, Fernando's only opposition was the resentment of his stepmother, Elizabeth Farnese, who wanted her own son by Philip,

Carlos[17], to be the one King of Spain. While Carlos did obtain the titles to the Spanish territories in Italy, as well as his mother's claim to the Italian duchy of Parma, tensions were still rife between the two brothers. Before he became king, Fernando and his wife Barbara de Braganza constantly found themselves ostracized and shunned by Elizabeth and most members of the court who wanted to stay on Elizabeth's good side.

Barbara, an Infanta of Portugal, was disfigured by smallpox and hideously overweight. While Fernando and Barbara's marriage might appear to have been yet another match made in the holy name of politics, Fernando was as devoted to his queen as his father was to his wives. This devotion was confused with servitude and Barbara was thought to hold the same spellbinding influence with Fernando as Elizabeth Farnese had held over King Philip. After Fernando's accession, the people joked that 'Queen Barbara had succeeded Queen Elizabeth'.

Although Fernando was very well-liked because he was the first Spanish king in fifty years who could actually speak fluent Spanish, he did lack political expertise, having always been excluded from any important chores by his father and stepmother. He did, however, take advantage of the widespread prosperity of his reign by engaging in grand gestures of charity toward his less fortunate subjects and by constructing a grand new royal palace in Madrid.

While much of his life was marked by unstable moods, resulting in sudden flashes of temper and long periods of depression, his sanity did not lapse until after the death of Barbara in 1758. Keeping himself secluded in the palace, he began to develop a morbid fear of death, believing that he would die if he ever stopped to lie down. There were accounts that he tried to commit suicide, once with a pair of scissors and another time by trying to hang himself with a

[17] She would eventually get her wish. Carlos succeeded Fernando as Carlos III. Luckily, Elizabeth would live to see it.

noose he fashioned out of his bed sheets. Also like his father his physical appearance eventually began to deteriorate. He refused to shave or bathe, and sometimes met both his ministers and foreign dignitaries half-naked in his nightclothes. Living only on watery soups, his health steadily worsened until he died in 1759, almost exactly a year after his dear wife.

Further Reading

Bergamini, John D. *The Spanish Bourbons: The History of a Tenacious Dynasty* (New York, 1974)

Green, Vivian *The Madness of Kings: Personal Trauma and the Fate of Nations* (Sutton, 1993)

Lynch, John *Bourbon Spain, 1700-1808* (Cambridge University Press, 1989)

MARIA I

Reign: *February 24, 1777–March 20, 1816*
Born: *December 17, 1734*
Died: *March 20, 1816*
Buried: *Basilica de Estrela, Lisbon*

Although it is easy to think of most monarchs as cynical wielders of an autocratic authority supported by the twin pillars of religion and custom, many were raised to see their station as God's representative on earth as much more than simply rhetoric. The relationship between a monarch and their God was very real, and more than a few obsessed over God's opinion of their policy and lifestyle. Queen Maria of Portugal was consumed by this very royal terror of the divine beyond the point of madness.

Maria's father, King José I of Portugal, was not born with a talent or even an interest in politics, so instead the real ruler during his reign

became his favorite minister, the Marquis of Pombal. Although Pombal raised Portugal to the Enlightenment and was the perfect image of the 'new European', he was almost like a medieval warrior-king in his ruthlessness. One staunch political enemy of Pombal implicated in an assassination attempt against José was punished with having each of his bones broken at Pombal's own personal command.

When Maria succeeded José, her husband and uncle Pedro took a place by her side as co-ruler, King Pedro III. While in theory they were meant to hold equal authority, Maria was in fact the true monarch. Pedro was more concerned with keeping up his flawless attendance record at Mass than making decrees and was said by many who met him to have been too naïve to make a good king. Maria at least had enough of a hold on things to have been able to effectively dismiss Pombal, whom she loathed from the beginning, and set free many of his political prisoners. Rescinding so many of these acts, all made by her enemy yet in the name of her cherished father, was not so easy for her on the inside. Her first reported episode of madness occurred when she scratched out her own signature on an act reversing one of her father's laws, crying out that she was in Hell.

Maria's condition was worsened by a horrific series of deaths that she could only interpret as God's punishment for betraying her father. Pedro died in 1786, followed in 1788 by Maria's eldest son José who died from smallpox after Maria refused to have him vaccinated[18]. Her daughter Mariana followed them not long afterwards. Eventually, of the seven children parented by Maria and Pedro, only one, João, remained alive and healthy.

As her family slowly dwindled around her, Maria became prone to deep periods of depression, accented by severe insomnia and intestinal problems. Two years after the deaths of José and Mariana, Maria completely lost her hold on reality: she was consumed by

[18] The Church initially opposed smallpox vaccinations, while it was also commonly believed then that vaccinations were more often fatal than helpful.

visions of being in Hell. João was made regent in 1799 while Maria was handed over to Dr Francis Willis, the same doctor who had treated the madness of King George III of Britain. Even the no-nonsense Willis was eventually forced to concede while Maria's visions of her damnation became all the more vivid and horrifying, both to her and those around her. One British guest at Maria's court wrote, 'The most agonizing shrieks, shrieks such as I hardly conceived possible, inflicted on me a sensation of horror such as I had never felt before. The Queen herself, whose apartment was only two doors off from the chambers where we were sitting, uttered those dreadful sounds. "*Ai Jesus! Ai Jesus!*" did she exclaim again and again in the utterances of agony.'

When Napoleon, who already held the Spanish royal family as state prisoners, attacked Portugal, Maria's family had little choice but to flee to Brazil. Maria, whose recovery now seemed impossible, was shut away in a Carmelite convent in Rio de Janeiro. After over two decades of near complete abandonment, she died there, but her body was eventually returned to her homeland.

Further Reading

Gribble, Francis *The Royal House of Portugal* (London, 1915)
Nowell, Charles *A History of Portugal* (Van Nostram, 1952)

IBERIA IN FILM AND LITERATURE

The prolific nineteenth-century French novelist and playwright Alexandre Dumas wrote a novella on Pedro 'the Cruel' which is collected with two other novellas *Praxède* and *Jehanne le Pucelle*. As far as I can tell, no published English translation exists.

The 2001 Spanish film *Juana la Loca*, titled by foreign distributors as *Mad Love*, exists on DVD with English subtitles. An earlier movie also concerning Queen Juana exists titled *Locura de amor*, made in Spain in 1948, and which itself is based on a nineteenth-century play by Manuel Tamayo y Baus. A more contemporary drama about Juana, *Juana del amor hermoso*, was written by Manuel Martinez Mediero. An English version by Hazel Carzola is titled *A Love Too Beautiful*.

In the early 1800s, a novel about Sebastian titled simply *Don Sebastian: An Historical Romance* was authored by Anne Maria Porter.

Friedrich Schiller's play about Don Carlos depicted him, wrongly, as a martyr for the Protestant cause against his tyrannical father Philip II. No trace of madness can be found in Schiller's Carlos.

Olivia Leigh has also written a novel, published in 1966, about the reign of Carlos II titled succinctly *The Cretin Wore a Crown.*

FRANCE

FREDEGUND

Reign: *584–597*
Died: *597*
Buried: *Basilica of Saint Denis (in effigy)*

Once the rich province of Gaul fell from the orbit of the Western Roman Empire to the 'barbarian' hordes sweeping across Europe, it was settled by a Germanic people, the Franks, who would in time give the land their name. After the Frankish king Clovis died, the area of modern France was split into a handful of kingdoms and bequeathed to Clovis's quarreling sons. The descendants of Clovis, the Merovingian dynasty, would remain dissatisfied with their own tiny slices of territory throughout the generations. For centuries, brothers and cousins fought and connived and intrigued against each other, giving shape to the story of one of the bloodiest royal families in history.

Our subject Fredegund fitted in easily with this violent clan. She came from a family of low rank and had worked as a servant to Queen Audovera, wife to King Chilperic of Neustria, a Merovingian kingdom in what is now northern France. Whether or not Fredegund did anything to invite his attentions, Chilperic quickly fell deeply in love or lust with her. Not content with having Fredegund as another of his mistresses, Chilperic waited for a way to get rid of his distracting wife. When Audovera broke canon law by not having a godmother to hold her newborn daughter after her baptism, Chilperic used this little incident as an excuse to divorce Audovera and exile her to a convent. Yet, as far as Fredegund was concerned, this was not enough to ensure her grip on Chilperic. Sometime after becoming Chilperic's new bride, Fredegund sent an assassin to murder Audovera in the haven of the nunnery itself. Audovera and Chilperic's daughter Basina was also later condemned to the holy life, but fortunately Basina did not share her unlucky mother's ultimate fate.

The remedy provided by Audovera's death was only temporary. Chilperic later resolved to marry a Visigothic princess named Galswinth and even promised her father that he would 'put away' all his other lovers (some of whom he may have been bigamously married to, which was a Merovingian tradition), including Fredegund. In spite of Chilperic's promise, Fredegund still resided in the castle and mocked and threatened the terrified princess, who became so distressed she tried to get permission from her husband to return home to Iberia. Chilperic refused, jokingly putting down Galswinth's paranoia, but her fear of Fredegund was justified soon enough: Fredegund lovingly persuaded Chilperic to let Galswinth be garroted by a servant. The matter did not end there, though. Galswinth's sister was Brunhilde, who happened to be married to Chilperic's brother, Sigibert, king of the Merovingian kingdom of Austrasia. Brunhilde was not at all willing to forgive or forget Fredegund's involvement in her sister's murder, starting a vicious feud between the two queens that would become the stuff of legends.

More than once throughout their long rivalry Fredegund tried to silence Brunhilde. One story claims that, after Fredegund became queen regent, she sent twelve assassins against Brunhilde and her sons, but one of them lost his nerve at the last minute and gave the others away. When the man stupidly returned to Fredegund, she ordered that his nose and ears be cut off. To rub salt into the fresh wounds, Fredegund let him live so he could spend the rest of his life as a ridiculed deformity. An anecdote makes her even less lenient to another failed assassin, who was sent disguised as Brunhilde's new confessor. When he too returned without blood on his hands, she ordered that he have his feet and hands chopped off.

After Sigibert died, allegedly at the hands of assassins also hired by Fredegund, Chilperic invaded Austrasia and banished Brunhilde to a convent while confiscating her estates. He also had his heart set on capturing and killing his nephew and Sigibert's heir, Childebert, but the boy was hidden in a game sack by a loyal nobleman and spirited away to safety. Still, it must have satisfied Fredegund that at least her hated rival was finally out of her hair forever. We can only imagine Fredegund's shock when she discovered that her stepson Merovech had married Brunhilde in Rouen, professing his eternal devotion to her like a lovesick teenager. At Fredegund's urging, Chilperic stormed Rouen only to find that the odd couple had taken refuge in a church and invoked sanctuary. Not quite furious enough to commit blasphemy, Chilperic sweet-talked the honeymooners into coming out, swearing that he would do nothing to separate them. Either they foolishly believed him or else they reluctantly realized that they did not have that many options at hand.

While Brunhilde was able to escape and plot to get back her kingdom, Chilperic sentenced his disobedient son to spend the rest of his life in a monastery. Merovech's lust for Brunhilde would not be quenched by the promises of a spiritual life or by his father's wrath, however, and he soon escaped the monastery with a faithful servant. Eventually he made his way to Tours, where he broke into the cathedral there and threatened to kill all those in the building until the bishop, Gregory (who also happened to be the historian who recorded many of these events), provided him with sanctuary. Gregory agreed, but when Chilperic approached, Merovech lost confidence in the Church's power to protect him from his father's fury and fled again. With Chilperic on his heels, Merovech tried to meet with Brunhilde, but the Austrasian nobility, with good reason, stopped him from seeing her. With nowhere else to run, he hid out in a farmhouse in Rheims where he begged his friend and servant to put him out of his misery. With a touching loyalty, the servant obliged his young master. When Chilperic and Fredegund realized what had happened, they rewarded the servant for his loyalty by having him deprived of his hands, feet, ears, and nose.

Fredegund treated her other stepson, Clovis, no better. When her children by Chilperic died from an epidemic of dysentery, she accused Clovis of casting a spell against them in jealousy. Apparently Chilperic seconded her accusations without a thought. Clovis was then imprisoned and later stabbed to death, supposedly while praying in his cell. Another anecdote says that her own biological children did not earn much more regard. A short while after her daughter mocked her because of her peasant origin, Fredegund told the girl she could borrow a jewel of her choice from Fredegund's own chest. Once the girl put her head under the chest's massive lid to look, Fredegund slammed the lid on her daughter's neck. The girl was only saved when her screams reached a nearby servant who saved her life.

Yet Fredegund seemed to reserve some warm feelings for her children. After the aforementioned dysentery caused her two young sons to fall ill, Fredegund burned the tax rolls to the cities in her private possession and passionately urged her husband to lower taxes, since the deaths of their children were certainly God's punishment for their tyrannical ways. 'God has endured our evil goings-on long enough. Now we are going to lose our children,' Fredegund said. 'It is the tears of the paupers which are the cause of their death, the sighs of orphans, the widows' laments. Yet we still lay up treasures, we who have no one to whom we can leave them. Our riches live on after us, the fruits of rapine, hatred and accursed. Now we are losing the most beautiful of our possessions! Come, then, I beg you! Let us set light to all these iniquitous tax demands!'[19] There may be some truth to this story and it may well indicate what kind of ruler she truly was, given Fredegund's high esteem later on as queen regent, but the story of how she became regent is not nearly as flattering.

Fredegund had taken the Mayor of the Palace[20], Landeric, as her lover. This arrangement went on well enough right under Chilperic's nose, until one day Chilperic snuck up behind Fredegund and playfully whacked her on her bottom. Perhaps not expecting to see her husband that day, she instinctively replied, 'Why do you do this, Landeric?' Instantly realizing the truth, the king went off to his daily hunt without a word, probably to contemplate what to do with the treasonous lovers. A panicked Fredegund ran to Landeric and together they got a couple of Landeric's men drunk and encouraged them to go out to kill the king on the pretext of some private grievance. Taking Chilperic off-guard during his hunt, they managed to stab him to death and Brunhilde's son, who had become King Childebert II of Austrasia, got the blame for it.

Since her son Lothair was too young formally to rule, she took on the regency of the kingdom. Curiously, despite her violent and sadistic reputation, she is depicted more or less as a good, respected ruler, albeit one with a streak of ruthlessness, notable even for her time. One nobleman, Leudast, rebelled against her regency but was defeated and wounded in battle. Fredegund ordered her physicians to treat him until he was well enough to serve as an example. Gregory of Tours writes, 'At the personal command of the queen, [Leudast] was placed flat on his back on the ground, a block of wood was wedged behind his neck, and they beat him on the throat with another piece of wood until he died.'

Fredegund did not shy away from any aspect of ruling any more than she shied away from punishing traitors. Following old Celtic

[19] Unfortunately, the two small boys were still carried off by the plague.

[20] The Mayors were, in a sense, the Prime Ministers to the kings. As time went by, the Merovingian kings became little more than puppets, and the Mayors their puppet-masters.

and Germanic traditions that saw nothing wrong with women following their men to the battlefield, she led an army alongside Landeric against Childebert II, who tried to capture the Neustrian capital of Soissons. She even devised the tactic that won them the field: she urged the troops to disguise themselves with foliage and tree branches. This strategy would be referenced centuries later by William Shakespeare in *Macbeth*.

But despite the occasional war and rebellion, her only real troubles, as far as we can tell, came mostly from her private war with Brunhilde, who had ironically also become regent in her own country. Despite Brunhilde's best efforts, in 597 Fredegund died peacefully, although rumors of poisoning shrouded her death. Brunhilde, on the other hand, met a far less merciful demise. Fate, helped along by more Merovingian interfamilial violence, killed off Brunhilde's son Childebert and his sons, leaving her with four royal great-grandchildren, all of whom were under age. In 613, Fredegund's son, now Lothair II, bribed the generals of Austrasia into surrendering the country to him. Well into her sixties, Brunhilde was 'led through the [army] ranks on a camel. Finally she was tied by her hair, one arm and one leg to the tail of an unbroken horse, and she was cut to shreds by its hoofs at the pace it went.' Her body was then burned and the ashes scattered to the four winds. Even if we suppose that the stories of Fredegund's cold-bloodedness were exaggerated, we can see the tale of her feud with Brunhilde as historical evidence that the nice guy does, in fact, finish last.

Further Reading

Gregory of Tours (trans. Lewis Thorpe) *History of the Franks* (Harmondsworth, 1974)

Scherman, Katherine *The Birth of France: Warriors, Bishops, and Long-Haired Kings* (Random House, 1987)

Wood, I.N. *The Merovingian Kingdoms, 450-751* (Longman, 1994)

CHARLES VI

Reign: *September 16, 1380–October 21, 1422*
Born: *December 3, 1368*
Died: *October 21, 1422*
Buried: *Basilica of Saint-Denis (in effigy)*

As a young man, Charles was an athletic and handsome prince, renowned for his boundless generosity and his habit of treating anyone amiably and like an equal, even servants and peasants. For years France had been devastated and exhausted by the so-called Hundred Years' War, ignited when King Edward III of England decided to force his hereditary claim on the French throne despite the opinions of the French themselves. They looked hopefully toward Charles when, at the age of just twelve, he inherited the throne, but sadly for the French this optimism in Charles would prove to be misplaced. Charles was plagued by a horrific mental illness, quite possibly schizophrenia, for most of his adult life, making what would normally be a personal tragedy into a national catastrophe.

When he came to the throne, the only complaint people had with the gallant and strapping young king was his preoccupation with sex. When Charles met with Isabeau of Bavaria, the young daughter of a German noble, on July 14, 1385 during a 'date' of sorts, he ordered that they be married only a few days later. She did not know a word of French and he could not speak any German, so hormones must have been the deciding factor. Although it would not turn out to be a happy marriage, their passion never really dimmed. Isabeau would eventually bear Charles twelve children.

Three years after the marriage, Charles was declared of age and began to rule formally. The State had formerly been in the hands of his uncles, who used their influence to further their own personal ambitions and indulge in feuds. Even when invested with the crown, Charles's interest in politics stayed minimal. He instead preferred spending his days on horseriding, archery, and, of course, sex. Any real power was delegated to Queen Isabeau and Charles's brother, Louis, the future Duke of Orléans. Gossip would later hint that the two were lovers, although the contemporary evidence does not quite agree.

The signs of Charles's insanity did not fully manifest themselves until 1391 when he came down with a strange illness resembling typhoid that caused him to lose his hair and nails. According to an observer, other men in the royal court came down with the disease as well, so we can only guess what effect, if any, it had on Charles's state of mind. Despite his all too recent and incomplete recovery, that summer Charles decided to go on a campaign against John IV, the Duke of Brittany, who had angered Charles by giving shelter to a fugitive who had tried to kill a royal official. Even with the protests of his uncles and advisors, the oppressive heat of that summer and the recurring fevers he still suffered, Charles went ahead with his plans to march against Brittany. Just before the campaign started, a contemporary wrote that the king seemed to suffer from more than just fevers: sometimes he would utter gibberish and make strange gestures.

These little unexplained outbursts did not trouble Charles or his companions, as they went on the campaign without any hesitation. Not far into the trek, though, Charles was left shaken by a bizarre incident. While they were riding through a forest, an old beggar came rushing up to the king's party. He claimed to know that the king was about to be betrayed and killed and cried out, 'Ride no further, noble king! Turn back!' The king's men chased the beggar off into the forest, but Charles was visibly disturbed. Later in the day, as the heat began to take its toll on everyone, an exhausted page dropped a lance he was carrying, making a loud clattering sound. Startled, Charles drew his sword and began stabbing at his own men, screaming, 'Forward against the traitors! They wish to deliver me to the enemy!' Charles managed to kill three or four of his own knights before he could be overpowered. Wrestled off his horse, the king collapsed to the ground in a seizure, eyes rolling and completely mute. His men had to return him to the palace in an ox cart where he lay in a coma for two days. When he finally regained consciousness, he seemed fully recovered but was still haunted by the memory of his actions, for which he begged forgiveness.

On January 28, 1393, Charles's peace of mind would be tried yet again. That evening, Isabeau hosted a masquerade where the men were dressed in linen costumes saturated with pitch to make them appear as though they were covered in hair like 'wild men.' Because of the flammable nature of the material, torches were forbidden, but heedless of the ban the Duke of Orléans and his attendants entered the ballroom carrying lit torches. Suddenly a spark fell on one of the costumes, starting a fire that killed one man instantly and led to the deaths of three others. Charles himself was one of the 'wild men', but he was saved from a fiery death by the quick thinking of the Duchess of Berry, who simply threw her massive skirt over Charles's body.

Even if narrowly missing a horrible death did not have a decisive effect on Charles's condition, he did suffer a severe relapse later that year, forgetting who he was and claiming he was not the king, but a man named Georges[21]. Whenever Charles saw his coat of arms, he would become agitated and try to erase it. He also could not recognize his wife and family, and started developing a hostile reaction to the very sight of Isabeau. 'Who is that woman, the sight of whom torments me?' Charles asked an attendant when Isabeau entered the room, 'Find out what she wants and free me from her demands, so that she may follow me no more.' Luckily Charles's revulsion of his wife and queen did nothing to extinguish his usual lust. A mistress, Odette de Champdivers, was arranged for him when Isabeau became too frightened to share her husband's bed when he was in one of his 'difficult' phases.

From then on, Charles's life was marked by recurring lapses into insanity, alternating from virtually comatose states to times spent consumed with sheer mania, and ever-shortening periods of lucidity. In his energetic phases, he would often dance obscenely and make lewd gestures to anyone in his sight. He would also rush around the palace, screeching that his enemies were chasing him. This behavior became so frequent that workers were hired to wall up certain exits from the palace to offset the chance of the king getting away.

The most tragic aspect of Charles's illness was that in his moments of sanity he was fully aware of when the madness was about to set on him. Suspecting he was the victim of sorcery, as did many others, Charles once cried out, 'In the name of Jesus Christ, if there is any one of you who is an accomplice in this evil I suffer, I beg him to torture me no longer but let me die!' Fearful of a recurrence of what happened with his first bout of delirium, Charles once ordered himself disarmed as he felt his hold on reality collapsing.

How much Charles's condition actually affected the course of French history is debatable. Despite his illness and the people eager and willing to rule through him, Charles was not entirely docile. For instance, he had met personally with the King of Bohemia and Holy

[21] One theory holds that, through the logic of a schizophrenic, Charles was associating himself with St Georges, the patron saint of France.

Roman Emperor, Wenceslas IV, over the Great Schism dividing the Catholic Church. But it is impossible to deny that the later years of Charles's reign were disastrous, thanks in no small part to his illness.

Behind the mad king's throne, Jean the Fearless, the new Duke of Burgundy, and the Duke of Orléans launched a private feud. This conflict escalated until, finally, on November 23, 1407 Orléans was ambushed and brutally murdered. The king tried to get Orléans' son, the new Duke, and Burgundy, to come to a truce. Burgundy confessed to the crime but insisted he only did it for the sake of the king's well-being. This little truce was a transparent farce, however, and in a short while outright civil war had erupted between the factions backing Burgundy and Orléans.

As if this was not terrible enough, the English king, Henry V, decided to devote himself to taking on his great-grandfather Edward III's claim to France and jumpstarting the Hundred Years' War. Henry's aggression culminated in the decisive Battle of Agincourt on October 24, 1415. The small English force led by Henry was, with the help of their Welsh longbowmen, able to defeat the much larger French army, hopelessly hampered by the archaic rules of chivalric combat. The battle concluded with the deaths of 7,000 Frenchmen and the capture of the best of France's nobility.

Meanwhile Queen Isabeau had made peace with Burgundy, and may have taken a new lover, Louis de Bosredon, the chamberlain to the late Duke of Orléans. The rumors of her affair with this man may have had some substance, as in 1417 at Charles's personal order Bosredon was arrested, tied into a sack and drowned in the River Seine. Later that same year, Isabeau was sent away from court, officially for 'the dissolute behavior of her ladies-in-waiting' but quite possibly for more scandalous reasons. Even in exile, she managed to encourage Burgundy, with whom she kept close contact, to meet with her young son, the future Charles VII, who had become dauphin on the deaths of his two elder brothers. Burgundy was suddenly attacked and assassinated in revenge for Orléans' death before Charles's very eyes. Furious at this betrayal and bribed by the English with the promise of a generous pension, Isabeau publicly declared that her son, the dauphin, was a bastard and not merely in the purely derogatory sense.

With the Treaty of Tours signed on May 21, 1420, Charles's daughter Catherine was married to Henry V and it was decided that the first son born of their union would inherit the crowns of both England and France after the deaths of their living monarchs. Charles concurred – or was forced to concur – with Isabeau's condemnation of their son the dauphin. He proclaimed that he disinherited his son because he had 'rendered himself unworthy' to be king, but by now all knew that the poor, mad king was himself at the mercy of the English invaders.

Charles would not have to live long with the indignation. Soon after Catherine gave birth to an heir, also named Henry, and the death of Henry V from illness, Charles himself would die from a fever on October 21, 1420. The new Henry, still an infant, would be crowned as Henry VI, the King of England and France. It would soon become clear later in life that Henry VI also suffered a mental infirmity, neither as colorful nor as constant as his grandfather's but just as crippling to himself and his country. Although it is uncertain if Henry VI was the victim of Charles VI's poisonous genes, it is ironic that while a king's madness helped lead to France's fall to the English, another king's madness would do at least a little to help pave the way for France's independence.

Further Reading

Curry, Anne *The Hundred Years War* (Basingstoke, 1993)

Famiglietti, R.C. *Royal Intrigue: Crisis at the Court of Charles VI, 1392-1420* (AMS Press, 1986)

Green, Vivian *The Madness of Kings: Personal Trauma and the Fate of Nations* (Sutton, 1993)

Jacob, Ernest Fraser *Henry V and the Invasion of France* (Hodder & Stoughton, 1947)

CATHERINE DE' MEDICI

Reign: *December 21, 1560–August 15, 1563;*
May 30–September 6, 1574
Born: *April 13, 1519*
Died: *January 5, 1589*
Buried: *Basilica of Saint Denis (in effigy)*

If a list of history's great peacemakers were written, it is unlikely it would include the name Catherine de' Medici, even though her actions and letters demonstrate that, despite always having more than a few ambitions on her mind, her one unwavering dream was for peace in France. As she herself wrote in another of her many letters, 'It seems to me that one ought to quit everything else, and to employ every means to avert the storm of war.' Despite such sympathetic motives, a list of history's greatest villains is far more likely to feature her name. French legends depict Catherine as a heartless conniver, more than willing to resort to ruthless intrigue or even murder to further her own ends. The most imaginative stories have her armed with a fantastic arsenal: poisoned gloves, clothes and even incense. While the accusations of Machiavellian tactics levied against Catherine at least have more weight than her reputation as a mass murderer, she was really no more ruthless and pragmatic than many of her contemporaries. She had the misfortune of coming to the fore during one of the most combustible periods in French history, that of the religious wars, and at the same time she was handicapped by both her gender and her foreign blood. If circumstances had been slightly kinder to Catherine, she would probably have been fondly remembered as a fighter for peace rather than by the name 'Madame Serpente'.

Catherine was a scion of the Medici, the notorious Italian clan that for centuries steered the destiny of Florence and produced two Renaissance Popes. In spite of such a distinguished family, her childhood was not a comfortable one by any standard. Both of her parents, Lorenzo de' Medici and Madeleine de La Tour d'Auvergne, died within two months of her birth. The orphaned girl was raised by her puritanical aunt, Clarice Strozzi, who probably instilled in Catherine what would become her lioness's loyalty to her husband and family.

As if the loss of both parents were not enough of a shock, Catherine's childhood was about to take another turn for the worse, putting her life in jeopardy. The Medici were deposed and exiled from the city they had called home for centuries by a new republican government, which at once found itself under siege by Austrian and papal armies. Catherine, still only a child, was sent as a hostage for the Republic of Florence to use to keep her family, including Pope Clement VII, in line. Eventually she was sent to the Convent of La Murate, where even under those dire circumstances she spent the happiest days of her life under the doting care of the nuns. However, the risk of facing a horrible fate hovered over her head as the radicals in the Florentine government argued that killing her or handing her over to the Republic of Florence's mercenary troops as a 'gift' was a good way to break the city's ties with the hated Medici.

Late one night three Florentine senators appeared suddenly at the Convent to ask that Catherine come with them. Thinking that this was her end, Catherine agreed to go with the senators, but only if she were allowed to dress like a nun before they left, making the senators' presumed motive to take her to a quick death a rather more tricky political maneuver. Such a cynical but brilliant decision is rendered all the more impressive by the fact that Catherine was only eleven years old at the time.

Much to Catherine's relief, it turned out that the senators only wanted to transfer her to another convent. There she continued living in the grip of anxiety until, finally, the Republic of Florence released her and she was allowed to go to Rome to live with her uncle the Pope. While Catherine escaped death, she could not escape the fate that awaited many girls in that age: being married off for her family's benefit. In 1533, Catherine was engaged to marry Henri, the Duke of Orléans. This turned out to be a lucrative deal on the part of the Medici because Henri soon became first in line to inherit the throne of France from his father, King François I. Future king or not, Catherine quickly became disenchanted with her royal groom, with whom she had fallen in love, when she found out he had a mistress, Diane de Poitiers, whom he preferred far more than his stout Italian bride, despite the fact that she was about two decades older than Henri himself. Worse, for the first few years of the marriage Catherine could not become pregnant and soon the entire court was taking bets on when Henri would ship Catherine off in exchange for a more fertile bride. Just as at La Murate, Catherine displayed her inborn instinct for survival and worked day and night to get into her father-in-law's good graces. The strategy worked: under King François' protection Catherine stayed on in the French court and in 1543 gave birth to the first of her many children with Henri, whom she tactfully named François, after her guardian. According to the legends about her, it was Catherine's desperation to mother children that led her to study the occult. It is true that Catherine did have a lifelong fascination with the 'black arts', but whether or not her mystical knowledge helped her become a fertile wife is open to interpretation.

Little François was followed by seven more children, all of whom Catherine showered with an attention uncustomary for royals of the time, fussing over the slightest detail of their upbringing, hygiene (with the unshakable belief in the benefits of clean air and physical exercise that she exhibited in her private correspondence, Catherine betrays a rather modern understanding of healthy living) and education. She even practically tutored her own daughters, as well as the young Scottish queen Mary Stewart, who for political reasons was being raised alongside the royal children in the French court. She personally arranged their lessons in Latin, theology, history, music and other subjects worthy of royalty. The Renaissance was alive and well in the daily curriculum of Catherine's children.

In the meantime, Catherine had lost her greatest ally. On July 25, 1547, King François died, leaving Catherine's husband to ascend to the throne as Henri II. If Catherine hoped that Henri's new holy role would force him to treat her with more respect, she was badly mistaken, for instead Diane de Poitiers became even more attached to Henri than ever. Diane attended state ceremonies side by side with Henri in extravagant dress and adorned by the crown jewels. Sticking to her strict, traditional upbringing, Catherine quietly suppressed her feelings about her husband's affair, even though Diane received so much attention and ceremony it seemed she was the *de facto* queen. After Henri's death, Catherine tellingly wrote that although she was 'hospitable' to Diane 'never has a woman who loves her husband liked his whore'.

Reading Catherine's writings, there is little room for doubt that Catherine's feelings for Henri stretched beyond loyalty into love and that his neglect caused her incomparable anguish. Still, the relationship between Catherine and Diane was almost strangely sisterly, even if condescension and resentment lurked just beneath the surface. Diane played no small role in tending to Catherine's children and even personally nursed Catherine back to health during a harsh bout of scarlet fever, despite the highly contagious and potentially fatal nature of the disease. But Catherine finally drew a line in the sand when Diane played adviser to the king. Angered over Diane's heartless advice on foreign policy toward her home country,

Catherine coolly said to her, 'I have read the histories of this kingdom and I have found in them that from time to time at all periods whores have managed the business of kings.'

Catherine did not have to languish behind the scenes for long. While her husband was off on a military campaign, she was briefly made regent. Although she was concerned for her husband's welfare, even going so far as dressing like a widow for the mortal danger Henri was in, she went at her new role with a passion, reading through all the books on politics she could find in a day. Over the short course of this regency, she finally discovered her one true calling. When Henri wrote to her, telling her to ask the Parlement of Paris to raise more money for the war, an observer noticed that when she presented herself before the Parlement she 'spoke with such earnestness and eloquence that everyone was moved'. The populace was also taken with Catherine, feeling pathos for the dutiful and modest queen overshadowed by the king's ostentatious harlot. If Catherine's career were limited to these days and she was spared from having to deal with the chaotic years to come, her place in history might have been viewed in a more positive light, albeit a dimmer one.

Tragedy would at last propel Catherine to greater political influence, whether she wanted it or not. According to legend, the prophet Nostradamus, whom Catherine sponsored as part of her growing fascination with the occult, made a veiled prediction about King Henri's death, a tragedy that actually came to pass during a tournament held to celebrate the marriage between his and Catherine's daughter, Elizabeth, to the King of Spain, Philip II. While he was personally jousting in the tournament, from the arena Henri declared to Catherine that he would go for one more bout 'for love of her'. In that one extra fight, Henri's opponent's lance broke and pierced the king's eye, penetrating as far as his brain. Taken to his bed, Henri suffered in a feverish, delirious state, constantly attended by Catherine and doctors who could only try to lessen the king's agony. Mercifully, he died after ten agonizing days, leaving the crown to his sickly, fifteen-year-old son François. Despite a very short-lived attempt to get Antoine de Bourbon, husband to Jeanne III, Queen of Navarre[22] and a descendant of King Louis IX, onto the throne, François and his wife, Mary Stewart, were crowned King and Queen of France in 1559. Catherine then had the satisfaction of arranging to have Diane de Poitiers banished from court and from her life.

For the rest of her life, Catherine would dress in black to reflect her perpetual mourning for her lost husband. One contemporary who saw her soon after Henri's death writes:

> She was in her room which was entirely draped in black . . . There were no lights except for two candles burning on an altar draped in black. The bed was covered the same way. Her Majesty was garbed in the most austere dress: a black robe with a long train which had no ornamentation except an ermine collar . . . She had a black veil on her head which covered her completely even to her face.

However, Catherine did not have the luxury of complete isolation. Her son King François II had become a cipher in the hands of the staunchly Catholic and vastly ambitious Guise family, which included François' mother-in-law, Marie, queen regent of Scotland.

The Guises, who clung proudly to their claim that they were direct descendants of Charlemagne himself, were distressed by the growing numbers of French Calvinists, also known as Huguenots. Although an edict passed in 1532 condemned Protestantism as a heresy and commanded the murder of any and all such heretics, the seemingly unchecked spread of Protestantism in Germany, Scandinavia, Scotland

[22] Navarre was a small kingdom sandwiched between France and Spain that had, despite the overbearing Catholic presence in those two countries, adopted Protestantism as the state faith.

and the Netherlands cast a shadow over Catholic France. The death of England's devoutly Catholic queen Mary Tudor and the accession of her Protestant half-sister Elizabeth went further to plunge Catholics in France into a panicked frenzy. Fears of an English and Huguenot collaboration against the Church and State in France were whispered everywhere, from the royal court to the village. This nationwide anxiety finally went to a boil when a group of Huguenots tried to break into the king's apartments to 'liberate' François from the clutches of the Guises. The plan backfired and instead the brave crusaders succeeded in triggering the arrest of one of the most prominent Protestants in France, the Prince of Condé, the King of Navarre's brother.

The plan to take the king hostage was a pointless endeavor at any rate, because after reigning for only about a year and a half, François succumbed to his myriad illnesses in December of 1560. In his last days, François was heard to utter, 'Lord God, how heavy is this crown which I thought you had granted as a gift.' This awful burden was passed right into his mother's hands. Catherine had enough political capital to be declared regent on December 21, 1560 for her younger son Charles, now King Charles IX. Still, the Duke of Guise, who remained suspicious of Catherine's open plan to placate the Huguenots, would remain a bitter enemy.

In the face of the holy chaos that consumed France in the years of her regency and afterwards, Catherine insisted on only one thing: mutual tolerance. She attempted to form a national council on theology that would equally represent both Catholics and Protestants and also refused to let the Inquisition get a foothold on French soil. Perhaps motivated by first-hand memories of the war-torn state into which her home of Florence had collapsed, Catherine began to devote herself completely to the task of keeping the claws of the Catholic and Huguenot factions sheathed.

It would be difficult to believe that anyone would not despair at the condition France fell into and would not try to remedy it if they were in a position to do so. Huguenots were subjected to almost daily torture and public humiliation and then put to death either at the hands of local authorities or their own godly neighbors. Likewise, in towns burning with the Protestant passion, Catholic priests were dragged into the streets and murdered, images of saints were torn down and destroyed, and churches and altars were desecrated by mobs. In Paris itself, one account says, 'At Saint-Eustache a schoolboy unhappily laughed during a sermon. An old woman saw him and pointed him out. He was killed on the spot.'

Even though Catherine tried to soothe the country's religious fervor by pardoning Condé and passing the Edict of Toleration, which made the practice of Protestantism legal with conditions[23], her hands quickly became tied. A new and ultra-Catholic government, the Triumvirate, formed by the Duke of Guise, the Constable of Montmorency and Marachel St. André, took control of affairs and reduced both Catherine and Charles IX to the status of virtual prisoners. Everything Catherine wanted so desperately to avoid came to pass. A massacre of Huguenots occurred in Vassy on January 29, 1562 where a congregation of Huguenots were harassed and then attacked by Guise's followers. Some 1,200 were slaughtered.

Alarmed, the Huguenots appealed to the Prince of Condé (his brother, Antoine, had proven himself worthless when it came to politics), whom they titled 'Protector of the Churches'. With the financial support of Protestant rulers in Germany and Queen Elizabeth I of England, Condé mobilized his forces and prepared to strike. Guise in turn tried to invoke the aid of Spain. Catherine, less than happy but not surprised that Condé rewarded her mercy with this small treason, had no choice but to back her enemy, Guise, at least for the moment.

This holy war, which would be only the first of many carried out before 1598, came to a quick conclusion with the death of Antoine

[23] Preaching Protestant ideas anywhere other than in open fields or in one's own home was still a crime.

de Bourbon in combat and the assassination of Guise at Orléans. It was with Guise's untimely demise that the black legend of Catherine de' Medici begins in earnest, with contemporaries accusing her of secretly arranging the death of Guise. Certainly she was Guise's most bitter enemy in the political arena and had a good deal to gain from his removal, but so did many others. But even if Guise's blood was on Catherine's hands, she had acted too late. The country was already bankrupt and even the royal court was heavily in debt. Catherine, whose reputation had already lost much of its initial lustre, was forced to consent to a further restriction on the rights of the Huguenots. The economic problems were of course blamed on her.

Her political failures were surpassed only by the pain of her personal life. On October 3, 1568 her daughter Elizabeth died trying to give her husband the King of Spain a male heir. In grief, Catherine wrote, 'God has taken away every hope I have in this world.' However, Catherine's political instincts soon overcame her sense of loss. Not long after Elizabeth's funeral, she opened negotiations to marry her youngest and most rebellious child Marguerite to Elizabeth's widower.

Marguerite, who was most assuredly no one's pawn, was as intelligent and strong-willed as her mother, but in time they became all but open enemies. Already Marguerite had taken the new Duke of Guise, the tall and handsome son of Catherine's late arch-enemy, as her paramour. After negotiations with Philip II of Spain came to nothing, Catherine saw in Marguerite, known across Europe for her exquisite and almost supernatural beauty, a bargaining chip to use to finally satisfy the Huguenot faction. For that to happen, Catherine had to worm her way into the good side of Jeanne of Navarre, recently widowed by the death of Antoine in the wars. Jeanne was a far more determined and devout figure than her husband, eager to give the Huguenot cause any support she could at any price. Catherine thought that she could make even the bull-headed Jeanne complacent by marrying Marguerite to her son, Henri de Bourbon, heir to the throne of Navarre (and possibly to the French crown to boot). With good reason, Catherine might have hoped Marguerite could lead her princely groom back to the warm and welcoming arms of Mother Church.

Catherine was so determined to see this match become a reality that she traveled personally to Navarre to discuss the matter with Jeanne. Although she was initially dead set against the match and probably was a match for Catherine in the art of diplomacy, Jeanne decided to agree. Not long after Catherine left for France, Jeanne became sick and died. Once again, stories would claim that she was a victim of the sinister machinations of Catherine, who is said to have poisoned Jeanne through her food, clothing or even through her perfume. The question of what exactly Catherine had to gain from Jeanne's death beyond removing a powerful and royal Huguenot, especially after Jeanne consented to Catherine's only real demand from her, did not stop the rumor from spreading.

The angriest protest to the union, actually, had not come from Jeanne, but from Marguerite, who wanted instead to marry her dashing Duke of Guise. While Catherine had no problems with sacrificing her daughter's desires to the interest of France and peace, Marguerite demanded a say in the matter, much to her mother's chagrin. One record says that after a ball, Catherine and Charles took Marguerite aside and, once they were alone with her, they beat her until she finally relented to the marriage arrangements. Right afterwards, Catherine spent an hour fixing up Marguerite's dress which had become dishevelled in the attack, to keep the scene from becoming a public scandal.

The crucial wedding, on which so much rode, took place on August 17, 1572. The ceremony was performed under the open sky because church law forbade a heretic to marry in a cathedral. Up until the pivotal moment Marguerite radiated contempt and defiance: the king himself had to push Marguerite's head forward when she was asked for her vows because she refused to do so. Nevertheless, after ten years of almost continuous fighting and massacres, this union of a royal Catholic with a Protestant prince must have seemed a blessing, an omen of promising things to come, in the middle of an age of bloodshed and fanaticism. Catherine was also pleased with her ongoing negotiations to marry her youngest son, the Duke of Alençon, to Elizabeth I (she may have been less optimistic if she had known Elizabeth liked to refer to Alençon as 'my frog'). Underneath all the joyous wedding festivities and hope for a brighter, less violent future for France, there was still a pulsing tension. The hatred between Catholic and Huguenot was still as hot as ever, however much Catherine denied it, and the fact that the *crème de la crème* of Huguenot leadership had shown up in Paris for Prince Henri's wedding raised tension to a fever pitch.

One of these leaders was the Admiral de Coligny, who had fought in the religious wars on the Huguenot side and had become, despite Catherine's best efforts to prevent it, an important advisor to Charles IX. Coligny was an adamant advocate for French intervention in the Netherlands, even if it would entail a war with Spain. Although Catherine, who still held no small influence over her son the king, was able to convince Charles to at least postpone his decision on the idea, Coligny's words were always buzzing in the king's ear.

Then, on August 22, Coligny was shot in the arm by an unknown assassin, wounding him badly. Again, to the French the scheming Catherine de' Medici was naturally to blame, but other plausible suspects included the Duke of Guise, the King of Spain and any passionate Catholic in power. On the brutally hot day that followed, Coligny refused to leave Paris, putting his life under the king's protection. The royal family, including Catherine, Charles and his brother the Duke of Anjou, were terrified of a Huguenot uprising in the city in outrage over the assault on Coligny. The story goes that Catherine and Anjou coerced Charles into demanding the deaths of Coligny and the Huguenot leaders around him, but the extent of Catherine's involvement is questionable even if what eventually did happen was meant to happen.

In fact, it is uncertain exactly what followed, thanks to gossip and hearsay, but the St Bartholomew's Day Massacre was set in motion. Soldiers led by the Duke of Guise stormed Coligny's place of residence and butchered his guards. Then, bursting into the Admiral's chambers, they fell on Coligny who was simply lying in bed half-asleep. Instantly they stabbed him repeatedly and threw his body through a nearby window out onto the streets.

The murder of Coligny was like a spark in a tinderbox. As the oppressive summer night drew on, soldiers and civilians alike went on the rampage, rioting across the city and choking the Paris streets and the River Seine with fresh corpses robbed of clothing and belongings. Catholic men, marked by the white crosses they wore on their hats, barged into Huguenot households and butchered their sleeping inhabitants. Shops run by suspected Huguenots were looted and burned to ashes. The slaughtering and rioting went on in Paris for three days, unchecked by local authorities who could not or would not help.

Meanwhile, King Henri of Navarre and his brother, the newly named Prince of Condé, were held as 'guests' – really state prisoners – at the Louvre. They were given three days to convert to Catholicism or else have the privilege of a martyr's death. To them, religious devotion was not a good enough reason to give in to the grave, so the two young men gave in to the Mass.

The massacre, however, was not to go without dire consequences, something Catherine must have realized from the outset. Outraged Huguenot leaders in the fortress city of La Rochelle, where Huguenot resistence was strongest, refused to pay taxes to the government. Anjou, who thought of himself as a warrior-prince past his age, led an army into La Rochelle to give the Huguenots a lesson in obedience. Despite much difficulty and heartache, La Rochelle was subdued and the Huguenot leaders were forced to a humiliating treaty, but this victory was swiftly negated by an unforseen defeat. Although Henri of Navarre remained a hostage, Condé escaped safely into Protestant hands in Germany and quickly repudiated his conversion, claiming with justification that it was only made under duress.

With the increasing tension between Catholic and Protestant and memories of the Huguenot Massacre, Catherine's reputation blackened at a steady rate. Through all the slander, however, she retained her remarkable sense of humor. When she read a venomous pamphlet titled *The Life of St Catherine*, a pseudo-biography of her life filled with stories of witchcraft and sexual degeneracy, she laughed and commented that, if only the authors were brave enough to interview her in person, she could have given them much more interesting stories than the ones they had invented.

Whether or not this growing infamy concerned her, Catherine devoted herself to her chief concern outside peace: her children. She continued trying to get Alençon, a teenager, married to the now middle-aged Queen Elizabeth, even though Elizabeth, who got to see the prince personally, confessed to her advisors that she found Alençon's smallpox-scarred face 'a major difficulty'. She also began to negotiate to get her other – and obviously favorite – son Anjou onto the throne of Poland. Poland had an electoral monarchy with a council of noblemen choosing the country's king from a number of native and foreign candidates with the right bloodlines. In this venture, she was much more successful than she was with marrying her youngest son off to the 'Virgin Queen', and the Polish council declared Anjou their king and Grand Duke of Lithuania on May 9, 1573. Unfortunately, for all the endless negotiating, the prize was not to last. A year later Charles, who was like his late brother physically weak despite their mother's loving care, came down with a terrible illness where one of the symptoms was said to have been sweating blood. On May 30, Charles IX let go of life and Henri of Anjou was declared King of France. The new Henri III had no qualms with leaving Poland, a country he never outgrew his dislike and contempt for, but was in no rush to claim his native land's throne. Despite his mother's pleadings, he took a tour of Italy that lasted months before he finally came back to Paris.

Catherine's beloved Henri turned out to be an emotionally unstable lush, constantly switching between extravagant self-indulgence and pious self-loathing. The lionhearted warrior-prince the people called 'the young eagle' had all but vanished into thin air. Whether Catherine saw any of this through the haze of passionate motherly love is left for us to guess, but she must have been aware on some level of the disastrous effects her son's decadence had on morale and the economy. Catherine often traveled, conducting state and diplomatic business on her son's behalf. Indeed, so incredible was the energy that Catherine channeled into her political work that it was said one of her secretary's arms became lame from so much writing. She wrote constantly back to Henri during her travels with motherly advice. One such letter pleads, 'I beg you to control your finances very carefully in order to raise money for your service without having to rob your people.' It is sound and sensible advice, but unfortunately for Catherine and France Henri was enraptured by his male favorites, contemptuously called his *mignons* by everyone in the know. Although Catherine wrote to her son endlessly, telling him about the important affairs she was conducting and asking for his approval on this-and-that, he never once wrote back. Yet with most of her children dead, Catherine's love for Henri only deepened. In one letter, she claimed, 'If ever I were to lose you, I would bury myself alive with you.' At one time, when he recovered from a nasty illness, Catherine then wrote, 'He is my life . . . I bless God for restoring him to me, and I pray that it may be for longer than my own life so that so long as I live I may see no harm come to him.'

With this kind of deep-rooted devotion reserved for one son, no wonder Catherine's other surviving son, Alençon[24], was more than a little resentful. During her brief regency that occurred after Charles's

[24] After Henri came to the throne, Alençon became the new Duke of Anjou, but to avoid confusion his earlier title will continue to be used.

death and before Henri returned to France, Alençon and Henri of Navarre had become close friends, so close that Catherine came to question her son's loyalties. Eventually the dangerous pair were imprisoned at the Louvre on Catherine's orders. The duo did try two escape attempts: once through an unattended gate, and another time dressed in women's clothes. Unfortunately, Catherine's hold over Henri of Navarre and Alençon only tightened, causing the scandalmongers to start referring to the two men as Catherine's 'chickens.' But despite Catherine's best attempts, these chickens eventually flew the coop. Alençon raised his own private army, determined to support the Huguenots (more out of loyalty to Navarre and a desire to have a shot at stealing his brother's throne than any religious motivation), while Navarre himself recanted his conversion and became the new favorite champion of the Huguenot cause[25].

The Huguenots rallied around their new savior and the religious wars started fresh. German mercenaries, sent to aid the rebellion, instead made their main concern robbing rural towns and villages. As enemy forces came within sight of Paris, Catherine desperately drew up a peace settlement all parties found unsatisfactory. While the Church found it too beneficial to the despised heretics, the Huguenots thought it too generous to be trustworthy.

Although Alençon was more or less forgiven for his role in the latest serious outbreak of war, once again he involved himself in the affairs of the grown-ups. No longer wanting to steal his brother's throne, but still craving some kind of prestige, he threw himself even deeper into the risky politics of the Netherlands. Protestants in the Netherlands were anxious for Alençon, heir presumptive to the French throne, to support their rebellion against Spain, hoping that Alençon's involvement would inevitably pull France into a decisive war. This was exactly what

[25] This decision was a political, not a religious one. When he inherited the French crown and was proclaimed Henri IV, he would once again renounce Protestantism and convert to Catholicism.

Catherine feared, so it must have been with mixed feelings that she received word of Alençon's sudden death on June 10, 1584. But while the death of this stupid prince solved one potential crisis, it opened the door for another: with no sign of King Henri III bearing sons, the Protestant Henri of Navarre was now heir presumptive to the French throne. The response from the Papacy to this ugly threat was immediate: Pope Sextus V excommunicated Navarre and his brother.

Catherine rushed to Navarre to try to avert the future storm by securing Navarre's conversion to the old faith. Navarre received his former captor with open arms, but said to her frankly, 'Madame, you grow strong on this trouble. If you had peace, you would not know how to live.' Catherine, justifiably paranoid, pretended to embrace him while secretly searching for any weapons he might have had on him. Recognizing what she was doing, Navarre laughed heartily and said, 'You see, madame, I keep nothing hidden.' Although Catherine must have mustered all of her skills as a politician in her conversations with Navarre, he refused to consider repenting his Protestantism (at least for the time being) and Catherine had to return to Paris empty-handed.

In opposition to Navarre, the Duke of Guise, who like his father became a spokesman for the radical Catholics, put Navarre's uncle, Charles de Bourbon, a 64-year-old cardinal, forward as a candidate for the crown. With Spain's backing, the Guise family formed the Catholic League, which enjoyed tremendous political and popular support. Ignoring his mother's wishes as usual, Henri III, although he balked at the Guises' usurpation of royal authority, quickly tried to take over the situation by declaring himself its nominal head. To show his loyalty to the cause, he signed the Treaty of Nemours, which revoked all rights that had been granted to Huguenots and ordered all Huguenots in the realm to renounce their heresy within six years or risk exile. With that one treaty signed by her own precious son, all of Catherine's hopes for religious tolerance were dashed forever.

This radical reversal sparked the longest phase of the religious wars, the War of the Three Henris (since King Henri III, Henri of Navarre, and the Duke of Guise, also named Henri, were the combatants and all represented different factions). Anti-royalist Catholics rallied in the end, driving King Henri out of the city and installing a pro-League government, the Sixteen. Although Henri, with the aid of loyalist troops, was able to at least get back some resemblance of authority, the Duke of Guise was the real master of France. Like his father before him, though, death would cheat him with victory on the horizon. On Christmas Eve 1588, at Blois Guise was ambushed and murdered on the king's orders, spending his last breath right before Henri III's apathetic eyes. Catherine, who had fallen ill with pneumonia, was horrified at the news of the murder of Guise and dreaded its political impact. Desperate, she tried to see Cardinal Charles, who had been led away to prison at Henri's orders. Rather than listening to this woman who was once praised glowingly by the Paris Parlement, the cardinal screeched at her, 'You will be the death of us all!' This was Catherine's final defeat.

Stricken with pneumonia, Catherine was forced to retire to her chambers as her grip on life slowly waned. She died on January 5, 1589 at the Louvre, the same site of the infamous massacre that would come to be blamed on her and her sons. Although she had dedicated all her life to her adopted country France, one contemporary noted that after her death, 'She was not spoken of any more than a dead goat.' Meanwhile in Paris that night the people marched through the streets, laughing and dancing, filled with joy at the death of a woman who was already declared 'Madame Serpente'.

Further Reading

Knecht, R.J. *The French Wars of Religion, 1559-1598* (Longman, 1989)
Mahoney, Irene *Madame Catherine* (Victor Gollancz, 1976)
Noguères, Henri (trans. Claire Eliane Engel) *The Massacre of Saint Bartholomew* (Allen & Unwin, 1962)
Young, G.F *The Medici* (Charles Boni, 1930)

HENRI III

Reign: *May 20, 1574–September 19, 1589*
Born: *September 19, 1551*
Died: *August 2, 1589 (assassination)*
Buried: *Basilica of Saint-Denis (in effigy)*

During the wars between Catholic and Huguenot that tore France apart, Henri, the favorite son of the indefatigable queen Catherine de' Medici, was not shy about taking on the role of protector of the Catholic Church. Indeed, Henri presented himself like one of the warrior-kings of old, fighting heroically and selflessly against the dark forces that threatened to consume both Church and State. Once he inherited the French throne from his brother Charles, this noble image would crumble away, leaving behind only the 'King of Trifles'.

Through her usual skillful diplomacy, Catherine secured Henri the throne of Poland[26]. While Catherine mourned the departure of her most favorite son, Henri balked at the strict constitutional limitations imposed on Polish monarchs that contrasted so badly with the virtually absolute power enjoyed by French kings, and could not help but relentlessly mock the unfashionable clothing and rustic customs of his new subjects. So great was Henri's contempt for the country his mother worked hard to give him that, when word of King Charles's death reached him on June 12, 1574, he fled the royal apartments through a secret exit like an escaped criminal.

Although he had been officially declared King of France on May 20 and had received letters from his mother urging him to return to Paris immediately, he detoured to take an unofficial 'tour' of Italy on the way home. In Venice, he was pampered by the government and showered with jewels, exotic perfumes and enamels. Distracted by such luxury and crowds of Italian sycophants, it was months before the king finally came home to claim his own throne.

The French would have cause enough to regret him coming at all. Henri soon surrounded himself with a clique of young male courtiers whom wagging tongues christened the *mignons*. Following the personal example of their king, they dressed in fashions so effeminate they verged on transvestism. At one ball, the king appeared dressed in pearls, rogue, and with earrings that reached down to his shoulders. In exchange for their devotion, and quite possibly sexual favors, Henri showered his *mignons* with jewels, silk and even lands. In gratitude, they gave him disastrous political advice that proved to be the bane of Catherine, who flooded her son with letters offering common sense advice that went unheeded. The unending party that was Henri's court continued without a stop, no matter what mother had to say. The king and his men's lifestyles so bankrupted the court that it found itself unable to pay for meals and clothing for palace servants.

[26] The Polish monarchy was elective, not hereditary.

While his mother's advice could not change his ways, tragedy would. Henri had a lifelong mistress, Marie de Cleves, to whom he was so devoted that he once wrote a love letter to her in his own blood. She died suddenly, leaving the king in an emotional shock that lasted for days. When he 'recovered', he exchanged his silk shirts and silver bracelets for a black shirt. He then joined the Battons, an order of flagellant monks, and following their practice whipped himself publicly up and down the streets of Paris. One Austrian ambassador was so distressed by the morbid spectacle that he wrote, 'I am afraid that everything is not golden here.'

Extreme religious piety was not enough to attract all the king's energies. Over time, he began to alternate between his flamboyant lifestyle and his hobby of pious self-loathing. Yet Henri's religious awakenings did not bring on the concept of matrimonial fidelity. Instead of trying to make a male heir for the dying Valois dynasty with his long suffering queen, Louise de Vaudemont, Henri spent many of his nights with his *mignons* or at the Parisian brothels.

Like his two late brothers, François and Charles, Henri soon became the victim of illness. He began to be struck by long periods of physical exhaustion so intense he could barely write, accompanied by delusions of persecution. He started to speak often of divorcing his barren wife and marrying a new woman who would bear him many children who would, in due time, 'piss on the graves' of his enemies.

In 1588, those enemies would prove themselves to be very much alive. Despite the best efforts of Catherine, the Catholic League, led by the ultra-Catholic Duke of Guise, took power in all but name. While a mob of furious Parisians waited outside, Catherine and Guise tried to hammer out a treaty in the same room as Henri, who said nothing to help negotiations but instead wept uncontrollably in the background.

Days later, both Catherine and Guise were shocked to discover that Henri had secretly escaped from Paris and was somehow able to drum up enough loyalist troops to take a stand for himself. On

December 23, 1588, the king ordered that Guise meet with him for negotiations. Unsuspecting, Guise obliged the king, not noticing that Henri had ordered archers to be positioned outside all possible exits. When Guise made it through the door to the king's chambers, the king's bodyguard, hidden behind curtains, rushed out to him and attacked him with a sword. Bloody and mortally wounded, Guise was able to crawl as far as the king's bedroom before all life drained out of him. It was claimed that Henri stared at Guise's corpse afterwards, but his only comment was, 'I never noticed he was so tall.'

In the summer of the next year, Henri, at one time the savior of Catholicism in France, became the victim of assassination by a fanatical monk named Jacques Clément. With Henri died the Valois dynasty that had ruled France since the thirteenth century, but this was of little concern to the French people, who rejoiced at the violent death of their effeminate king. In his place, the people welcomed the ascension of the Bourbons, who would become France's most famous royal dynasty, but would almost come to an end with an even nastier fate than the Valois.

Further Reading

Knecht, R.J. *The French Wars of Religion, 1559-1598* (Longman, 1989)
Mahoney, Irene *Madame Catherine* (Victor Gollancz, 1976)
Waldman, Milton *Biography of a Family: Catherine de Medici and Her Children* (Longman, 1936)

LOUIS XVI

Reign: *May 10, 1774–September 21, 1792*
Born: *August 23, 1754*
Died: *January 21, 1793 (executed)*
Buried: *Basilica of St. Denis*

Tasteful depravity, iron etiquette and wasteful extravagance in the face of starving subjects all spring to mind whenever the names Louis XVI or Marie Antoinette are mentioned. Yet so much about Louis and his wife, like Marie's callous phrase 'Let them eat cake', are only the results of years of slander. In truth, Louis and Antoinette were surprisingly human, but have been distorted into monstrous caricatures. Thomas Paine, one of the most ardent supporters of the early stages of the French Revolution, admitted that it was really not Louis who deserved the wrath of the French people, but the archaic institution he was born into. Even so, Louis and his young family had to be the sacrificial victims to satisfy a nation's thirst for futile revenge.

Louis was born on August 23, 1754 in the Château de Versailles, the celebrated and fabulously adorned residence of his great-grandfather Louis XIV 'the Sun-King'. He was the son of the Dauphin Louis, the heir to King Louis XV, and Marie Josephe of Saxe. Louis did not begin life marked for future greatness, but was eclipsed in every way by his elder brother, the Duke of Burgundy, who won his parents' devotion with his charismatic personality and sharp wit. Louis, in sharp contrast, was shy, sensitive and seemingly slow-witted, but he was also warm-hearted and compassionate. Unfortunately, Louis still had a hard time leaving a good impression on anyone because of his pathological bashfulness, always giving people the opinion that he was both too soft and too cold. He never could dress himself well or adjust to the inflexible etiquette that dominated life in Versailles, leading one observer to state that he 'looked like some peasant shambling behind his plough'. Nevertheless, after tuberculosis claimed the life not only of the young Duke, but also of both their parents, Louis, at the age of twelve, was shoved onto the national stage.

As the new Dauphin, the matter of Louis' marriage became one of the utmost importance. King Louis XV decided on Marie Antoinette, the youngest daughter of Empress Maria Theresa of Austria, to serve as the Dauphin's bride. This marriage would be a quick but lasting way of ending the centuries-old feud between the Habsburg and Bourbon dynasties and soothing the festering tensions between Austria and France. If the Empress was deeply troubled about the prospect of sending her daughter into a land where, even as queen, she would be distrusted and despised as a foreigner from an evil nation, she gave no sign.

Once young Marie arrived in the country, the king, very well known for his amorous appetites, asked a French official who had seen Antoinette if her breasts were properly developed yet. The official gave a flattering description of the future Dauphine, but skirted the issue of her cleavage.

'That's not what I meant,' the king interrupted. 'I'm talking about her breasts.'

The official replied, 'Sire, I did not take the liberty of looking at them.'

'Then you're an idiot. It's the first thing one should look at in a woman.'

As for the young couple themselves, both were understandably nervous, but fifteen-year-old Louis even more so. He had an overwhelmingly neurotic fear and awe of women, probably due to the fact that the only women he had up until then encountered were his mother, sisters, and his spinster aunts. Also his father always resented the widely publicized sexual adventures of Louis XV and made sure Louis would be taught from the start to dread the opposite sex. There were also reports that the Dauphin suffered a physical deformity called phimosis, which made erections painful and could only be cured by circumcision. According to this theory, the very idea of such an operation terrified Louis so much he did not consent to it for years, but the young king's timidness as well as sexual inexperience on both Louis' and Antoinette's parts alone could have ensured that their marriage for the first few years was completely celibate. The fact that etiquette at Versailles demanded that married couples sleep in separate rooms must have made an already awkward sex life (or lack thereof) even stranger.

Much later, after Louis had become king, Marie's brother Joseph, the future Austrian Emperor, came to Versailles for a casual visit. In private, Marie confessed her sexual problems with Louis to her brother. Joseph, always the practical man, wrote to his brother Leopold, 'Ah, if only I could have been there once. I should have put things right. He ought to be whipped to make him ejaculate, as one whips donkeys.' Even without Joseph's helpful intervention, the marriage was finally consummated sometime in 1773, three years after the wedding ceremony. On December 19, 1778, Marie gave birth to her first child, Marie Thérèse Charlotte. Three more children would follow: Louis Joseph Xavier François, born on October 22, 1781; Louis Charles, the future Dauphin and Louis XVII, born on March 27, 1785; and Sophie Beatrix, born on July 9, 1786, who died only a year later.

In the meantime, King Louis XV came down with smallpox himself and died on May 10, 1774. Louis, who had just entered adulthood, responded to the news of his grandfather's death and his own ascension by stating, 'I feel the universe is going to fall on me'. His words would prove almost prophetic.

Most admitted that the kingdom Louis was handed had seen much better days. France's once ample colonial holdings had been all but wiped away by the military disasters that marked Louis XV's reign, which in turn led to economic disaster. This lack of national wealth did not, however, dampen the luxurious lifestyles of the aristocracy, who found they did just as well living off credit. In Louis' lifetime, the saying was that one measured a gentleman's wealth not by what he owned, but by what he owed. While the aristocrats were spending more and more they did not have, the middle classes lost work, the poor lost bread, and inflation gained ground. The seeds for revolution had already been planted, if not nourished.

Despite his reputation as an idiot trapped in an old mindset, Louis as king was able to sense change in the wind and tried his hand at serious reform. Unfortunately he was unable to make it last, but not throught a want of trying. Louis and Antoinette occasionally mingled with the populace, something that had not been dared since the time of Henri IV, the Bourbon dynasty's revered founder, and Louis frequently busied himself with charitable acts. He tried to set a model for frugality for the aristocracy by cutting corners in the royal household's budget and setting examples like buying the expensive copy of the first *Encyclopedia* second-hand. Unfortunately, this was all eclipsed by the massive gambling debts Antoinette tended to pile up as well as the audacious spending habits of his brothers, who could always rely on a helping hand and an open wallet from their sibling. Louis himself cannot escape guiltless: despite his penny-pinching, he could not help indulging himself now and then, such as when he had hundreds of live animals imported for his favorite hunting resort at Fontainebleau.

As 'modern' as Louis tried to be, his upbringing made him believe in his divine right to rule. Yet he could not find it in himself to be the model of the absolute monarch like Louis XIV. Even in adulthood he was shy and easily embarrassed, preferring to toy with clocks, teach himself about the latest trends in architecture and read about the newest scientific advancements than meddle in the endless rituals of etiquette that were the *raison d'etre* for the glamorous residents of Versailles. He seemed to enjoy the company of sailors more than that of dukes, and once when a sailor apologized for using coarse language in the king's presence, the king put him at ease with a grin. Louis was not at peace with politics and as his situation grew from bad to horrifically bad, his confidence dwindled, in spite of – or perhaps because of – his belief in his right to rule. Increasingly he became able to act only under pressure from his wife, brothers or ministers. Toward the end he may have even suffered a complete breakdown. He did not joke entirely when he said to one of his resigning ministers, 'How lucky you are! Why can't I resign too?'

Secretly Louis, who spent hours busying himself with engineering projects, yearned to be a simple craftsman. He had a good deal of admiration for the simple, practical man who could make the most out of his environment, as demonstrated in his favorite novel, *Robinson Crusoe*. It might have been this passion for the man struggling against nature, the pioneer-hero, that inspired Louis to become involved with America. Of course, Louis' eventual entanglement with the future United States of America was not just a matter of personal whim. France still had important colonies in the Americas that were threatened by the overwhelming British presence. Louis authorized a secret loan of 2,000,000 livres to the American rebels, but his sympathy for the brave American leaders had its limits. When a woman at his court chattered incessantly about the greatness of Benjamin Franklin, Louis eventually gave her a gift that spoke volumes: a chamber pot with Ben's face painted on the bottom.

Louis' desire to keep France's support for America under wraps changed after the rebels won a sweeping victory at Saratoga, finally throwing the odds firmly toward the rebels' favor. French support of the Americans' war effort, Louis decided at last, would now be quite direct, even if it meant open war with the British. Louis could not have foreseen that, in a way, his backing of America would have indirect but catastrophic consequences for himself and his family.

By the mid-1780s, after the United States of America at last became a fact, in France all things American became in vogue. Among the French intellectuals, updates on the 'American experiment' (in democratic, republican government) were excitedly discussed in the salons and in the academies: it was something radical and daring, a defiant step past aristocratic supremacy and rigid class structure. The fact that there were rich landowners in America who, outside of a lack of titles, were almost a match for Europe's nobles in privilege and prestige was unimportant. The ideals of social equality and liberty that the new republic pursued with audacious vigor became the envy of the French elite, and it was not long before the belief that these heroic goals could easily be transplanted to France spread like wildfire.

This was not the France of Louis XIV. It became clear enough that any attempt to play the role of the absolutist would be risky, but Louis could not break away from his royal hubris. The war with Britain that resulted from French support of the American rebels left

France heavily in debt while the rise of inflation was coupled with the aristocracy's rising debts. In an attempt to heal these financial wounds and place more of the economic burden on the shoulders of the landed rich, Louis tried to institute a land tax that was not only unpopular among the nobility, but also the rural populace. The Parlements, the local governments, pounced on the tax, which came as a surprise to no one who knew the political landscape. When Louis claimed his customary right to supersede the Parlements' objections, they responded by denouncing his actions and refusing to give him any more tax revenue. Furious at this defiance of his right to rule unhindered, Louis banished all delegates of the Parlement of Paris from the city. Later, he was forced to reach a compromise and recall the Parlement, but the damage to his reputation and to the populace's goodwill toward him was already done. Despite the name, the Parlements of France did not have as much of a voice in government as the Parliament of Britain, but they were still seen traditionally, especially by the middle classes, as the people's only representation to the king. When he silenced the Parlements, people said that Louis was striving to silence the people.

Yet matters could only get worse from there. On April 29, 1788, the Parlement of Paris broke a term of the compromise that stated it would continue to collect a tax from the nobility. Louis responded by stripping them of their right to challenge the monarch's decrees. Even though the Parlements really did not have the general populace's interests at heart, revolts erupted across France as the people clamored that the Parlements' rights be restored by a king that could not refrain from tyranny. The French Revolution had begun.

To replace the Parlements and earn popular approval for his plans for monetary reform, in 1789 Louis called the Estates General. This was an ancient law-making body which, although it supposedly represented France's three 'estates' or classes (the aristocracy, the clergy, and the commoners), had not been in place since 1614.

Unfortunately for Louis, the Estates General were no more a reliable tool than the Parlements, as the delegates let themselves stew in their own class resentment. On the heels of this political blunder, personal tragedy struck: on June 4, 1787, Louis' eldest son died after a long and painful bout of tuberculosis.

Devastated by his son's death, Louis was unable even to pick up the pieces as his plans fell apart. The Third Estate, the one representing the working class, moved to have the Estates General renamed the National Assembly and was determined to draft a bold new constitution for France. When persuasion failed, Louis tried threatening them with military force, but it was much too late. The other two Estates had joined the National Assembly by the end of June. The year 1789 brought with it more catastrophes. By then nearly half of the workers of Paris were unemployed. Soldiers, lacking both morale and paychecks, were revolting with peasantry suffering from a want of bread at their side. Something had to give under all this pressure and that something at last collapsed on July 14, 1789.

A crowd of Parisians – peasants, workmen, fishwives, students, soldiers – attacked the Bastille, the ancient fortress-prison reserved for enemies of the State, believing that the Bastille was being used to house weapons for the army to use against the people. As the crowd marched on the fortress, the commander of the tiny troop guarding it refused to give it up to the mob. However, the crowd overwhelmed the underarmed defenders, not without casualties of their own. For his defiance, the captured commander was murdered and his body mutilated. The other officers were captured, beaten and butchered by the crowd, drunk with their own victory. At the time, the Bastille held only a few petty criminals and madmen, all of whom were set free by the crowd. While not the most substantial of conquests, to the people of Paris the act was a vastly successful and symbolic one, a clear sign of the People throwing off their chains and trampling over an oppressive, archaic government.

'All Frenchmen are my children,' Louis said to his brother, the

Count of Artois (and the future King Charles X), when he suggested that he join him in fleeing France. 'I am the father of a big family entrusted to my care.' Louis would not, or perhaps could not, see the ever decaying state of affairs for what it was. The only person his 'children' loathed more than him was his foreign wife, whose reputation, poor to begin with, was made even worse by a scandal known as the 'Affair of the Queen's Necklace'.

In 1786, an impoverished woman who claimed descent from the old Valois dynasty, the Countess de La Motte, began forging letters 'proving' that she was an intimate member of Marie Antoinette's inner circle as well as the queen's lover. With this 'evidence' in tow, she convinced the Cardinal de Rohan, a less than holy priest who had inadvertently earned Marie Antoinette's resentment, that she was the best chance the cardinal had of making amends with the queen. La Motte even went so far as to hire a woman who bore an uncanny resemblance to Antoinette, to have a secret meeting with Rohan in the gardens of Versailles. In the course of her swindle, La Motte tricked Rohan into buying an extravagant diamond necklace that was worth 1,600,000 livres (the equivalent of a country estate) to ease his way back into the queen's favor. La Motte, of course, took the necklace for herself. Antoinette had refused to buy the necklace before because of the exorbitant cost and because of her need to reform her image as a spendthrift, so she was furious when the necklace's makers innocently mentioned the purchase to her. As word of this leaked out and the scandal unfolded, Antoinette's already shaky reputation came under fire.

Once La Motte was exposed and arrested, it was rumored that she was nothing but an unwitting pawn, a victim of Antoinette's deceptiveness and greed, instead of the other way around. Pamphlets were circulated, painting vivid portraits of Antoinette's alleged hedonistic lifestyle or depicting her as a half-insane nymphomaniac. One such pamphlet, titled 'The Austrian Woman On a Spree', leaves behind no detail in describing Marie Antoinette's role in orgies with her servants and brothers-in-law. Another, 'A Historical Essay on the

Life of Marie Antoinette', claimed to be an autobiography of Marie Antoinette where she freely describes herself as 'barbaric Queen, adulterous wife, woman without morals, soiled with crime and debauchery'. The pamphlet's 'Antoinette' goes on to write that she tutored herself in new sexual positions with the help of her brothers-in-law and went on to try them out with her loyal young maids, leaving, of course, no detail untold.

As more and more aristocrats, sensing the coming storm, began to flee the country, becoming the first of the *émigrés*, the people began to throw off all the old customs and fashions. Steel, considered the metal of choice for the romanticized American pioneer, replaced silver on gentlemen's coats. Diamonds, cologne, perfumes, and silks all became sneered upon as staples of an old and irresponsible way of life. Even the wealthiest came to wear simple jackets and dresses, adorned now with the tricolor of liberty: red, white, and blue. This was one fashion statement that could not be ignored: hapless people seen not wearing the tricolor in one way or another could be proclaimed 'enemies of the Revolution' and were liable to be beaten or even killed by a crowd of concerned patriots.

Even the French language was not safe from the new Revolutionary spirit. The polite second person pronoun, *vous*, fell out of use and everyone, even royals, were expected to use and receive the familiar *tu*. 'Monsieur' and 'Mademoiselle' were replaced by the humbler 'Citizen' and 'Citizeness' and as the Revolution gained steam one could actually be thrown into prison for addressing a lady as 'Mademoiselle' instead of 'Citizeness'. Curtseys and other traits of etiquette were also frowned upon by all, high or low. The tiniest facet of life had to reflect the French people's new-found liberty and equality, superficial as it may have been.

On October 5, the royal family felt the new anti-monarchy sentiment in a very brutal way. Very early in the morning, a crowd of armed women, protesting bread shortages, led by a disheveled, blood-soaked man named Nicholas Jourdan marched on the palace of Versailles. Finding the gate unlocked and little opposition, they broke into the palace and began stealing everything in sight or breaking whatever could not be carried away. Any guard or servant that tried to stop them or even happened to get in the way was murdered outright, their blood daubed on the faces of their killers. Crying out 'Death to the whore!' they found Antoinette's bedroom and, after failing to find the queen as well, ripped apart her furniture and her linen. The queen, as well as her children and Louis' sister Elizabeth, were lucky enough to have been alerted and managed to get to safety, at least for the moment, but it was agreed that the only way to soothe the rioters was for the king to appear before them.

Louis himself stood on a balcony above the furious crowd and tried his best to pacify them. Although there were a few shouts in the king's favor, most of the mob bellowed for the queen. Calming herself, Marie took her husband's place on the balcony in a dressing gown she hastily put on in the confusion, her then four-year-old son holding one hand and her eleven-year-old daughter holding the other. As soon as they came within view, another shout, 'No children!', went up. Marie Antoinette turned momentarily to help her children back into the building and then turned back to the mass of faces below her. Her composure was confident despite several muskets that were aimed directly at her from below. Perhaps realizing that this frightened mother was not the devilish harlot they hated, the crowd regained their humanity for a moment and the guns vanished.

Their work had not yet finished, however. Once a relieved Antoinette turned back from the crowd, a new demand went up: 'The King to Paris! The King to Paris!' The entire royal family found themselves herded into a carriage bound for Paris and surrounded by the unpredictable mob. For the first time in a very long time in French history, the people now ruled a king. Surrounded by marching and dancing women, many singing patriotic songs and firing guns off into the air, the carriage slowly lurched toward a capital that had long been neglected by the Bourbon kings. Along the trip one of the crowd would sometimes shout harsh death threats at the royal family, especially the infamous Antoinette. At one point the little Dauphin peered out of the carriage window and cried out to the mob, 'Mercy for Mama! Mercy for Mama!'

The Assembly decided to put the displaced little family in the dusty Parisian palace of Tuileries. Overnight they decided to strip Louis of his powers of law-making, veto and declaring peace or war. Even worse, Louis found himself deprived of his very independence as it quickly became painfully clear that the 600 guards given to him were not only there to protect his life, but to keep the royal family in the palm of the Assembly's hand. Even the household servants were now mostly spies on the Assembly's payroll.

While Louis and his family suffocated in their gilded cage, the Assembly busied themselves with the task of dismantling the France that was. In November 1789, all church property was confiscated by the government. Priests who refused to swear allegiance to the State were liable to be deported or, worse, given up to the tender mercies of a patriotic mob. Many of these patriots, not content with the government's measures, took matters into their own hands by burning down cathedrals and smashing religious icons. Priests and nuns were beaten, humiliated, and sometimes killed to the delight of the people. Louis, who undoubtedly heard word of these atrocities, must have realized with a chill that it was chiefly the Christian God that gave him his place as the King of France. With Christianity in peril, so was his now no-longer-sacred life.

Even Louis now had to admit that his so-called 'children' were throwing quite a tantrum. Hans Axel von Farsen, a handsome Swedish adventurer who worked as an intermediary between Louis and King Gustavus III of Sweden, secretly collaborated with Louis and royalist sympathizers to spirit the royal family out of Paris to a town that bordered on the Netherlands, where they expected to come under the protection of loyal soldiers under the Marquis de Bouillé. There is evidence that he had been Antoinette's lover for some

time, which is believable, since he was both a close, sympathetic friend and a very attractive alternative to her asexual husband who had now been driven to a nervous breakdown by the horrors of recent years.

At ten o'clock in the night of June 20, 1791, Louis and Antoinette prepared their children and, with the help of Farsen and a handful of trusted servants, secretly hurried out of the castle. At two o'clock in the morning, they exchanged carriages and moved onward, disguised as Russian travelers and provided with forged passports and identification papers. At two-thirty, they reached the town of Chaintrix and spent the night anxiously at the house of a royalist.

At the next destination, Pont de Summevelle, they expected to find royalist soldiers who could escort them most of the way. Fate took a hand, however, and their chariot broke after hitting a post, costing them time they could not afford to lose. Once they finally arrived, Louis and Antoinette were horrified to find no one awaiting them. The accident and other minor delays had caused them to be extremely late and thirty minutes before they came the troops decided they could no longer wait without arousing suspicion. Another group of soldiers were arranged to meet and escort the royal family, but, weary of their activities, a local citizens' militia detained them. The helpless Bourbons had no choice but to continue their journey unprotected.

It was at the town of Varennes, only thirty miles and roughly three hours from their final destination, that the royal family was captured by local authorities while waiting for fresh horses for their carriage. Vanquished in body and spirit, and perhaps regretting his own betrayal of the trust he once placed in the French people, Louis was returned with his family to Tuileries in Paris and on September 14, 1791 signed with a bowed head a new constitution drafted by the National Assembly.

The atmosphere at Tuileries now became unbearable. Antoinette, in despair, found comfort only in Farsen's arms, who meanwhile continued to work night and day to conceive more plans to save his love and her family, but to little avail. Louis refused to accept the Assembly's plans to reduce him to a constitutional figurehead and secretly wrote to foreign governments, pleading for any kind of support. When the Assembly urged Louis to accept a number of anti-clerical laws, including an act to deport any priest spoken against by at least twenty citizens, he instead denounced the Assembly's authority. On the same evening that he refused to approve the laws he wrote to his confessor Père Hébert, 'Come to see me. Never have I needed the consolation of religion so much. I have finished with man; my trust is now in heaven. Disasters are foretold for tomorrow.'

On June 20, 1792, an enraged crowd smashed their way into the Tuileries, unhindered by the guards who simply stepped aside. Standing his ground, Louis placated the crowd by donning the red cap of liberty. Also, despite the likely possibility of poison, he drank a glass of wine a man from the crowd offered him, saying as he took the first sip: 'People of Paris, I drink to your health and that of the French nation!' The crowd, forgetting all of their dark intentions, cheered for their king.

Whatever advantage Louis gained with his bravado was quickly lost once a man named Maximilien Robespierre and other radicals in the government ignited an insurrection on August 10. The citizens of Paris gladly took the invitation to revel in bloodshed that night. One observer at the time claimed he saw a crowd carrying human heads on pikes: 'I noticed with horror young people, in fact children, throwing the heads in the air and catching them on sticks'. The same day, the Tuileries was again stormed by a mob. The 900 soldiers guarding the palace ran out of ammunition and were massacred. During the attack, the royal family managed to flee to the meeting place of the National Assembly to plead for their lives. Unfortunately, that very night the National Assembly had caved in to the demands of the radicals and robbed Louis of all his legal powers. It was decided also that the royal family was to be transported to a new prison known as the Temple. With the nations of Europe now opening hostilities with the Revolutionary government, the royal family was now a liability at best.

For five days, Parisian mobs broke into prisons and slaughtered their inhabitants, all mostly prisoners condemned as enemies of the State. Louis and Antoinette were always aware of the danger that lurked all about them, posed by both the murderous crowds and the new extremist government that came to power, the Convention. This threat that hung over Louis' head was made all too painfully apparent after one of the Convention's first official acts: the abolition of the monarchy.

As conspiracies, a few urged on by Farsen who was determined to at least rescue Antoinette, kept being formed with the goal of freeing, if not restoring, the king and as foreign troops marched on French soil, the royal family was pulled into greater risk. In the afternoon of December 11, Louis was called before the Convention to be put on trial as an enemy of the people. The charges were varied: some were real, in particular his secret communications with hostile governments, but others were ludicrous. For instance, Louis' past charity was turned into a weapon when he was accused of 'distribut[ing] money among the populace for the treacherous purpose of acquiring popularity and enslaving the nation'. Meanwhile the citizens who were shot and killed while storming the Tuileries on August 10 were made into martyrs by the government , victims of Louis' tyranny.

The Convention debated on three matters regarding Louis' ultimate fate: whether Louis was guilty of the crimes of which he was accused; if he should be put to death; and if the people's approval should be sought for the verdict. On the first question, out of 749 members thirteen abstained, twenty-eight were absent, and the rest voted for a guilty verdict. On the other two questions, a majority voted against seeking the people's approval for the death penalty. When Louis heard that his cousin, the former Duke of Orléans, now calling himself Citizen Phillipe Egalité, had voted for his death, Louis was visibly shaken and muttered, 'I didn't believe there were such men.'

Louis was placed in solitary confinement for six weeks but, before January 21, 1793, the day marked for his death, he was finally allowed to see his family one last time. In tears he left them, possibly because he almost certainly knew that they would follow him. On the appointed day, he was led to the scaffold, leaning weakly on the arm of his confessor, where the guillotine waited patiently for him. As difficult as it might be to believe today, the guillotine was invented to ensure a clean, humane death, but it would not be so for Louis. The fat on his neck slowed the descent of the blade. A young soldier, just out of his teens, then snatched the bloody head of King Louis and made obscene gestures with it for the entertainment of the watching crowd. For a moment, the crowd was silent, perhaps stilled by something that remained of their ancient reverence for the monarchy, but then, as though they had just shifted from one dream into another, they shouted in unison, '*Vive la République!*'

To Louis' family, the State would be no kinder. After the execution, Antoinette (now mockingly called the 'Widow Capet' by the populace), her children, and her sister-in-law Elizabeth lived on in the Temple with the awful knowledge of what had been done to Louis. On July 3, Antoinette would suffer an even more terrifying loss. Officials came to Antoinette's cell to take away the Dauphin, Louis, who was then only seven years old. Antoinette clutched the boy to her, arguing and pleading with the men to just let her son stay. After about an hour, Antoinette, with what she knew was one last embrace, surrendered her confused and terrified son to his fate. On September 1, Antoinette herself was transferred to a new prison called the Conciergerie. Instead of a room, she was now in a tiny cell, with only a worn screen to give her privacy.

Farsen never forgot her and wrote often to the Austrian government, urging them to fund another escape attempt. One was made on September 2, by men disguised as guards, but one of the conspirators betrayed the others to the authorities even as Antoinette was being led out of the prison. With the plot exposed, she was moved into an even smaller cell, unlit except by a street light outside the prison.

Her own turn to be put on trial at last came on October 12. She was accused by the State of many crimes, including encouraging the guards to shoot innocent civilians on August 10 by getting them drunk. The Dauphin, who was given up to the custody of a cobbler, was even forced to sign a statement against his mother, accusing her of forcing him to mutilate himself and making him try to have sex with a syphilis-infected prostitute.

Confronted with such charges, Antoinette turned the tables on her accusers. Even broken down by months of emotional scarring and physical neglect, Antoinette found one bit of strength left in her. When the prosecutor pointed out that Antoinette did not immediately respond to the charges made against her about her son, she replied in a tense voice, 'If I have not replied, it is because Nature itself refuses to respond to such a charge laid against a mother.'

Then she turned to the jury and said, 'I appeal to all mothers who may be present.' A number of women in the jury responded to Antoinette's plea with cries of outrage and disgust, directed for once toward the prosecution. But despite her last passionate stand, she was unanimously found guilty and sentenced to die in the same way as her husband.

On the day of her execution, she was taken to be transported in a cart (Louis was taken to the scaffold in a carriage). At the sight of her final conveyance, her bowels loosened and she had to ask to relieve herself against the prison wall. As she later climbed the steps to the scaffold, she accidentally stepped on her executioner's foot and whispered, 'Pardon me, monsieur. I did not mean it.' After the deed was done and the 'harlot' was dead, Farsen wrote sentimentally, 'It fills me with horror that she was alone in her last moments with no one to whom she could give her last wishes.'

By May 1794, the Revolutionary Tribunal, no longer bothering with the niceties of trials as they had done with Louis and Antoinette, ordered the death of Elizabeth on grounds that she was guilty of treason against the people. After her own execution, her body was stripped, the clothes confiscated by a very needy State, and her body was thrown naked into a mass grave.

The Dauphin, having fulfilled his sole purpose by testifying against his mother, was taken from the cobbler and spent his eighth year of life in a dirty, small cell. Outside of occasionally being fed and given water, he was completely ignored by his guards. His waste was never removed from his cell and his clothing and bed linens were never cleaned or changed. Left to infection and lice, he became extremely ill. The Dauphin, hailed as King Louis XVII by royalists since his father's death, died alone with a twisted, sickly body in filth and neglect. He too was thrown unceremoniously into a mass grave.

His sister Marie-Thérèse was the only one of the small family to survive the Revolution. Although she too was imprisoned, no real attempt was ever made on her life. Public sentiment eventually swung around to mourn the monarchy and the once hostile crowds would often gather outside her cell window at night, singing sad songs of remorse. In the winter of 1795, she was given over to the custody of the Austrian government as part of a political agreement.

In the meantime, the most powerful man in the French Republic, Robespierre, continued the 'Reign of Terror' against the old aristocracy of France. So-called 'enemies of the State' were condemned to die without trial underneath the guillotine's blade until the Reign of Terror finally claimed its last victim: Robespierre himself. For Louis and more than 3,000 others the end of the nightmare had come too late.

Further Reading

Cronin, Vincent *Louis and Antoinette* (Morrow, 1975)
Fraser, Antonia *Marie Antoinette: The Journey* (First Anchor, 2001)
Hibbert, Christopher *Days of the French Revolution* (Morrow, 1980)
Richardson, Joanna *Louis XIV* (Weidenfield & Nicolson, 1973)

NAPOLEON

Reign: *May 18, 1804–April 6, 1814*
(as Emperor of the French; abdicated);
March 20–June 22, 1815 (again abdicated)
Born: *August 15, 1769*
Died: *May 5, 1821 (possibly murdered)*
Buried: *Hôtel des Invalides, Paris*

In a stone, scarcely furnished house in the city of Ajaccio in Corsica, Letizia Ramolino, wife of the poor, title-less nobleman Carlo Maria Strada Malerba Buonaparte, gave birth to her second child that would survive into adulthood, Nabulio. At the age of thirty-nine, Carlo Buonaparte died from cancer on February 24, 1785, leaving Letizia alone with Nabulio and his seven siblings in near poverty. No one could have guessed that this boy from a poor family in Corsica would one day not only be proclaimed Emperor of the French, but would also change, for better or for worse, the course of history.

The first step in Nabulio's path toward destiny came in 1779 in the guise of a full scholarship to the Royal Military School in France. Letizia raised Nabulio to believe firmly in the cause of Corsican independence from French rule, so the bittersweet fact that Nabulio's scholarship was officially provided by the King of France must not have rested easy on him or his mother. Nevertheless, he naturally could not pass up this perfect opportunity for himself or his family, although he was always very close to his siblings and was said to have departed from them all, especially his elder brother Joseph, with badly restrained tears.

It is not too hard to imagine the difficulties, the hardships, and the humiliations that were faced by a short, scrawny child who spoke broken French in a heavy Corsican accent in a school mostly filled with the sons of French aristocrats. His substantially bloated ego, unrestrained contempt for all things French and outspoken support for Corsican independence did not help him make friends or spare him from the taunts and punches of bullies. Although Nabulio became studious and spent many evenings learning the writings of classical authors such as Tacitus and Plutarch by heart, his teachers did not hold out much hope for him. One school report said plainly but prophetically that this particular pupil was 'domineering, imperious and stubborn'.

Regardless of his instructors' feelings, Nabulio (who eventually got into the habit of signing his name with the Gallicized 'Napoleon Bonaparte') went on to enroll at the Ecolé Militaire in Paris at the age of fifteen. Even by then it was typical for him to be harshly punished for disciplinary problems. In the fall of 1785, just after his father's death, which now burdened him with the duty to help care for his family, he graduated and joined the army artillery. Yet his studies did not necessarily come to an end. In fact, he spent much of his time in the army studying history, politics and military tactics, particularly those of the ancient Greeks whom he deeply admired.

Despite his obvious passion, it seemed that his military career was doomed to come a crashing halt when he was charged with failing to suppress a riot in Corsica and exiled back to Ajaccio. Astonishingly and in the first of a series of inexplicable turns of luck, Napoleon was not only later recalled to France, but also granted full French citizenship. Dearer to him, however, was his recent election at home to the position of lieutenant colonel of the 2nd battalion of Corsican Volunteers, which he asked for leave from the French army to accept.

He decided to stay in Corsica for some time, supporting his family and staying with the Corsican Volunteers. It escaped Napoleon's attention that he needed to ask for an extension of his leave and he ended up being put on trial for desertion. All seemed dire and the only thing Napoleon had to plead was his need to support his family as the second-eldest brother. Nonetheless, fate was once again on his side. Instead of being found guilty, he found himself promoted to captain.

Disaster was bound to catch up with Napoleon sooner or later and finally it did in a very harsh way. Napoleon's brother Lucien had accused the immensely popular governor of Corsica, Pasquale Paoli, of treason and pro-British sympathies in front of a Jacobin Club, who promptly sent word of the allegations to the revolutionary government in Paris. Paoli's arrest was immediately ordered and the loyal Corsicans reacted to the news with a vengeance. A mob started to congregate outside the Bonaparte home, determined to have their revenge on the turncoat Lucien and his Francophile brother Napoleon. The entire family had no choice but to sail to France from their beloved homeland in the middle of the night on June 1792 even as rioters smashed their property to pieces. Now Napoleon had to sustain himself and his family in a strange land on a captain's meager pay.

Meanwhile the new republican government of France, having abolished the monarchy and put King Louis XVI to death, had brought down the wrath of Britain, Holland, Austria and Spain on their heads. Disastrous as all this was for the French people, in such an atmosphere a military man with Napoleon's skill and energy could thrive. He was soon promoted again, to major, and gained suitable recognition for his adept defense of the port city of Toulon from the British Royal Navy. This spectacular success led him to become brigadier general at the age of just twenty-five.

After the fall and execution of Robespierre, Napoleon was briefly imprisoned thanks to his friendship with Robespierre's brother, Augustine. This proved to be only another temporary distraction, and it was not long before Napoleon was pardoned and attending the lavish parties hosted by one of the men now heading the new regime in Paris, Director Paul François de Barras. The Director was a man of the world with an appetite for extravagance that expressed itself in full at his frequent parties, which were both the joy and scandal of the top Parisians. Undoubtedly the uptight, socially awkward Napoleon felt out of place at Barras's decadent affairs, but it was at one such celebration that he met the one true love of his life, Joséphine.

Joséphine, whose full name was Marie Josèphe Rose Tascher de la Pagerie de Beauharnais, was, like Napoleon, the child of an obscure, hardluck aristocratic family from outside France (her family had lived in Martinique for a number of generations). She came to France for an arranged marriage with a nobleman, Alexandre de Beauharnais, by whom she had two children, Eugéne and Hortense. After being neglected and psychologically abused by her husband, she sought and won a divorce on grounds of some public libels he made against her. In the days of the Reign of Terror, both she and her ex-husband, who got himself ensnared in Jacobin politics, were imprisoned and left to wait for the guillotine's mercy. Her neck was saved by the timely fall of Robespierre, but her ex-husband was not so lucky.

In the brighter and freer days after the Reign of Terror had run its course, Rose, as she was known at the time before Napoleon insisted that she call herself Joséphine, sought security and wealth by sharing her bed with the most influential men in France, especially

Barras himself. It was at Barras' château, the Chaumière, that Joséphine outraged, delighted and influenced French high society with her daring fashions that almost bordered on nudity. Exactly how Napoleon, with his conservative Corsican upbringing, could fall for such an independent woman with a 'distinct' reputation is a mystery, although, as we will see, it took some denial on his part.

But it is undeniable that he did fall recklessly in love with Joséphine, a love that flows in his endless stream of love letters. 'I awake every day with thoughts only of you', was just one of the many, many sentiments expressed under Napoleon's pen. On Joséphine's part, she realized that a married life was a sound life, especially if it was to a quickly ascending star on the political scene. Despite the whispered warnings from her friends, Joséphine agreed to marry Napoleon, who had in 1794 been put in charge of the Army of Italy. On March 6, he and Joséphine were to be married in a civil ceremony. The groom was hours late and arrived, distracted and impatient, to an anxious, unsettled bride. On their records, both of them were conscious about the fact that Joséphine was older than Napoleon by six years and lied about their ages (Joséphine claimed to be four years younger, Napoleon one year older). Napoleon also named Paris, not Ajaccio, as his birthplace in the records. So much for pride in his homeland.

Napoleon's love for Joséphine did not fade, even after their honeymoon. On the contrary, it was only given fuel. Tongues wagged over how Napoleon would caress and fondle Joséphine in full public view in highly sexual ways. He also came to adore Joséphine's children, treating them as though they were his own. Napoleon even went as far as giving Eugène a high position in his army.

Unfortunately for Joséphine, Napoleon's affection was not shared at all by his family. Letizia never stopped referring to Joséphine as 'the whore', while Napoleon's siblings were not shy in expressing their loathing of Joséphine to Napoleon and even to Joséphine own face. Worse, Joseph Bonaparte made a crusade out of exposing Joséphine and his efforts were far from in vain. Not only did Joseph start finding proof that Joséphine was still having regular rendezvous with one of her old lovers, a dashing young soldier named Hippolyte Charles, but she and Charles had both invested heavily in a company that illegally sold poor quality goods to the French army. If Napoleon harbored any suspicions of his own, he repressed them brilliantly. In his eyes, Joséphine was as saintly as ever.

As dear as Joséphine was to him, the invasion of Italy in the name of the Republic consumed more of his waking hours. The French in their patriotic fervor had conceived the most ingenious excuse yet for declaring war: the noble need to spread democracy to nations still suffering under the yoke of tyranny. Of course, the real reason for the invasion of Italy was the need for the strained French government to refill its coffers and Napoleon gladly obliged. Riches, priceless art, and other treasures were promptly snatched from Italy's ancient cities and shipped to French hands. Unfortunately, although Napoleon was well received in some parts of Italy (especially by those who hated the Spanish and Austrians far more than they did the French), the suffering of the Italian people was the only price for these goods. In what would be a common theme in all of Napoleon's campaigns, towns and villages would be left devastated during the combat and brutal measures would be taken against dissenters at Napoleon's command . One village that remained in revolt against the French occupation had most of its inhabitants massacred at Napoleon's personal order. Napoleon would later proclaim without irony, 'I do not wage war as a profession. No one in fact is more peaceful than I.'

In the midst of all this avarice and slaughter, love still held firm in Napoleon's heart. He wrote to Joséphine once a day, every day for 127 days. Whenever she failed to respond immediately, which was often, since the muscular Hippolyte Charles frequently insisted on her undivided attention, he would become paranoid and agitated.

Eventually, it dawned on Joséphine that even Napoleon's devotion had its limits and she had to do what she could to ease any doubts he might have about her, especially with Joseph crusading to discredit her. She agreed to meet Napoleon at Milan, but she thoughtlessly decided to take Charles with her. Unfortunately, Joseph insisted that he accompany both of them on the carriage ride, creating one of the most awkward and bizarre family situations in known history.

On February 19, 1797, Pope Pius VI was forced to agree to cease supporting the Austrians in any way or form. This was the decisive victory for Napoleon and by April he was at last able to march his troops into Austria. By April 18, Austria agreed to the Treaty of Leuben through which France acquired Belgium, Holland, the Ionian Islands and the west bank of the Rhine. France did agree to concede Venice and a few other Italian territories to Austria, but it was still a major victory for a weary France. Overnight the Bonapartes went from poverty to prominence with Napoleon now the new hero of the Republic.

This warrior of democracy had this to say in a conversation after his return: 'Do you really think that I triumphed in Italy to aggrandize that pack of lawyers that form the Directory? What an absurd idea! A republic of thirty million people, that is what the French people want today. But that fad will pass, just like all the others. What they really want is glory to gratify their vanity, but as for liberty, they do not know the meaning of the word.' Although barely-concealed sentiments such as this must have made the Directory aware of the danger Napoleon represented, they nevertheless readily agreed to Napoleon's new scheme: the conquest of Egypt.

In name, Egypt was a province of the Ottoman Empire, but in fact it was virtually independent. The practical reasons for an invasion of Egypt by France were that it was a way to block Russia and Austria's encroachments on the dying Ottoman Empire and, most importantly, it would give France leverage against Britain's trade empire, especially Britain's grip on India. After winning the Directory's approval, Napoleon went at his plan with demonic energy. He ordered the making of French, Greek and Arabic printing presses for Egypt, and planned to bring with him translators, engineers, astronomers and other scholars to make the most out of the trip. Egypt was not only ripe for conquest, but also had educational value for Napoleon's busy mind.

For all of Napoleon's meticulous preparations, the Egyptian adventure did not run smoothly from the start. The army's supplies were meager and the soldiers were struck hard by dysentery as soon as they set foot on Egyptian soil. Nevertheless, under Napoleon's brilliant leadership they were able to take Cairo, but this triumph was dashed when the British all but annihilated the French fleet at the Battle of Abukir Bay[27], leaving Napoleon and his forces stranded.

Undaunted by this minor catastrophe, Napoleon continued working to establish a firm French presence in Egypt. He forbade his troops to loot on pain of death and tried to present an image that would be favorable to the Egyptian people. Unfortunately, when pressed for cash, Napoleon dashed his own popularity by undertaking a number of hated measures, including a tax for mosques. The Egyptians inevitably saw past Napoleon's benevolent façade and, before Napoleon's appalled eyes, an insurrection was rising fast.

Unfortunately, Egypt became not the only problem facing Napoleon. Before departing from France, a maid confessed her knowledge about Joséphine's indiscretions to Napoleon. Not missing a golden opportunity, Joseph gleefully confirmed it and on top of it all sent his brother evidence he had uncovered about Joséphine and Charles's illegal financial speculations. Nasty but hard to refute rumors about against dissenters chased Napoleon all the way from Paris to Cairo. Overwhelmed, Napoleon struck back the only way he

[27] Also commonly known as the Battle of the Nile.

could: he would cheat on his deceitful wife himself.

After going through his pick of Egyptian women, Napoleon then chose the twenty-year-old wife of a French lieutenant, Pauline Fourès, whose husband was conveniently given orders to return to France. With him out of the way, Napoleon flaunted his affair with Pauline to all the officers to negate the threat to his masculinity that Joséphine's well-known affair posed. The ploy worked for him at least. After the campaign was over, Napoleon would claim, 'In Egypt, I was relieved of the restraints of an obnoxious civilization.'

Meanwhile the Ottoman Empire also needed to save face and declared war on France to save the province that belonged to them only in their imagination. In retaliation, Napoleon took the offensive into Syria, even with Egypt slipping through his fingers. Poor planning, superior enemy forces, and the bubonic plague conspired to turn Napoleon's elaborate plans sour. With a seriously depleted army, Napoleon fled back to Egypt, only to find open revolt against the French occupation everywhere he turned. After having hundreds of war prisoners shot in Cairo and winning a temporary victory against British and Russian naval forces, Napoleon decided to scrap the entire Egyptian venture and fled the country, leaving behind his army and a good number of his officers without money and supplies in a country that despised them. He had also left behind the bodies of 10,000 men who did not live to see their homeland or their families again.

As far as Napoleon was concerned, however, those 10,000 lives were not wasted. Once he returned to France, he found that even though the Egyptian plan had ended in failure, he was greeted by jubilant crowds, cheering his name. At thirty years old, Napoleon had at last made his mark.

The reception he got from his dear brother Joseph, who eagerly held even more proof about Joséphine's sins in his hands, was not what he expected. Aware of the incriminating evidence Joseph had ready, Joséphine stormed into Napoleon's house with her two children in tow and pleaded for his forgiveness. Perhaps because he really did still love her despite himself, Napoleon forgave her and agreed not to end the marriage. However, he made it painfully apparent that the days of his devout faith in her were over.

Just as Napoleon had predicted, the French began losing their own faith in the principles of the Revolution. People once again addressed each other as 'Monsieur' or 'Mademoiselle' instead of 'Citizen' or Citizeness', and the days when failing to do the latter was a punishable offense were long dead. The *émigrés* started to return to France in droves and in their wake the people began to mourn for the Bourbons while the Directory was bogged down in partisan quarrels. A coup was in the making and Napoleon of all people was in the best position by far to make it happen.

Napoleon already had the support of one of the Directors, Emmanuele Sieyès. His brother Lucien had also wormed his way into one branch of the government, the Council of Five Hundred. Apparently no one noticed that Lucien had lied to qualify for the office: he claimed he was thirty, which was the minimum age for qualification, when in reality he was twenty-four. Nevertheless, the coup began when the Council of Agents exceeded their powers by putting Napoleon in command of all troops in and around Paris. Of all the politicians and lawyers aware of this act, none dared or cared to point out that it was an unconstitutional act on the part of the Council. The death knell of liberty was sounded, beginning not with a foreign invasion, as the Revolutionary government once envisioned, but with startling apathy at home. Realizing that the government's collapse was inevitable, Director Barras announced his resignation.

Napoleon made an appearance at the Council of Five Hundred, where Barras's letter of resignation had just been read. The politicians there, enraged by the events that were unfolding beyond their control, literally mauled Napoleon, shouting, 'Down with the

tyrant!' Only his burly bodygaurds were able to save Napoleon from a thrashing or worse at the hands of the rabid politicians. As Napoleon fled, Lucien led troops into the building, shouting that the Councilmen's lives were being threatened by Jacobin rebels. Utterly helpless, the Councilmen left the scene in a blind rush.

Meanwhile Sieyès and another politician named Pierre Roger-Ducos urged the Council of Ancients to draft a new constitution, which would place a 'temporary' triumvirate with Roger-Ducos, Sieyès and Bonaparte at the head of the Republic. The whole affair was called by the historian Alexis de Tocqueville 'one of the most badly conceived and executed *coups d'etat* imaginable'. Yet it was successful, especially for Napoleon who was named First Consul and over time was able to edge Sieyès and Roger-Ducos out of power. With the help of his brother Lucien, whom he appointed Minister of the Interior, Napoleon was able to pass a new constitution, the Constitution of the Year VII[28], which dissolved the Directory and the legislative bodies of the old constitution, replacing them with new bodies that were to be far more dependent on Napoleon's whims. The constitution was voted into place by a staggering majority, thanks to Lucien who managed to 'lose' three and a half million votes against the constitution.

Even with this careful charade, it became clear that not everyone in France was consumed with a feverish love for Bonaparte. On Christmas Eve 1800, a cart holding two large barrels exploded on the Rue St-Niçaise, killing and maiming a number of passers-by. The cart was positioned to trap Napoleon's carriage, which was headed toward an opera house. The assassination attempt was mistimed and Napoleon and Joséphine, both of whom rode in separate carriages, narrowly missed the explosion. The incident left a stark impression

[28] During the Revolution, the old Gregorian calendar was replaced by a new calendar that started off at the year the Revolution began and held new names for the months. The calendar stayed in place until the year 1806.

on Joséphine who was close enough to hear the blast. A crippling fear of riding in carriages would stick with her for the rest of her life.

As ruthless as the attempt was, there was reason enough for it. Even with the machinery of a purportedly 'republican' constitution, Napoleon's rule was far more totalitarian than King Louis XVI's had ever been. Elections became carefully rigged courtesies. For instance, Napoleon was later made Consul for life, despite an overwhelming number of opposing votes. The soldiers and the police had only one boss that mattered: Napoleon. Freedom of the press was a charade at best, with dissenting newspapers shut down and their defiant editors arrested for libel. Writers whom Napoleon himself once burned the midnight hours studying, such as Tacitus and Rousseau, were banned from school curriculums. History itself was rewritten according to criteria devised under Napoleon's instructions. Even plays could not be performed without meeting with Napoleon's own approval. By November 6, 1804, all pretenses were finally dropped and with yet another rigged vote the people of France named Napoleon Bonaparte their Emperor.

The coronation for the new Emperor, held on December 1, was a grand affair with more than adequate pomp and ceremony, rivaling if not surpassing anything the Bourbons could have done. Pope Pius VII was invited personally to crown Napoleon and Joséphine Emperor and Empress, although Pius only accepted the invitation after Napoleon went to great lengths to threaten him. Beneath all the glitter were very real tensions among the Bonaparte clan. Lucien and Letizia were both absent from the ceremony while Joseph and Louis glared with loathing at their anointed brother.

Napoleon had grand designs for all his siblings. In his plans his brothers and sisters were to be the foundation for a new royal dynasty of Europe and as such Napoleon showered them with titles and kingdoms. Joseph was made King of Naples in 1806 and later King of Spain in 1808; Elisa was made Grand Duchess of Tuscany; Louis was made King of Holland in 1806; Pauline was made

Duchess of Guastalla; Caroline, after Joseph went to claim the Spanish throne, was made Queen of Naples; and the youngest sibling Jerome later had a kingdom, Westphalia, created for him out of Germany. In exchange for these magnificent favors, Napoleon naturally expected his siblings to marry to match their new standing and to be obedient to his every wish. Even with Napoleon as Emperor and the most dangerous man in Europe, though, the Bonaparte siblings never stopped being a match for their dear brother. As Madame Devaisnes wrote, 'The Emperor is truly rendered unhappy by his family. They are all acting like a pack of devils deliberately bent on tormenting him.'

As the eldest sibling, Joseph was, in accordance with tradition, the head of the family since their father's death. Even as his younger brother skyrocketed into power, Joseph anticipated that Napoleon would at least respect his role in the family and remember the hard times through which he had helped steer the family. So it was an unthinkable slap in the face when Napoleon declared before the coronation that, as long as Joséphine remained without child, his heir would not be any of his brothers, but his nephew Napoleon Louis Charles, born in 1802. When Joseph complained bitterly that he was being overlooked, Napoleon was outraged. 'How dare he speak to me of his rights and his interests!' he raged. 'To do this before me, his brother, to arouse his jealousy and pretensions, is to wound me at my most sensitive point . . . It is as if he had said to an impassioned lover that he had fucked his mistress . . . my mistress is the power I have created. I have done far too much to achieve this conquest to permit someone else to ravish or even covet her.' In his mind, Napoleon had enough good reasons for excluding his once cherished big brother from the succession: '. . . [H]e was not born in a high enough social position to have warranted such an illusion on his part . . . He, like myself, was born in a common position. But I raised myself by my own abilities. He, on the other hand, has remained exactly the same since birth.'

Joseph would not lie down and take Napoleon's simple explanations. Instead, he threatened to boycott Napoleon's coronation. This protest only infuriated Napoleon who thundered that he would disown Joseph, brother or not, unless he came. In the end, Joseph appeared at the coronation, where he glowered at Napoleon all throughout the ceremony. Joseph was not even satisfied after Napoleon offered him the throne of Naples. By this point, their relationship could only deteriorate.

Lucien, despite his many illegal services for Napoleon, was on even worse terms by the time of the coronation and afterwards. Although Napoleon had no issues with his family accumulating wealth in a France still ridden with poverty and unemployment, he asked them to at least try to be subtle. The *dolce vita* was too tempting for Lucien, however, and the money leaked from his wallet. To further his lavish lifestyle, he brazenly embezzled money from the government, but went too far when he started coveting Napoleon's 'mistress'. His greatest offense was when he published and distributed a pamphlet against his brother titled *Parallels Between Caesar, Cromwell, Monck, and Bonaparte*, paying for the publication of the pamphlet with government funds. Even then, Napoleon gave Lucien a chance to redeem himself by making him ambassador to Spain. Unfortunately, Napoleon underestimated his brother's recklessness. King Carlos IV of Spain offered Lucien five million francs' worth of diamonds and some valuable art if he would draft a treaty in Spain's best interests. Napoleon tore up the treaty and lambasted Lucien, who in the meantime anticipated Napoleon would be unhappy with his services and fled Madrid with all his bribe treasure in the middle of the night.

Lucien again invoked Napoleon's anger by impregnating and then marrying his mistress, an actress and divorcée named Alexandrine Juoberthon. Even the corrupt Lucien could not be swayed from his vows by the bribes and threats Napoleon heaped on him to try to convince him to break up the marriage. Eventually,

Napoleon lost what little patience he had and exiled Lucien and Alexandrine to Italy. Even this final break was not enough to make Lucien surrender to his brother's meddling nor did Lucien lose his family's sympathies. During the coronation, Napoleon was astonished to discover that the reason for his mother's absence from the ceremony was because she chose instead to stay in Italy with Lucien. Later on, Lucien fled to Britain with his wife and child, where, while he lived under an official but loose house arrest, he was treated by the British government and people like a hero.

Brother Louis, while always a favorite brother of Napoleon, was mentally ill, due to an advanced case of gonorrhea, making him inclined toward depression and a violent temper. Regardless, Napoleon let him marry his stepdaughter Hortense and made him King of Holland. Louis treated Hortense badly, keeping her from leaving their residence to visit her mother and trying to bully her into renouncing her French citizenship for Dutch as he had done with all French nationals in Holland (unlike any of them, she never relented). Her household staff was filled with spies, paid to keep detailed records on her activities for Louis. When word came out that Napoleon planned to make Louis' son his heir instead of him, Louis was incensed. He became even more so in April 1808 when his third son Charles Louis Napoleon (the future Napoleon III) was born and Hortense had used the pretext of her pregnancy to go to Paris, and now refused to return to Holland with her newborn son, ignoring the letters Louis furiously wrote to her. Worse, Napoleon took in Hortense and his new nephew, promising Hortense that he would protect her from her mad husband.

About his sister Caroline, Napoleon once said, 'Of my entire family, it is Caroline who most resembles me.' This explains why, out of all the Bonaparte sisters, Caroline was the one to cause him the most heartache. Besides being an implacable critic of Joséphine, Caroline also married against her brother's wishes. The man was a cavalry officer named Joachim Murat, who not only was way below

Napoleon's high standard for in-laws, but was also a former lover of Joséphine's. At Napoleon's darkest hour, it would be Caroline and her loutish husband who would betray Napoleon to his enemies.

Finally there was the baby brother of the family, Jerome Bonaparte, who at the tender age of nineteen had already made a mockery of his brother's dynastic plans by returning from a trip to the United States with a souvenir: a bride, Elizabeth Patterson, a middle-class girl from Baltimore. After hearing the happy news, Napoleon proclaimed, 'If he brings her with him, she will not set foot on French territory. If he comes alone, I will overlook his error.' Trusting that his brother's heart would melt after seeing Elizabeth, Jerome planned to sail from America with his bride, who was then with child. Unfortunately, Jerome found that not a single accessible port in Europe was untouched by his brother's decree. At last, Jerome told Elizabeth that he would confront his brother in person and get him to accept the marriage. 'Rest assured', he said in a letter to her, 'your husband will never abandon you. I would give my life for you and for my child.' As far as husbandly devotion went, though, Jerome was made of weaker stuff than Lucien.

Jerome was told in plain terms that if he kept up the silly nonsense with the American girl he would be disowned from the family and exiled from all of Napoleon's territories. If he instead relented to big brother's best interests, all his debts, which were quite substantial, would be paid and he would be rewarded handsomely with a fatter allowance and royal titles. Jerome agreed enthusiastically and never wrote or spoke to Elizabeth again, who had to return to Baltimore broken-hearted and with an unwanted bastard of quasi-royal blood.

Over time, Napoleon's own marriage began to hit bottom. As Napoleon carried on affairs of his own, some more successful than others, Joséphine became the target of his frustrations. One frightful episode occurred when Napoleon took Joséphine to view a few hundred acres of woods he had purchased. On the way the small carriage the two were riding in went into a gully and Joséphine, always nervous in carriages since the assassination attempt of 1800, became hysterical and begged to be let out. Embarrassed by his wife's genuine terror, Napoleon screeched at her, accusing her of ruining the trip on purpose. When the coach driver finally stopped the carriage for Joséphine's sake, Napoleon leapt out of the coach and attacked him with a riding whip.

While his personal life yielded mixed results at best, the world seemed to be completely at his mercy. In addition to being the Emperor of France, Napoleon crowned himself the King of Italy on May 26, 1805. Although the defeat of French forces at Santo Domingo and the sale of the Louisiana territory to the United States put an end to Napoleon's plans for the Americas, and Napoleon's schemes for the invasion of Britain came to nothing, French troops occupied the Netherlands and Switzerland and prepared to cross the Rhine. After a number of resounding victories against Austrian and Russian forces, Napoleon built a firm French presence in Germany. His main German allies, the electors of Bavaria and Württemberg, were promoted to kings with his blessing and the west bank Rhine territories were annexed to France. Further the Act of Confederation, signed on July 12, 1806, dissolved the ancient Holy Roman Empire and reorganized many of its former territories into the French-controlled Confederation of the Rhine. With the stroke of a pen, Napoleon dismantled an institution that had lasted for nearly 1,200 years. His foreign minister, the brilliant Charles Maurice de Talleyrand-Périgord, was livid, realizing that the dissolution of the Holy Roman Empire, as crippled and meaningless an institution as it was, meant that the balance of power in Europe was disrupted. Yet Napoleon would not be denied.

Among those angered by the French reorganization of Germany was King Friedrich Wilhelm III of Prussia, who saw that the new order in Germany was deliberately made unfavorable to his country. He wrote a lengthy letter to Napoleon that left out no detail of his personal outrage. Napoleon only scorned the letter, dismissing it as 'a pathetic pamphlet against France'. This cockiness was swiftly warranted once French forces trampled the Prussians at the Battle of Jena.

Despite this steady stream of successes, Napoleon's one obsession remained strangling the life out of the British Empire. He concluded that the best way to thrash the British was not through his armies, but through their wallets. Napoleon issued the Berlin Decrees, which put in place a complete blockade against Britain. Unfortunately, such a blockade was easier to declare than to enforce. Napoleon was willing to threaten England's major trading partners, Portugal and Denmark, and even to dispatch troops to sack Copenhagen, but the blockade was violated on a daily basis within his own empire, even by his own royal siblings.

Nevertheless, other triumphs set Napoleon's mind at ease. At the Battle of Friedland, Napoleon beat back Russian forces and secured Poland, while promising the Polish aristocracy to restore independence to Poland, which had been divided between Russia, Austria, and Prussia since 1772. Of course, even though he kept a Polish countess, Marie Walewska, as his mistress, he had no intention of giving Poland the autonomy it craved and instead installed an obvious puppet government.

Over the matter of Poland, Napoleon met with Tsar Alexander I at the River Niemen on June 25, 1807. Alexander, who felt Russia had a traditional right to Poland, loathed Napoleon before he met him, but after their first meeting the two forged a warm friendship. They were even seen to embrace in public. In a letter to Joséphine, Napoleon wrote glowingly, 'I am content with Alexander and he must be with me! If he were a woman, I do believe I could make him my mistress.' However, it was not going to be the sort of friendship that would stand the test of time. One night Napoleon had a dream that a bear ripped open his chest and ate his still beating heart. Although Napoleon consulted many occultists to try to find an interpretation, he could never make what would seem to be the obvious connection between the bear and Russia. But, for the present

time, Alexander agreed to sign the Treaty of Tilsit, which cemented France's dominion over western and central Europe.

France's rapid expansion appalled the world, but in particular it worried Talleyrand. The talented minister soon resigned, saying, 'I do not want to be, or rather, I no longer wish to be the executioner of Europe.' Napoleon pleaded with him to stay, since he held Talleyrand, with him from almost the beginning, with almost superstitious regard, but Talleyrand was adamant. He was eventually replaced by a mere yes-man, Jean Baptiste Nompère de Champagny. In the state-sanctioned newspapers, it was written that Napoleon was forced to 'dismiss' Talleyrand.

Although the loss of his talented foreign minister did worry Napoleon, especially with his superstitious belief that the individuals that had been with him since his first accomplishments were like living good luck charms, he decided to carry through with his plans for Iberia. Portugal had been a thorn in Napoleon's side because it was such a staunch ally of Britain and refused to give up its partnership with Britain even under the weight of Napoleon's threats. On November 30, 1807, a force led by a young officer named Jean-Andoche Junot attacked Lisbon to capture the Portuguese royal family. But by the time Junot arrived, he found that the royals had already escaped on a ship to Brazil. Also, thanks in part to Junot's incompetence, the British were able to drive the French out of Portugal by August of the next year.

However, a golden opportunity to take Spain had presented itself when King Carlos IV appeared before Napoleon on his knees, begging for help. Fearing that his son Fernando was scheming to depose him, Carlos had abdicated on March 19, 1808, making his heir King Fernando VII. Carlos instantly regretted this decision and begged Napoleon to restore him. After getting both King Fernando and Carlos to meet him on French territory, Napoleon tricked Fernando into repenting his accession: at the same time he convinced Carlos to make him regent of Spain. After pulling off this sleight of hand, Napoleon invited the Spanish royal family to become 'guests' (really state prisoners, although they were treated lavishly) of the French government.

Even with Spain now under his boot, Napoleon did not dare annex it or make himself its king. He offered the Spanish crown to Lucien on condition that he divorced his wife and disowned his child by her, but Lucien was steadfast in his loyalty to his bride. When he received Lucien's inflexible reply, Napoleon grumbled, 'Lucien is acting more self-righteous than the Pope!' Louis and Jerome, realizing that Spain would present many more difficulties than their own cushy kingdoms, also declined. Joseph said no at first, but when Napoleon asked him a second time he reluctantly agreed, even though he had developed a love for the Neapolitan countryside. After handing Naples over to Caroline, Napoleon named Joseph King of Spain and the Indies on May 6, 1808. It would turn out to be the worst decision Joseph made in his life.

Joseph was handed a Spain that raged against its oppressors. Although Napoleon was able to coerce the Spanish parliament, the *cortes*, into making Joseph's crown legitimate, the gesture meant almost nothing. Joseph was never regarded by his Spanish advisors and officials as anything but a mere puppet of Napoleon. Almost daily riots erupted, demanding the restoration of the Spanish royal family while terrible acts of defiance, including mob attacks against French soldiers that ended in slaughter and mutilation, occurred with alarming frequency. Joseph did genuinely care about his responsibilities and often begged Napoleon to ease his oppression of the Spanish people, but Napoleon only laughed at his brother's presumption and continued putting the screws on the Spanish.

Although the occupation of Spain would prove to be a disaster in every possible sense in the word, Napoleon correctly saw himself at the apex of his power. The one-time poor, bullied schoolboy milked his prestige and lived up to his imperial status, spending much of his private time on huge hunting expeditions and entertaining the most expensive court in Europe. He particularly enjoyed chess as a hobby, although he was really quite terrible at it, but of course no one ever felt the need to win a game against the Emperor nor call him on the fact that he clumsily cheated nearly every time.

Despite all appearances, though, the confidence his people had in their chosen Emperor was beginning to wane. Some even began to talk openly about the possibility that the Emperor was out of his mind. Certainly Napoleon's impulsive personality lent credibility to these rumors, but there was also the one secret that the Emperor was trying to hide: he was epileptic. Joséphine was able to bribe into silence anyone who witnessed one of Napoleon's episodes, but it could not be kept secret forever.

Festering unrest in Spain or not, Napoleon's only concern for the time being was the issue of the succession. His nephew Napoleon Louis Charles had died, but Louis and Hortense still had two other healthy sons. Yet Napoleon yearned for a son of his own and he knew that the middle-aged Joséphine was no longer able to bear children. Napoleon still cared for Joséphine and her children and, as he did with Talleyrand, Napoleon believed that his marriage to Joséphine had brought him his good luck. Eventually his desire for a son overrode his own love and superstition. On December 15 1809, a ceremony for the divorce was held where Napoleon was seen embracing Joséphine and her children and weeping with them. When the other Bonapartes heard the news, they celebrated well past midnight.

Napoleon's fondness for Joséphine and her family never dimmed. Joséphine was allowed to take up residence at the ancient Château de Navarre and was granted an annual income of five million francs. The French never forgot their 'Rose' and she became even more of a celebrity as the ex-Empress. Not only was she graceful and amiable, but, even though her homeland was Martinique, she was French through and through. Napoleon's choice for a new bride, Marie Louise, was quite foreign. Like the hated Marie Antoinette, she was an Austrian princess and had the further handicap of being the daughter of Napoleon's enemy, Emperor Franz I.

The whole situation with Napoleon was agony for Marie Louise. Although she willingly entered into the marriage, she saw the engagement as a heroic sacrifice on her part to help save her homeland from the tyrant that had humiliated her country on the battlefield and threatened the life of her father. As for Napoleon, he was characteristically frank about the reason for his match. He stated bluntly, 'I am marrying a womb'. Marie Louise fulfilled Napoleon's basic expectations by March 19, 1811 when she bore Napoleon a son, Napoleon François Joseph Charles, whom Napoleon created King of Rome at birth.

As for the child's uncle, the King of Spain, catastrophe was at hand. Napoleon had to intervene to save Joseph from a rebellion, blaming his brother for it while ignoring Joseph's vocal pleas for leniency toward the Spanish people. Napoleon did not help salvage his brother's credibility when, on June 22, 1811, he decreed that all his siblings ruling as monarchs in Europe would be reduced to the status of princes and princesses. Before that, he had pushed his brother Louis over the edge by dethroning him and annexing Holland to France. Napoleon no longer felt accountable to anyone, not even his family.

By November of that year, Napoleon's seemingly inexhaustible good fortune would at last run out. Tensions, mainly stemming from France's occupation of Poland, grew worse between Napoleon and Alexander of Russia until finally on November 10 French forces crossed the Russian border. Tsar Alexander wrote a letter pleading for peace, but Napoleon replied that he would accept nothing less than total capitulation.

For his Russian campaign in 1812, Napoleon led the Grande Armée, the largest army until then assembled in Europe, but here was a campaign where size was a disadvantage. Rather than confronting Napoleon's 450,000 troops head on, the Russians lured Napoleon deeper into the country, emptying villages and towns of

food and supplies and burning crops as they went. The marches were made worse for the French by the erratic weather, which alternated between withering heat and monsoon-like rain, and by incompetent planning. Food supplies rapidly ran out and the medical staff were painfully underfunded. Surgery had to be done by torchlight since lamps were not paid for and, worse, men with no experience were asked to perform complicated surgical procedures. As morale inevitably went to pot, Napoleon did little to restore confidence. He hysterically accused his generals of incompetence, all the while refusing to even consider the option of retreat. When Napoleon received a letter from Tsar Alexander that offered to open negotiations, Napoleon exclaimed, 'Alexander is poking fun at me!'

After a couple of skirmishes with Cossacks and Russian forces, Napoleon finally reached Moscow, only to find it was as silent as a graveyard. Undaunted, Napoleon set up headquarters at the Kremlin and ordered his troops to occupy the city, suspecting Alexander was trying his hand at a waiting game. During the night, Russian troops came out of hiding and set fire to the entire city. Quickly the horrible truth dawned on Napoleon: Alexander had chosen to let the ancient Russian city burn rather than let Napoleon claim it. At first Napoleon was still determined to stay his ground, but finally on October 3 he realized that for his own survival he had no option but to retreat. Struck by the coming Russian winter and hounded by Cossacks, the Tsar's men, and even hordes of angry and armed Russian peasants, Napoleon's army, now reduced by deaths and desertions from 450,000 to 102,260 men, made its slow and painful way back to France.

Napoleon was used to looking down at seas of smiling, cheering faces. This time he received a cool welcome from the subjects of his new empire. Napoleon was finally forced to admit that the French were getting sick of him and his endless war-games. His cherished long-term schemes of one day conquering all of South America and moving the Vatican to Paris were now more impossible than ever. The Russian campaign was just the start of a stern lesson in reality.

Sensing Napoleon's weakness, the Allied forces against him set down their plans for an invasion of France and a final strike against Napoleon. Soon Napoleon found he had no choice but to recall Joseph from Madrid and restore Fernando VII to the throne of Spain. The resources of his empire were now stretched almost to the breaking point.

This was not the worst of it. Napoleon was distressed to discover that his brother Jerome had fled his kingdom of Westphalia, allowing Allied forces to march into Germany unhindered. If this betrayal was not appalling enough, Napoleon also quickly discovered that his own sister Caroline and her husband had joined the Allies. Knowing he was no longer fighting for personal glory, but for the life of his empire, a weary Napoleon met the Allies at the Battle of Leipzig, which ended with the loss of Germany and opened the way to Paris for the Allies themselves. Napoleon struggled to the last, but in the end Paris surrendered.

By April 11, 1814, Napoleon was forcibly obliged to abdicate and sign away all of his rights, and those of his heirs. Lacking any remorse for the devastation his ambition had wreaked on France and Europe, Napoleon claimed, 'Born a soldier, I could get on very well without an empire, but France cannot get on without me.' Despite Napoleon's confidence in France's dependence, Talleyrand was already helping France do exactly that by paving the way for Louis Stanislas Xavier, the brother of the late King Louis XVI, to take the throne of France as Louis XVIII[29]. Napoleon tried to kill himself using a vial of poison he had always kept around his neck, but found that over the years it had lost its potency and he only succeeded in making himself sick for a couple of days. When his brother Jerome heard of this, he revealed his true gratitude by exclaiming, 'The

[29] Supporters of the Bourbon dynasty referred to Louis XVI's son and heir who died at an early age in a Revolutionary prison as Louis XVII, even though he was never formally crowned.

Emperor, after having caused all of our problems, has survived!'

In the aftermath, Jerome and Louis were allowed to live in France. Joseph Bonaparte, on the other hand, eventually went across the Atlantic to New Jersey. Caroline's husband Murat was later executed by the Allies after breaking their treaty, and Caroline herself drifted away into obscurity. Joséphine, on the other hand, was allowed to retain both her residence and her income. She even became close friends with Tsar Alexander, who offered her a palace in St. Petersburg which she graciously declined. She never forgot her husband and the two would write to each other often during his exile, but Joséphine would not live to see Napoleon's last desperate quest for glory. She died on May 29, 1814, her funeral extraordinarily well-attended.

Napoleon himself, the Allies decided, would be banished to the small Mediterranian island of Elba, but he would be granted sovereignty over it, along with a small personal guard. Despite this nicety, it was an exile and 400 men were assigned to guard Napoleon. Marie Louise, who had gone to live with her father Emperor Franz and had taken her son with her, sometimes wrote to him, but ignored his requests for a visit. Napoleon liked to believe she was prevented from doing so out of spite by her father, but in reality, she had already taken a lover, the Count of Niepperg.

Although the restored Bourbon government agreed to provide Napoleon with a generous annual income for the rest of his life, the money soon slowed to a halt. This annoyance, and the belief that there was enough popular support awaiting him in France to reclaim his throne, led Napoleon to end his exile by suddenly landing at Cannes on March 1, 1815 with a number of his own guards who had remained loyal. By March 20, in an incredible reversal of fortune, he was back in control of Paris. The day before Louis XVIII, fearing he would share the same fate as his brother, had taken flight to the Netherlands. This was the start of the 'Hundred Days', Napoleon's last desperate grasp for empire.

In spite of the return of his supernatural luck, Napoleon had severely overestimated the desire of the French to put up with him again. Although Napoleon had done much to distance himself from the radical Jacobins, the aristocracy feared that his restoration signaled a return to the darkest, bloodiest days of the Revolution. The rest of France remembered Napoleon's apocalyptic thirst for power. Demonstrations, complete with students and other youths defying attempts to conscript them into the armies, were held against Napoleon, despite his weak pleading that he only wished to use force to restore a fragment of France's former glory.

It was inevitable that the Allies would prepare for a second invasion of France to rid themselves of Bonaparte forever. Without as much confidence as he once had, Napoleon fought the Allied forces in Belgium and was initially able to push them back, but when fighting the British under the Duke of Wellington at the legendary Battle of Waterloo on June 18, 1815, a Prussian army arrived to reinforce the beleaguered British. The tables irrevocably turned and Napoleon fled back to France.

The Parlement of Paris, under pressure from the Allies, formally requested that Napoleon abdicate. He agreed, but insisted that his son, who was still in Austria with his mother, be made the new Emperor of the French. His request was brushed aside and Louis XVIII was once again returned to Paris. On July 3, after spending some time in hiding at Hortense's residence, he boarded a vessel bound for the United States, but the ship was intercepted by the British. The Allies determined that, this time, Napoleon should be banished to the tiny and distant Atlantic island of St Helena. By then Napoleon was well into middle age and his dreams of worldwide conquest had bitterly faded. Still, he was not yet ready for such a forced retirement. After hearing about the Allies' decision, he cried out, 'I appeal to history!'

At St Helena, the former Emperor of the French resigned himself to a quiet life of routine, spending most of his time playing cards, horseback riding, or trying to learn to read and write English (he did it very badly). For most of the time he spent his days at his

assigned quarters, Longwood House, since he was not allowed even to walk around the small island without an armed escort, as much for his own protection as the world's.

After years of living dully if peacefully, by 1818 Napoleon was becoming mysteriously ill. The physicians' treatments only worsened his condition and all observers agreed that the great general and self-made emperor was dying. On his deathbed, the last words he muttered were 'Joséphine' and 'My son'. Although it was at first assumed that he died from natural causes, it was learned that he had been poisoned day by day with small doses of arsenic and cyanide. The murderer was not an agent of one of Napoleon's many old enemies or an assassin sent by King Louis XVIII, but his closest companion on St Helena, a Frenchman named Gharreu Tristan de Montholon. Ironically, his motive was not political: he probably only wanted the fortune Napoleon had promised him in his will. With surprising unity, the Bonaparte family legally blocked Gharreu from taking the prize.

Destined for a life of obscurity and poverty, Napoleon ended up doing far more to change Europe and the world than most born and bred monarchs. Indeed, the effects of his accomplishments on France, Europe, and the world are felt to this day. He had given France an empire, although he displaced and destroyed countless lives in the process. As Talleyrand said, 'What a grand and noble role he could have played. But that true glory he simply did not understand.'

Further Reading

Erikson, Carollyn *Joséphine: A Life of the Empress* (St. Martin's Press, 1999)

Schom, Alan *Napoleon Bonaparte* (Harper Collins, 1997)

Schom, Alan *One Hundred Days: Napoleon's Road to Waterloo* (Harper Collins, 1993)

Seward, Desmond *Napoleon's Family* (Viking, 1986)

FRANCE IN FILM AND LITERATURE

An 1843 opera and a nineteenth-century play by Sir Henry Taylor titled *St. Clement's Eve* have both focused on the character of Charles VI. Naturally, King Charles is also depicted in Shakespeare's play *Henry V* and subsequent cinematic adaptations, but without too much madness. Charles also had an 1843 opera named for him. Alexandre Dumas wrote a novel about the life of Charles VI's queen, *Isabel de Bavière*.

Catherine de' Medici and her children, including Henri III, were featured in another Alexandre Dumas novel, *Queen Margot*, which in France has twice been adapted for film: in 1954 and in 1994. Catherine's rival for her husband Henri, Diane de Poitiers, was the subject of a MGM production, titled simply *Diane*, in 1956 and naturally Catherine herself is an important character. Novels based on her life include *Sur Catherine de Médicis* by Balzac and *The Italian Woman* by Jean Plaidy. The ever prolific Alexandre Dumas wrote a play titled *Henri III et sa cour* which was novelized into the English language as *The King's Gallant* by Henry Llewellyn Williams in 1902.

An attempt to capture the events of the French Revolution in one film was made with 1989's *La Révolution Française*. Naturally Louis XVI is an important aspect of the film. Although not directly concerned with the life of Louis XVI himself, 1996's *Ridicule* examines court life and political intrigues within his court at Versailles. A 1938 film, titled *Marie Antoinette*, centers around her alleged affair with Farsen and the republican schemes of the Duke of Orléans. The film is mostly remembered for Norma Shearer, who performed the role of Marie Antoinette. Victoria Holt wrote a pseudo-autobiography for Antoinette, who also features heavily in the 2001 film *The Affair of the Necklace*, which focuses on La Motte, how she engineered the scam that led to the purchase of the diamond necklace, and its effects on the public image of the French monarchy.

There are, unsurprisingly, numerous novels and films that feature Napoleon to one degree or another, but by far the most prominent is Leo Tolstoy's *War and Peace*. Napoleon was the subject of another novel by Balzac, a novel by Anthony Burgess titled *Napoleon Symphony*, and another novel by Simon Leys, *The Death of Napoleon*. The 1937 film *Conquest* starred Greta Garbo as Countess Marie Walewska, who tried to seduce Napoleon into granting Poland independence while Marlon Brando played Napoleon in 1954's *Desirée*. The 1970 film *Waterloo* portrays Napoleon's return to power, the Hundred Days, and his consequent fall, while the naval aspect of the Napoleonic wars is vividly described in the novels of Patrick O'Brian.

THE BRITISH ISLES

MAELGWYN (MAGLOCUNUS, MALGO) 'THE TALL'

Reign: *534–549 (?)*

In the turbulent Dark Ages that were the sequel of the demise of the Western Roman Empire, one needed not only the benefit of blood, but also to be made of stern stuff to be a king. Maelgwyn, who ruled over the kingdom of Gwynedd in what is today northern Wales, was the perfect man for his age. He has even been proposed as the king upon whom the legend of King Arthur might be based.

The scarce records that survive all suggest that he was a dashing, powerfully-built man who, like many Welsh kings, took an active interest in the arts and patronized countless bards and poets at his court in Deganwy. Nevertheless, in his work *The Ruin of Britain*, a contemporary monk named Gildas wrote: 'You are last in my list, but first in evil, mightier than many both in power and malice, more prolific in giving, more extravagant in sin, strong in arms but stronger still in what destroys a soul.'

Certainly the fact that, while possibly still in his late teens, Maelgwyn raised an army against his uncle, the last king, and killed him for his throne would not have secured a good reputation, even in those vicious times. He did apparently repent this murder and other sins and vowed to retire from the kingship to become a monk. There is a suggestion that he even went so far as to take the vows, but he never surrendered his crown to anyone.

Although both Gildas and the twelfth-century historian Geoffrey of Monmouth say he had flings with men, he was even more notorious for his way with women. Not only was he said to have been a sort of Dark Ages playboy, but one legend states that he murdered his nephew and his first wife in order to marry the wife of the said nephew.

In the prime of his life, Maelgwyn died from cholera, which must have delighted his critics and fulfilled their prophecies that God would strike him down for his crimes, but Maelgwyn was strong and popular enough for the legacy he left for his sons to go unchallenged. His son Rhun succeeded him unhindered, while his other son Brude went on to become a king of the Picts in what is now Scotland.

Further Reading

Snyder, Christopher A. *An Age of Tyrants: Britain and the Britons, A.D 400-600* (Sutton, 1998)

Gildas (trans. Michael Winterbottom) *The Ruin of Britain and Other Works* (Phillimore, 1978)

Monmouth, Geoffrey of (trans. Sebastian Evans) *The Chronicle of the Kings of Britain* (Dent, 1963)

ETHELRED II 'THE UNREADY'

Reign: *March 18, 978–December 24, 1013 (deposed); February 3, 1014 (restored)–April 23, 1016*
Died: *April 23, 1016*
Buried: *Old St Paul's Cathedral, London*

King Ethelred II is best known by his mocking sobriquet, 'Unready', which was an inexact attempt to recreate the Old English pun of his name, translated as *æthel*, 'council', and *ræd*, 'noble', hence 'noble council.' The nameplay in the original Old English was *rædless*, 'without council'. A far more appropriate nickname would have just been 'luckless' or 'unlucky'. Although Ethelred did have his fair share of bad advice, he was in fact a scrupulous lawmaker and a decent king. He just had the atrocious fortune to sit on the English throne during the worst Viking raids Anglo-Saxon England had seen since the days of his heroic ancestor, King Alfred the Great. Unfortunately for himself and England, Ethelred was no Alfred.

Ethelred's string of bad luck began even before the Vikings became a serious nuisance. When his father King Edgar died, it was Ethelred's half-brother Edward, then in his early teens, who ascended to the throne. Ethelred himself was probably only seven when Edward was declared king by the *witan*[30], but there was strong enough support for the boy, centering around Ethelred's officious mother, Elfrida, and the most influential nobleman in the kingdom, Alfhere. Edward, who did not help himself by continuing his father's despised policies toward monastic reform and being an ill-tempered brat, was ambushed and stabbed to death while visiting his stepmother and half-brother. Of course, no one believed that this was just a tragic coincidence: rumor had it that Elfrida and Alfhere arranged the assassination in order to install Ethelred as a puppet king, and there can be little doubt that Ethelred's supporters were responsible. Although Elfrida was never really formally accused of the crime and Alfhere was too powerful to be brought down easily, there was still the urgent need for both of them to wash their hands, bloodstained or not, of the affair. They gave Edward an exquisite funeral and, once miracles were reported to have occurred around his tomb (reports they may have helped along), he became called 'the Martyr', even though in life he was never a saint.

Despite the rocky start to his reign and his very young age, Ethelred's tenure as king at first went smoothly. Calamity came two years later, when Viking raids began afresh, culminating in a siege on London itself in 982. A welcome period of tranquility followed, but

[30] The *witan* were a council of elders who traditionally elected the new king in the Anglo-Saxon kingdoms.

it was soon shown that this was only the eye of the storm when, in 987, the attacks began again. After the disastrous Battle of Maldon, where an English army was defeated by Danish forces led by Olaf Tryggvason, Ethelred pushed for negotiations with the bloodthirsty Norsemen. The end result was that the English had to agree to what was, in essence, extortion. Ethelred offered to pay 22,000 pounds of gold and silver to Olaf as well as provide an indemnity against paying compensation for their past attacks. Olaf agreed to the bargain, probably because he was more concerned at the moment with his designs on the Norwegian throne than making further excursions against a country already thoroughly sucked dry, but attacks led by other Vikings not under Olaf's jurisdiction continued to wreck England.

Ethelred tried a variety of ineffective measures to put off further Norse invasions, but none were as self-defeating as the St Brice's Day Massacre, which was carried out on November 13, 1002. Every Dane in England, even women and children, was to be put to the sword by order of the king. The extent to which this Herodian measure was carried out cannot be known, but it did much to spoil any remaining support Ethelred may have had among the Anglo-Danes, who had been a sizeable community in northern and eastern England since the days of Alfred the Great. It could also have sparked an international incident. Among those murdered, according to one account, was Gunhilda, sister to King Sven of Denmark, and her husband. Allegedly to avenge this death (it is unclear whether or not the murder actually occurred or if it was just *post facto* propaganda), Sven began to orchestrate even more devastating raids against England, beginning in 1003.

Sven's attacks marked a new decade of terrible fighting, each bloody battle followed by a cycle of humiliating defeat and expensive extortion, which exhausted the people's morale and wrecked the economy. In the long run, Ethelred had to rely on an army of Scandinavian mercenaries to protect the kingdom, led by a man named Thorkell, himself a former Viking raider. It was already too late. In 1013 Sven returned, this time to invade England once and for all. By the end of that year, Sven had captured London and Ethelred had fled to Normandy.

For once in his life, though, Ethelred was going to have a turn of good luck. Sven, already an old man by the standards of the age, died from illness by the first week of February the next year. The *witan*, who never lost faith in Ethelred despite his many blunders, unanimously voted to deny Sven's son Canute's claim to the English throne and recall Ethelred. Unfortunately, Canute would not back down from the prize and Ethelred's son and heir, Athelstan, was killed in the inevitable fighting. Drained and broken by his political failures and personal tragedy, Ethelred died, leaving behind a country in turmoil. His formidable second wife, Emma of Normandy, went on to marry the conqueror Canute, but would one day restore the native monarchy with her young son by Ethelred, Edward the Confessor. Despite this amazing recovery, the days of Anglo-Saxon England were numbered and it would be only fifty years from Ethelred's death that the arrival of a new power, the Normans, would change the face of England forever.

Futher Reading

Henson, Donald *A Guide to Late Anglo-Saxon England: From Aelfred to Eadger II* (Anglo-Saxon, 1998)

Humble, Richard *The Saxon Kings* (Weidenfield and Nicolson, 1980)

Loyn, Henry Royston *The Vikings in Britain* (Cambridge University Press, 1980)

MACBETH

Reign: *August 15, 1040–August 15, 1057*
Died: *August 15, 1057 (killed in battle)*
Buried: *Iona*

Although he will forever be known as the tragic villain of Shakespeare's play, Macbeth was in his own time a well-loved king. The King Duncan he usurped was not the innocent, benign ruler painted in the play, but was widely hated and immensely inept. Neither was Duncan murdered while a guest of Macbeth, but killed 'properly' on the field of battle while fighting against an army raised by Macbeth and his half-brother, Thorfinn, Earl of Orkney.

Most sources indicate that Macbeth's reign was mostly a peaceful and prosperous one and that he was an unusually generous man. One account claims that, while on a pilgrimage to Rome, he showered

gold coins on a crowd of peasants. Nevertheless, Duncan's son Malcolm, backed by the king of England, Edward the Confessor, was able to take the throne by force and drive Macbeth into the independent kingdom of Strathclyde.

There Macbeth was able to put up a strong resistance for three years before he was finally vanquished. His stepson and heir Lulach continued to rebel and press his own claim to the throne, but he too eventually failed, earning him, perhaps unfairly, the sobriquet 'the Fool.' The overthrow of Macbeth is widely considered a turning point in Scottish history, signaling an end to the ancient Celtic way of life and the full beginning of Anglo-Norman dominance.

Futher Reading

Aitchison, N.B. *Macbeth: Man and Myth* (Sutton, 1999)

Borce, Hector *Chronicles of Scotland* (the main source of the Macbeth legend) (W. Blackwood and Sons, 1938–41)

Ellis, Peter Barresford *Macbeth, High King of Scotland, 1040-1057* (Blackstaff, 1980)

WILLIAM II
'RUFUS'

Reign: *September 9, 1087–August 2, 1100*
Died: *August 2, 1100 (assassination?)*
Buried: *Winchester Cathedral*

Just as William the Conqueror heralded a new Norman epoch in English history after the Battle of Hastings, so did his sons start a proud tradition of family bickering for the English royals. William's eldest son Robert, who was quite bluntly disliked by his father, spent his nights carousing with a rough crowd of aristocratic thugs who kept a steady supply of prostitutes of either gender at hand. His brother William, always the preferred son, did not have a better reputation. He had a violent temper and a fiery red face to match that earned him a nickname that would stick with him throughout his life and into posterity: 'Rufus', the Red.

William the Conqueror did nothing to quell the brothers' natural rivalry when he split his hard-won dominions between them on his death. Robert inherited the duchy of Normandy, while William was crowned King William II of England. Years of backstabbing and warring against each other later, the brothers negotiated for peace in 1091. But they were united only because their youngest brother Henry had begun to scheme against them both.

Stout and muscular, William was always dressed in the latest continental fashions, which the English chroniclers of the time blasted as too effeminate. His habit of wearing his blond hair long was also enough to send the monks of the time into spasms of moral outrage. Yet one anecdote that survives suggests that perhaps William's fashion sense was not as developed as he thought it was. When a servant brought him a pair of shoes, his famous bad temper flared up once the servant told him that the shoes cost only three shillings. 'You son of a whore!' William screamed, 'Since when does a king wear shoes as cheap as that?' The servant did procure a new pair, but one that was even cheaper than the last, a fact he did not bother the king's handsome head with. Laying eyes on the shoes, the king exclaimed, 'Now these are more fitted to our royal majesty.'

Church writers in particular enjoyed spending rivers of ink accusing William of wallowing in decadence. Gleefully they wrote that he sought to emulate the Emperor Caligula by dressing like a woman and hosting orgies. At the same time they were writing pages about his lechery, they were also implying that he was a homosexual, a suspicion spurred on by his refusal to marry. Certainly these stories should not be automatically dismissed, but it must be kept in mind that William went out of his way to offend the clergy, whose chronicles make up most of the historical records of the period.

His worst offense against the servants of God was leaving the position of Archbishop of Canterbury open after the death of the last archbishop, something that let him collect the church revenues for himself. The clergy begged him time and again to appoint a popular cleric named Anselm to the office, but William refused until one day he fell almost mortally ill. Thinking it was a sign of God's ire, he went through with the appointment, but even God could not scare William into liking Anselm. The two bickered over political and church matters until William finally pleaded with the Pope to depose Anselm, but his requests were denied. By 1097, matters between king and priest became so tense that Anselm left England in a huff.

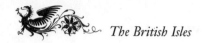

After that incident, the clergy did not have long to make William their whipping boy in their chronicles. While hunting in the New Forest, William was struck down and killed by an arrow that was apparently meant for a deer. History's verdict is that William's death was a freak accident, although arguments that he was murdered at the command of one of his brothers persist, particularly in the case of his younger brother Henry, actually in the New Forest at the time of Rufus's death. Whatever really happened, and perhaps the accident story is the more likely, Henry was not slow in taking advantage of his brother's demise and was able to arrange his own ascension to the English throne with Robert still away on Crusade.

William II has been somewhat forgotten, shuffled between the reigns of his Genghis Khan of a father and his brother Henry I, known as 'Beauclerc', who went on to become one of the more successful and refined kings in English history (for one thing, Henry, unlike his brothers and father, was literate). All that really remains is that his image as a bad-mannered transvestite, and the fact that his death inspires interesting conspiracy theories. Still, one wonders what would have become of his reputation had he lived long enough to step on fewer or more clerical toes.

Futher Reading

Barlow, Frank *William Rufus* (Methuen, 1983)

Grinnell-Milne, Duncan *The Killing of William Rufus: An Investigation in the New Forest* (develops the theory that Henry was responsible for William's death) (David & Charles, 1968)

STEPHEN

Reign: *December 22, 1135–April 7, 1141 (deposed); November 1, 1141 (restored)–October 25, 1154*
Born: *1097 (?)*
Died: *October 25, 1154*
Buried: *Faversham Abbey, Kent*

Concerning the reign of King Stephen, the *Anglo-Saxon Chronicle* is quite definite:

Every great man built himself a castle and held it against the king . . . They surely burdened the unhappy people of the country with forced labour on the castles and when the castles were built, they filled them with devils and wicked men . . . I do not know how to, nor am I able to tell of all the atrocities nor all the cruelties that they wrought on the unhappy people of this country. It lasted throughout the nineteen years that Stephen was king, and always grew worse and worse.

Another chronicler of the time wrote: 'These things we suffered nineteen long years for our sins. It was said openly that Christ and his saints were asleep.'

Exaggerated as these drastic descriptions may be, King Stephen's reign was one spoiled beyond repair by civil war and split loyalties. The string of crises had its genesis in a succession dilemma suffered by his predecessor, King Henry I. Henry had fathered at least twenty-five illegitimate children (one chronicler writing at the time said eloquently that Henry was truly 'the father of his country') but had only two legitimate sons, William, Henry's designated heir, and Richard, both of whom died in the wreck of the White Ship in 1120. Henry made his barons swear an oath to support his daughter Matilda, the widow of the Holy Roman Emperor Heinrich (Henry) V, as his successor. Not only did the barons balk at the idea of being ruled by a woman, but they detested Matilda's new husband, Geoffrey, Count of Anjou, since Anjou was the traditional enemy of Normandy in France. It was assumed by the barons that Geoffrey would be the one holding the reins if Matilda got to the throne, and that they would never allow.

So when Stephen de Blois, Henry's nephew through his sister Adela, came to London and secured the city's support by promising to grant it a degree of autonomy, the barons rallied around him. He also managed to gain the all-important support of William, the Archbishop of Canterbury. A story that on his deathbed Henry changed his mind and nominated Stephen as his true successor was spread and accepted by many, even the Pope.

Although she was dismissed as a pawn of her husband, Matilda, who still referred to herself as the 'Empress' due to her first marriage, was not a woman to be denied. She had more than enough of the personality of her grandfather, William the Conqueror, in her. Seeing an unmissable opportunity, she returned to England in 1139,

claiming that her purpose was only to pay a friendly visit to her stepmother, Adeliza. In the meantime, her half-brother, Robert, Earl of Gloucester, was busy raising an army to fight and die in her name. Then Stephen's own brother Henry, the Bishop of Winchester, and nobles alienated by Stephen threw their lot in with Matilda. By February of 1141, Stephen was beaten and could be found not on the throne, but imprisoned in leg irons at Bristol.

Ruling under the title 'Lady of the English', Matilda seized virtual control of the government but, with Stephen off the board, she sorely overestimated the strength of her position. Arrogantly she cut the autonomy granted to London by Stephen, in order to tap into the city's hefty tax revenues, and alienated her own supporters with unpopular taxes. Before she could be crowned as queen, Stephen's wife, also named Matilda, spurred on an army of loyalists from Kent, which signalled the end of Matilda's brief reign. With her popularity evaporated and Robert captured in battle, Matilda was forced to free Stephen in exchange for Robert's liberty. Although Stephen was once again on the throne, Matilda managed to remain in England until she found herself trapped by Stephen's forces in Oxford. There she made a daring escape by climbing down a rope from an open window and, dressed in white to camouflage herself against the snow, bolted on foot until she managed to get on a boat to Normandy. Even from the Continent, Matilda kept pressing her claim, first for herself and then for her son Henry.

With the civil war still boiling, Stephen's authority was never as sure as it once was. But for all the problems of his reign and the missteps Stephen took, the chroniclers say that he was always a gentle man, which was perhaps why he was such a failure as a ruler of feudal England. At one time a boy named William Marshal, who would go on to advise and defend the future kings of England Henry II, Richard I, John, and Henry III, was a hostage in Stephen's court in exchange for the good behavior of his father, one of Matilda's backers. Marshal's father rebelled anyway, bragging that it would only take a little while to make another son. Stephen, who always treated Marshal as his own child, was openly disgusted by such behavior and refused even to consider harming the young Marshal. But even with such empathy and benevolence, or perhaps because of it, Stephen simply could not handle a situation that had spun out of his control.

In the end, the long, gray years of war and rebellion exhausted Stephen's spirit. The young Henry, now the Duke of Normandy and the Count of Anjou, began to rally massive support in England. Stephen's own son and heir, Eustace, had died from what may have been an epileptic fit in 1153. After that, Stephen knew the fight was over. He agreed to make Henry his undisputed heir and then went into virtual retirement in Kent where he died from a ruptured appendix one year later. The death of Stephen would pave the way for the Plantagenets, England's longest and perhaps most famous royal dynasty, who would oversee more anarchy and bloodshed than Stephen ever did.

Futher Reading

Chibnall, Marjorie *The Empress Matilda: Queen Consort, Queen Mother and Lady of the English* (Oxford University Press, 1991)

Cronne, H.A. *The Reign of Stephen, 1135-1154: Anarchy in England* (Routledge, 1993)

Donald, Matthew *King Stephen* (Hambledon & London, 2002)

JOHN

Reign: *April 6, 1199–October 18, 1216*
Born: *December 24, 1167*
Died: *October 18, 1216*
Buried: *Worcester Cathedral*

Once upon a time in the French province of Anjou, an old story goes, the Count encountered an exotically beautiful woman hailing from an unknown land. The Count was entranced by the woman and soon married her, despite the mystery surrounding her and her lack of a dowry. They lived well enough as husband and wife for some time and, in due course, she bore the Count heirs, but the Count's bliss was ruined by suspicions revolving around his wife's peculiar behavior. For one thing, she rarely went to Mass and, when she did, she always found some excuse to leave before the Consecration. One Sunday, the suspicious Count finally resolved to discover the truth and ordered his knights to somehow detain his wife in the church for the duration of Mass. Just as she was rising to leave, one of the knights stamped his foot firmly

on her cloak. When the priest lifted the Host as part of the ritual, the woman screamed in pain and, flinging off her cloak, literally flew out of the window, taking two of her children with her, but leaving the other two behind. Despite what had happened, the Count raised the two children as his heirs.

The Countess, the story finishes, was Masuline, the daughter of Satan, and when she witnessed the Consecration, a sight no demon can bear, she fled back to hell. From the two remaining children were descended the Angevin dynasty, better known to us as the Plantagenets, that would rule England from 1154 until 1485.

The sons of Henry II, the first Plantagenet king, knew the tales about their Satanic origins and took them in their stride. 'Don't deprive us of our heritage', Henry's son, King Richard I, joked. 'We cannot help acting like devils.' After all, the legend explained perfectly why Henry II and his sons had such manic energy, which they channeled into ruling, as well as such unpredictable tempers. To take just one example, one day when Henry II overheard a member of his court generously praising his enemy King William the Lion of Scotland, Henry leaped on his bed, tore off the linen, and thrashed around on the floor, tearing out the stuffing of his mattress with his teeth.

The demonic traits of the Plantagenets seemed to have reached a pinnacle with Henry II's youngest son, John. Today he is remembered, at best, as the bungling, corrupt villain of the Robin Hood legends and Sir Walter Scott's novel *Ivanhoe* or, at worst, the vindictive tyrant whose actions made the Magna Carta necessary, but even a few hostile critics admit he was an able and attentive administrator. However, he was the victim of his Plantaganet temper, a man who never wasted time caring about his own reputation or the opinions of his most powerful subjects. As one chronicler of the age summarized him: 'He feared not God, nor respected Men.'

It has been thought that John's flaws sprang from the fact that as the youngest of seven children, he was at core a spoiled child. This is probably true, but he might have been cursed with a deep

insecurity from an early age since his parents, King Henry II and Eleanor of Aquitaine, were both such towering, frightening figures to anyone, adult or child. John was also raised in awe of his elder brothers, Henry, Richard, and Geoffrey, all of whom were at least eight years older than him and were bound to inherit all of their father's lands, leaving John nothing, hence burdening him with the nickname 'Lackland'. In the Middle Ages, it was the custom for the youngest son of aristocratic or royal parents to be trained for the clergy since, as with John, all of the inheritance would go toward their elder brothers, but Henry was determined to find a real legacy for John. His plans in this direction were never successful, but by far the worst was his idea in 1185 to make John, not yet out of his teens, the King of Ireland.

Henry hoped that through 'giving' Ireland to John he could kill two birds with one stone: not only would John have no reason to complain that his father never provided for him, but Henry would also have a way of keeping his unpredictable Anglo-Irish nobles in check. Pope Lucius III declined to grant John the all too precious title of king, so John had to settle for the much less glamorous 'Lord of Ireland'. Either way, the title would have been merely an honorific. At the time, Ireland was still very much divided between the warring Irish kings and the nearly independent Anglo-Irish lords. It was an ugly situation for even the most able would-be conqueror, yet, when John came to the island to arrange his 'dominions', he brought his drinking buddies along and offended the Irish kings who had come to pay him homage by making fun of their unfashionable clothing and pulling at their scruffy beards, which had gone out of style back in London decades before. To no one's real surprise, it was less than a year before John was forced to go back to England empty-handed.

Despite this abysmal failure, young John stayed on guard for opportunity. His brothers were no less ambitious: several times they rebelled against their own father, often with the support of their mother Eleanor. Eventually the sudden deaths of his brothers Henry, the 'Young King'[31], and Geoffrey, the Duke of Brittany, strengthened John's position considerably, although Geoffrey had left a son, Arthur, who would complicate matters for John in the future.

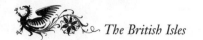

Richard, in the meantime, had heard rumors that his father had slept with and was planning to marry his intended bride, Alice, daughter of King Louis VII of France. Whether or not his father's alleged rendezvous with Alice infuriated him (quite possibly not, if the theories about Richard's sexual preferences are to be believed) or if, as seems more likely, he was lured by the throne to which his father still stubbornly clung, Richard raised an army with the new King of France, Philippe Augustus. On July 4, a sick and exhausted Henry was beaten and forced to recognize Richard as his heir apparent. Later Henry asked to see a list of those who had supported Richard in the rebellion. On the top of the list was John, the son Henry had believed would never turn against him. Shattered by this final betrayal, Henry retired to his castle at Chinon, France and died only three days later. The only son who stood by him on his deathbed was his bastard son Geoffrey Plantagenet.

Although Richard now had the scepter, he preferred the sword and went off on the Third Crusade, leaving his country in the hands of Hugh Longchamp, the Norman bishop of Ely. Richard made John take a vow to remain in Normandy, but Eleanor later coaxed Richard into releasing John from his oath. John quickly justified his brother's caution when he planned to exploit the fact that Longchamp was detested by the English people. This advantage was lost when the more popular Archbishop of Rouen, Walter of Coutances, was sent to take Longchamp's place, but an even better opportunity for a coup soon came along for John: Richard had been betrayed and held for

[31] To concede to his son after one of the brothers' rebellions, Henry II agreed to have his son Henry crowned, although he never held full power and is not considered a 'true' king in English history.

ransom by the Holy Roman Emperor, Heinrich (Henry) VI.

With a small army of Welsh mercenaries, John tried to occupy the throne, but those still loyal to Richard were able to keep him in check. John managed to hold on to some support, but in 1194 when Richard was released on ransom, John's chances fell apart and the few castles still in his possession surrendered. Like a fugitive he hid out in France but was finally caught and brought to Richard on his knees, pleading forgiveness. Richard graciously pardoned John without a second thought, but added: 'Think no more of it, John. You are only a child who has had evil counselors.' At the time, John was in his late twenties.

Vindication at last came for John five years later. After receiving a wound in battle against an unruly subject who was supposedly hoarding some recently discovered Roman gold (it turned out that the reports were grossly exaggerated), Richard died from gangrene on April 6, 1199. The only serious rival to the English crown left for John now was his young nephew, Arthur of Brittany. Doubtless John thought he had little to fear from a boy, but he did not take into account Arthur's formidable mother, Constance, and the backing Arthur was sure to gain from King Philippe of France, who was more determined than ever to put an end to the Anjou possessions in France. Fortunately for John, Constance decided to come to an understanding with John and stop pushing her son's claim. Also, at least for the time being, Philip agreed to leave John's continental possessions untouched so long as John acknowledged him as overlord of his French dominions.

As King of England, John was a less than awe-inspiring figure at five foot and five inches, but he proved in time that he was no one's sycophant. Scorning the company of uptight barons, John preferred the companionship of servants, mercenaries, laborers, and other low-class persons. Contrary to what we think of him today, he was in his own day known somewhat as what we might call with praise 'a man for the people'. At least John never hesitated to step on the toes of his barons, or those of his so-called 'overlord'. Unfortunately, the same attitude that won him the admiration of the common man proved to make for disastrous diplomacy.

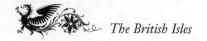

John divorced his first wife, Isabelle of Gloucester, by using a common strategy for medieval kings who wanted to dispose of unwanted wives: he got an annulment granted by the Pope because he suddenly 'noticed' that he and Isabelle were closely related cousins and thus barred from marriage according to canon law. His choice for a second bride was Isabel, daughter of Count Aymer of Angoulême. The new marriage made good political sense, since Count Aymer was a powerful nobleman in the Duchy of Aquitaine, whose allegiance could prove very useful for John in case Philippe ever tried to grab the rich province of Aquitaine for himself or if the notoriously quarrelsome Aquitaine nobles turned against John. There was one little problem: in order to marry John, Isabel's engagement to Hugh le Brun, Baron of Lusignan, was broken. The gossip went that Isabel had seduced John, either through feminine wiles or witchcraft (which, at the time, really amounted to the same thing). These stories ignored the tiny fact that Isabel was only twelve when John married her.

John's marriage to Isabel would have grave consequences in the near future, and it proved to be trouble from the start. Isabel, according to one first-hand account, wept bitterly when she heard that her engagement to Hugh le Brun was dissolved. Further, long into her marriage with John, it was rumored she began seeing quite a few lovers. One of them, a story says, was caught and killed, his corpse suspended over the bed where Isabel slept at John's personal order.

Whether or not Isabel was proving a good wife to John, her old fiancé, as was his right according to the customs of the era, asked for compensation that never came. Instead, out of pure spite, John instructed his officials on the Continent to bully Brun and his family at every chance they got, spurring Brun to appeal to his feudal lord, King Philippe. In 1201, John and Philippe met personally in Normandy where John satisfied Philippe by promising him he would give Hugh le Brun the means to address his grievances. John did give

Hugh le Brun his day in court but, with the petty vindictiveness that was such a strong part of his character, took the opportunity to charge him with treason against himself and the late King Richard (of which, to be fair, he was guilty). John encouraged him to try to prove his innocence via trial by combat against trained, seasoned royal swordsmen. Exasperated, Hugh le Brun went back to Philippe, who demanded that John grant Hugh le Brun a fair trial. After John did everything he could to delay another trial, Philippe became sick of John's excuses and, by April 1202, played his trump card and commanded John to come to Paris to be tried for his irresponsibility before a council of barons . When the arranged date came around, John simply did not show up.

Philippe's response was resounding and swift. He renounced all his feudal obligations to John, confiscated the English-held duchies of Anjou and Aquitaine and gave them to Arthur, who had been dependent on Philippe's guardianship since Constance had died, and sent an army to conquer Normandy for the French crown. John rushed to the Continent with an army of his own and succeeded in capturing Arthur, who soon conveniently disappeared. One report, repeated by William Shakespeare in his play *King John*, had it that John ordered Arthur blinded and castrated. Another, perhaps far closer to the truth and more likely, given John's personality, claimed John accidentally beat Arthur to death in a drunken rage and had his corpse dumped in the River Seine. The truth, though, was never discovered.

Regardless of whether it was premeditated or not, everyone suspected that John had somehow put his troublesome little nephew six feet under. This suspicion and the resulting anger, particularly among Arthur's subjects the Bretons, cost John more than any lost battle. In April 1204, death took Eleanor and with her any hope of reclaiming her Duchy of Aquitaine for the English crown. By 1206, all Angevin territories north of the Loire were lost to Philippe. In only a few years, the empire John's father had built was completely dismantled.

As if all this was not bad enough, John was about to invoke the wrath of an even more relentless enemy than King Philippe, Pope Innocent III, one of the most ruthless popes of the medieval era. Under him the Fourth Crusade sacked the Christian city of Constantinople, where countless churches and artifacts were destroyed or lost, and by his instructions the brutal persecution of the Cathar heretics in southern France were carried out. He was also the kind of pope who subscribed to his predecessor Gregory VII's self-described philosophy: 'Who can doubt that the priests of Christ are to be considered the fathers and masters of kings and princes and all the faithful?' Innocent was the worst kind of pope for someone of John's irreverence toward authority to have to deal with, but destiny, with its usual sense of humor, decided to throw the two against each other.

Innocent had appointed Stephen Langton as Archbishop of Canterbury, in spite of John's wishes to the contrary. Angry over this papal infringement of his royal prerogatives, John not only refused to give his blessing to Langton, but ordered that he not be allowed to set one toe on English soil. Innocent thundered against John and even threatened to put an interdict on England. The interdict was the nuclear bomb in the arsenal of the medieval Church: the priests of a country under an interdict were forbidden from performing any sacrament save baptismals and last rites. As he did with Philippe, John offered delaying excuses and meaningless concessions but, like Philippe, Innocent eventually lost his patience and imposed the interdict on March 28, 1208.

John's response was ingenious and yet typical of his shrewd thinking: he confiscated all church property but said he was willing to return it to its former owners . . . for a price. After all, now that the church was no longer fulfilling its role in England, why shouldn't the king have the right to take the church's property as his own? Enraged that John was making a profit when he should have been flooding the Vatican with letters begging for mercy, Innocent brandished another weapon, excommunication. Besides excluding its

target from the Church, the excommunication rendered the victim *persona non grata* to Christians everywhere. As dire a spiritual weapon as it was, it was even more effective as a political weapon: all feudal ties between vassals and their excommunicated king were dissolved, giving a pre-emptive blessing to all rebels and rivals.

When even by 1212 John showed no sign of giving the Pope his due, Innocent then adopted his role as king of kings and hinted that he was more than willing to officially depose John. While such a thing would have been little more than an angry gesture, one the Pope was more or less powerless to enforce, it also constituted an even more tempting invitation to any rival claimant to the throne or, in John's case, Philippe, who seriously thought of invading England and making his son Louis king.

Even John's stubbornness had to wane in the face of a papally-sanctioned invasion from France, but all of John's declarations of obedience to the papacy seemed empty to Innocent, who was already quite fed up with him. John deduced that only a grandiose and humiliating act would appease Innocent's hurt ego, so he humbly offered to make England and Ireland fiefs of the Vatican, in effect turning John into a vassal of the papacy. Innocent was overjoyed by this generous 'donation' and proclaimed to all Christendom that truly John was a just, Christian king. John's neglected and abused nobles saw this humiliating debasement of their country very differently.

Already the barons of England had been pushed to their limits. Even worse than the social embarrassment of having to kneel to a king who preferred the company of soldiers, ditch diggers, and the like to their own was John's mocking treatment of them, such as when he indulged in blackmail. John kept careful track of his nobles' transgressions, no matter how private or minor, and made sure that the wrongdoers realized they were at risk of facing royal disapproval. Of course, they could always find their way back into John's good graces, as long as they kept their money ready. One baron paid off the king so 'that he would keep quiet about the wife of Henry Pinel'.

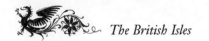

Just underneath this playful if audacious conduct were genuine fears of his 'overmighty subjects'. Even William Marshal, a faithful aide to his brother and father, was not immune to John's distrust. Another victim was William de Briouze, whose only offense against John seems to have been owing him money, although one story says that his wife Matilda brought up Arthur's murder in front of royal envoys. John's harassment of William and his wife culminated in John sending an army against him and demanding that William pay the cost of the expedition. William and his family managed to escape to Ireland, but were separated as Matilda and her children sought refuge in Scotland while William went to Wales where he sent messages to the king begging for a truce. Unfortunately, Matilda was betrayed by a Scottish nobleman and she and her eldest son were put in prison, never to be seen again. Gossip claimed that under John's orders William's family was starved to death.

By 1214, matters between the barons and John were more than tense. What proved to be the fuse for rebellion was John's attack on France that year in order to head off Philippe's designs on England. Even with the aid of his nephew, the Holy Roman Emperor Otto IV of Brunswick, the campaign ended in disaster and John had lost any respect the barons might have held for him. Threatening to depose him, the disloyal barons demanded that John reconfirm a charter of rights made under King Henry I. The original document from Henry I's reign was revised, forming what is known today as the Magna Carta. On June 15, 1215, John signed, under great duress, the Magna Carta at Runnymede near London[32]. Innocent was ill-pleased, to say the least, to see that the nobles of *his* domain were taking such

[32] Contrary to the popular story, John did sign a draft of the Magna Carta, rather than have it marked with the royal seal simply because he was illiterate. There is no proof that John was illiterate, but rather it is certain that John did receive at least part of a clerical education.

unwarranted liberties and he bellowed that the Magna Carta was 'contrary to moral law'. In the end, this cornerstone of English liberty only lasted ten weeks before Innocent fumed that 'the charter, with all undertakings and guarantees, whether confirming it or resulting from it, we declare to be null and void of all validity for ever.' John was the last one to argue with these words and, because it was signed under threat of force, he felt free to break with it. The Magna Carta itself, however, would not be forgotten by the English, and would be reissued in 1216, 1217 and 1225. Its provisions were often ignored or broken, but just as often were the basis for legal action or complaint.

It was not too long before the nobility turned on John again, with some barons inviting the dauphin Louis to come to England and take the throne, and in May 1216, he entered London. John was able to marshal some support and gain some success in the civil war which followed, but then a humiliating blow came in October when, while crossing the swampy area called the Wash in East Anglia with most of his belongings and treasures, an accident occurred, causing a great deal of the treasure, including the English Crown Jewels, to be lost in the waters. Not long after, John fell sick after having a hearty meal and stopped at Newark Castle. What seemed a routine illness turned out to be a fatal case of dysentery. The troublesome country was left to his nine-year-old son Henry who, despite the chaos and troubles at the end of John's reign, managed to stay on the throne with some help from the council of barons which ruled in his stead, a council which included one of John's old victims, William Marshal.

Further Reading

Bingham, Caroline *The Crowned Lions: The Early Plantagenet Kings* (David & Charles, 1978)

Jones, J.A.P. *King John and the Magna Carta* (Longman, 1971)

Warren, W.L. *King John* (University of California Press, 1961)

EDWARD II

Reign: *July 8, 1307–January 1327*
Born: *April 25, 1284*
Died: *September 21, 1327 (executed)*
Buried: *Gloucester Cathedral*

King Edward I was one of the great titans of British history, a true legend in his own lifetime. The epitome of chivalry and the ultimate medieval warrior-king, the first Edward, with a towering body and statuesque features, marched his armies into Wales and Scotland, subduing them, at least partially, to the English yoke, and earning himself the nickname 'Hammer of the Scots'. But even more daunting for Edward was keeping control over the notoriously tiresome English nobles: yet they too were made to revere and fear him. With such a heroic bearing, it is understandable why his son, the future Edward II, had such a terrible time of it. Not made to be a medieval king, much less a clone of his father, Edward paid the price for being born in the wrong place and at the wrong time to the wrong father.

With the death of his elder brother Alfonso, Edward became heir to the throne and the first royal heir in English history to be given the title Prince of Wales. Although he inherited his father's massive physique, was an athletic youth, and learned the art of war at his father's side on the Scottish campaigns, Edward was thought to be a poor replacement for his father from the start since his hobbies seemed odd for a royal prince at the time: swimming, theatre, boating, gardening and digging ditches. Although he had some talent for politics and fighting, Edward instead threw himself into anything involving the arts or working with his bare hands. Much to the disgust of his peers, these recreations determined his choice of friends. A contemporary wrote, 'He fraternized with buffoons, singers, actors, carters, ditchers, oarsmen, sailors and others who practiced mechanical arts'. Like his great-grandfather, King John, Edward suffocated under the stuffy airs of his fellow aristocrats and felt nothing but out of place among them. Edward did, however, find solace in one man: Piers Gaveston, the son of a Gascon knight at King Edward's court.

There is the persistent question of whether Edward and Gaveston were actually lovers. A strong claim can be made that they were not, even though the popular assumption runs otherwise: scholars theorize that the intensity of Edward and Gaveston's chivalric friendship has been misinterpreted through the highly sexual views of modern eyes. On the other hand, the attitudes of Prince Edward's contemporaries as well as the strong reactions of his father to the 'friendship' (when Edward asked his father to grant Gaveston some lands, one story goes, Edward grabbed him by the hair and beat him) all hint that, even if Edward and Gaveston were never actually really close in the sexual or romantic sense, many of their peers probably thought that they had been.

Worries that Gaveston's friendship with Edward was an ugly influence became strong enough for King Edward to exile Gaveston on Feburary 26, 1307. Prince Edward was forbidden from ever again contacting Gaveston in any form. That summer, though, while on another campaign to rid himself of some Scottish rebels, Edward I suddenly fell ill and died. As the new king, Edward immediately recalled Gaveston and named him the Earl of Cornwall.

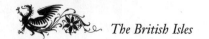

From the start Gaveston was a flamboyant, swaggering personality and, much to the disgust of the barons, he puffed up as the king blessed him with more and more royal favors. Although the nobles made their resentment and jealousy of Gaveston as visible as the sky, Gaveston refused to be intimidated by them. On the contrary, he made jokes about their private lives to their faces and flaunted his position as the king's favorite as Edward continued showering him with more lands and titles. Gaveston was even appointed regent when Edward traveled to France to collect his bride, Princess Isabelle, and was engaged to Edward's niece, Margaret of Gloucester, one of the richest ladies in the kingdom.

The resentment finally boiled over with a council of nobles forming to demand Gaveston's banishment on April 28, 1308. Reluctantly, Edward agreed, exiling Gaveston to Ireland, but managing to turn the tables on the barons by giving Gaveston the lucrative position of Lieutenant of Ireland at the same time. Nevertheless, Edward wilted without Gaveston and recalled him to England less than a month later.

Losses in Scotland and bad government finances were blamed on Gaveston and his power over the king. Spurred on by Edward's cousin, Thomas of Lancaster, a group of nobles pledged themselves to the noble cause of escorting the king's obnoxious friend (or lover) to the grave. No longer satisfied with yet another banishment, the rebels not only insisted that Edward set up a special council of nobles to take charge of the State, but also hand over Gaveston to be executed. The cause of Edward's supporters was lost when the Archbishop of Canterbury sympathized with Lancaster and excommunicated Edward. With Gaveston in tow, Edward fled to Scarborough but was routed by rebel forces. Hoping in vain for leniency, Gaveston surrendered, but the barons remembered all his old jokes, punchlines and all. Found guilty beyond a reasonable doubt by a kangaroo court, Gaveston was put to death on June 19, 1312.

As if this personal injury were not enough, the triumphant rebels did everything possible to clip Edward's political wings. Although Edward was still the undisputed king, power for the most part now rested in the hands of the twenty-one nobles who formed a body called the Lords Ordainer. Hoping to salvage his prestige and stir up fond memories of his father's reign, Edward made moves in 1314 against Robert Bruce, who had proclaimed himself King of Scots. Although his forces were large, they were badly disciplined and badly led, and on June 24 they were annihilated by Robert Bruce at the Battle of Bannockburn. As an encore to their triumph, the victorious Scots made demoralizing raids on England's northern counties.

Despite this, it was Lancaster, not Edward, who was blamed for England's misfortunes. The country was aflame with rumors that Lancaster had made a secret pact with Robert Bruce, ensuring the downfall of the English for his own benefit. Meanwhile Edward had found two new allies, Hugh Despenser and his son of the same name, who replaced the dead Gaveston as Edward's confidant and possibly lover. Under the Despensers' tutelage, Edward was encouraged to once again raise a hand against his disruptive subjects. By 1322, Edward gave in to their advice and at last discovered the backbone to get his revenge. After the barons tried to get the Despensers banished, Edward struck back with an army. Lancaster lost his head soon enough.

Drunk with triumph, Edward, the man who once enjoyed conversations with ditch-diggers and mercenaries, took on the mantle of a tyrant. Undoubtedly he was encouraged by the Despensers, who were eager to use their influence over Edward, but it is also likely that the murder of Gaveston and the humiliations he had suffered at the hands of the people whom he was raised to see as his to rule had unhinged Edward's mind.

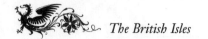

With Lancaster's supporters executed or exiled and Edward seeming to have paid for the respect that was once given to his father with blood, it seemed that he could finally rule in peace. Unfortunately, he underestimated his wife Isabelle, who always resented him for preferring the obnoxious Gaveston's company. Edward allowed Isabelle to leave for France to take their son, the future Edward III, to pay homage to the King of France for the Duchy of Aquitaine. This small and innocent decision turned out to be the worst of all Edward's mistakes. In France, Isabelle started an affair with Roger Mortimer, an English expatriate and former ally of Lancaster, and in September 1320 they landed in Suffolk with the goal of overthrowing the king.

The elder Despenser met his end on the battlefield. Betrayed by their own supporters who, disgusted with the Despensers, flocked to the queen and Mortimer, Edward and the younger Hugh Despenser went to Wales and tried to escape to the Continent on a boat. Unfortunately, contrary winds cut the voyage short and they were quickly caught. Hugh Despenser was put to death in a grisly fashion: he was hung, cut down while still alive, and had his genitals cut off, which were then burned before his eyes. Although this newest tragedy took its toll on Edward, who may have then suffered a nervous collapse, he still refused Isabelle and Mortimer's demands that he abdicate from the throne until they hinted that if he remained stubborn they would depose him anyway and disinherit his son. Finally he relented under pressure on January 25 and abdicated in favor of his son, even though he must have known it would mean his death.

With both the former and the new king in their power, Isabelle and Mortimer controlled England in the name of Edward III, but they stood on shaky ground. Not only was Edward III quickly coming of age and still sympathetic toward his father, but they also did not take into account the people's empathy for the old king, especially the Welsh, who always felt a special connection to their prince.

After a rescue attempt was made by the Welsh under Rhys ap Gruffydd, Edward was transported to Berkeley Castle where, according to an account by Raphael Holinshed, assassins sent by Mortimer and Queen Isabelle inserted a red-hot poker into Edward's anus, 'so that he died as he had lived'. Although the rationale for this horrific murder was that Edward's corpse would show no outward signs of physical harm, the highly symbolic nature of the account shows that associations between Edward and sodomy were current long before our time. Another story was circulated that Edward's allies faked his death and spirited him away to Lombardy, where without any regret he spent the rest of his days as a hermit. Wishful thinking, but an unsurprising story given the monarch's unusual history.

King Edward III never forgot his father. After he was forced to stand by while Mortimer had his uncle Edmund executed in March 1330, Edward III had finally had enough and secretly arranged to have Mortimer arrested for treason. Mortimer would suffer the traditional English punishment reserved for traitors, to be hanged, drawn and quartered; that is, hanged, cut down while still breathing, castrated and disemboweled. His lover and partner in power Isabelle was thrown into comfortable imprisonment at Castle Rising in Norfolk. Edward later had a new alabaster effigy placed above his father's tomb at Gloucester Cathedral, commemorating the grief a son felt for his father and a nation felt for their king, an elegant and moving monument which is still there.

Further Reading

Chaplais, Pierre *Piers Gaveston: Edward II's Adoptive Brother* (Oxford University Press, 1994)

Corstain, Thomas Bertram *The Three Edwards* (Doubleday, 1958)

Saaler, Mary *Edward II, 1307-1327* (Rubicon, 1997)

ROBERT III

Reign: *April 19, 1390–April 4, 1406*
Died: *April 4, 1406*
Buried: *Paisley Abbey, Renfrewshire*

Christened John at birth, Robert was the son of Robert Stewart, maternal great-grandson of Robert Bruce, the renowned hero of Scottish independence. When the elder Robert Stewart ascended to the throne after the death of his uncle King David II, becoming the first Scottish king of the Stewart dynasty, he was no longer the young, vigorous soldier he had been during the wars of independence against England. Well into his fifties and possibly suffering from venereal disease (he had fathered at least eight illegitimate children, most likely even more), Robert II suffered damaging physical and mental defects. First he relied on young John, but after a riding accident left John crippled, John's brother, the future Duke of Albany, also named Robert, took over most of the state affairs.

When Robert II's suffering finally ended at the age of seventy-four, John ascended to the throne and renamed himself

Robert, afraid that the name 'John' brought bad luck to kings, such as the old Scottish king John Balliol as well as the kings of that name in England and France. A change of name could not erase the tension between him and his brother Albany, a very real enemy Robert faced from the start. Robert's mother, Elizabeth Mure, was related to his father within the forbidden degrees of kinship. Although the Pope had granted a dispensation to allow the marriage, to some minds Albany, who was born by Robert II's second marriage to Euphemia of Ross, was the true heir.

Years of his father's misrule and his brother Albany's corruption had left Scotland in chaos. Growing clashes between the Highlands and the Lowlands meant that clan warfare was an everyday happening. His brother Alexander, 'the Wolf of Badenoch', ruled the north without dispute and was brutal even by the standards of the age. Just to display his power, Alexander hosted a great hunt for his guests where, after setting fire to parts of a forest, they hunted down the fleeing deer, boars and even clansmen. Meanwhile powerful aristocrats across all of Scotland exploited the government and channeled royal funds into their own private coffers.

Robert was by all accounts a generous, warm-hearted man, but, maybe because he was actually too kind, he was never the best of kings and the shoddy state of his kingdom soon sharpened his feelings of self-loathing and melancholy. He asked his wife Annabella to bury him under a dunghill when he died, with the epitaph, 'Here lies the worst of kings and most miserable of men.'

Realizing her husband's emotional state was doing Scotland no good, Annabella called a council of nobles and asked them to declare her nineteen-year-old son David 'Lieutenant of the Realm', giving him the same position of influence his father had held under Robert II. Unfortunately, maternal love blinded Annabella to David's many faults. For starters, he was a rowdy young man and careless enough to strike up a violent rivalry with his uncle Albany. After Annabella died in late 1401, removing her protective influence, Albany talked Robert

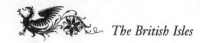

III into signing a warrant for his own son's arrest. Albany then left David to starve to death in a dungeon at Falkland Palace in Fife.

Robert's heir apparent was now his younger son James. Aware that Albany would probably try to rid himself of this son as well, in February 1406 Robert had James, then eleven years old, kept in Dirleton Castle to await a ship that would take him safely to France. Albany heard of the plot and sent armed men to take the prince under his custody, but while Albany's men were busy fighting with loyalist soldiers James's guardians sailed him on a small boat to the tiny, rocky island called the Bass Rock on the Firth of Forth. After nearly a month of anxious waiting, a ship from France finally did arrive, but then on the way across the Channel the boat was attacked by pirates who found the young prince and, realizing the importance of the human cargo, ransomed him off to the King of England, Henry IV.

Although James was given an excellent education at Henry's court and treated well under the unusual circumstances, he was still technically a state prisoner of the English and kept strictly in apartments at the Tower of London. He would remain there until he became thirty years old. When King Robert heard that his son was now in English hands partially because of a blunder on his part, he suffered a complete breakdown and died only a few days later after depriving himself of most food. Although his wish to be buried under a dunghill was not carried out, his request that he not be buried at the traditional resting place for Scottish kings at Scone was obeyed. He did not think he deserved the privilege.

Further Reading

Bingham, Caroline *The Stewart Kingdom of Scotland, 1371-1603* (Weidenfield & Nicolson, 1974)

Boardman, Stephen *The Early Stewart Kings: Robert II and Robert III, 1371-1406* (Tuckwell, 1996)

RICHARD II

Reign: *June 22, 1377–September 29, 1399 (abdicated)*
Born: *January 6, 1367*
Died: *February 14, 1400*
Buried: *Westminster Abbey*

King Richard II is remembered as a profligate autocrat, a man who was at the same time a dilettante and a despot. His grandfather was Edward III, whose reign was the apex of the culture of chivalry and marked the beginning of the Hundred Years' War against France. Edward III's eldest son and Richard's father, Edward the Black Prince, had a legendary standing due to his almost superhuman stamina in battle. Richard's mother, Joan of Kent, was infamous thanks to a later bigamous marriage to the Earl of Salisbury, William Montague, and Sir Thomas Holland, an ugly situation that called for the intervention of the Pope.

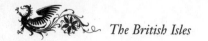

The Black Prince died before his father, whose otherwise glorious reign had been spoiled by the unimaginable horrors of the Black Death. Richard was only ten years old at the time of Edward III's death and found himself crowned the king of a country still reeling from the plague. A number of socio-economic changes followed in the wake of the plague (for one thing, there was more farming land available and the peasants had more leverage to demand higher wages and more freedoms): one of the remedies enacted by the government was the poll tax, which steadily increased over the first years of Richard's reign. This tax became the object of great resentment which broke into violence in the summer of 1381 when a man in Kent named Wat Tyler killed a tax collector who in summary fashion tried to ascertain if his daughter were old enough to pay the poll tax. When authorities tried to apprehend Tyler, the villagers rushed to his aid and it was not long before he found himself commanding a mob, then an army of tens of thousands of angry peasants. This was not a force to be underestimated, as they helpfully demonstrated. Having marched on London itself, they grabbed and murdered the royal treasurer and Simon of Sudbury, the Archbishop of Canterbury.

Still barely an adolescent, Richard fearlessly walked out to the ragtag army that was demanding radical reforms, at least for that era, and was still dangerous even though Wat Tyler himself had been killed. Richard solemnly promised to concede to their demands and the rebels dispersed, only to find Richard's promises broken, and their leaders hunted down and butchered. Despite this betrayal, the young Richard went on to become highly regarded by many from the lowest of the low to the nobility. Unfortunately, Richard's main problem as an adult was that he grew up believing his own press.

Once Richard became a young man, the nobles of the kingdom snickered behind the once fearless boy's back at his swanky French attire and his peculiar habit of bathing once a day. Some went on to claim that Richard had invented the handkerchief. Naturally, being king, Richard was free to adopt the splendor of the role without any obstacles. He enjoyed sitting on his throne while his courtiers stood around him, forbidden to make the slightest movement or the least sound, for hours on end. Yet despite this self-conscious royal air and his well-cultured tastes, the notorious Plantagenet temper did not miss making a mark on Richard. This was made all too clear when he threatened a bishop at court with a sword until the weapon was wrestled from his hands.

Like his unfortunate great-grandfather, King Edward II, Richard had also become very attached to a hated rake, Robert de Vere, the Earl of Oxford. De Vere was just one among the many fawning sycophants that Richard kept on call, who were resented all the more since Richard was still young and easily swayed. No matter how annoying his many flatterers became to the conservative nobility of the kingdom, Richard's power was protected by his affluent uncle, John of Gaunt, considered by many the true master of the land.

Taking advantage of an expedition John of Gaunt made into Spain to press his claim to the throne of Castile, a group of nobles, including Richard's uncle the Duke of Gloucester and his cousin (and John of Gaunt's son) Henry Bolingbroke, assumed power as the Lords Appellant. Richard was coerced into exiling many of his favorites, including Robert de Vere, who died while out of England. His remains were brought back on Richard's orders and then he had the coffin opened so that he could look upon what was left of his old friend. This account could be taken as evidence that Richard had a sexual relationship with Robert de Vere, but Richard was always as extravagant with his affections as he was with everything else. For instance, when his first wife Anne of Bohemia died in June 1394, he ordered the castle where she breathed her last to be demolished.

Officially, the power of the Lords Appellant declined when Richard declared himself of age in 1389, at the age of twenty-two. Nevertheless, the threat of another uprising always remained a threat that loomed over Richard and put in question his own fanatical belief that he was a divinely-ordained king: especially when the war-hungry nobility grumbled over his lasting peace treaty with France, ending for the time being the Hundred Years' War, and his marriage to Isabella, daughter of King Charles VI of France.

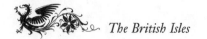

Finally, in 1397, Richard felt strong enough to humble his nobles and banished or executed the Lords Appellant, even going so far as arranging the murder of the Duke of Gloucester, a leading member of the revolt. Two remaining Lords Appellant, Thomas Mowbray and Henry Bolingbroke, accused each other of treason and were ordered to prove their innocence in a trial by combat, an ancient custom that was already on the decline in England. As famously depicted in Shakespeare's play, Richard abruptly called a halt to the proceedings and instead banished the two men: Mowbray for life, Bolingbroke for ten years.

Grieved by his son's disgrace and exile, John of Gaunt retired from public life, freeing Richard from one last check on his power, and died quietly in February 1399. John of Gaunt's estates were the largest in England and Richard saw no reason why he could not have them for himself. Disregarding not only custom but also common decency, Richard extended Bolingbroke's banishment to life and prepared to confiscate the lands he should have rightfully inherited. That May, while Richard was overseeing a military campaign in Ireland, Bolingbroke arrived on English shores, followed by an army. Bolingbroke claimed that his purpose in breaking his exile and raising swords against his king was simply to force Richard to give him his dead father's lands. This may even have been true, but as more and more support came his way the prize he sought became the crown itself. Although Bolingbroke's forces were small, it was a simple matter to bribe or coerce many into turning against Richard. Finally, at the Welsh castle of Flint on August 19, 1399, Richard was forced to surrender, but he retained the crown.

Regardless of what his intentions started out as, Bolingbroke now staked his claim to the throne of England before Parliament and claimed that Richard should be deposed for his alleged tyranny, a precedent set by the deposition of Edward II. Unfortunately for his dynastic pretensions, John of Gaunt was only the third son of Edward III. An older brother, Lionel, had a great-grandson through his daughter Phillipa named Edmund Mortimer, the Fifth Earl of March, who was still alive at the time, and had a better claim to the throne than Bolingbroke, having inherited his father Roger's claim as heir presumptive. Bolingbroke's party argued that Edmund's right to the crown should be discounted since it came through a maternal line (an argument ignoring the fact that two English kings, Stephen and Henry II, had already inherited their thrones through their mothers). More importantly, Edmund Mortimer was only eight years old at the time and no one was willing to risk their necks to defend the rights of a boy, especially with such an ambitious, charismatic figure like Bolingbroke at work. Unfortunately, Bolingbroke did not realize that he was setting a trend that would cause a great deal of misery and hardship for his descendants. This negligence would eventually be the death of the Plantagenet dynasty itself.

For the time being, Henry Bolingbroke's genealogical tampering was approved by a compliant Parliament. They decided that Richard had proved himself unfit to rule while Edmund's rights as heir presumptive were quietly swept under the rug. With no other real choice, Richard agreed to abdicate on September 29, 1399 and was forced to watch the traitor Bolingbroke sit on his throne as the latest in an illustrious line of Henrys. The very sight of it caused Richard to fall into a deep depression, possibly the result of a nervous breakdown caused from seeing his faith in his own majesty shattered.

Although the admittedly less than unbiased records state that the kingdom of England came willingly and easily to Henry's clutches, the price was very steep. Henry spent his reign and the rest of his life buried in fear. During Henry's reign heretics who questioned the wisdom of Mother Church were to be burned, something never allowed in the 'tyrant' Richard's time, and even a commoner from

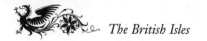

Cambridge named John Sparrowhawk was hanged and beheaded. His treacherous sin worthy of the full cruelty of the law? He had joked that it had not stopped raining since Henry IV seized power. Henry died in horrible pain from leprosy or a disease much like it, a sign many took to mean that he suffered under the burden of a tremendous, unrepented sin.

Richard might have been heartened to know that over the next few months his supposed crimes as an autocrat were quickly forgotten and he became viewed as the tragic victim of evil nobles. Unfortunately, it was this upsurge in popular support that marked him for death. In the winter of the next year, his captors left him in his cell to die from starvation. Shakespeare's play would do much to vindicate him, although Richard's own sad megalomania remains intact in these lines: 'For every man that Bolingbroke hath press'd / To lift shrewd steel against our golden crown, / God for his Richard hath in heavenly pay / A glorious angel . . .'

Further Reading

Bennett, Michael *Richard II and the Revolution of 1399* (Sutton, 1999)

Goodman, Anthony and Gillespie, James *Richard II: The Art of Kingship* (Oxford University Press, 2003)

Green, Vivian *The Madness of Kings: Personal Trauma and the Fate of Nations* (Sutton, 1993)

Saul, Nigel *Richard II* (Yale University Press, 1997)

HENRY VI

Reign: *September 1, 1422–March 4, 1461 (deposed); October 31, 1470 (restored)–April 11, 1471 (deposed again)*
Born: *December 6, 1421*
Died: *May 1471 (murdered)*
Buried: *Windsor Castle*

With Richard II deposed and murdered, the triumphant King Henry IV established what was to be known as the House of Lancaster, although it was still a branch of the centuries-old Plantaganet dynasty. The House of Lancaster reached its zenith in Henry V, whose renewal of the Hundred Years' War against France gave him an outstanding place in English patriotic legends and eventually won him the French throne upon the death of its current occupant, the mad king Charles VI. At last, fifty years after his death, it seemed King Edward III's attempt to press his hereditary claim to the crown of France had at last achieved fruition. Unfortunately, the dream was marred when Henry V died, worn down physically and mentally from the long months of rough fighting and bloodshed, leaving England and France to his son Henry, a nine-month-old infant.

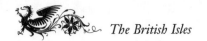

As often happens when only children are left to succeed their great-parents, things went awry almost immediately. Although he was disinherited through the contrivance of his mother Isabeau, Charles VI's nineteen-year-old son was acclaimed by loyalists as Charles VII of France. This new rival came to control much of southern France, while the northern provinces stayed under the crumbling authority of Henry VI's uncle, John, the Duke of Bedford.

Meanwhile in England, a regency council ruled in Henry VI's name until he would reach an appropriate age. Prominent in the council was Henry's uncle and 'Protector of the Realm', the Duke of Gloucester, and his great-uncle, Cardinal Beaufort. The two men split the council with their squabbling, even as the English cause in France continued to deteriorate under Bedford. By 1429, a strange peasant teenager who claimed to be instructed by the voices of saints, Joan of Arc, successfully led an army to victory at Orléans. This was only the first of a series of unexpected victories that would come to unite the French behind a firm sense of national pride. The English hoped to capitalize on the trial and death of Joan of Arc for heresy in 1431 by bringing the nine-year-old Henry to the Cathedral of Notre Dame to be crowned King of France on December 16 the same year. Unfortunately, the coronation only showed how doomed the English occupation of France was as riots burst out in Paris with such intensity that little Henry had to be spirited out of the country.

What cemented the reversal of Henry V's hard-won conquests was the decision of the Duke of Burgundy to make peace with Charles VII. Burgundy had been England's most crucial ally in France and his defection helped Charles VII to retake Paris on

November 12, 1438. As for the young Henry VI, when he heard Burgundy would no longer call him the King of France, he burst into tears.

Among the regency council, the bad luck in France led to a new conflict altogether. Even though subduing the French people or forcing Charles VII to relinquish all claim to the French throne seemed more and more of an impossibility with each defeat, Gloucester's faction argued that the war must move onward. Beaufort and his supporters, on the other hand, urged that, due to fading morale and a lack in funds, there was no choice but to put an end to the war in France. Perhaps because of his already powerful religious outlook, the young king, who declared himself of age just before his sixteenth birthday, threw his lot in with Beaufort. After that, the only thing that remained was to permanently rid himself of Gloucester. To that end, Gloucester's wife Eleanor was charged with witchcraft and imprisoned for life. Although Gloucester did his best to distance himself from his doomed wife and salvage his reputation, he, and by extension his supporters, became completely discredited.

As part of a new peace treaty with France he had drafted, Beaufort advised the king to marry Margaret of Anjou. She was the daughter of the Duke of Anjou, René, who claimed the titles of King of Sicily, Naples, Hungary, and Jerusalem, all pretty little titles with no real substance in them. René's court, nonetheless, was a major center of art and learning in France, although rather impoverished. Coming from such a background, Margaret was very well educated, but the arrogance of the ancient Anjou clan was in her heart. The instant this proud French woman stepped onto English soil she was widely detested but, on April 23, 1445, Henry VI and Margaret of Anjou were wed.

One part of the marriage agreement was that Henry had to agree to surrender the English-occupied territories of Maine and Anjou. When news of this leaked out, the people's resentment exploded and it seemed as if the long suffering Gloucester would finally rise to the forefront again. Together with an enemy of Gloucester's, the Earl of Suffolk, Margaret, who saw it as her duty to help maintain peace with France even at the expense of her adopted country, convinced the ever-gullible Henry that Gloucester was guilty of conspiracy. Gloucester was immediately thrown in prison where he died two weeks later, supposedly of natural causes, although some accounts maintain otherwise.

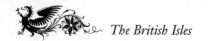

The English held out some hope that, despite the unpopular marriage and Beaufort's influence, Henry would suddenly transform into a great warrior like his father and effortlessly lead the English in taking back their lost lands in France. As he grew older, though, Henry VI began to display the qualities and interests of a devout monk, not a warrior or even a king. Obscenities, bawdy tales, and sexual quips were not to be tolerated in his presence, giving his court the atmosphere of a church. Once, when a courtier invited a female dancer to strip in the king's presence, Henry diverted his eyes away from the woman's topless body and rushed to his private rooms, crying, 'Fie, fie! For shame!' Instead of royal robes in the newest fashion, the king was more likely to wear embarrassingly modest clothing and even a hairshirt. With true Christian modesty, Henry always kept his temper well in control and treated everyone in his company, including servants, like equals. Unfortunately, he was also completely trusting and stupidly naïve, so much so that his only reliable talent was his knack for filling his government and court with the most self-interested, incompetent but silver-tongued men in England. He also happened to generously give away so many royal estates to his friends that there was a major dent in the government coffers.

The death of Cardinal Beaufort on March 15, 1447 did nothing to dilute the power of the pro-peace faction in the government. Margaret of Anjou gladly and skillfully filled the political void left by Beaufort, so much so that her signature had almost the same force of law as the king's. But while Margaret was astute, forceful, and charismatic, she lacked both restraint in financial matters and respect for her English subjects. So free was Margaret with the funds of the royal household that servants went without pay and sometimes no food could be found for the King and Queen's dinner. Soon enough, no merchant or banker trusted the government enough to give it loans.

As the war effort in France dragged on, people grumbled – with some justification – that Henry and his French bride had sold out the English. Worse, the soldiers that returned from the wars found themselves without pensions, so they had little alternative but to turn to robbery and murder to get their bread. War veterans were not the only ones with empty pockets. The faltering war effort had exhausted the government's treasury, causing a recession, while the corruption and ineptitude that festered under Henry VI and Margaret of Anjou only deepened the crisis.

No wonder that the people sought a champion of reform in the chaos, a role filled by Richard, the Duke of York. A stout, stern and above all competent man, his was not a dynamic nor even a likeable personality, but he was quietly considered by more than a few to be the rightful king of England, robbed of his crown by the deceitful House of Lancaster. After all, his mother Anne Mortimer was descended from Roger, the designated heir to Richard II before he was deposed. Although no one then, not even York himself, dared to voice their opinion that York really was the true king of England, it was believed that, as long as Henry VI remained without a son, he should become the heir presumptive. Given Henry VI's saintly behavior, rumors and jokes flew that Henry VI could not even bring himself to become well acquainted with his wife in the bedroom.

York was banished to Ireland in 1447 because of his sympathy for the Duke of Gloucester and his possible role in the mysterious death of one of the Queen's supporters, the Duke of Suffolk. Despite being trapped in Ireland, it was also believed that he was somehow involved in a violent insurrection caused by a commoner named John Cade in the summer of 1450. Eventually, backed by his own private army of mercenaries and war veterans, York came to London in August of 1450 to demand reforms and claim his rightful place on the Council, much to Queen Margaret's chagrin.

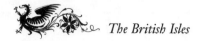

Instantly York found an enemy on the Council in the person of the Duke of Somerset, the Queen's most prominent supporter. He ordered Somerset's arrest with Henry's reluctant consent, but when the Queen saw Somerset being led away by guards she loudly intervened and commanded that they release him. She then took Somerset to the king to demand he rescind the order for the arrest. York had the misfortune to walk right into the middle of Henry and the Queen's argument. In the end, Somerset was freed and York was forced to swear an oath of loyalty to Henry on bended knee.

Circumstances, unfortunately for Margaret, were about to finally play out in York's favor. As the pressure from the war in France and the disputes in the Council mounted, Henry VI suffered a complete breakdown and drifted into a catatonic state. It is uncertain exactly what happened to Henry, but very likely he had inherited something of his grandfather Charles VI of France's mental condition through his mother. At the time of the catatonia, Margaret was pregnant and gave birth on October 13, 1453 to a boy, Edward. York's followers spread rumors that Edward was illegitimate, the unplanned result of an affair between the Queen and Somerset. These stories were given dangerous credibility when Margaret showed the infant Edward to the king, hoping it would stir him from his stupor and he would acknowledge the child as his own. He did not make a single move.

At the same time events in France were unfolding that would prove the worst disaster in a reign full of them. The dashing and talented Earl of Shrewsbury, John Talbot, who seemed to be a one-man army and the sole cause of a brief turnaround for the English cause, was killed in battle at Chillon. On October 19, 1453, the capture of the city of Bordeaux by Charles VII's men signaled an end to the Hundred Years' War. The only French territory that still waved an English banner was the port city of Calais. At last, the English had to make a permanent peace.

Somerset's influence waned while York's waxed during the king's madness and the final English failure in France. Although the birth of Prince Edward now barred him from the position of heir, it did not put a check on his growing influence. When it seemed clear that the king would not make a recovery in the near future, Margaret tried to assume the regency, but only alienated more people in the government with her presumption. She was furious to discover that Parliament nominated York as regent instead, giving him the valuable title 'Protector of the Realm'. Using his newfound authority, York once again ordered the arrest of Somerset, while Margaret was literally locked out of authority, forced to become nothing more than a nurse for her husband.

At the end of 1454, when York's regency was only half a year old, Henry recovered consciousness, at least to the extent that he was able to function normally. In the long run, though, he was even more weak-willed and absent minded than ever before. He even believed that his son might have been conceived by the Holy Ghost. Spurred on by his wife and York's numerous enemies, Henry dismissed York from the regency and released Somerset from imprisonment, but York knew that his position was still strong and no one would forget Henry's tottering sanity. Even more crucial was the knowledge that the Queen and Somerset would never forgive his actions against them while he was the Protector. Possibly for his ambitions, but more likely for his own survival, he called together his army and fought the king's forces at what would be called the Battle of St. Albans. England's most infamous period of civil war, the Wars of the Roses, had broken out, so called because of the belief that the rival houses of Lancaster and York took a red and white rose respectively as their symbols.

The result of this battle was stunningly conclusive. Somerset was killed during the fighting and Henry was forced to accept York as his chief advisor, a position that was made all the more necessary by the likelihood that Henry had suffered a minor relapse. Even in his daze of passivity and near-madness, Henry recognized the growing conflict between the Yorkist party and the Queen's followers and tried making March 24, 1458 a peaceful day of reconciliation. The effort was a comedy. The divide between the Yorkists and the Lancastrians grew ever wider, with the former continuing to slander Henry and the Queen while the latter plotted using military force to obliterate York.

The conflict broke out anew at Ludlow in April 1459, when a pro-Lancastrian army seized York's ancestral castle. York fled to Ireland, where his support had always been strong, abandoning his wife, daughter, and two youngest sons to the enemy. They were kept under house arrest while York's supporters made Calais their stronghold. After a decisive victory against the Lancastrians at Northampton in July 1460, York returned to England and bullied Parliament into naming him, not Prince Edward, as Henry's heir apparent. Henry, docile as ever even with his son's future in the balance, agreed, but Margaret would not stand for it. With an army of Lancastrian troops and Scottish soldiers provided by the queen regent of Scotland, Marie de Guise, Margaret met York at Wakefield on December 30. The tables were turned on the Yorkists and Somerset was avenged once York was beheaded for treason. To add insult to injury, Margaret placed a paper crown on York's head as it sat impaled on a lance. York's chief backer, the Earl of Warwick, was also beaten, but was able to escape and throw his lot in with York's increasingly popular son, Edward. In a drastic change of fortunes, the city of London, which always hated Margaret, opened its gates to Edward of York on February 27, 1461 and it was not long before Henry VI was deposed and Edward was proclaimed King Edward IV.

The Lancastrians tried to regain the upper hand at the Battle of Towton, a fight so savage that the field on which it was fought become known as the 'Bloody Meadow', but it was a wasted effort. With meager support from Scotland, Margaret continued the struggle, but Henry seemed to have lost interest in the outcome, assuming he had any to begin with. After a time, Margaret fled to Burgundy to try in vain to drum up further support from the Continent. Meanwhile Henry had been in Scotland, but was forced to leave and hide in a monastery in northern England after he outlived his political usefulness to the Scots. In the summer of 1465, he was betrayed and sent to become a state prisoner in the Tower of London. Undoubtedly this news did much to test Margaret of Anjou's iron resolve, but she did not know that a second chance for Henry VI was about to come from the unlikeliest of sources.

The Earl of Warwick had been alienated by Edward IV's treatment of him and Edward's unpopular marriage to a woman of low rank, Elizabeth Woodville. Eventually tensions between the two men grew so deep that Warwick orchestrated a revolt against the king he helped establish and even had Edward IV imprisoned in the Tower of London. After unsuccessfully trying to establish a junta consisting of himself and Edward IV's backstabbing brother, George, the Duke of Clarence, he negotiated to have Henry VI restored, promising to marry his daughter Anne Neville to Prince Edward. However, Henry was as much of a cipher as ever, and it was understood that Warwick would rule as regent. In fact, as Warwick went about the business of the State, Henry stuck to carrying out his religious devotions. Of course, Edward IV was not about to be cheated out of his hard-won throne and, after mustering armed forces from the Continent, he fought and killed Warwick in battle.

Reluctant to give up even a passing chance, Margaret and her son had gathered together the last of the Lancastrian resistance and on May 4, 1471, Edward's armies met them near Tewkesbury Abbey.

There the Lancastrian cause was lost when Prince Edward was either slain in the fighting or murdered at Edward's command. Margaret, whose indomitable will was at last shattered by the death of her only son, was captured and led in a triumphal procession through London, where passers-by bellowed obscenities and threw stones at her body. After spending some time as a state prisoner, Margaret was eventually sent back to France, where the former queen died in near poverty on August 25, 1482, a year before Edward IV's death and the beginning of the fall of the House of York.

As for King Henry, he was kept prisoner in the Tower of London throughout the Battle of Tewkesbury. He died sometime during May of 1471. The state-sanctioned reports had it that he perished from natural causes, but no one was fooled even then. When his remains were examined in 1911, they found evidence on his skull that he had died from a severe blow to the back of the head, verifying old rumors that claimed Henry had been killed by a blow to the head while he knelt and prayed. The irony is that the one king who never wanted to shed a drop of blood instead almost single-handedly brought his country into one of its worst periods of civil war.

Further Reading

Curry, Anne *The Hundred Years' War* (Macmillan, 1993)

Green, Vivian *The Madness of Kings: Personal Trauma and the Fate of Nations* (Sutton, 1993)

Haswell, Jock *The Ardent Queen: Margaret of Anjou and the Lancastrian Heritage* (Peter Davies, 1976)

Weir, Alison *Lancaster and York: The Wars of the Roses* (Jonathan Cape, 1995)

Wolffe, Betram Percy *Henry VI* (Methuen, 1981)

RICHARD III

Reign: *June 25, 1483–August 22, 1485*
Born: *October 2, 1452*
Died: *August 22, 1485 (killed in battle)*
Buried: *Leicester Cathedral (in effigy)*

Although recent attempts by historians have tried posthumously to rehabilitate the man, Richard III, thanks in no small part to the pen of Shakespeare, remains the greatest villain in English history. It is impossible to argue that his image has not been distorted over time, but it is almost as hard to deny that Richard III was nearly as remorseless and calculating as the stories claim, even by the harsh standards of his day.

Richard was short, but not stout, and had the dark hair of his father. Even though it is very unlikely that he was severely deformed – popular legend claims he was hunchbacked with one withered arm – he may have had a right shoulder that was slightly higher than the left. He was the youngest brother of Edward, the Duke of York, who became King Edward IV after the rival House of Lancaster was not only barred from the throne, but pushed to the brink of extinction, with the deposition and execution of King Henry VI and the death of his only son in battle.

Because of his unflinching support for his brother during the Wars of the Roses, Richard was awarded with enough lands to make him one of the most powerful men in the kingdom. He was also allowed to marry Anne Neville, daughter of the Earl of Warwick, who carried with her a hefty inheritance. Anne herself was in no position to object. Her father had brought about his own demise and his family's disgrace by betraying Edward IV in favor of restoring Henry VI, a plan which, although it did achieve a brief second reign for Henry, was nevertheless doomed to failure. For the sake of her own future and that of her family's, she had no choice but to marry into the winners' circle.

After decades of a weak, sickly and mentally unstable king, Edward IV seemed the perfect antidote for England. He was a tall, strapping, and animated man, who seemed to many to have been born with the virtues of kingship in him. Even his critics were won over with his friendliness and uncanny ability to always recognize the faces and names of everyone from his officers and ministers to his household servants. But he was also well known for his licentious lifestyle, particularly his all-consuming lust for women. He disgusted even his most loyal followers by falling in love with and secretly wedding a low-ranking woman named Elizabeth Woodville, who promptly went about getting profitable offices and titles for her relatives.

One of the Woodvilles' most passionate enemies was the king's brother, George, the Duke of Clarence, who was motivated by personal ambition more than anything else. Clarence had conspired with the Earl of Warwick to overthrow his brother; an act for which Edward had forgiven him. He continued to scheme against Edward, and to slander Queen Elizabeth until at last he was charged with treason and thrown into the Tower of London. At his own request, according to legend, Clarence was executed by being drowned in a barrel of wine, in order to die as he had lived. The Woodvilles' enemies immediately put about the story that only Elizabeth's seductive charms could have driven Edward into killing his own brother. Likely Richard, who started to distrust the Woodvilles himself, felt the same way.

Eventually the king's self-gratifying lifestyle caught up with him and he died, a fat shadow of his former self, on April 9, 1483, leaving his thirteen-year-old son, also named Edward, to become king. Richard arranged for himself to be proclaimed the Protector of the Realm and, using his newfound authority, had the Queen's brother, the Earl Rivers, arrested before the very eyes of Edward, who was traveling to London to prepare for his coronation. Whether or not Richard's plans at this stage were motivated by fear of the Woodvilles or by a genuine desire to take the crown is unclear, but either way, as he assumed the responsibility of escorting the new king to London, he played the part of loyal subject perfectly. Nevertheless, it was only an act, and Richard was already slowly manipulating events to his advantage. Under pressure from him, the Council decided to move Edward to the Tower of London, which was still primarily a royal residence and was not yet burdened by the bloody reputation it would gain during the Tudor and Stuart eras. Queen Elizabeth caught sight of what lay beneath Richard's posturing and went to Westminster Abbey with her other son, the Duke of York, where she claimed sanctuary and refused to consider leaving.

Coming events revealed that she had been insightful rather than paranoid. Furious at the opposition he found within the Council, mainly from Lord Hastings, Richard called a meeting on the morning of June 12, ostensibly to iron out the details of Edward V's coronation. Although he first came into the meeting with a broad, friendly grin, he abruptly left and returned later, looking anxious and angered. After remaining silent for a few moments, he turned to Hastings and asked, 'What do men deserve for having plotted the destruction of me, being so near of blood unto the King and Protector of his royal person and realm?'

Taken aback, Hastings replied, 'Certainly, if they have done so heinously, they are worthy of a heinous punishment.'

Richard then screamed, 'What? Dost thou serve me with ifs and ands? I tell thee, they have done it, and that I will make good upon thy body, traitor!'

Richard accused Hastings and some others present of plotting against his life in conjunction with Queen Elizabeth. Then, overstepping his legal authority, he immediately ordered the men's arrests. Hastings himself was beheaded only minutes after his arrest, without even the semblance of a trial. Later that day, Richard sent armed men to Westminster Abbey to collect the young Duke of York, brother to Edward V. Elizabeth refused at first, but, once she realized she had no alternative, she reluctantly surrendered the boy to his uncle's custody. It would be an act she would quickly come to regret, especially when she came to realize the extent of Richard's ruthlessness when her own brother, Earl Rivers, was executed on June 25, also without the right of trial.

At the Tower of London, the two boys' movements became more and more restricted. Richard dismissed most of their servants personally. The date of the coronation was pushed further back: at the same time the boys began to be seen less frequently until, that summer, they disappeared entirely, although the evidence suggests they survived past that point. Even the boys could sense what was in the air and their once carefree personalities became darkly mature. Edward V is even alleged to have said, 'Alas, I would my uncle would let me have my life yet, though I lose my kingdom.'

With the two little princes caged, Richard was free to pave his way to the throne with a brutal propaganda campaign against his own family. First it was claimed that Edward IV was the product of an affair his mother had (Edward and Richard's mother, the Duchess of York, was still alive at this time), but then, realizing that the late Edward IV's reputation as a womanizer was ripe for exploiting, Richard and his supporters spread the claim that Edward's marriage to Elizabeth Woodville was invalid because he had contracted a secret marriage earlier to a Lady Eleanor Butler. Although no solid proof was offered, Edward's character and the secrecy surrounding his own marriage to Elizabeth (it had been kept secret for about four months) made it all *seem* perfectly credible. On June 25, 1483, Parliament declared Edward's marriage to Elizabeth Woodville to be invalid and officially deposed Edward V, now turned overnight from a royal heir to a bastard. On July 5, Richard was crowned King Richard III alongside his wife Anne, in spite of the modest claim made by his most devoted follower, the Duke of Buckingham, that Richard would of course 'refuse such a burden'. It was around Richard's coronation that many believe that the king's nephews were secretly murdered, most likely at the order of their own uncle.

The most vivid account of the murder comes from Thomas More, who was writing at the time of Henry VIII's reign. Late at night, the story goes, while the princes slept in their single bed, one of the attendants assigned to them by their uncle, along with a burly man named John Dighton and one of Richard's retainers, Sir James Tyrell, crept into the princes' chamber. With Tyrell waiting outside the room, the other two men ensnared the boys in their bed linen and clothes and then smothered them with their pillows. More's account also claims that the two boys were buried inside the Tower under a specific spot. In the late seventeenth century, the skeletal remains of two young boys, with scraps of velvet on them, were discovered by accident exactly at the area More described.

Examinations further verified that the skeletons did indeed belong to the 'Princes of the Tower' and in time the remains were buried at Westminster Abbey. Yet there are those today who discount More's writing as Tudor propaganda and argue that Richard III could be innocent of his nephews' deaths.

One of the points made by Richard III's tireless defenders is that after Parliament had the boys declared illegitimate, their deaths were unnecessary. However, as long as the boys lived, they were tempting prizes for Richard's enemies and any ambitious would-be kings. Having spent his formative years at the peak of the Wars of the Roses, Richard was very cautious of any possible rivals and understood that those sharing his royal blood were automatically the most hazardous menaces.

But even with the princes dead, Richard still had his adversaries. With rumors of the brothers' deaths flying, the eldest daughter of Edward IV and Elizabeth Woodeville, also named Elizabeth, was now considered the rightful monarch of England. Only the fact that England was not yet ready for a female ruler kept Princess Elizabeth from becoming a serious direct threat, but her potency as a political tool was clear. The squeamishness about being ruled by a woman also hindered Margaret Beaufort, the indomitable Countess of Richmond, who lived through the Wars of the Roses. She was descended from John Beaufort, the son of John of Gaunt, who was himself the son of King Edward III. However, John Beaufort's mother was Katherine Swynford, who did not legally marry John of Gaunt until after John Beaufort was conceived. Even though the Pope later legitimized the children of John of Gaunt and Katherine Swynford, to many the Beauforts were still an illegitimate line.

However, Margaret was also married to Edmund Tudor, who could claim direct descent from the old Welsh kings of Gwynedd and Deheubarth, giving him an almost sacred bloodline that ran back to before the Anglo-Saxon invasions. That gave their son Henry Tudor an appealing mystique. Henry was even fond of bragging that King

Arthur himself was an ancestor of his. Despite the young man's links to both Edward III and the most legendary of Celtic heroes, Richard was not about to be intimidated by a young upstart who was living in poverty as an exile on the Continent. In fact, Richard would only ever refer to Henry Tudor as 'that unknown Welshman.'

Although Richard actually proved himself a talented and pious monarch, the foundations of his authority soon began to decay. Stories of the princes' murders detracted from whatever skills Richard brought to the table. In fact, word of the ultimate fate of the princes shocked even the cynical foreign courts. King Louis XI of France was heard to have sworn he would not stand to have any dealings with a man who stooped to murder children of his own blood. The Duke of Buckingham, who staunchly supported Richard at the start, suddenly started plotting with Margaret Beaufort to put Henry Tudor on the throne. Why Buckingham changed allegiances so suddenly is unclear, but one theory, supported by the timing of Buckingham's switch, is that even he was disgusted by the murder of the princes. Meanwhile Queen Elizabeth had been secretly keeping in touch from Westminster Abbey with Henry Tudor's supporters and had agreed to a plan to marry Princess Elizabeth to Henry Tudor to strengthen his claim to the throne.

These plans were finally put into execution on October 10, 1483 with an uprising backed by Buckingham himself, but contrary winds kept Henry Tudor from arriving in England with his own men as planned. After his forces were routed, Buckingham was found hiding in a cottage and executed. Richard, for all the ferocity of his reputation, could not bear to see his former friend and ally before or during his execution.

Buckingham's rebellion, although on the surface a dismal failure, accomplished one great thing for Henry Tudor. While before he was a curiosity at best on the major political scene, he had at last made his presence and ambition known. It also forced Richard to recognize the threat the Princess Elizabeth and her sisters would pose if they ever married Henry Tudor or anyone else with a rival claim. He bullied Queen Elizabeth to put the princess and her other daughters under his protection. Perhaps losing all hope with Buckingham's defeat and death, Queen Elizabeth consented to handing over her daughters to a man she must have believed was involved in her sons' deaths, but tellingly she demanded that Richard swear in public that he would do nothing to harm her daughters. Even more tellingly, Richard did so.

Personal tragedy had already struck and weakened Richard's grip on the English throne even further. His only son and heir, Edward of Middleham, died suddenly at the age of eight. Meanwhile Queen Anne was slowly dying of tuberculosis and was much too weak to have another child. There is evidence that Richard was a devoted husband to her and, unlike many of his royal predecessors, there is no indication that he had any extramarital affairs (he did have at least four illegitimate children, but they were all conceived before his marriage). However, Richard's political instinct superseded any affection he might have kept for his wife. Even as Anne lay on her deathbed, Richard wooed Princess Elizabeth, hoping to steal Henry Tudor's best opportunity for himself. The Princess Elizabeth, herself showing some shrewd if cold thinking, responded to Richard's advances kindly, if not provocatively.

Finally, Queen Anne succumbed to her illness on March 16, 1485. Even though Richard made a believable show of grief, people remembered his past ruthlessness and knew how much he had to gain with Anne out of the way. A widely circulated story of the time, repeated by Shakespeare, claimed Richard had Anne poisoned to get her safely six feet under.

Henry Tudor, once again urged on by his mother and by the Woodvilles, knew he had to act fast. A new force led by Henry landed at Wales on August 7 and confronted Richard on August 22 at the Battle of Bosworth. Henry did not join the fray personally, but Richard did and was killed in battle after being deserted by a number of allies, while trying to get within sword's length of Henry. Tradition claims Richard's crown was found under a hawthorn bush, which remained an important symbol to the Tudor dynasty. Richard's body was stripped and had a halter put around its neck, as with criminals. It was carried on a mule to the Abbey of the Grey Friars' in nearby Leicester, where it was buried. Much later, when the monasteries and convents were shut down during Henry VIII's reign, Richard III's grave was smashed and his remains thrown into a nearby river. In recent years, the Richard III Society, a group devoted to reforming Richard's shoddy image, paid for a memorial to be raised at Leicester Cathedral.

Even though another nephew survived, by his late brother the Duke of Clarence, the House of York, and by extension the Plantaganet dynasty that had held the throne of England for over three centuries, lost its hold on England, giving way to the renowned but short-lived House of Tudor.

Further Reading

Cheetham, Anthony *The Life and Times of Richard III* (London, 1972) (for the argument that Richard was innocent of the murders of his nephews) (Weidenfield & Nicolson, 1972)

Drewett, Richard and Redhead, Mark *The Trial of Richard III* (Sutton, 1984)

Ross, Charles Derek *Richard III* (Methuen, 1981)

Weir, Alison *The Princes in the Tower* (The Bodley Head, 1992)

HENRY VIII

Reign: *April 22, 1509–January 28, 1547*
Born: *June 28, 1491*
Died: *January 28, 1547*
Buried: *Windsor Castle*

Henry VIII is one of those rare monarchs who is remembered, almost paradoxically, for both his skillful kingship and capricious tyranny. When anyone today envisions 'Bluff King Hal' they might conjure up the image of a gluttonous monstrosity of a man who used up six women in succession to satisfy his desires. Yet when he inherited the throne at the ripe age of seventeen, he was considered the perfect Renaissance prince: amiable, extroverted, intelligent and chivalrous. His very physique was the stuff of medieval legends: observers commented on his athletic prowess and muscular limbs, which Henry put to use in his frequent wrestling matches and jousts.

Henry also had a powerful mind and through his highly-structured education mastered Latin, Greek and French. His chief intellectual interest was theology for Henry was, despite what has been made out of him, a deeply religious man. He was even awarded the title 'Defender of the Faith' by the Pope after he co-wrote, with Thomas More and John Fisher, a popular treatise titled *Defence of the Seven Sacriments* which was a rebuttal of Martin Luther's treatise *On the Babylonish Captivity of the Church*. Music and dancing were more relaxing passions of his, and it is said that he composed the music for 'Greensleeves' along with about thirty other songs. Finally, Henry had inherited a realm that was, after decades of instability in the monarchy, financially and politically secure, as well as a major player in the European arena.

However, a dark note was sounded even at the very start of his reign. His father Henry VII was always unpopular for his parsimoniousness and two of his ministers, Edmund Dudley and Richard Empson, were loathed by the people for imposing heavy taxes. Soon after Henry VIII ascended to the throne, the two men were tried for treason and executed. Although it is possible that they really did entertain treasonous designs, it is more likely Henry had the men beheaded in public to increase his own popularity.

Henry's insecurity may have been in part due to the fact that he was never raised to be a king. His older brother, Arthur, was the first Prince of Wales, but died from tuberculosis while still a teenager. Arthur's wife, Catherine of Aragon, daughter of the renowned Queen Isabella and King Ferdinand of Spain, was kept in England after her husband was laid to rest and, to keep England's alliance with Spain strong, Henry VII on his deathbed made his son swear to marry Catherine. Henry, who from all indications had already fallen in love with his brother's Spanish widow, happily agreed and the two wed on June 11, 1509.

Although pious and dutiful, Catherine also had a touch of her mother Isabel's fierce spirit which would come to torment Henry in more turbulent days. But for the time being, the two made for an excellently matched couple. Catherine learned how to get a word in despite her husband's arrogant and misogynistic bearing, while Henry found he could always rely on his wife through thick and thin, even on the battlefield. When Henry sought to imitate King Henry V by waging war against France late in 1513, James IV of Scotland tried to take advantage of Henry's absence by launching an attack against England. Catherine, who was made regent while Henry was in France, sent an army under the earl of Surrey against James IV at the Battle of Flodden, where James and much of the Scottish nobility were struck down. As a bizarre token of love, Catherine sent James's cloak, still caked with mud and the late king's dried blood, to Henry. Few wives ever bestowed such a gift upon a husband.

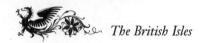

Unfortunately, something called Henry's 'Great Matter' ate away at what might have otherwise been a content marriage. Henry VII always felt unsafe on his throne, having usurped it from the ancient Plantaganet dynasty with what basically amounted to right by conquest, and remained painfully aware that he had a much weaker blood claim to the throne than some still living. This fear was passed on to his son, who was well aware that the Plantaganets lived on in the de la Pole family, descendants from King Richard III's brother, George, the Duke of Clarence, and in Edward Courtenay, the grandson of Katherine, a daughter of Edward IV. To preserve the Tudor dynasty, and also to prevent dynastic turmoil from plunging the realm into civil war, Henry had to have a son to call his heir.

Catherine was more than willing to please her husband in anything, but she could never answer his deepest desire. She had borne six children by 1518, but only one, a daughter Mary, born on February 18, 1516, survived long past infancy. The king did have a son, Henry Fitzroy, created Duke of Richmond, by his mistress Elizabeth 'Bessie' Blount, but his illegitimacy was a serious consideration. Although little Henry Fitzroy was given an upbringing fit for a royal prince, Henry yearned for a son born in wedlock and Catherine was by now growing past childbearing age.

With perhaps a push by his influential advisor Cardinal Wolsey, Henry came to believe that Catherine's failure to bear a healthy boy was divine punishment for marrying his brother's widow, an act forbidden in

Leviticus 20:21: 'If a man shall take his brother's wife, it is an unclean thing; he hath covered his brother's nakedness; they shall be childless.' Long before, Henry VII had requested and received a papal dispensation to allow Henry to marry Catherine on the grounds that her marriage to Arthur was never consummated, but Henry began to suspect that it had been. Also around this point Henry had fallen for Anne, the sister to one of his long-time mistresses, Mary Boleyn. Anne was wiser than her sister, who ended up being discarded by Henry once he became bored with her, and refused to succumb to Henry's increasingly desperate advances even as she seductively encouraged them. Although later propaganda exaggerated Anne's influence in the drastic decisions Henry was soon to make, it is hard to believe that Anne's stubborn demands for a commitment did not play any part whatsoever.

Certainly Henry was very much infatuated with the beautiful, witty Anne Boleyn. Like a teenager, he wrote to her each day with new love letters and chivalrous pleas for her to come to his bed. In comparison to dull and obedient Catherine, Anne had a fiery personality that was a match for Henry's, and there lay her novel appeal. Anne was well aware of her advantage and was rumored to have said, 'I am resolved to have him whatsoever might become of his wife.'

It looked as if Anne would get her wish. Henry soon sent Cardinal Wolsey to negotiate with Pope Clement VII in hopes of annulling his marriage to Catherine. Unfortunately, at that same time the Pope was at loggerheads with the Holy Roman Emperor and King of Spain, Charles V, who just happened to be Catherine's nephew. So severe had matters become between the two men that Charles's armies sacked Rome, not discriminating between the palaces of Rome's richest citizens or the most well-adorned cathedrals. The Pope was understandably terrified of further antagonizing the Emperor and so granting Henry's request for an annulment seemed impractical at best. By that time, Catherine and Henry had long stopped living together as wife and husband, against

Catherine's own wishes.

On May 30, 1529, Wolsey and a papal legate, in the Pope's name, oversaw proceedings to examine the case for an annulment. Catherine appeared at the trial, defending her own cause by bringing up the papal bull that validated her marriage to Henry and continued to claim that she never had intercourse with Arthur. When it was made clear that her arguments would only be ignored, she knelt before Henry, who had been present for the entire trial but said nothing, and pleaded, 'I have been to you a true, honorable and obedient wife, ever conformable to your will and pleasure.' She begged that he punish her in whatever way he saw fit for any crimes she may have accidentally committed against him, as long as he accepted her as his lawful wife again. Henry said nothing. After waiting a few minutes for a reply, Catherine rose and left the room without a further word, not even acknowledging the order of a court official to return, and instead commented to her reluctant attendant that this was no impartial trial. Much to Henry's frustration, the papal legate then adjourned the hearing, derailing any real decision.

The spoiled child that lurked within Henry's mind demanded instant revenge. Catherine became all but a prisoner on her estate in the English countryside, but most of Henry's wrath fell on Wolsey whom he somehow held accountable for the entire affair. All the years Wolsey had spent as one of Henry's most loyal and useful ministers meant nothing in the end. Without further ado he was exiled from court and died in disgrace, with his secretary Thomas Cromwell taking his place at Henry's right hand.

An ambitious man who read his master's mind well, Cromwell promised Henry that he would work hard for an annulment, no matter what the Pope had to say. It is telling that Anne at least had faith in the prospect of an annulment, because while accompanying Henry on a diplomatic voyage to France late in 1532, Henry and Anne finally made love for the first time. Afterwards Anne became pregnant and Henry, overjoyed at the prospect of a son, married Anne secretly on

January 25, 1533. On May 23 that year, the new Archbishop of Canterbury, Thomas Cranmer, finally annulled the marriage between Henry and Catherine without any word from the Pope.

Heedless of the dignity of his former wife, who still clung to the title of Queen of England, and public opinion, which turned resoundingly against Anne Boleyn, Henry tried to hold a public coronation for Anne as queen in London. The whole thing erupted into a fiasco as the crowds cheered 'God save Queen Catherine!' and, seeing that Henry and Anne's initials unfortunately adorned their coach as H & A, began chanting 'HA! HA!' The Pope, in turn, was not amused by Cranmer and Henry's disregard for his holy authority and had the king excommunicated.

Although it is an oversimplification of Henry's complex character, and the history of the Church in England, to say that England's break with Rome was solely the result of the Anne Boleyn affair, it is safe to argue that Henry had developed a megalomaniacal understanding of his own ordained role by this point in his reign (if he had not before). For good reason he carried a bracelet with the inscription: 'To die rather than change my mind'. He earnestly believed that he was following God's will, even when it conveniently coincided with his own, so it was not important if former allies and loved ones died for the sake of his own desires. It was not just his wish to have legitimate sons that motivated him to end his long marriage to Catherine, a woman he seemed to have loved at least at one time, but also a fervent belief that God Himself did not want the marriage to continue. But it is interesting to note that, after moving on with his relationship with Anne Boleyn, Henry avoided the very sight of Catherine after the annulment. Despite his own assurance in the rightness and the divine approval of his actions, throughout his life Henry would show a reluctance to face his own conscience.

Urged on by Cromwell, as well as driven by jealousy over his own authority, Henry pushed a bill through Parliament titled the Act in Restraint of Appeals which rendered the Pope's authority in England null and void. The Act of Supremacy soon followed, making King Henry VIII the spiritual head of the Church of England. Now not only did Henry hold dominion over his subjects' bodies, but also their souls.

The tragic but unavoidable result of these two acts was that remaining true to the Pope now became treason. Even the King's friends and counsellors were not immune to arrest and execution on account of Henry's self-made promotion. Among the many killed was Henry's own advisor and personal friend, Sir Thomas More. Outside Henry's court, a pre-modern McCarthyism followed, with hundreds of Englishmen writing to Cromwell's agents, accusing their neighbors, friends and even relatives of harboring secret papist loyalties. These papists, high and low, were hunted down and hanged for daring to deny their king his rightful spiritual authority.

Although it was Henry and, to an even greater extent, Cromwell who were to blame for the persecutions, the popular Catholic imagination held that the Protestant monster Anne Boleyn had ensnared the king with witchcraft and plotted to plunge all the English into heresy. As a result, many stories, encouraged by traditional Catholics, were circulated: a few, such as the claim that Anne had six fingers on one hand, survive to this day.

Unfortunately, even Henry's allegedly infinite love for Anne began to wane. The first sign of trouble was when, on September 7, 1533, Anne gave birth to her eagerly anticipated child, the future Queen Elizabeth I, but not a son. Meanwhile the chivalrous prince to whom Anne had succumbed soon vanished, leaving behind only Henry the overbearing husband. Through his own eyes, Henry saw the woman he loved as a firecracker turning into a nag. Whereas Catherine used gentle persuasion and quietly looked the other way on the matter of Henry's flirtations and infidelities, Anne loudly objected to Henry's indiscretions and fought with him tooth and nail over the smallest matters of politics and Scripture. If Henry was at first attracted to Anne's standoffishness, after marriage he found it insufferable.

Anne's worries that she would be replaced as easily as Catherine were suddenly coming true. Just as she was a lady-in-waiting to Catherine when her affair with Henry began, so did he begin to flirt openly with one of her own ladies-in-waiting, Jane Seymour. Worse, Jane's personality resembled Catherine's in its meekness. In spite of the fact that Parliament passed an Act of Succession that declared the Princess Mary a bastard and made Elizabeth heir to the throne in lieu of a son, court observers wrote that Henry was tired of Anne's 'unwomanly' personality and perhaps he even secretly felt regret at deserting his sweet, loyal Catherine. Anne's only hope in keeping her position secure was giving Henry what he desperately wanted: a healthy son. Unfortunately, she had miscarried her child after Elizabeth.

After a long illness, which some Catholics claimed was caused by Anne having her poisoned, Henry's first wife and love Catherine died on January 7, 1536, which might have made Anne feel slightly more safe. Catherine's last letter to Henry, unanswered, ended with, 'Lastly, I make this vow, that mine eyes desire you above all things.' Henry and Anne answered the news of her death by wearing bright yellow at court and spending the afternoon at a dance. Even Anne on that day might have felt a touch of dread. She learned she was pregnant once again, but she knew well that her marriage, and maybe even more, depended on the successful delivery of a prince.

Instead, on January 29, Anne miscarried. By her own explanation the shock of hearing about a severe accident the king had while jousting brought it about. When the fetus was examined, it was discovered that, had it been born, it would have been the prince Henry so needed. Once the complete story reached him, Henry only said, 'I see that God will never give me male children.'

Once again, Henry saw God's hand at work. This time he was being punished for turning his back on the saintly Queen Catherine and allowing himself to be seduced by the wicked whore Anne Boleyn. Just as he once thought Catherine's consummation of her relationship with Arthur was to blame for his invoking the anger of God, so must he have angered God again by leaving his true wife. It was never any fault of his own that God always seemed angry with him or that his marriages seemed to turn out badly. His record with wives in particular was something that Henry felt reflected badly on him and his manhood, since it could be taken that he was not as virile as he liked to advertise. Once when an Austrian ambassador tried to argue against marrying Anne Boleyn by suggesting that having another wife would not necessarily guarantee a son or even another pregnancy, Henry stammered, 'Am I not a man like other men? Am I not? Am I not? . . . I need not give proofs of the contrary, or let you into my secrets.'

Whatever was going on in his mind or his bedroom, after the miscarriage Henry resolved to dispose of Anne in favor of Jane. He almost certainly began to believe the whispered rumors that she was a witch. 'When the Duke of Richmond went to say goodnight to his father', one account goes, '. . . the king began to weep, saying that he and his sister, meaning [Mary], were greatly bound to God for having escaped the hands of that accursed whore, who had determined to poison them.' Henry left the problem of Anne Boleyn in the hands of Cromwell, who had the idea of charging Anne with adultery, a crime that, for a queen, was tantamount to treason. With the same indifference he showed Catherine, Henry tried to completely detach himself from the woman he once desperately loved, refusing to see her or write to her during the trial.

Although there have been some arguments that Anne actually was guilty of adultery, it is almost certain that the trial Cromwell engineered was nothing but a means to an end and that Anne was guilty only of minor indiscretions. Five men at court, even Anne's own brother, George, were arrested and accused of having their way with the queen. One of the accused men, a court musician named Mark Smeaton, was put to the rack until he confessed, but was the only man to do so. Eventually, Anne too was arrested and taken to the Tower, where she was charged with adultery, incest and conspiracy to murder the king, all crimes punishable by death. The horror of the situation took its toll on Anne's sanity, who found herself placed in the same room she had slept in with Henry the night before her coronation[33]. At the horrible irony, she burst into tears and cried out, 'It is too good for me', before falling into a fit of hysterical laughter.

The traditional punishment for treason in England was a horrific one for those not lucky enough to be of the nobility. The unlucky victim was drawn and quartered, which involves being hanged, cut down while still breathing, castrated, disemboweled, and then finally quartered. George, because of his noble birth had the privilege of being tried before his aristocratic peers and the right to be put to death by beheading even for treason; the others had no such fortunate right. Henry, however, spared them the horrors of such a death, instead allowing them all the 'nobler' execution of beheading. Even though there was no need and it actually nullified the charge of adultery, Henry curiously ordered Archbishop Cranmer to annul his marriage to Anne, thus making his daughter Elizabeth a bastard. Perhaps Henry felt that his marriage to Catherine of Aragon was true in God's eyes after all? If so, however, he did nothing to change the fact, leaving his other daughter Mary a bastard as well.

By the morning of May 19, Anne Boleyn was dead, beheaded by an expert swordsman from Calais. All the accounts say that she met her death with superhuman calm, but Henry was not there to observe it. Instead, with his usual extraordinary callousness, Henry married Jane Seymour just one day after the execution. Having a legitimate son by Jane was now more urgent than ever, since his illegitimate son Henry Fitzroy had died, but still the shocking coldness of the timing is important for anyone seeking to comprehend Henry VIII's psychological make-up.

If Anne's enemies thought that her denouncement and death and the rise of a new queen would bring an end to anti-papist sentiment,

[33] Traditionally, a king or queen must spend the night before their coronation at the Tower of London.

they were much too optimistic. Deciding to take financial advantage of the reforms, Henry dissolved a few hundred monastic houses that year, with more to come. Even what was considered by many the holiest site in England, the shrine of Thomas Becket, was not immune to Henry's zeal and greed. The jewels that were left by pilgrims in honor of the shrine's saint were confiscated and the relics present were obliterated. The remains of Becket were tried posthumously for treason against King Henry II, a king Becket had defied in his lifetime, and then burned and scattered to the winds.

In the face of all this desecration, Henry was just as vehemently intolerant of radical Protestantism. One Protestant preacher, John Lambert, was invited to dispute the Catholic doctrine of transubstantiation, the belief that the bread and wine of the Communion actually become the body and blood of Christ, with the king himself and ten bishops. Faced with the king's mastery of Greek and Latin and encyclopedic knowledge of Scripture, Lambert crumpled, but refused to recant. Cromwell then sentenced him to be burned at the stake for heresy.

Despite Henry's hostility toward the Protestant doctrines then circulating in Germany and Scandinavia, the staunchly conservative Catholic majority in northern England were driven over the edge by his treatment of religious houses and a rebellion that would become known by the rather sympathetic name of the Pilgrimage of Grace ignited. When the rebellion was crushed, Henry was at first willing to negotiate and even issued a general pardon that some stories attribute to the intervention of Queen Jane. Henry, however, broke the promises he made to the ringleaders, a new uprising began, and this time he was not nearly as merciful. Massacres were carried out at the king's command, leaving hundreds of corpses scattered across the countryside. Among the men specifically singled out for execution was Robert Aske, an original leader of the Pilgrimage, who had actually tried to prevent the second insurrection.

Soon after this bloodshed, Henry at last achieved his lifelong desire. Jane gave birth to a son, Edward, on October 12, 1537. Unfortunately, this also cost Jane her life: she died of puerperal fever nearly two weeks later. Henry was visibly grieved at the news but, even with a prince to take his throne at last, he was not quite ready to retire to widowhood.

Getting married once more, even for Henry, was easier said than done. By the time of Jane Seymour's death, Henry was no longer the catch of Christendom. His once athletic physique had by then deteriorated into a monstrously fat bulk. Now he was riddled with gout and other aches and illnesses: most particularly a sore, ulcerous leg. His reputation as a capricious tyrant, and tales of Anne Boleyn's execution, had swept across Europe to make him seem an even less attractive prospect of marriage.

Even worse, the Pope renewed his excommunication in 1538 and declared Henry deposed, leaving Henry's throne vulnerable to foreign invasion or internal intrigue. With more reason to fear for his crown and throne than ever before, Henry was determined to save himself by ridding the kingdom at last of the scattered remains of the Plantaganet dynasty. The twelve-year-old Edward Courtenay and his parents, the Marquis and Marchioness of Exeter, were thrown into the Tower. Edward Courtenay would not leave the Tower until he reached adulthood. Two sons of the Countess de la Pole, Geoffrey and Henry, were also charged with treason and arrested, as was Henry de la Pole's little son, who would never be seen again.

What really shocked both the English people and foreign observers was the fact that even the aged Countess was arrested for treason and sentenced to beheading. What made it all the more horrifying was that a young, inexperienced executioner was hired for the job. A witness to the execution wrote starkly that the executioner 'hacked her head and shoulders to pieces' instead of giving her the clean blow of a professional.

The excommunication and deposing also meant that Henry would be wise to find a wife who could bring him a valuable foreign alliance to protect himself from the ambitions of the French or the Habsburgs. The situation grated on Henry, since this would be the first time in his life he would not know his wife before marrying her. Various prospective matches were arranged by Cromwell, with portraits of the candidates being brought before the king. In the end, he selected the daughter of a German duke, Anne of Cleves, who was about half his age. Whatever Henry's hopes for his new bride were, he complained after first laying eyes on her that she was 'nothing so fair as she had been reported.'

After Henry reluctantly went about the nuptials and the wedding night, Cromwell anxiously greeted him the next day and asked, 'How liked you the queen?'

Henry replied, 'I liked her before not well, but now I like her much worse.' The king complained that she had brown skin and sagging breasts and claimed that her ugliness was such that he could not bring himself to become aroused.

Because of her strict upbringing, Anne was very naïve about such things and literally did not know any better. While having a conversation with other English ladies, she said, 'When [Henry] comes to bed, he kisses me and taketh me by the hand and biddeth me "good night, sweetheart" and in the morning, kisses me, and biddeth me, "Farewell, darling". Is not this enough?'

Anne was certainly not enough to raise Henry's flagging passions. History once again repeated itself when Henry became infatuated with one of Anne's ladies-in-waiting, Katherine Howard, a not terribly bright but strikingly attractive young woman, only five years older than the Princess Mary. Despite her naïvety, Anne was pragmatic enough to realize the best way to handle the situation was to step aside, and she consented to a divorce on July 10, 1540. Henry became immensely grateful to the once loathesome Anne and developed such a strong friendship with her after the divorce that she was referred to as the king's 'good sister'. As tokens of his appreciation, Henry granted her both a large English estate and a generous allowance.

Thomas Cromwell, the shoddy matchmaker, was not so lucky. Taking advantage of Henry's ire at Cromwell over the Anne of Cleves issue, Cromwell's enemies – and by that point he had many – seized their chance. Despite his ten years of loyal service to Henry, Cromwell was arrested on charges of heresy (probably true) and plotting to seize the throne by marrying the Princess Mary (probably not). Feverishly Cromwell wrote lengthy letters begging the king for an audience. The king, of course, ignored them all.

Henry wed Katherine Howard only eighteen days after the divorce, and on the very same day Thomas Cromwell was beheaded. Rejuvenated by his pretty and youthful bride, Henry showered her with trinkets, dresses and perfumes. He was not aware, though, that Katherine Howard was not another Jane Seymour. Before the marriage, she had been lovers with two men, Henry Maddox and Francis Dereham, the latter of whom she later confessed 'used me in such sort as man doth his wife many and sundry times.' Of course, people in those times were no more chaste than they are today, but Katherine was also foolish and indiscreet.

Much worse, after the marriage to Henry, Katherine started an affair with one of Henry's courtiers, Thomas Culpeper, a brutal thug of a man. It was said that Culpeper once raped a peasant woman while she was held down by his attendants and then killed a man who tried to save her. It was a wonder that the two reckless lovers were able to carry on for as long as they did, but the sword of Damocles came down at last on November 2, 1541 when Dereham's past with the queen came to light and he was put under torture. To save his own skin, he implicated Culpeper, who was promptly arrested and sentenced to die. Katherine was immediately stripped of the title of queen and placed under house arrest. Henry, unable to believe his pretty wife's betrayal, was utterly grief-stricken, bellowing for a sword with which to kill Katherine personally. He then vowed that all the happiness 'that wicked woman' gained from her sexual romps with Culpeper would not equal the suffering she would feel on the rack. His raving against her stopped only when he finally collapsed into sobs.

Like Anne Boleyn before her, Katherine became morbidly resigned to her fate and even asked for a block to be brought to her so she could practice resting her head before the big day. By the morning of February 13, 1542, she was dead. Again, Henry did not see her before she died, or mark the day of her execution. The treachery of his fifth wife seemed to have been the last straw and finished his evolution toward becoming the antithesis of the idealistic, young prince he once had been. A French ambassador wrote that Henry said aloud 'he had an unhappy people to govern whom he would shortly make so poor that they would not have the power to oppose him.' Certainly, like its king, England had seen better days. Recession and devalued currency had wearied the English people, while religious turmoil continued unabated.

Despite a pledge never to marry again, he took a sixth wife, Katherine Parr, a 31-year-old and twice-widowed woman, who became a nurse rather than a lover to him. At the time, that is just what the old king needed. Both his legs had become so ulcerous that he could hardly walk and needed a sedan chair to climb stairs. Yet these significant physical problems did not slow him from trying to recapture the glories of his youth. Henry accepted the Holy Roman Emperor's offer to join a campaign against France, but insisted that he lead the campaign himself. The whole thing was more or less a disaster, and Henry was lucky he survived.

Katherine, meanwhile, spent her time trying to reconcile Henry and his children and served as a beloved companion to the ailing king, but at one point even she was in danger from Henry's whimsical anger. One time Katherine heard a rumor that Henry was annoyed with her and suspecting that the cause was a theological argument she had recently had with him, she went to see him to apologize.

Deciding to test her, Henry said, 'Not so, by Saint Mary. You are become a doctor, Kate, to instruct us and not to be instructed by us.'

Realizing what she had to do, Katherine deferred to Henry's judgment as much as she could and confessed that, as a woman, it was her duty to relent to him on everything, especially matters of faith.

Katherine passed the test. Henry took her hands and, smiling, said, 'And is it even so, sweetheart, and tended your argument to no worse end? Then perfect friends we are now again as ever at any time heretofore.' Katherine saw that she may have quite literally saved her own life when guards later came under orders to escort her to the Tower. Henry then arrived on the scene, screeching that no one was to lay a hand on this loyal, beloved wife.

Although Henry by now seemed only to want to rest, he had one more heartache to experience : the sinking of the *Mary Rose*. Having come personally to see the warship join battle against the French, he listened instead with horror as the screams of the hundreds of men aboard reached him. Consumed by the illnesses which prematurely aged him, Henry died at the age of fifty-five. His sixth and last wife, Katherine Parr, went on to marry a man she loved, Thomas Seymour, but died after a little over a year of marriage after giving birth to a daughter, Mary. Henry's nine-year-old son, Edward, was left to inherit the throne from his larger-than-life father. At his own request, Henry was buried next to Jane Seymour, the wife who died giving him what he wanted most, a son.

Further Reading

Erickson, Carolly *Great Harry* (Summit, 1980)

Fraser, Antonia *The Six Wives of Henry VIII* (Weidenfield & Nicolson, 1992)

Green, Vivian *The Madness of Kings: Personal Trauma and the Fate of Nations* (Sutton, 1993)

Lacey, Robert *The Life and Times of Henry VIII* (Weidenfield & Nicolson, 1972)

Morris, Christopher *The Tudors* (Severn House, 1955)

'BLOODY' MARY I

Reign: *July 19, 1553–November 17, 1558*
Born: *February 18, 1516*
Died: *November 17, 1558*
Buried: *Westminster Abbey*

Even though Mary was the first anointed queen regnant of England (the previous two queen regnants, Matilda in the twelfth century and Mary's immediate predecessor Jane, were never crowned), her time in power is often eclipsed by her renowned half-sister, Elizabeth, a fact that would have galled Mary had she lived to see it. When Mary is not overlooked, her name is associated with the anti-Protestant burnings that occurred with disturbing frequency during her reign, accounts of which are famously collected in *Foxe's Book of Martyrs*. As undeserving as Queen Mary I may be of the reputation of the fanatical murderer 'Bloody' Mary, her reign was fatally marred by bad choices, the most catastrophic of which privately and politically for her was her decision to marry Prince Philip of Spain.

Mary was the only child of Henry VIII's first wife, Catherine of Aragon, to live past infancy. Although she frustrated her father's dynastic plans by daring to be born female, Henry was at first a doting if distant father, nicknaming Mary his 'pearl'. Mary's mother was a deeply religious and old-fashioned woman and, although Mary was given an education worthy of a Renaissance prince, she was also taught by her conservative Spanish tutor, Juan Luis Vives, to view her sex as a fatal handicap. In fact, Vives had written a treatise, *On The Instruction of a Christian Woman*, where he states that any girl must be taught to understand that she is 'the Devil's instrument, not Christ's'.

When Mary was only eleven, the chaos over Henry's plan to declare that he had never been legally married to Catherine began. Yet this did not at first threaten Mary's own position, since it was not to Henry's advantage that Mary be declared a bastard and decrease her value on the marriage market, nor was the Church particularly unforgiving to those children whose parents were illegally united but who had married in good faith. But doubtless these considerations did nothing to ease the terrible trauma Mary suffered as a result of the divorce. Even worse, Mary would not find a friend in her new stepmother, Anne Boleyn.

To Anne, Catherine and Mary were living dangers to herself and her newborn daughter, Elizabeth. Anne, deciding to make an immediate strike against her would-be rivals, played a hand in Mary's loss of her independent household and staff in 1533 and her forced move into the household of her infant half-sister Elizabeth, where she was treated like a lady-in-waiting to the baby girl. These humiliations were nothing compared to the Act of Succession passed by Parliament when Mary was nineteen, which officially made Elizabeth heir presumptive to the throne and left Mary a bastard, stripping her of her royal title.

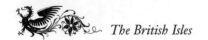

Despite the humility Vives tried so hard to instill in her, Mary did not shelve her Tudor pride during this crisis. She wrote a manifesto to the Council, claiming she was happy to move into her sister's household, but 'her conscience would in no wise suffer her to take any other than herself for princess'. In another letter to her father, she stubbornly signed, 'Your most humble daughter, Mary, Princess'. She also refused to defer to the little Elizabeth in any way, which ended in her being punished by having her personal possessions taken away. Her governess happened to be Anne Boleyn's aunt, who was chastised by Anne's uncle, the Duke of Norfolk, and Anne's brother George for giving Mary 'too much respect and kindness'.

The reality that Anne was hated by sections of the populace while Catherine was hailed as the true Queen of England did nothing to soften Anne's loathing for Catherine's defiant daughter. In time, Mary was forbidden to write to or visit her mother, the reason being that Catherine was thought to be secretly encouraging Mary to be obstinate. Although most of the stories that Anne plotted to kill Mary were only rumors, it was attested that Anne muttered once that she would make Mary a maid of honor in her household and then either 'marry her to some valet' or 'give her too much dinner' (that is, poison her). How much weight Anne's threats had is uncertain since she was known for a bad temper, but Anne never stopped bearing down on Mary.

As for Henry, he shoved his 'pearl' under the rug. Once when Henry came to pay a visit to Elizabeth, Mary was shut up in her room and ordered not to come out and see her father. She tried to send a message to him, asking him to at least let her see him and kiss his hand, but it was ignored. As soon as she learned that Henry was preparing to leave, she snuck out of her room and climbed to a terrace on the roof. When she saw him mounting his horse, she knelt down where she was. Catching sight of her, Henry nodded and tipped his hat to her, then rode away.

Whether it was a rare sign of fatherly affection or a gesture of admiration for his daughter's tenacity, Henry's attitude toward Mary promptly took a turn for the worst. While she had previously been a nonentity, Henry later came to share Anne's view that Mary was an obstacle to the validity of his marriage to Anne, and to Elizabeth's legitimacy. Mary was told in no uncertain terms that she must acknowledge Elizabeth as heiress presumptive and Anne as Queen of England or she would face imprisonment in the Tower – or worse. To make matters even more dire for Mary, her mother died on January 7, 1536, leaving her alone in an increasingly hostile world.

Anne Boleyn's eventual fall from grace, conviction and execution on trumped-up charges of adultery saved Mary from an implacable foe, but it did not erase the consequences of Henry's second marriage or the birth of a new heiress. Even though Mary wrote self-deprecating letters to her father begging to be restored to his favor, Henry continued to demand that Mary acknowledge the Act of Succession and the invalidity of his marriage to Catherine of Aragon or he would arrange for her to be arrested for treason. Henry even sent a small pack of nobles to bully Mary into compliance. She merely answered their demands by saying that, although she was loyal to her father as both his daughter and his subject, she could do nothing that would insult God or the honor of her late mother. At Mary's quiet insolence, the men became angry and barraged their king's daughter with threats. One man bellowed that if his daughter was ever as willful as Mary, he would have cracked her skull open against a wall.

Not quite willing to put the neck of the king's daughter and the Holy Roman Emperor's cousin in jeopardy, the Council tried to give Mary one last shot at survival. They sent her a document explicitly stating that her parents were never married in the eyes of God and that the Pope had no authority in England. Willing to embrace what she saw as holy martyrdom, Mary entertained the idea of not signing but, at the urging of the Emperor's ambassador, who convinced her that by staying alive she remained a tool for God to use to restore England to the old faith, she relented and gave the document her signature. However, she also secretly signed a protest, affirming that she had signed only under threat of force. Nonetheless, the ploy worked: Mary was restored to her father's favor and allowed to regularly visit the court. It also helped that Henry's future wives, most particularly Jane Seymour and Katherine Parr, tried to mend old wounds between the bitterly divided Tudor siblings (who by the fall of 1537 included a boy named Edward mothered by Jane Seymour) and their imperious father.

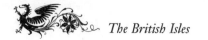

By early adulthood, Mary was a popular and adored figure, famous for her acts of charity and her pious personality. This saintly reputation also came from her virginity: partially because of the questions surrounding her legitimacy, all marriage negotiations involving her failed. Mary tried taking her spinsterhood as a point of pride but, as her enthusiasm for her future marriage with Philip would reveal, it brought her endless anguish.

In the court, her naïvety and innocence was the focus of many stories and rumors. One time during a masque, Henry VIII decided on a whim to test his daughter's famed blamelessness. As a sort of party game, he asked one of his courtiers to talk to Mary and throw blatant sexual innuendos and dirty puns into the conversation. The whole time, as eavesdroppers snickered, Mary chatted happily with the man, completely oblivious to the double meanings he used. Another story, told by one of Mary's ladies-in-waiting, described how one day Mary's chamberlain was flirting with Mary's maiden of honor, calling her his 'pretty whore', unaware that Mary was overhearing them in the next room. Afterwards, while this maid was helping Mary into her dress, Mary affectionately referred to the poor girl as a 'whore'. The hurt maid found that she had to explain to a puzzled Mary, at the time queen and well into her thirties, what exactly the word meant. But even while young, Mary did have a blemish on her reputation here and there. One of her favorite pastimes was gambling and she tended to rack up considerable debts. She also inherited the Tudor love for display, showing an attraction for ostentatious clothing and jewels that rivaled even her father.

Although she would later be called unattractive and ugly, in her youth she was deemed a prize beauty with a slim figure and beautiful red hair, although one ambassador described her voice as 'manly'. When she was young, observers thought that she showed external signs of her father's formidable personality. One of these features was the piercing gaze Mary used whenever in conversation. Witnesses took this as the sign of a powerful character trait. The cause actually might have been that Mary had inherited her father's affliction, far-sightedness, which forced her to peer closely at everyone.

Near the end of his life, King Henry composed a will that made his once despised daughter Mary second-in-line to the throne behind her half-brother Edward, even though she was still illegitimate in the eyes of the Protestant church and the law. Next to her in the line of succession stood Elizabeth, who had also been rendered a bastard by Henry's tortuous marital history, and past her the descendants of his sister Mary and her husband Charles Brandon, the Duke of Suffolk. When Henry gave up his life on January 28, 1547, Edward, who was only nine years old, was declared king with the Council, headed by his maternal uncle, Edward Seymour, the Duke of Somerset, ruling England in his name. With this, Mary's life once again hit bottom. Despite being only a nine-year-old boy, Edward was already a fanatical Protestant. So in touch with his righteousness was Edward that, when he was only eight years old, he asked his stepmother Katherine Parr to chastise Mary for attending 'foreign dances and merriments which do not become a most Christian princess'.

Whereas Henry had simply wanted a break with Rome and was more likely to defend than denounce Catholic traditions, Edward with his advisors sought to make England a thoroughly Protestant realm. Because of that aim, Mary's Catholicism became a political embarrassment at best and a lightning rod for conspiracy at worst. Mary's status as a powerful landowner, due to her considerable country estates in East Anglia, only aggravated anxieties about her. Once again Mary found herself banished from court and the target of harassment from the government she stood one day to rule.

As usual, Mary was not about to give in to political coercion. Not only did she openly continue to practice her religion, she also invited the local people to come to her residences to hear Mass with her. Although Somerset made a promise that Mary would continue to be allowed to practice her religion if she became more discreet, the Council was not entirely willing to honor it. Worse still for Mary, Somerset was removed from power: he had annoyed his Protestant supporters by being too moderate and had turned public opinion against himself by having his brother Thomas executed for treason. The more ambitious John Dudley, Earl of Warwick and the future Duke of Northumberland, took his place as head of the Council.

The hostility Northumberland showed to Mary once he took control of the Council became so intense that Mary began plotting to flee to her cousin Charles V in Austria for protection, something she had previously considered during the dark days under her father. English history might have been very different if her plans had come to fruition, but the sudden death of the Austrian ambassador, Franz van der Delft, who was masterminding the plan, spoiled matters at the last minute. Charles V himself became reluctant to approve a further attempt. After all, Mary was by far his most valuable political pawn in England, and if she were out of the country should Edward die childless it might well prove a lost opportunity for her to become queen. Further, Charles was heard to comment that, 'If death were to overtake her for this cause, she would be the first martyr of royal blood to die for our holy faith, and would for this earn glory in the later life.' A safe Mary in Austria was useless to both Charles and the Church, but a persecuted Mary in England was valuable. Unaware of these considerations, Mary kept her faith in Charles V as a father figure and never stopped hoping that one day she could escape to his court where she would practice her faith in peace.

The noose tightened once word of the aborted escape attempt reached the Council. Mary was forbidden to hear Mass even in private and two of her chaplains were arrested. When Mary heard about the ban, she vehemently wrote to the Council that, while she would concede to such a law out of respect for her sovereign and brother, 'none of your new service shall be said in any house of mine, and if any be said in it I will not tarry in it an hour'. She began to keep a priest hidden in her household away from the Council's spies. The only thing keeping Northumberland and the Council from putting Mary under arrest was fear of irritating Charles V or of causing a Catholic rebellion to erupt.

Northumberland was soon cursed with another problem. Although he had plans to declare the king of age on his sixteenth birthday, Edward, who was never very healthy, came down with tuberculosis in 1553. In May of that year, Edward signed the Device for the Succession, which negated the terms of his father's will and barred Mary and Elizabeth from the throne on account of their illegitimacy. This made an heir of Edward's cousin, Jane Grey, who was as much a Protestant as Edward. After weeks of agony, Edward died on July 6 and Northumberland's plans to make Jane queen succeeded – for the time being. That Northumberland had the foresight to marry Jane to his boorish and spoiled son Guildford Dudley was just icing on the cake, but then the tables were abruptly turned. Although he tried to keep Edward's death a secret for as long as possible, Mary caught wind of what Northumberland was up to and fled to Norfolk, a hotbed of pro-Catholic sentiment.

Northumberland tried to arrange for the capture of Mary while cementing the new regime, but at every step he underestimated both the hatred the English people, especially Londoners, held for him and the escalating popularity of Mary, who had already proclaimed herself the rightful Queen of England. In a matter of days, Mary was riding on horseback through camps filled with loyal soldiers, humbly thanking them for their support and genuinely overwhelmed by their devotion to her. The decisive moment for Mary was when the crews of four ships at Yarmouth mutinied in her favor. Realizing then that Northumberland's cause was lost , most of the Council yielded in the face of public opinion and on July 18, after fleeing through the night from London, they put out a reward for Northumberland's arrest. Deserted by the same soldiers he tried to raise against Mary, Northumberland reluctantly surrendered and made a phony show of newfound loyalty to Mary. To everyone's delight, except his own, he was arrested and condemned to death, although Mary later mitigated his punishment from drawing and quartering to beheading.

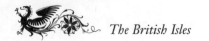

Mary proved even more considerate to the fifteen-year-old Queen Jane, whose reign had lasted only nine days. Recognizing that Jane was only being used as a pawn by Northumberland and had been reluctant to accept the throne in the first place (in fact, when she learned that she had been deposed, Jane said only, 'I am very glad I am no longer queen'), Mary gladly promised to spare Jane's life, despite their serious religious differences. Of course, Jane had to be imprisoned in the Tower and even formally sentenced to die for treason, but Mary had no intention of having the sentence carried out and even planned, once her crown was more secure, to release Jane. She was also lenient to many of Northumberland's supporters, especially those who had defected to her early on, which only raised her already astronomical popularity among the populace. As one foreign visitor noted with surprise, 'The inestimable joys of the people cannot be reported.'

When Mary became queen regnant at the age of thirty-seven, she discovered a kingdom that was almost bankrupt from the excesses and corruption that had started during her father's and her brother's reigns. Mary had gained valuable experience of governing from being a wealthy landowner, but it became painfully clear that although she had the iron will and razor-sharp intellect of the Tudors, she lacked their pragmatism and shrewdness. She could be dangerously single-minded in all matters, especially religion, and would often sacrifice sound policy for the sake of pursuing what she felt was right on an emotional level.

For the time being, Mary yielded to the advice of her councilors and put a leash on her desire to bring England back into the Catholic fold. She promised that she did not mean to impose Catholicism on everyone or otherwise 'compel or constrain other men's consciences', at least not until Parliament declared on the matter. Until then, Mary's most pressing concern was the provision of a Catholic heir to the throne, since Elizabeth showed no signs of renouncing Protestantism. The best choice was Edward Courtenay, one of the last remnants of the Plantaganet dynasty, who was imprisoned under Henry VIII's reign but had recently been released as part of a general amnesty Mary offered to political prisoners in the Tower. Courtenay was only twelve when he was jailed and twenty-seven when he was released, so he was by that time an emotionally stunted man. Mary could barely stand him and, although she restored his family's estates and titles to him and showed him some favor, it is unlikely that she even considered marrying him, despite the political value of such a match.

With a push from Charles V, Mary began to consider marrying Charles' son, Prince Philip of Spain. When word of the proposed marriage came out, the English, both Mary's councilors and the commoners, were horrified. Such a match would surely force England into becoming a satellite of the Habsburg Empire, especially if a male heir were born. Although English custom did not bar a married female monarch from ruling alone, it decreed that women must submit their property to their husbands, so people assumed Mary would hand England itself over to Philip as her dowry. Despite her own conflicting feelings about the submission a Christian woman should show to her husband, Mary tried to assure everyone that she would not surrender her own God-given authority to her husband, whoever he was, but few were convinced. Even worse, the insular English were terrified of the coming Spanish swarm. Exaggerated tales of the Spanish Inquisition circulated around England, convincing the masses that Philip would bring this horrible oppression to the English people. Although the Austrian ambassador was quick to bribe members of the Council into endorsing the match, the people could not be so easily bought.

Even Mary harbored a few doubts, at least at first. Although Philip was in essence a dull and gloomy man, rumors of his many amorous adventures reached Mary, but she was inclined to accept Charles' half-hearted explanation that these were only exaggerated youthful indiscretions. The age difference also worried her: Philip was twenty-six, eleven years younger than herself. Mary's reservations about the match were dissolved when she saw a portrait of Philip sent from the Continent, that depicted a dashing if small and slender man. She might also have felt that her throne would be more secure with both a husband and a child heir. If such fears for her throne weighed in on her, they were mostly generated by the presence of her much resented half-sister, Elizabeth.

Elizabeth's existence alone was a painful reminder to Mary of why she had suffered so much neglect and abuse throughout her childhood. Mary still could not forget that it was for Elizabeth's sake that her mother's marriage and her legitimacy were trampled on, nor forgive her half-sister the months she spent acting as her servant. Nor could Mary ignore the fact that Elizabeth, being young, pretty and Protestant, was becoming a more attractive alternative to her old and Catholic sister. Mary was fond of stating snippily that Elizabeth had 'the face and countenance of Mark Smeaton, who was a very handsome man'. When Elizabeth's mother Anne was charged with adultery, Smeaton was the only man among the accused who confessed under torture. Ironically, it was universally agreed that Elizabeth resembled the late Henry VIII much more than Mary did.

Elizabeth knew that it was in her best interests, if not for her own survival, to get into her sister's good graces, so she gave Mary the impression that she sincerely wanted to convert to Catholicism. Overjoyed, Mary presented Elizabeth with gifts, among them a coral rosary that Elizabeth would never use. When Elizabeth agreed to Mary's request that she attend Mass with her, however, Elizabeth made no secret of her reluctance and 'complained loudly all the way to church that her stomach ached, wearing a suffering air'. Mary took note of Elizabeth's insincerity and was deeply insulted.

For the time being, though, Mary had more pressing concerns. Parliament objected to her plan to marry Philip, forcing her to appear before them and plead her case. She argued that, being sovereign, it was within her right to choose her own consort, regardless of the momentous impact of such a decision. 'If you try to force me to take a husband who would not be to my liking,' she said to Parliament, 'you would cause my death, for if I were married against my will, I would not live three months and would have no children, and then you would be sorry!'

The marriage treaty agreed upon between Mary and Charles V went out of its way to keep Philip's nose out of the English government under any conceivable development. Nevertheless, many were understandably afraid of what would occur if Mary died, leaving an English prince in the tight fist of Philip and the Habsburg clan. Finally, the national anxiety came to a head in the spring of 1554, when Sir Thomas Wyatt hatched a plan to kidnap Mary and separate her from her pro-Habsburg advisors. Edward Courtenay, who was involved, ended up betraying the other conspirators, but they went through with an armed uprising regardless. However, Courtenay's betrayal dealt a deathblow to the plan, and by February 7, 1554, Wyatt's attempt to take London had failed. Anxious to soothe Charles V's anxieties about sending Philip to England after such a recent revolt and because Jane's father, the Duke of Suffolk, had backed Wyatt, Mary reluctantly ordered Jane's execution, which was carried out on February 12 after efforts to convert her to Catholicism had failed.

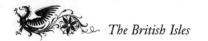

Jane was not the only one to suffer because of Wyatt. Elizabeth, whom Mary believed at least knew of the rebellion and perhaps gave it her blessing, found herself in serious danger. Despite pleading illness, Elizabeth was ordered to return to London andwas placed in the Tower, the same grim structure where her mother had waited to die years earlier. The terror Elizabeth must have felt with her mother's execution weighing on her mind as she was led to the Tower was surely agonizing. No wonder, when Elizabeth was brought to the steps of the Tower, she sat down despite the heavy rain of that day and declared, 'Here landeth as true a subject, being prisoner, as ever landed at these stairs.' She refused to budge for a long time, even with the pleas and threats of her captors at her back. Despite the intense interrogations that followed her imprisonment, Elizabeth stuck to her claim of innocence and betrayed no sign of guilt. Elizabeth's interrogator complained to Mary about Elizabeth's agile mind and argued that nothing incriminating could be got from her.

Mary chalked the failure of the interrogations up to Elizabeth's stubbornness and refused to release her, sound evidence to her guilt or not. Elizabeth, meanwhile, had become an archetypical maiden in distress in the public eye. A five-year-old boy started regularly to bring Elizabeth flowers during her walks in the Tower garden. It was a sweet, innocent gesture, but Mary would not tolerate it once she heard of it, imagining that conspirators sent Elizabeth secret messages inscribed in code on the petals. 'I can bring you no more flowers, Lady,' the boy quietly told Elizabeth one afternoon.

Any apprehensions Mary may have had concerning Philip soon dissolved, or were at least soothed, on July 23, the day she finally met her future husband, strategically accompanied by ladies-in-waiting older than herself. Finding her groom as handsome as she imagined, she chatted excitedly with him throughout the day and eagerly anticipated the marriage scheduled for two days later. Philip, on the other hand, was less impressed with this middle-aged bride and found the whole thing an unpleasant political chore. Philip's Spanish companions joked about Mary's missing teeth and bad breath. One asked, 'What shall he do with such an old bitch?' The English were no more thrilled at the presence of 'Jack Spaniard'. Spanish visitors found that London merchants never failed to overcharge them for goods. Fights broke out on an almost daily basis, often leading to bloodshed, and on one occasion a mob of Englishmen gathered together with the sole purpose of killing as many Spanish as possible.

Even in the face of all the unnerving hatred, Mary still felt more secure with her staunchly Catholic husband and hurried on with her religious agenda. On November 30, Mary and Philip pressured Parliament into placing England back under papal authority. By December 18, the old heresy laws were restored, making heresy, including Protestantism, punishable by burning at the stake. The rationale for this appalling method of execution was that heretics would receive a taste of Hell and repent just before they died. Ultimately, Mary reasoned, it was a matter of bringing salvation, not pain, to lost souls.

While there were certainly some in the government, including the papal legate Reginald de la Pole, who feverishly urged on the burnings, Mary was without a doubt the driving force behind them. She even personally admonished a sheriff who spared one heretic who repented while being tied to the stake. Over the course of Mary's reign, 240 men and sixty women perished in the flames: some radical Protestant preachers, others uneducated country folk who just did not know the sacraments or the Lord's Prayer. Usually gunpowder was tied to the victim, so it would explode and end the victim's agony before long. More often than not, though, the gunpowder failed and the victim was left to feel the flames. One victim, a former Protestant bishop named John Hooper, burned alive for almost an hour.

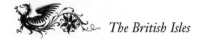

The persecutions and deaths only brought resentment against Mary to a fever pitch and any trace of her former popularity evaporated forever. With resistance to her policies now centering around Elizabeth, Mary soon had no choice but to end Elizabeth's unlawful imprisonment, but she did make sure Elizabeth would remain a virtual prisoner at court where it would be harder for her to become the focus of a Protestant uprising. Although Prince Philip himself, who wanted to be in the good graces of the woman nearest to the throne, tried to make peace between the sisters, Elizabeth was kept at heel at all times. One day Elizabeth furiously wrote a letter protesting her treatment to Mary, referring to the queen with the familiar pronoun 'you' instead of any of the appropriate honorifics. Mary was not amused. She eventually cut the correspondence short by writing to Elizabeth that she would no longer allow herself to be 'molested' by any further letters.

In the spring of 1555, the very thing which made Elizabeth a threat, her place as heir presumptive, was put at risk, much to Mary's joy. At last she was pregnant, or so she thought. In actuality, she might have had a tumor, which was what was believed at the time, or, more likely, she was experiencing a psychosomatic condition called hysterical pregnancy, where a woman exhibits most of the physical signs of pregnancy, even a swollen abdomen, while not actually carrying a fetus. The 'pregnancy' went on for about twelve months, with the doctors claiming that a miscalculation of the birth date was at fault, but everyone except Mary herself suspected the truth. Mary became a laughing stock at home and abroad, while she came to believe she was being punished by God for some unknown offense. A prayer book of Mary's that survives today shows stains, perhaps from tears, on the page titled *A Prayer for a Woman with Child*. By August, Mary resumed her period and even she had to face the barren truth.

Humiliated by the false pregnancy, exhausted by the hostility of the English and sick of his ugly wife, Philip was eager to leave for the Continent and used the fact that he had recently inherited the Netherlands as an excuse. Despite his wife's pleas, he left to sail for Flanders on August 29. She wrote lengthy letters to him, which he responded to less and less frequently as time drew on. The only news about Philip she got were rumors that her husband had abandoned his sober personality and embraced a life devoted to racking up debts and attending balls with attractive, young mistresses on each arm. Even Mary's patience and devotion for her husband were plainly finite. Once she was overheard remarking, 'God sent oft times to good women evil husbands'.

Despite any resentment she nurtured against Philip, she felt even more alone in the arena of public opinion. Pamphlets were published and distributed across London painting Mary as the Babylonian Whore. Her pregnancy and her attempts to bring back Catholicism were openly ridiculed; the nursery rhyme, 'Mary, Mary, quite contrary', is believed to have been about Mary's reign. Philip, who had become King of Spain in his absence after Charles V's abdication, did return on March 1557, but only to ensure Mary's support in a war against France, which was a disaster and ended with England losing the last of its territorial possessions in France, the city of Calais. After the conclusion of the war, Philip soon left his wife again on the excuse that he had to attend to matters on the Continent. Mary would never see him again.

That winter, she did think she was once again pregnant by him, but it turned out to be another false alarm. Defeated, Mary surrendered herself to depression and illness. To a servant, she said, 'When I am dead, you will find Philip and Calais engraved on my heart'. As her body began to fail her, her ministers urged her to nominate Elizabeth as her heir. Mary knew that Elizabeth would undo everything she had worked for, so she put off naming her heir apparent until, at last, it was clear she would not have long to live.

With a heavy heart, she gave the half-sister she had loathed all her life the key to erase all her accomplishments. Whether or not Mary feared that Elizabeth would become more successful in history's eyes than she was is something we could never know. Bedridden with influenza and consumed with self-loathing, Mary died on November 17, 1558. The last terms of her will, including her humble request to be buried near her mother, were completely ignored by Elizabeth, who proclaimed upon hearing the news of her sister's death, 'This is the Lord's doing, and it is marvelous in our eyes'. Throughout Elizabeth's lifetime, Mary would stay buried under an unmarked grave.

Further Reading

Erickson, Carolly *Bloody Mary* (Doubleday, 1978)
Morris, Christopher *The Tudors* (Severn House, 1955)
Loades, D.M. *Mary Tudor: A Life* (Oxford University Press, 1989)
Weir, Alison *The Children of England: The Heirs to King Henry VIII, 1547-1558* (J. Cape, 1996)

GEORGE III

Reign: *October 25, 1760–January 29, 1820*
Born: *June 4, 1738*
Died: *January 29, 1820*
Buried: *Windsor Castle*

Even though he was really a harmless, prudish man, whose court was thought by all to be the most boring in Europe, he is usually remembered as either the tyrant who made the American Revolution necessary, described in the American Declaration of Independence as 'a prince whose character is marked by every act which may define a tyrant', or as an incoherent madman as shown in the play *The Madness of King George*. As if he were consciously trying to fight the unfortunate reputation that dogged the other members of his family, the Hanoverians, he lived a simple, moral life and expected the same, in vain, from his siblings and children. Tragically, a rare hereditary illness called porphyria would make George famous for madness, not piety.

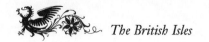

George's father was Frederick, Prince of Wales, heir to King George II. Although Frederick was an educated man, devoted to the arts and sciences, his family loathed him to an unusual degree, largely due to his extravagances and huge debts. The Vice Chamberlain of the Household heard Frederick's mother, Queen Caroline, say as her son passed a window, 'Look, there he goes – that wretch! that villain! I wish the ground would open this moment and sink the monster to the lowest hole in hell!' His father once called him 'the greatest beast in the whole world', and even his sister Caroline hoped that 'he may die and we may all go about with smiling faces and glad hearts'. Frederick was, in spite of his family's opinions to the contrary, a careful and devoted father to George, ensuring his children received a thorough education in literature, history, and languages.

The future George III lost his father on March 31, 1751 at the age of twelve. Frederick's parents did not even bother putting on a show of grief. Afterwards young George was left in the hands of his mother Augusta of Saxe-Coburg, a domineering woman who kept all of her children on a short leash. It was perhaps she who instilled him with such straitlaced sensibilities that overcame even his sensual Hanoverian blood.

Or did they? One of the great traditions of the Hanoverian family was the secret marriages which occurred among the men with amazing frequency. Although, as will be seen, George did everything in his power to put his foot down on this family custom, he may have yielded to it at least once. Recently unearthed evidence suggest that George had in secret married a Quaker girl named Hannah Lightfoot on April 17, 1759. It was even suggested that they had a son, also named George, who was sent to South Africa where he died apparently childless. As ironic as a secret marriage entered into by bland George III of all men is, and as intriguing as the possible implications it would have for the current royal family of England are, the case for it is far from sound.

If such a marriage did happen, it was covered up so well that George succeeded to the throne after his grandfather George II's death on October 25, 1760 without any nasty rumors taking root. In fact, after the reigns of the first two Hanoverian monarchs, both sour old men, the young and likeable George III seemed a breath of fresh air. He was deemed 'the most amiable young man in the world' and was appreciated for his rare lack of pretension. None of this saved him from being mocked for the same strange conversational tics that helped make him seem more like a man and less like a king, such as when he constantly ended his sentences with 'hey, hey' or 'what, what.' He could also be quite tactless, although he never seemed to have any malicious intent. To start off a conversation, he sometimes liked to point out how fat the other person had grown since he last met them. One day, when meeting with a man whose native county was Yorkshire, he asked, 'I suppose you are going back to Yorkshire?' Without a second thought, George added before the man could reply, 'A very ugly county, Yorkshire.'

Even if his strange conversational tics suggest otherwise, George's everyday life was based on the strictest guidelines. He always rose at six in the morning and went to bed exactly at ten at night. He rarely ate rich foods, avoided alcohol, exercised often to fight his natural tendency toward plumpness, and was far more likely to spend his free time working on his collections of model ships, books, and clocks than gambling. Various fields, such as architecture, literature[34], and music sparked his interest, but he became particularly well known for the fascination he had with agriculture,

[34] George III had an opinion of Shakespeare that many people might find understandable. When he heard that a German translation of Shakespeare's plays was being attempted, he exclaimed: 'The Germans translate Shakespeare! Why, we don't understand him ourselves. How should foreigners?'

which went so far that he designed model farms around Windsor, earning himself the nickname 'Farmer George'.

Although George was infatuated for a time with Sarah Lennox, the teenaged daughter of the Duke of Richmond, he ended up bowing to family tradition by picking a German wife, Charlotte Sophia of Mecklenburg-Strelitz. Some were puzzled by George's happy acceptance of his bride: cruel jokes were made about Charlotte's ugliness and she was known by the unflattering nickname of 'Monkey Face'. However, in terms of the new queen's personality, the match could not possibly be more perfect. A rigid and introverted woman, she made few friends at the English court, but all the better for her to live solely for her husband. She accepted, if not encouraged, his Spartan lifestyle, and over time fulfilled her duty to the dynasty and to Britain by giving birth to fifteen children.

Even with such a large brood and the convention among royals that the raising of one's children was a task best left to others, George and Charlotte were hands-on parents. Much to their surprise (and annoyance), his ministers often found George playing with his children, sometimes even crawling around on the floor with the toddlers. Yet the royal couple were as stern parents as any who wanted to turn their children into upstanding, moral adults. Charlotte kept her daughters in a gilded cage until the day they could be married off. They were rarely allowed to be in the company of men and the queen, afraid of being alone, kept her daughters unwed for as long as possible. It is no surprise that all of Charlotte's daughters grew to resent her and hate the lives they were given. One spinster daughter, Elizabeth, wrote, 'We go on vegetating as we have done for the last twenty years of our lives.'

George could be every bit as hard on his sons, making certain that their tutors understood to never spare them a beating when necessary, and the eldest sons, Crown Prince George and Frederick, got the full brunt of George's determination to stamp out any early traces of hedonism in them. Of course, thanks to their overly strict childhood, George III's sons turned out every bit as indolent as he feared. The most scandalous instance of this was when one of his sons, Ernest Augustus, the future King of Hanover, was rumored to have been the father of his sister Sophia's illegitimate child.

George would have probably argued in his defense that his boys constantly found poor role models in their paternal uncles and one of their aunts. Edward, the Duke of York, was a playboy who, when he was not chasing women, passed the time in playing vicious practical jokes. William, the Duke of Gloucester, was banished from court for marrying secretly, a crime shared by the youngest brother, Henry, the Duke of Cumberland. His brothers' habit of marrying against his consent led George to pass the Royal Marriages Act of 1772[35], which invalidated any marriages made by any member of the royal family before the age of twenty-five without the monarch's consent. Perhaps the worst embarrassment to George came from his sister, Caroline Matilda, who was married off to the insane Danish king, Christian VII. Caroline had a quite open affair with Johann Friedrich Struensee, Christian's physician, who, once Christian became all but an invalid, started to take the reins of Denmark's government. A coup orchestrated by Christian's stepmother and half-brother resulted in Struensee's execution and Caroline's banishment. George allowed her to take up residence in their ancestral land of Hanover, but Queen Caroline refused to let George take her back to Britain. Disgraced and embittered, Caroline died on May 11, 1775, at the age of just twenty-three.

Britain had been a constitutional monarchy since the Bloodless or Glorious Revolution of 1688 that drove the hated Catholic King James II off the throne and installed the Protestants Queen Mary II and William III. However, the monarch still had a certain role to play in the actual government and George seemed to handle political matters well enough. However, his liking for conservative and moderate policies brought him into opposition with the Whigs, who made their policy

[35] The Act is still in full effect to this day.

out of advocating popular economic and social reforms. Worse, George was saddled from 1770 to 1783 with Lord North, considered by many to be the worst Prime Minister in British history.

The most devastating crisis to shake North's government was the growing unrest caused by taxation on the American colonies. Although George himself advocated a firm but generally diplomatic course of action, the government fought back with an iron fist and war eventually broke out with the Battle of Bunker Hill on June 17, 1775. The dispute between the colonists and Britain became about far more than simply taxes and another war with France followed, brought on by King Louis XVI's backing of the rebels. Finally, the American war came to its conclusion at Yorktown on October 19, 1781, where George Washington's forces defeated the largest British army stationed in North America. Lord North resigned following the battle, dealing a death blow to the already dwindling support in Parliament for a continued war. Even though George commented bitterly that 'it may not in the end be an evil that [the colonists] become aliens to this kingdom', he eventually warmed to the idea of American independence and the war formally ended when both parties signed the Treaty of Paris on September 3, 1783.

The problem of the Revolutionary War paved the way for another memorable political crisis during George's reign. To gain more recruits for the army and navy, Parliament considered the Catholic Relief Act of 1778, which rescinded the draconian requirement that all men who volunteered to join the army had to swear an oath that they were Protestant. To our modern minds, this would seem a rather minor push against a disturbingly intolerant system. At the time, though, it was taken as a sign that the government was beginning to swing toward Catholicism. On June 2 1780, the London Protestant Association marched on Parliament with a petition against the Act, leading to widescale rioting in the city. Catholic churches were attacked and burned while Irishmen were harassed and beaten. Named after the writer of the original petition, George Gordon, the riots continued for seven days before they finally ended once military force was used. As many as 850 lives were lost before the disturbances were quelled.

George himself would be more directly touched by violence on August 2, 1786 when a woman named Margaret Nicholson, approaching the king on the pretext of handing him a petition, stabbed him with a dessert knife. The weapon was so dull it did not even pierce the skin and only cut his coat. When the king's guards tackled the woman, George protested, saying, 'The poor creature is mad. Do not hurt her. She has not hurt me.' If George was disturbed by the incident, he showed no sign. Instead he revealed the same cheerful calm in 1794, when an arrow struck through his private carriage, and in 1800, when he was shot at in a theatre.

What really cut through George's skin was the conduct of the Prince of Wales, who even as a teenager showed signs of becoming a royal louse. George tried his best to keep control over every aspect of his son's lifestyle, but once he turned twenty-one the Prince gained his own income and household. George's anxieties about what his son and heir could do to tarnish the monarchy's reputation proved absolutely justified when the Prince secretly married Maria Fitzherbert, a Catholic, an illegal act for members of the royal family. The marriage was made invalid with the passing of the Royal Marriages Act and in 1795 the Prince of Wales was lured by promises of a larger income into marrying his cousin, Caroline of Brunswick. The miserable, catastrophic marriage between the desolate Prince George and the headstrong Caroline sadly ended up causing more scandals than even George could have imagined.

George himself would one day become the center of embarrassing attention, which surely would have horrified him. In the summer of 1788, he became bedridden with sharp stomach pains, breathing difficulties and leg cramps. He seemed to make a full recovery soon after, but his behavior became increasingly erratic. There still did not seem to be any particular cause for alarm but then, on August 16, his illness returned with a vengeance. Along with almost unbearable pain in the stomach, the whites of his eyes became yellow and his urine dark but, far worse, his mental state became completely unpredictable.

Unable to concentrate, and given to moments where he would talk incessantly, George ordered that a servant read to him in a loud voice to try to counter this, but George would only talk over him. He soon found himself completely unable to control his speech. At church, he stood up during a sermon, threw his arms around his wife and daughters, and shouted, 'You know what it is to be nervous. But was you ever as bad as this?' Another time he babbled, 'I am nervous. I am not ill, but I am nervous. If you would know what is the matter with me, I am nervous.' The most tragic thing was that George was always painfully aware of his madness's onset. Once he laid his head on his son Frederick's shoulder and burst into tears, exclaiming, 'I wish to God I may die, for I am going to be mad.' Although the king still had times of self-control, he complained even in his lucidity of worsening vision problems and stiffness in his limbs, and talked so incessantly that he ran his throat raw and often had hallucinations. Once he thought his pillow was his deceased son Octavius. Sometimes he would become violently temperamental, shouting 'What! What! What!' at the top of his lungs while other days he would sink into a deep, brooding depression.

Naturally, the family found it rather hard to cope. At dinner one night, George suddenly leapt up from his seat, grabbed the Prince of Wales by his collar, and slammed him against a wall. He sometimes shouted insults at Queen Charlotte and frightened her so much that she started to spend her nights in a separate bedroom. He would also often treat Charlotte as if she were an imposter queen and Elizabeth Spencer, the Duchess of Pembroke, one of Charlotte's maids of honor, was the genuine article. He talked about Pembroke quite frankly, expressing thoughts his normal prudish self would repress, and whispered lewd if flattering things to her face.

An army of physicians and quacks was rallied to treat the King. According to medical theories at the time, the king could be cured if the 'black humours' were drawn from his brain. To accomplish that, leeches were pressed against his skin and blisters burned on his feet. Of course, the quackery never worked and probably only exacerbated the problem. For certain members of the government, the king's sickness had an additional sense of urgency. Backed by the opposition party, the Whigs, the Prince of Wales declared he would seek a regency in his father's name. Unless the king could be proven fit to rule, the Prince would get his wish, thus giving the opposition supremacy.

Finally the government called upon Dr Francis Willis, a former clergyman who turned to medicine and ran a mental institution in Lincolnshire. George, who always had a distrust of doctors, met Willis with a suspicious eye. When George was told that Willis was once in the clergy, he said to Willis, 'I am sorry for it. You have quitted a profession I have always loved, and you have embraced one I most heartily detest.'

Willis replied calmly, 'Sir, our Saviour Himself healed the sick.'

'Yes, yes, but He had not 700 pounds for it, hey!'

Believing that the key to restoring sanity was in once again instilling in his patient a sense of control, Willis treated George like a juvenile delinquent. If George became rowdy and bellowed, Willis would shout him down. Whenever George refused to eat, tore off his clothes, became violent or just knocked his sheets off his bed, he would be confined in a straitjacket and gagged.

What was the matter with the king? The most widely regarded modern diagnosis was made in 1969 by Ida Macalpine and Richard Hunter, two psychiatrists, in their book *King George and the Mad Business*. By examining his symptoms and similar physical problems shared by other members of the family, including the strange illness that killed George's sister Caroline Matilda, they deduced that George may have suffered from porphyria, a rare hereditary blood disease that can lead to paralysis and excruciating pain in the stomach and limbs as well as, in its very worst cases, hallucinations and mania. The telltale symptom for porphyria is dark colored or purple urine, which George often exhibited.

More likely because of a remission in the disease than Willis's treatment, George slowly began to recover, and was declared fit to rule by February of 1789, killing off the Prince of Wales's hopes of becoming regent. Sadly, even with this clean bill of health, George would never be the same again. He stayed physically frail and his vision continued to steadily deteriorate. He also threw the court and the government into a panic when he suffered a minor relapse on February 13, 1804.

Even with his sanity restored, the next years of George's rule would be dark ones. Napoleon Bonaparte had conquered George's ancestral land of Hanover and was determined to land in Britain or at least cripple the country economically by imposing trade embargos across Europe. The relationship between the Prince and Princess of Wales increasingly became a match made in Hell. Worst of all, the advent of the Industrial Revolution in Britain dragged the country into a period of marked social unrest.

Then there were tragedies closer to home. Amelia came down with tuberculosis by 1810 and had to be tended by her sister Mary. After Amelia died that year, George suffered a severe relapse. This time there seemed little hope of another recovery, so the Prince of Wales was at last made regent on February 6, 1811.

The king was shut away in Windsor Castle like a bad secret, where he continued his rapid physical and mental decay. Queen Charlotte was far from sympathetic. About the Queen's visits to him, their daughter Mary wrote, 'her unfortunate manner makes things worse'. As the king continued to fall apart, Charlotte could no longer bear the sight. After 1812, she never visited him again. However, her absence went unnoticed, because George had entered a fantasy world long before then. Wandering the halls of Windsor aimlessly, he had conversations with people who were long dead, including his lost children, Octavius and Amelia. At times, it seemed he even lost all sense of self. Once he remarked sadly, 'I must have a new suit of clothes and I will have them black in memory of King George III, for he was a good man.' He did not even respond when he learned that Queen Charlotte had died in late 1818. Two years later, he would follow her to the grave. Despite the illness and the neglect he suffered, he had lived to the age of eighty-one, becoming the longest reigning monarch in British history until his granddaughter Queen Victoria.

Further Reading

Andrews, Allen *The King Who Lost America: George III and Independence* (Doubleday, 1971)

Green, Vivian *The Madness of Kings: Personal Trauma and the Fate of Nations* (Sutton, 1993)

Hibbert, Christopher *George III: A Personal History* (Viking, 1998)

Macalpine, Ida and Hunter, Richard *George III and the Mad Business* (Pantheon Books, 1969)

THE BRITISH ISLES IN FILM AND LITERATURE

For Macbeth, there is of course William Shakespeare's play, even though the protagonist there is different to his real-life counterpart. The numerous adaptations and twists on the story/legend of Macbeth are too numerous to mention here.

Besides the original literature and many subsequent adaptations of *Robin Hood* and *Ivanhoe* which hold less than flattering depictions of John, there is also James Goldman's play, *The Lion in Winter*, a drama about the turbulent relationship between King Henry II, Eleanor of Aquitaine, and their sons. It was made into a 1968 film with Katharine Hepburn and Peter O'Toole, and a television mini-series in 2003, with Patrick Stewart and Glenn Close. One of Shakespeare's lesser-known histories is titled *King John* and centers around the murder of Arthur of Brittany.

Edward II was the subject of Christopher Marlowe's play *Edward II*. Derek Jarman directed a film also titled *Edward II* in 1991, which was based loosely on Marlowe's play and used the story of Edward and Gaveston as an allegory for the modern gay rights movement. A novel also focused on the tragedy of Edward II, *Men Loved Darkness: A Romance of Chivalry*, which was published in 1935 and was written by M.G. Richings.

One book offers the reader a chance to share in Richard II's lavish lifestyle: *To The King's Taste: Richard II's Book of Feasts and Recipes Adopted for Modern Cooking* by Lorna Sass. There was also a novel, *Within The Hollow Crown*, written by Margaret Barnes and published in 1947. Most famous of all is Shakespeare's play, which has been adapted for the stage and the screen numerous times.

Another part of Shakespeare's cycle of plays about the English monarchs is the three-part play *Henry VI*.

Following that is perhaps the most famous of Shakespeare's historical plays, *Richard III*, which has also been heavily adapted. One recent adaptation, made in 1995, stars Ian McKellen and stages the story in a fascist, 1940s England. A novel by Rosemary Hawlin Jarman, *We Speak No Treason*, gives a sympathetic portrayal of Richard.

Henry VIII, beside being the subject of another of Shakespeare's histories, has also recently been the topic for a pseudo-autobiography by Margaret George titled *The Autobiography of Henry VIII: With Notes By His Fool, Will Somers*. The saga of Henry and Anne Boleyn's relationship is told in Charles Jarrott's film *Anne of the Thousand Days*, based on a play by Maxwell Anderson and starring Richard Burton. Another person sacrificed for Henry's desires, Sir Thomas More, is the protagonist in 1966's *A Man For All Seasons*, directed by Fred Zinneman. All of Henry's wives are portrayed in 1971's popular BBC mini-series, *The Six Wives of Henry VIII*.

Mary, Bloody Mary by Carolyn Meyer is another pseudo-biography, this time about Queen Mary as a child. Mary also features heavily in the first episode of the classic BBC mini-series, *Elizabeth R*.

Alan Bennett's play, *The Madness of King George*, and the consequent 1994 movie, focuses on the first onset of madness of King George III.

SCANDINAVIA

ERIK 'BLOODAXE'

Reign: *933–934 (deposed)*
Born: *ca. 885*
Died: *954*

As his sobriquet suggests, Erik was a vicious but talented Viking lord, yet he was condemned to live in a time that was rapidly passing his kind by. The Dark Ages were giving way to the more stable Middle Ages, while his homeland of Norway was making the transition from a pagan backwater to a Christian kingdom. Indeed, Erik may very well have been one of the last great Vikings. In the Norse saga *Fagrskinna*, he is described as 'well-built and good looking . . . surly and taciturn, covetous and reckless, but a great and very successful warrior.' Such were the times, though, that martial skills were no longer enough to ensure success as a king.

Of the twenty sons of Harald 'Fair-Hair', the first king of a united Norwegian kingdom, Erik was the eldest and his father's favorite. Naturally then, even at a time when the law of primogeniture was not yet widely accepted among the monarchies of Europe, Erik came to take his father's throne. Apparently, he did not feel too secure on it, because soon after King Harald's death he murdered eighteen of his brothers.

With so many competitors for the crown, and being born at a time when familial affections were a liability, especially for the scion of a royal family, we can perhaps excuse Erik's spree of fratricides, but his people were not so understanding. Soon enough Erik was deemed a butcher and a tyrant, hard accusations for such a harsh age. His half-brother Haäkon, who was away being educated at the court of the King of England, Athelstan, and thus safe from Erik's bloodstained hand, was propped up as Erik's rival on his return to Norway . His experiences at the sophisticated English court not only made Haäkon more worldly than his brother but also a Christian, while his brother clung to the old pagan beliefs abandoned by much of Europe. A relic in his own homeland, Erik was overthrown in favor of Haäkon and was banished from Norway in 934.

However, the world had not yet been bled dry of opportunity for a warrior of Erik's stature and ability. After spending a few years sharpening his reputation on piracy, Erik established himself in the Orkneys, a cluster of islands off the coast of Scotland that had been home to Norwegian settlers since 874. From the Orkneys, he managed to continue leading piracy expeditions against anyone unlucky enough to come across him.

In 947, another opportunity knocked for Erik. Although the *witan*, or ruling council, of the kingdom of York in northern England had pledged their allegiance to the new southern English king, Eadred, the Archbishop of York, Wulfstan, invited Erik to claim the throne for himself. It is strange that a Christian priest would ask a mass-murdering, thieving heathen to rule his kingdom, but Wulfstan was very much at odds with King Eadred and hungry for any rival who could stand up on his own.

With Wulfstan's backing, Erik started his reign in York without much effort, but unfortunately not many people were ready to tolerate him any more than had the Norwegians. Not only did the English threaten to take back the kingdom, but Olaf Sitricson, one of many Viking chieftains established at Dublin, laid claim to York and stormed it with a healthy army backed by the King of Scotland, Malcolm I. Erik was beaten and York was Olaf's by 948.

Fortunately, Olaf proved as hated a ruler in York as Erik was in Norway, and he was soon exiled, leaving Erik to merely step in and take his old position again, undoubtedly with Wulfstan's ever-ready support. Even a tough, battle-hardened king like Erik, who was probably now into his sixties, must have looked forward to a quiet life by this point, but it was not to be. King Eadred managed to capture and jail Wulfstan, cutting off Erik's chief source of support.

Without Wulfstan to prop him up on the throne, Erik was once again driven out of York by 954. While making his way back to the Orkneys with his followers, he was ambushed by an English army and killed in the fighting. His wife Gunhild, described in some stories as a sorceress, and her sons Godred and Ragnfred, kept control over the Orkneys. For all his struggles and ambitions, Erik ended his life by just becoming proof for that old adage: 'He who lives by the sword, dies by the sword.'

Further Reading

Lawson, Karen *A History of Norway* (Princeton University Press, 1948)
Thomson, William P.L. *History of Orkney* (Mercat Press, 1987)

HARALD IV 'GILCHRIST'

Reign: *August 28, 1130–December 13, 1136*
Born: *1103*
Died: *December 13, 1136 (assassinated)*
Buried: *Christ Church, Bergen*

Although he was given a nickname that meant 'Servant of Christ', King Harald IV was never a man known for his piety. It is unsure if he came to Norway in 1127 as a skilled con artist or a lost heir, but either way he was destined to bring civil war to Norway. What Harald claimed when he traveled to Norway and presented himself to the royal court was possibly an unlikely truth, but also just as possibly a careful lie. He had said that the Norwegian king, Magnus 'Barefoot', had fathered him on a young Irish barmaid when he visited Ireland in 1103.

Despite the less than prestigious background of his mother, the fact that Harald was very much Irish in appearance and that his language of choice remained Gaelic (throughout his life he could speak only a broken Norwegian),meant that his claim to be the illegitimate son of the old King Magnus was entertained by the living king of Norway, Sigurd, Harald's alleged half-brother. Harald was bad-tempered and cocky, but he also had a magnetic personality, so Sigurd, soon won over by his charisma, gave Harald a chance to prove his royal heritage beyond a doubt through the medieval ritual of trial by ordeal. Without the slightest reluctance, Harald jumped at the chance, even though it meant he had to walk over red-hot plowshares. Apparently Harald passed this test without serious injury, for next he was given a lofty position in Sigurd's court. King Sigurd did have the foresight to force Harald to swear an oath that he would never challenge the claim of his own son Magnus to the throne. It was a prudent precaution, perhaps, but a naïve one.

After the death of Sigurd in 1130, Harald was popular enough to summon a *thing*, or council, and coerce them into proclaiming him King of Norway, even after the young Magnus had already been crowned. From then on two rival courts existed side by side in Norway. To clear up the confusion, civil war finally broke out in 1134. Although Harald was driven out of the country at first, he quickly enlisted the ambitious Danish king, Erik II, to his cause and then the course of the war was decided. Magnus was captured, stripped of his authority, blinded and then imprisoned in a monastery. Even with his throne assured, Harald was no more merciful to Magnus's followers. One bishop who could not reveal to Harald the location of some treasures hidden by Magnus when he was king was hanged like a common criminal after he refused to pay the hefty fee Harald demanded in compensation.

Magnus was not the only rival Harald had to cope with. Sigurd Slembediakn, an adventurer, claimed, like Harald, to have been an illegitimate son of King Magnus 'Barefoot' and, also like Harald, he 'proved' his special blood through trial by ordeal. This time, Harald refused to repeat old King Sigurd's mistake by acknowledging this new Sigurd. Instead, he had him subjected to a mock trial and condemned to death for a suspected murder that had taken place during his travels.

Late one night at his prison, Sigurd was taken out to a river by Harald's men where a boat waited for them. He was told that the king had ordered him to be transported to another jail, but Sigurd was no fool and realized that they were there to drown him. Acting on his instincts, he managed to overpower the guards through brute force and consign his escorts to the fate they had intended for him.

Much to Harald's dismay, Sigurd then went into hiding. Harald cannot have been too concerned since he allowed himself a few peaceful nights of debauchery while Sigurd was still on the run. One night, Harald's royal apartments were broken into by Sigurd and a handful of followers. They murdered King Harald in his sleep and managed to escape before the guards took notice. After the deed was done, Sigurd liberated the old King Magnus, now called 'the Blind', from his monastery and propped him up on the throne.

Unfortunately, Sigurd did not account for the sons of his old rival, legitimate and illegitimate, who were all simultaneously proclaimed king: Inge Crookback, Sigurd II Mund and Eystein II. Although all three were very young, they had considerable support behind them and Sigurd was driven out of Norway and forced to resume his old occupation of adventuring. If he entertained thoughts of once again pushing for the crown, he did not have the chance. Eventually Sigurd's skills failed him and he ended up in enemy hands, where he suffered a horrific death by slow torture.

Further Reading

Lawson, Karen *A History of Norway* (Princeton University Press, 1948)

Sturlusun, Snorri (trans. William Morris and Eirík Magnusson) *The Stories of the Kings of Norway, called The Round World (Heimskringla)* (B. Quaritch, 1893-1905)

CHRISTIAN II

Reign: *July 22, 1513–January 20, 1523*
(as King of Denmark and Norway);
November 1, 1520–August 1521
(as King of Norway)
Born: *July 1, 1481*
Died: *January 1559*
Buried: *St Canute's Church, Odense*

Despite sometimes being remembered as 'the Cruel', King Christian II's name also conjures up stories of a 'man of the people'. He even fell in love with a less than aristocratic woman named Dyveke, the daughter of a widowed Norwegian shopkeeper originally from Amsterdam, Sigbrit Willumsdatter, and kept her as his mistress for as long as she lived. Christian's sympathy for the common man went hand in hand with his pathological distrust and loathing of the aristocracy and the clergy, which eventually culminated in the infamous Stockholm

Massacre, an event that helped push Sweden along the path toward independence.

Since the Kalmar Union of 1397, the countries of Denmark, Norway and Sweden were peacefully united under one monarchy, thanks to dynastic circumstances, , which, by the time of Christian's father, King Hans, had become Danish. To prepare him for his future role, Hans made Christian, then in his late teens, Viceroy (and eventually king) of Norway, where he had first met Dyveke. Even at such an early age, Christian was given to unpredictable mood swings and wild outbursts of temper, and was suspicious of everyone in power. Distrustful, and perhaps a bit apprehensive, of the native Norwegian nobility, he stripped many of them of their titles and lands, conferring them instead on his Danish friends.

After inheriting the Danish throne from his father on February 21, 1513, Christian decided for politics' sake to marry Isabel, the sister of the Holy Roman Emperor, Charles V, on August 12, 1515. Christian's love affair with Dyveke was known even to the Emperor himself, who made two demands: first, that Christian banish Dyveke from court, and, second, that he shave off his uncouth and unfashionable red beard. Christian did neither, but Isabel was sent off to her Danish groom regardless. Like an unwanted pet, the new bride had nothing to do but sulk as Christian refused to leave Dyveke's side.

Isabel luckily found help from an unexpected source, Dyveke's own mother. Sigbrit had a place at the royal court where she not only was seen to advise the young king, but even to lecture him whenever he did something she found grating, including not performing his marital duties with Isabel. Sigbrit would stay an important advisor to Christian II even after tragedy struck with the death of Dyveke in the summer of 1517. Christian needed to hold someone accountable for the death and, rightly or wrongly, a nobleman named Torbern was accused by Christian of giving Dyveke a basket of poisoned cherries. Following an old Nordic ritual, Christian had Torbern tried by twelve peasants from a village. Found guilty, Torbern's punishment was also a homage to ancient custom: his hand was chopped off.

That same year, the Kalmar Union had begun to unravel in Sweden. Sten Sture, the young and much loved Viceroy of Sweden, had the Archbishop Gustav Trolle, a rival of Sture and a staunch supporter of Christian II, imprisoned. It was a direct challenge to Christian's authority, one that had to receive a loud answer. On January 29, 1518, Christian led his army to Stockholm, but was forced to the negotiating table when he discovered that his army lacked supplies. A temporary truce was agreed upon by both parties and Christian graciously invited Sture to a conference in Denmark. To Sture's surprise, Christian even offered hostages to ensure his good intentions. He remained wary of Christian, however, and made an exact counter offer inviting Christian to discuss terms in Sweden. Sture's fears would be vindicated. Although Christian seemed to agree to Sture's demands at first, he broke his oath once Sture's hostages were handed over and fled to Denmark with them securely in tow. One of those hostages was the nobleman Gustav Vasa, who, unknown to Christian, would play a large role in the years to come.

Returning from Denmark with fresh men, Christian fought Sture at the Battle of Börgerund on January 19, 1520. This time Christian had the upper hand and Sture soon died from wounds inflicted during the fighting. Sture's wife, Christina Gyllenst, refused to surrender Stockholm until September 7, after the Danish navy had worn down the city's resistance through a blockade.

The first day of that November, Christian decided to capitalize on his victory and had himself formally crowned as King of Sweden. Underneath the happy and regal face he put on for the coronation festivities, however, Christian was terrified of more problems from another Sten Sture and felt that, in order to safeguard his interests and even his life, the entire Swedish nobility had to be obliterated. On November 7, various noblemen and women, as well as the leading citizens of Stockholm, were summoned with no explanation to the royal palace. Once everyone was assembled, the exits were suddenly sealed and the Archbishop Trolle emerged. With a booming voice, he accused all present of crimes against himself and, by extension, the Church. Therefore all there were not merely guilty of treason against their king, but heresy.

As punishment, Trolle ordered that they pay a ludicrous, impossible sum, 500,000 marks, in compensation and allow themselves to be judged and condemned at the king's pleasure. After a brief period of imprisonment and a kangaroo court where all were sentenced to die, they – eighty-two people – were led on November 8 to Stortonget, the main public square, and beheaded. Sture's corpse, and that of a deceased child of his, were dug up and burned along with the bodies of the victims. The slaughter extended outside of Stockholm as Christian allowed his soldiers to sack the countryside, including the religious houses. One group of nuns who fell prey to Christian's men were said to have been brutalized and then drowned.

Strangely enough, Christian followed this gleeful bloodbath with a friendly tour of the Low Countries in the summer of the next year. He made the most of his tour, as he hobnobbed with famous Flemish artists and had dinner with the celebrated Dutch humanist Erasmus. However, Christian betrayed something of his brusque philosophy with Erasmus when he said to him, 'Mild measures are of no use. The remedies that give the whole body a good shaking are the best and surest.'

This journey must have deeply inspired Christian, for his actions afterward were more like those of an enlightened monarch. For instance, he outlawed the practice of selling and trading peasants like cattle, quite a radical act at the time. But despite his newfound progressivism, the Swedish, now led by Gustav Vasa, who had escaped imprisonment in Denmark to find that his father was among those killed during the Stockholm Massacre, began to rebel against Denmark the same year Christian was busy with his tour.

Although Christian was determined not to let Sweden slip through his fingers, his efforts to keep a grip were in vain. The Stockholm Massacre had shattered any desire for the Kalmar Union that was left. Finally, at Strägnäs on June 6, 1523, Gustav Vasa was crowned the King of Sweden, thus breaking all ties with Denmark and Norway. Before that fateful outcome, though, the Swedish war for independence had already proved the final blow to Christian. After years of dodging his dangerous shifts in temper and coping with his condescending treatment, Christian's nobles formally renounced their loyalty to him on January 20, 1523 and replaced him on the throne with his uncle Frederick. On April 13, with Sigbrit and his family, Christian sailed away from Copenhagen to Germany. As his boat moved toward the horizon, a crowd of people came out of their homes and watched the royal family flee the country in a thick silence.

Christian remained in Germany, hoping for financial and military aid from his brother-in-law the Emperor, but he always came away empty-handed. While waiting day and night for any good word from the imperial court, Christian personally heard Martin Luther preach on one occasion and may have even been so moved he converted to Lutheranism, but pragmatism overcame piety and he just as quickly renounced the new faith so as not to annoy the staunchly Catholic Emperor. If that was his reason, it was a futile gesture. Charles V refused even to pay the dowry he owed to Christian for the marriage to Isabel and so the former royal family lived in near poverty while Christian tried to gather an army of mercenaries to help recover his throne. Despite the dire circumstances and Christian's past treatment of her, Isabel stayed loyal. When Christian's uncle, now King Frederick I of Denmark, offered Isabel a pension if she returned to Denmark without her husband, a kind offer made out of fear that she could actually convince her brother to restore Christian to the throne, she replied, 'Where my king is, there is my kingdom.' Unfortunately, Christian would not benefit from her steadfast devotion. She died not long after the German banishment at the age of twenty-six, followed shortly by their son Hans.

By late 1531, Christian had at last assembled an army of mercenaries ready to try to reclaim his throne and landed at Norway. The Norwegians, willing to prove their loyalty to him, proclaimed him king on November 29. Unfortunately, this turnaround was not to last. Danish forces loyal to Frederick I invaded Norway and Christian had no choice but to surrender the kingship on July 1, 1532. Christian hoped to negotiate a satisfactory settlement with his uncle, who seemed eager to comply, but unfortunately he did not suspect that the same trick he once tried to use on a young man named Sten Sture was now being pulled on him. On the pretext of meeting with his uncle, Christian allowed himself to be taken to Denmark, but was then thrown into a dirty cell in Sønderburg Castle. Later he was transferred to Kalundburg Castle, where he received much better treatment and was even allowed servants of his own, but he would remain a prisoner there for seventeen more years before he died an unhappy and obscure death.

Perhaps the personal tragedy and political failure that dogged him for the last decades of his life were just punishment for the atrocities he inflicted, but many rulers before and since have participated in similar deeds and still their reputations have survived their deaths almost unscathed. The career of Christian II may prove that the ends, not the means, are what separate heroes from villains in history's eyes.

Further Reading

Dunkley, E.H. *The Reformation in Denmark* (S.P.C.K., 1948)

Lauring, Palle (trans. David Hohnen) *A History of Denmark* (London, 1972)

ERIK XIV[36]

Reign: *September 30, 1560–January 26, 1569*
Born: *December 13, 1533*
Died: *February 26, 1577 (murdered)*
Buried: *Västerås Cathedral, Domkryka*

The Vasa dynasty that spawned Erik was stuck in a precarious situation when he came to the throne. His father Gustav was the spearhead of a movement to break away from Denmark and Norway, all united under a single monarchy since the Kalmar Union of 1397. To put a firm foundation to Sweden's independence, Erik's father Gustav Vasa was crowned King of Sweden on June 6, 1523, but even after that he seemed to have cause to fear his own nobles, who never forgot

[36] The number 'XIV' was more based on Johannes Magnus's fictional *History of the Goths*, which Erik translated himself when he was later imprisoned, than on actual historical fact that would have made Erik only about the seventh king of that name. Erik probably believed in the accuracy of the *History of the Goths*, but the use of XIV gave the new Swedish monarchy a stronger sense of continuity.

that the Vasas actually had nothing more to recommend them to kingship than any other Swedish aristocratic family.

As though he was trying to compensate for the Vasas' mediocre origins, Gustav saw to it that Erik had an education his sharp mind could make the most out of. By the time he was an adult, Erik became fluent in Latin, French, Finnish, German, Spanish and Italian, and even picked up a little Greek and Hebrew. He also took an active interest in architecture, science and rhetoric, and proved to have a special gift for the latter. When he came to the throne, he was only twenty-seven and was a handsome and energetic man, if somewhat neurotic, moody and over-conscious of his royal prestige. For one thing, he was the first Swedish king to adopt the honorific of 'Majesty'. Few suspected at the time that these were more than character flaws, but symptoms of an illness that would develop as his reign moved on, a mental sickness also shared by his brother Magnus, who became helplessly insane in adulthood.

Even before he was crowned and anointed, Erik had his heart set on Queen Elizabeth of England as his consort. Erik's obsession with her made him one of her most persistent suitors, and he pestered her with lengthy love letters in Latin. When it came to Erik's attention that Elizabeth supposedly had a lover, Robert Dudley, he contemplated having him assassinated or challenging him to a duel. He was only dissuaded from the latter idea when he was told that a man like Dudley was made unworthy by his lowly birth to be so challenged by a king. Despite Erik's persistent wooing, the 'Virgin Queen' never failed to live up to her reputation. She always found the young king irritating and presumptuous, but never so much as when he made preparations, which were never completed, to sail to England to court the queen in person. The English people, though, were a bit warmer to the idea. When word of the possible voyage got out, shopkeepers in London sold woodcuts that depicted the Queen of England and the King of Sweden sitting side by side on twin thrones. Still given the cold shoulder by Elizabeth, Erik tried to make her jealous by hinting in one of his letters about marriage

negotiations with her cousin, Mary, Queen of Scots, and a German princess, Christina of Hesse. Inevitably, though, even Erik could take the hint. Much to the dismay of his subjects, he instead married Karin Månsdotter, a barmaid and the daughter of a jailer.

Matters more important than love demanded Erik's attention. Despite the fact that Sweden was opening hostilities with Poland, his brother Johan asked for the hand of Katarina, a sister of the Polish king. Even worse, he gave his new father-in-law a substantial loan at the exact same time he claimed to be too poor to help fund Erik's military campaign in Estonia. Holding back his suspicions, Erik reluctantly gave his blessing to the couple in the spring of 1562. When that summer Poland and Sweden were on the verge of war, Johan indiscreetly brought his marriage forward to October 4 that year, which proved the final straw with Erik. Under the Articles of Aborga that had been composed by King Gustav to clip the wings of the aristocracy, Johan was judged guilty of treason and was determined, after being condemned by a meeting of his peers or a *rikstag*, to have forfeited his place in the succession, his property and his life. Erik was feeling fraternal enough not to claim the last thing, but he did have his brother and his sister-in-law placed under house arrest at Gripsholm on August 12. Their servants, on the other hand, were not so lucky. About thirty of them were executed for 'encouraging' their master's misbehavior.

Perhaps affected by his brother's actions, even though Johan was probably guilty more of stupidity than treason, and by the war with Poland, which eventually dragged in Denmark as well, Erik's behavior became increasingly unhinged. Fiercely protective of the dignity of the crown, Erik deemed that painting the royal arms upside down was a punishable offense and one time he had his chamberlain arrested for accidentally breaking the royal scepter. Erik believed that anyone who whispered, laughed or cleared their throat in his presence was mocking him since he started to think that not only the nobles at court, but his own servants disrespected and despised him. When he lost the notes to a speech he was going to make, Erik screamed at his secretaries for scheming behind his back to make him look like a fool.

Jöran Persson, the king's right hand and an ambitious man of middle class origins, worked hard to make the situation that much worse. Under Jöran, men were constantly fined or even sentenced to die for crimes of treason against the king, real and imagined. He was never reluctant to apply torture to the occasional servant who needed some encouragement to confess their master's and mistress's involvement in a conspiracy, even if such evidence had to be embellished now and then.

At last Erik completely lost his sanity on May 26, 1566 when he visited his rivals, the influential Sture family, who had been imprisoned at Uppsala Castle along with a few other political prisoners. The king at first begged the forgiveness of Svante, whose son Nels had been implicated in a plot against the monarchy[37]. Then Jöran walked to Erik's side, whispering something in Erik's ear. No one but Erik heard what Jöran said, but whatever it was it immediately caused Erik to rush out of the castle. He returned later, visibly agitated, and got into an argument with Nels Sture himself. The argument did not last long before Erik suddenly brandished a knife and stabbed Nels to death. Without a word Erik then ran outside and leaped on his horse, shouting orders as he rode off that every prisoner inside the castle was to be put to death except a 'Herr Sten'. None of the guards were sure whom he meant, but two men with that name were spared the coming massacre thanks to that one incoherent order.

Hallucinating that he was pursued by relentless enemies, Erik rode his horse aimlessly around the countryside. An old tutor of his found him and tried to calm him, but Erik, imagining he was an assassin, killed him. Afterwards, he rode into a forest, where he roamed throughout the night in terror. When Erik finally returned to his castle, he blamed Jöran, perhaps not unjustly, for what happened at

[37] Specifically Nels Sture had met secretly with a group of other nobles to discuss their grievances against the king.

Uppsala Castle and had him stripped of his powers, imprisoned and sentenced to be executed. He also freed his brother Johan but, when Johan came to pay his respects, Johan had a relapse. Believing that he had been deposed and Johan was now king, Erik knelt to him, while Johan was trying to do the exact same thing to Erik.

Although he suffered long moods of depression, Erik seemed to have recovered his senses by January of 1568. Unfortunately, his madness was not forgotten and finally the nobility was pushed to drastic action when Erik not only pardoned the hated Jöran, but gave him a title and raised him to the nobility. Erik's paranoid fantasies were at last fulfilled when his brothers Johan and Karl raised the standard against him. Jöran was captured and murdered through slow torture. Erik himself was finally deposed, leaving his brother to be crowned King Johan III.

As for the former king, he was shuffled from prison to prison, each one worse and more degrading than the last. Although he still had the presence of mind to translate Johannes Magnus's *History of the Goths* from Latin into Swedish , the increasingly harsh conditions he endured at last caused him to lapse into complete insanity. He died on February 24, 1577 from arsenic poisoning, a fact verified by a modern examination. His wife Karin and son Gustav were somewhat luckier. Karin was generously given a fairly large Finnish estate by the Swedish government. Gustav moved to Russia where he half-heartedly entertained notions of reclaiming his father's throne until he died in 1607.

Further Reading

Roberts, Michael *The Early Vasas: A History of Sweden, 1523-1611* (Cambridge University Press, 1968)

Green, Vivian *The Madness of Kings: Personal Trauma and the Fate of Nations* (Sutton, 1993)

CHRISTIAN VII

Reign: *January 14, 1766–March 13, 1808*
Born: *January 29, 1749*
Died: *March 13, 1808*
Buried: *Roskilde Cathedral, Domkirke*

The Lex Regia of 1665 gave the monarchy of Denmark more power than almost any other in Europe at the time. All of Denmark and all Danish possessions were considered the private property of the king, to do with as he pleased. Any and all major political acts could pass only with his personal approval. Fortunately for the people of Denmark, these incredible privileges were rarely abused. King Frederick V, reclusive and debauched as he was, had the good sense to curtail his own influence. Unfortunately, his son and heir, who would become King Christian VII, suffered from severe mental illness, causing the absolutist power of the Danish monarchy to fall into unlikely hands.

Although much of Christian's insanity probably derived from biological sources, he also had to endure a bleak childhood that no doubt had much to do with his problems in adulthood. His mother, Louisa of Hanover, died when Christian was only a toddler. He gained a stepmother, Juliana of Brunswick, but she preferred to pour her attentions into her own sickly son by King Frederick, named after his father. After he turned six, Christian was put under the charge of Ditlev Reventlow, a rough and physically intimidating man who beat Christian until he collapsed to the floor for the slightest offense, even for just forgetting something. Contemptuously Reventlow liked to call his young charge his 'doll'. Once Christian reached adolescence, his life improved once he was given a new tutor, Elie-Solomon Reverdil, a kindly Swiss scholar who would find himself taking care of a prince who was already badly educated and emotionally stunted by Reventlow's abuse.

Reverdil tried his best to turn the tide and make up for the years under Reventlow, but Christian remained a poor and difficult student. Given a pathological obsession with his masculinity because of Reventlow's beatings and demeaning insults, Christian hated his short and slender body and sought to toughen it through exercise and by subjecting himself to a great deal of physical pain. In fact, Christian's habits bordered on the sadomasochistic even in adolescence. One of his favorite games as a boy involved mock executions and tortures. He even had his own 'toy' rack on which he asked his playmates to beat him until he bled.

Another of Christian's typical pastimes involved playing pranks on women in his court. He threw sugar over the head of his dreary grandmother Sophia Magdalena and hurled a hot cup of tea in the face of one noblewoman. He did enjoy reading, but only cheap French novels about romance and adventure. Often he tried to imitate his literary heroes and prove his manliness by prowling the streets of Copenhagen with a gang, harassing passers-by and beating up watchmen. On a wall in his bedroom, Christian proudly kept as a trophy a club he stole from one watchman he and his friends successfully thrashed .

On November 11, 1766, Christian was wed to Caroline Matilda, the sister of King George III of Britain. By then, he already had a favorite mistress, Sløvet Katherine, who accompanied Christian everywhere in public and was created a baroness. On top of this, Christian believed that staying faithful to his new bride would be unfashionable and make him the subject of ridicule. As a French ambassador commented, '. . . how can [Matilda] please a man who quite seriously believes that it does not look well for a husband to love his wife?'

Although Matilda found herself isolated in the strange Danish court, a problem not helped by her libertine husband, she found a formidable ally and substitute mother in her lady-in-waiting, Madame von Plessen, who railed against Christian's treatment of Matilda. Plessen frequently referred to Christian as the 'Sultan' and was heard to say aloud, 'His Majesty's conduct towards the Queen was of the kind only tolerated in brothels.' Plessen encouraged Matilda to play the angry wife in retaliation and reject Christian's advances, but this only succeeded in turning Christian's frigid apathy toward his wife into bitter hatred. Still, they must have been able to put up with each other enough since on January 28, 1768, Matilda gave birth to an heir, the future Frederick VI.

Christian was not unaware of what Plessen whispered about him and started to plot his revenge. One snowy day while the royal court were enjoying themselves at a park just outside of Copenhagen, Christian graciously offered Plessen a ride in his sled. Thinking he wanted an opportunity to apologize to her for his treatment of both her and Matilda, Plessen stepped on but, just as soon as she settled into the sled, Christian rushed off at a breakneck speed. Suddenly he forced the horses to a stop, making the sled overturn. Christian managed to leap out, but Plessen was not so fast and fell into a ditch.

Pretending to be trying to pull her up, he pushed her down a slope, pulling off her dress and tearing her clothes as his companions, who were told by Christian what he was planning, laughed hysterically at the sight. After that 'accident', Christian removed Plessen from Matilda's household without giving her a chance to say farewell to her mistress, but he was so afraid of the queen's reaction that he gave the order from another palace.

Matilda would score a victory against her husband eventually. Christian's affair with Sløvet, never popular to begin with thanks to her lower class background, began to spark outrage when he appeared in public everywhere with her but not his wife. He even dismissed Reverdil, since he objected to the affair after Christian gave Sløvet her own castle. Something was finally done about the Sløvet 'problem' when the Prime Minister convinced Christian that the populace was in revolt and could only be satisfied by Sløvet's banishment. Christian, who like all braggarts was really a coward at heart, not only agreed to the banishment, but had Sløvet sent to a women's prison where she would be kept in a tiny, dirty cell for three years. He cried when he heard stories about the nightmare existence he put her in, but did nothing to end it.

By June 6, 1768, Christian decided on a whim to embark on a diplomatic tour of England and France, without his wife. Although Matilda looked forward to seeing her homeland and family again, Christian refused even to think about taking her with him, much to her anger. Instead he allowed the new court physician, Dr. Johann Friedrich Struensee, a middle-class German doctor brought to the court by one of Christian's friends, to join in the travels. Struensee had a corpulent but very tall form that complimented his brilliant mind and his extravagant personality. One intriguing trait he had that was commented on was the habit of reading in bed by the light of two candles kept in the hands of a human skeleton.

When Christian arrived in the British Isles, his reputation had already preceded him and he helped along the gossip by behaving in a less than regal manner. Aloud he uttered after he reached Canterbury, 'the last king of Denmark who entered Canterbury laid that city in ashes and massacred its inhabitants.' In London, Christian and his compatriots spent their evenings at balls, plays, and other social functions, where he continued to make a bad impression, especially on his uptight brother-in-law King George III. One lady observed that, at an opera no less, Christian 'picked his Nose which you know is neither graceful nor royal'. Another night, when Christian came to see a comedy titled *The Provok'd Wife*, Horace Walpole wrote to a friend 'he clapped whenever there was a Sentence against matrimony – a very civil proceeding when his wife is an English princess!' Like modern rock stars, Christian and his compatriots completely trashed their lodgings once they were through with them. After weeks of this kind of behavior, Christian had overstayed his welcome as far as his brother-in-law was concerned. George III one day invited Christian to a 'farewell party'. Fortunately, even Christian could take the hint. The Danish king would find a friendlier and livelier reception across the Channel where King Louis XV and his courtiers at Versailles indulged him with expensive gifts and nights of debauchery. But the people in Louis' court began to notice that something was odd about the Danish king: for one thing, Christian would on occasion start babbling in an almost completely incoherent speech.

Although he had abandoned her for this trip, Christian returned from his journey with a new appreciation for his wife, perhaps brought on by his newfound love for all things English. Although he did keep a new favorite mistress, Birsette von Gabel, Matilda discovered that she could excite Christian's attentions by playing on his craving for masculinity. She became fond of dressing up in a man's riding outfit, something that was always guaranteed to arouse Christian's interest.

That October, Matilda fell ill and Christian, overcome with concern for his now precious wife, put the trusted Struensee in charge of her treatment. At first, Matilda refused to let him see her, since she associated Struensee with those riotous friends of

Christian's she hated, but she became intrigued by Struensee's open, personal approach[38] and his methods, which were so very different from the quackery that passed for professional medicine at the time. Under his watch, she made a full recovery, and Struensee was promptly rewarded with even more prestige.

As the symptoms noticed in Louis XV's court grew worse and Christian began to slide into madness, Matilda came to call on Struensee more and more. She even allowed Struensee to vaccinate Prince Frederick against smallpox, which was considered a dangerous procedure at the time. The two became closer until at last the nineteen-year-old queen became so entranced with the doctor that she began an affair with him. If Christian had the presence of mind to understand that his wife was cheating on him right under his nose, he gave no sign. In fact, the three of them became a strange sort of family, having dinners and appearing at public functions together. As Reverdil, who was eventually recalled to court to take care of the mentally deteriorating king, wrote, '[Matilda] hardly took her eyes off [Struensee], insisted on his presence at all gatherings, and allowed him, publicly, to take liberties which would have ruined the reputation of any ordinary woman, such as riding in her coach and walking alone with her in the garden and woods.' Even more drastic to Denmark was Christian's own faith in the doctor. On July 15, 1771, Christian gave Struensee's orders as much 'validity as those drawn by our own hand'. Now it was this middle-class German doctor, not King Christian VII, who ruled Denmark.

Although Struensee and Matilda worked hard to make sure that no one outside the court knew how badly Christian's mind had deteriorated, it was obvious to anyone who had any degree of access to the king's presence that he was even less fit to rule than

[38] Struensee's techniques were literally revolutionary for the time. In those days upper class etiquette forbade doctors even from asking their royal patients about their symptoms.

before. Christian was consumed with hallucinations so vivid he was no longer certain of even his parentage. Sometimes he thought he was really the son of the King of Sardinia or that Empress Catherine II of Russia or even his wife Matilda was his real mother. He was convinced at least that he was illegitimate, although examinations between Christian VII's portrait and that of his father Frederick V show enough of a striking similarity to disprove his illusions. He did sometimes become faintly aware that Matilda was having an affair, but he swore she was sleeping with the King of Prussia, not Struensee.

Christian's sadomasochism began to reach new heights. He would run around for hours on end until he became completely exhausted. Fancying that he could make his skin invulnerable to gunfire, he kept burning and freezing it to accomplish this. It became a normal habit for him to bang his fists against walls until they bled. On several occasions he vandalized his own royal apartments, smashing windows and breaking up furniture. One day he threw everything from one of his rooms out of a window to the ground below and had to be physically stopped from throwing a friend and a dog down as well.

Christian's most colorful fantasies involved a tough-as-nails mistress named La Roquer, who accompanied him on expeditions into Copenhagen where they broke into houses and murdered their inhabitants, and threw themselves into drunken fist fights. One servant, Muranti, indulged Christian by wrestling him, but others were not so ready to accept Christian's desperate challenges.

Once at dinner he threatened a minister and a friend of Struensee, Count Enevold Brandt, shouting, 'I am going to thrash you, Count, do you hear me?' Brandt said nothing as Matilda and Struensee lectured the king like a child for his outburst, but Christian continued raving, 'He is a poltroon, and I will make him submit to my will.' Later that evening, Brandt quietly walked up to Christian's room and challenged him to a fight. Brandt, a powerfully strong man, took Christian down effortlessly and 'battered him without pity . . . he cursed him, wrestled with him and reduced him to asking for quarter. At last he left him much bruised and even more terrified.'

Luckily no emotion ever stayed on the king's mind for long. Christian's moods frequently shifted from mania to depression, from megalomaniacal fantasies to suicidal urges. Often he stayed in a stupor and, during dinner, if he began to stir, Reverdil was instructed to lead him away to his room. Once when Reverdil took Christian outside for a walk, the king spoke of his overwhelming desire to kill himself and added sadly, 'There is a noise in my head' and 'I am not quite myself.'

Meanwhile Struensee had been made a Count and in Christian VII's name he introduced radical reforms into Denmark. For the first time, illegitimate children were no longer to be treated like second-class citizens, an end was brought to the censorship of the press, and other sweeping reforms were brought to church and state. Struensee's influence was even felt in how the Crown Prince was raised. He was given a playmate of his own age whom he had to treat as his equal and a little garden that he alone was responsible for, things historians alleged helped make him into a better king. If Struensee's progressive policies sparked more resentment than he bargained for, the indiscreet affair with Queen Caroline Matilda really conjured the demon of bad public opinion. The outrage got worse after Matilda gave birth to a daughter on July 1, 1771, Princess Louise, whom gossip christened the child of Struensee. Vicious as these rumors were, they may have had a solid basis; a careful look at the portraits of Louise and Struensee reveals more than several common physical traits. Matilda herself was conscious of the harsh rumors spreading around and said to one of her ladies-in-waiting, 'I know what you say of me, I don't care – to be unfaithful to a husband one has been forced to marry is not a crime.'

The distant noise of a coming coup could be heard so vividly that during a dinner party one night Struensee, Matilda and their friends calmly discussed what they would do if they were made to flee the country. Their gloomy expectations were finally fulfilled around four in the morning on January 18, 1772, when Christian's stepmother Juliana, half-brother Frederick and a small group of nobles tried to get to Christian's room, but were stopped from entering by an imposing valet. When the valet proved unmoved by bribes and threats, Juliana nearly fainted while Frederick collapsed terrified into a chair. Only one of the conspirators, Count Carl Rantzau, had the presence of mind to convince the valet that a revolt was breaking out and that they had to warn the king right away. When they were finally allowed into the king's presence, Juliana repeated to Christian that the people were uprising. Already frightened half to death by this strange crowd of people who were suddenly standing over his bed, Christian cried out, 'Terrible! Terrible! Where should I go? What should I do?'

Juliana replied with a reassuring smile, 'Sign these papers and Your Majesty's life will be saved.'

Christian noticed that his wife's name was on these mysterious papers and for a minute refused to sign. He then tried to get out of bed to leave, but someone pushed him back down and the pen was forced into his hand. Easily frightened, Christian signed all the papers without a further fuss. These were only to be the first of many papers Juliana and her faction would ask him to sign. Christian never had any idea what he was signing, but he found the task a fun chore and became delighted when Juliana told him that some of the papers even had to do with executions.

The condemned men were to be Struensee and Brandt, now both imprisoned in small cells at the Citadel. Matilda, meanwhile, was placed under a life sentence of imprisonment at the palace of Aalborg. Christian, who never knew about the arrests, kept asking for his wife and one night he escaped from his apartments. Before the guards finally caught up with him, he was on the verge of boarding a coach to go off looking for his dear Matilda.

Days after he found himself in prison, Struensee renounced his own Deism and became a Lutheran. There were allegations that Struensee's change of heart came more from the hope that his newfound religious convictions would inspire a pardon. If that was his plan, it was a bad one. On April 27, 1772, he and Brandt were beheaded before the very eyes of Juliana, who crowed that she was only unhappy that Matilda would not be joining her lover.

Had he lived, Struensee might have been pleased to see that his liberal policy was sorely missed. Although the junta set up by Juliana rescinded most of Struensee's reforms, she and her son Frederick became so unpopular she found herself obliged to revive many of the doctor's measures or run the danger of a coup herself. The people of Denmark had come to appreciate the doctor's progressive philosophy only after he was already out of power and dead. Matilda had good cause to bitterly reflect on the fickleness of human nature. She would, fortunately, win a significant victory when the courts decided that Prince Frederick, who resembled Christian in any case, and Princess Louise were both legitimate.

Matilda might have remained a prisoner of the Danish government for her entire life if her brother had not put diplomatic pressure on the country. Always eager to preserve her already tenuous grip on the government, Juliana complied with George III's requests with a bowed head and released Matilda, but the courts annulled her marriage to Christian VII, so she was no longer legally the Queen of Denmark. As though separation from her son and one-year old daughter were not punishment enough, Matilda's sister-in-law, Charlotte, put her foot down and made George promise not to allow Matilda with her sour reputation to set one foot on British soil. Denied even the comfort of her homeland, Matilda had no choice but to go to her family's ancestral duchy of Hanover. On May 11, 1775, at the age of only twenty-three, she died there from either typhus or possibly porphyria, the hereditary illness that would drive her brother George mad.

Back in Denmark, Juliana and Frederick's regime finally came to a crashing halt when Prince Frederick, at the age of sixteen, came before his father with a document dissolving Juliana and Frederick's government. Just as he had been with the papers that brought about the fall of Streunsee, Christian was oblivious to the document's significance and Prince Frederick came to rule Denmark as regent.

Afterwards, Christian VII's only purpose was to sign necessary papers or make rare public appearances, but other than that he would be left to roam the palace corridors or make faces at passers-by from a window. Unlike George III in his darker days, Christian was never given treatment for his condition, which today might be diagnosed as schizophrenia. His son went on to become a fondly-remembered ruler and an enlightened monarch, something that might justly be attributed to the effect the doomed Streunsee had on his upbringing.

Further Reading

Chapman, Hester *Caroline Matilda, Queen of Denmark, 1751-1775* (Cape, 1971)

Nors, P. *The Court of Christian VII* (Hurst & Blackett, 1928)

Green, Vivian *The Madness of Kings: Personal Trauma and the Fate of Nations* (Sutton, 1993)

SCANDINAVIA IN FILM AND LITERATURE

A psuedo-autobiography of Erik Bloodaxe, *The Lost Diary of Erik Bloodaxe, Viking Warrior*, was written by Steve Barlow.

August Strindberg wrote a play about Erik XIV as part of his *Vasa Trilogy*, which later inspired a 1974 television movie in Sweden based on the life of Erik XIV.

A novel by Per Olov Enquist about the situation between Struensee and the family of Christian VII, titled *The Visit of the Royal Physician*, was translated into English by Tina Nunnally. Christian VII's wife, Caroline Matilda, is the protagonist of Norah Lofts' novel, *The Lost Queen*.

GERMANY AND AUSTRIA

WENCESLAS (WENZEL OR VÁCLAV) 'THE DRUNKARD'

Reign: *June 10, 1376–August 21, 1400 as Holy Roman Emperor*
Born: *February 26, 1361*
Died: *August 16, 1419*
Buried: *Cathedral of Saint Vitus, Prague*

Perhaps the only important and remarkable thing to come out of the reign of Wenceslas was the outbreak of a religious movement known as the Hussite Revolution. Wenceslas himself was, from all reports, a lazy, temperamental man, spoiled utterly by a crown that was handed to him at the age of just two. Apathetic toward what he had inherited, Wenceslas instead made the bottle his chief concern and it was perhaps this attitude that helped along one of the most important religious movements of the age.

Wenceslas was declared the King of Bohemia and the Romans, titles that more or less singled him out as the imperial heir to his father, Emperor Charles IV of the Holy Roman Empire. Despite being uninterested in anything political even at that age, the Empire was handed over to Wenceslas in his teenage years. While his father must have been too blinded by paternal affection to see the flaws in his son, the tempestuous German princes whose dominions comprised the Empire would not be so forgiving.

As Voltaire once pointed out, the Holy Roman Empire was not holy, Roman nor even really an empire, except in the most generous definition of the word. For the most part throughout its history, the Holy Roman Empire was really only a confederation of loosely united German states. The decrees of the Emperor, although sanctioned by the Church, were, like his grandiose pretensions of being the heir to the Roman emperors of ancient times, not binding on the German princes. Even then, Wenceslas ignored his government in Germany and remained in Prague throughout his life, causing the already tenuously united German states to collapse into civil war. Jealous of his own power, Wenceslas even refused to remedy the situation by appointing a *Reichsverweser*, or imperial governor, to take care of German affairs in his absence.

As for his reign in his own homeland, it was a little bit more successful, although enough distractions were caused by the threat of ambitious relatives, particularly his grasping half-brother Sigismund, King of Hungary. Wenceslas's cousin Jobst, backed by Sigismund, started a rebellion against him and even managed to throw him into prison for a time before he was freed by German aid. Later, however, Wenceslas was coerced into giving Jobst a high position in the government. As his authority waned, he became more and more of a drunk, which was a vicious cycle that only made him less capable of keeping control. Yet Wenceslas did not completely neglect the position that he was born into. Stories claim that Wenceslas used to roam the streets of Prague in disguise, looking for merchants who cheated their customers. If he found one, he would order the man to be arrested and thrown off a bridge to his death.

Ecclesiastical affairs sometimes also excited Wenceslas's flagging interest. In Wenceslas's era, Europe was divided by the Great Schism that split Christendom between two rival Popes, one in Rome and the other in the French city of Avignon. The papal turmoil embittered Wenceslas and many others to the Catholic Church, so when a man named Jan Huss preached at Bethlehem Chapel in Prague in Czech, not Latin, and had the audacity to put the absolute authority of the Church under question, Wenceslas lent a sympathetic hand, at least at first.

By the fall of 1400, unfortunately, Wenceslas lost even more of a grip on things. The German princes, sick of their lazy and incompetent Emperor, literally 'fired' Wenceslas from his imperial job and chose the Elector of Palatine to become Emperor Ruprecht III. Two years after this, King Sigismund finally made his move and Wenceslas found himself this time deposed from the Bohemian throne and imprisoned. Eventually he was restored, but what power he had left he was forced to delegate to a council of noblemen. Crushed by these latest humiliations, he finally succumbed completely to his alcoholism.

Thanks in large part to his drunken ennui, Wenceslas did not lift a finger when his religious hero Jan Huss was ordered to stand trial before the Catholic Church. Although he was given a letter of safe conduct by King Sigismund, the bishops charged Jan Huss with heresy and, during the Council at Constance, Huss was burned at the stake on July 6, 1415. Huss's movement continued to grow rapidly, even without him.

Four years later, on July 30 in Prague, a crowd led by a Hussite priest protested a recent arrest of a number of Hussites. When a stone was supposedly thrown at the priest, the crowd went mad and broke into the hall where the town council was meeting. Some of the council members managed to escape, others were not so lucky. Seized by the crowd, the unlucky politicians were hurled out of the window down onto the streets below to their deaths. Present at the carnage was Jan Zizka, one of Wenceslas's own attendants and a man who would soon become the champion of the Hussite Revolution.

As for Wenceslas, when word of what happened reached the royal court, he went berserk. After one of his own courtiers had the bravery or stupidity to suggest that Wenceslas was to blame for what happened, he attacked him with a dagger and was only barely kept from killing the man. Suddenly, Wenceslas collapsed to the ground, suffering a sudden stroke. His left side paralyzed, Wenceslas was bedridden for days until he died from a second stroke, mercifully spared from witnessing the religious uprising that was to come.

Further Reading

Kaminsky, Howard *A History of the Hussite Revolution* (University of California Press, 1967)

Spinka, Matthew *Jan Huss: A Biography* (Princeton University Press, 1968)

RUDOLF II

Reign: *October 12, 1576–January 20, 1612*
Born: *July 18, 1552*
Died: *January 20, 1612*
Buried: *St Vitus' Cathedral, Prague*

Melancholy is an 'illness' that was often diagnosed among Renaissance royals, especially the Habsburgs. Although it is debatable whether or not a strong genetic disposition toward depression was introduced into the Habsburg bloodline by Queen Juana of Spain, the Habsburgs long had a strong inclination toward dark moods. Rudolf II was no different, and in fact the stories and rumors of his 'insanity' in the end led to him becoming Emperor in title only. However, to regard him as being crippled by his madness would be a mistake. On the contrary, his Bohemian court was a noted haven for intellectuals, artists, occultists, and theologians and to this day his reign is remembered in Prague as a 'Golden Age'.

Rudolf's father, Emperor Maximilian II, went against the Habsburg grain by being a good-humored man. At his wife and cousin Maria's insistence, Rudolf and his younger brother Ernst were sent to spend their adolescence and teenage years at the court of their uncle and Maria's father, Philip II of Spain. By nature, Philip was Maximilian's near opposite with his cold, righteous personality, and Philip's court became even more dismal than usual with the successive deaths of his deranged son Carlos and his young queen Elizabeth in 1568. When Rudolf and Ernst returned to Austria, their father found them remote like their uncle and 'ordered them to change their behavior', but, since both already had a tendency toward despondency, the habits the princes learned at the Spanish court only made them seem even more unapproachable.

Eventually, an acute bout of illness made Maximilian aware of his mortality, so he designated Rudolf as his heir by naming him King of the Romans[39] as well as King of Hungary and Bohemia. On October 12, Maximilian died and Rudolf was immediately chosen as the new Emperor. From the start Rudolf was in some ways a gifted leader, but he could be cantankerous, something he took out on foreign dignitaries, who would often find themselves shut out of the court. Favorite targets for his anger were always the helpless papal envoys. Although there is little doubt Rudolf remained a devout Catholic throughout his life, memories of the rigid indoctrination he received at the Spanish court galled him as an adult and he often treated the papal nuncios to a cold shoulder, while rewarding Protestant visitors to his court with rich gifts and his full attention. He was just as distrustful toward his own ministers. Rudolf would sometimes abruptly dismiss them from their posts, only to call them back and restore their positions soon afterwards.

Not long into his reign, he blamed the turmoil of Vienna, the traditional capital for the Austrian Habsburgs, for his bad health and relocated the imperial government to the Bohemian capital of Prague. But another, and perhaps more eroding, source of stress than the noisy Viennese crowds was his private life. Rudolf was consumed

[39] Despite the electoral theory behind the imperial office, a reigning Emperor could use this title to name his heir apparent.

with a phobia of marriage and was frightened he would invoke God's anger by failing in his marriage vows because of his irrepressible lust, so instead he gave himself sexual relief in an unending series of mistresses. For a number of years, though, it was speculated that Rudolf would marry his cousin Isabella, but Rudolf could not bring himself to it. When Isabella was instead engaged to marry Rudolf's brother, Albert, Rudolf became furious with jealousy and a gulf opened up between the two. Worse was his relationship with his other brother Matthias, the heir apparent since the death of Ernst. Matthias provoked Rudolf's hatred with his badly concealed scheming and, in turn, Rudolf made certain Matthias was aware of his resentment by refusing him permission to marry.

With increasing frequency Rudolf began to fall into lengthy periods of depression and anxiety. By 1600, something was clearly wrong, as Rudolf had attempted suicide at least twice and had started suffering hallucinations. Court physicians wrote that Rudolf needed to be treated for 'great feebleness, dizziness, and flux in the head' as well as 'melancholy and serious disturbances'. Besides the expected recommendations that the Emperor change his already irregular diet and be bled, the physicians concluded that the Emperor was the victim of witchcraft and possession, but making such a diagnosis of the Holy Roman Emperor of all people was not a wise thing. Therefore, it was delicately decided that Rudolf was somehow only a 'little' possessed. Apparently Rudolf agreed with the diagnosis, stating, with the spiritual self-loathing only a true Habsburg could muster, 'I know for certain that I belong to the Devil.'

Far direr than Rudolf's troubles were those of his illegitimate son, Julius Caesar, the child of his favorite mistress Catalina Strada. Julius was the most favored of all Rudolf's bastard children and had a prestigious title, Duke of Krumau, handed to him but, as Rudolf's paranoia escalated, relations between father and son became strained. Once when Julius came to Prague to visit his father, Rudolf did not come out to greet him, but instead spied on him from a distance.

The key to his father's sudden distaste lay in Julius's outrageous lifestyle. When he was not chasing after women or squandering his money, Julius went into intense outbursts of rage. During one of these periods, he attacked his mistress with a knife and hurled her out of the bedroom window. She survived, thanks to a pond that broke her fall, and immediately made her way to the home of her father, a local barber.

After Julius learned that his mistress had survived and recovered fully from the fall, he ordered her to come back to the castle. Defying even the son of the Emperor and his local lord, the barber refused to let his daughter leave his home. In retaliation, Julius had the barber arrested and threatened to have him executed unless his daughter willingly came to him. The mistress's mother finally relented, but begged Julius to swear an oath not to harm her daughter again. He did so, and she, reluctantly submitting to the inevitable, allowed her child to return.

That same night, either some new slight offense triggered Julius's rage or he wanted revenge against the barber's daughter for not returning to him of her own free will in the first place. Whatever the reason (and does a man of Julius's mental state need reasons?), he commanded his mistress to put on a nightgown and lie on his bed. Then, erupting into a frenzy worse than ever before, he mutilated her face with a knife, gouging out her eyes and smashing her teeth, and cracked open her skull. For three hours, he mangled her body, and shreds of her clothing and flesh were later discovered scattered across the room.

The next morning rage gave way to remorse. Julius prepared what little of his mistress he could gather for burial with his own hands and spared no expense for her funeral. He did not change his clothing or bathe before the funeral, so her blood and gore stayed on him. After his mistress and victim was buried, he stayed trapped in a trance, walking around his castle listlessly for days.

Word of what had happened was sent to Rudolf, who ordered

that his son be confined indefinitely, but imprisonment did nothing to improve Julius's state of mind. When he was out of his near-catatonic state, he would rave incoherently, smash whatever he could lay his hands on, and tear off his clothing. Like his father, the physicians theorized that Julius was the target of sorcery. Whatever was the real cause of his violent madness, it seemed to finally claim his life on June 25, 1609.

In two years' time, Rudolf himself would also lose much because of his own 'madness'. Stories about Rudolf had spread across Germany and Austria, leading many to think that Rudolf was simply incapable of ruling. Afraid that the centuries-old Habsburg monopoly on the imperial office would draw to a close because of the scandal and that the Holy Roman Empire would fall to one of the Protestant princes of Germany, a meeting of the Habsburgs in Vienna decided that Matthias should rule as regent. Guided by the family, Matthias forced Rudolf to sign over the titles of King of Bohemia and Hungary in addition to his legal authority. Rudolf was allowed to retain the title of Emperor, but not one of the powers associated with the office. With the generous pension allowed him by his hated brother, Rudolf retired for the rest of his life to Hradcany Castle in Prague where he spent the remainder of his years as a recluse with his collection of exotic animals and court of scholars and occultists.

Further Reading

Evans, Robert John Weston *Rudolf II and His World: A Study in Intellectual History, 1576-1612* (Oxford University Press, 1973)

Midelfort, H.C. Eric *Mad Princes of Renaissance Germany* (University of Virginia Press, 1994)

Vurm, Robert B. (trans. Helena Baker) *Rudolf II and his Prague: Mysteries and Curiosities of Rudolfine Prague* (Prague, 1997)

FRIEDRICH WILHELM I

Reign: *February 26, 1713–May 30, 1740*
Born: *August 14, 1688*
Died: *May 30, 1740*
Buried: *Friedenskirche, Potsdam*

In 1701, Friedrich (Frederick) III, the Elector of Brandenburg, won a superb promotion when he was named King Friedrich I of the newly formed German kingdom of Prussia. Although Friedrich I took pains to imitate the profligate glories of the court of Louis XIV at Versailles, Prussia, being the 'new kid' among the European nations, was generally regarded as a forgettable backwater. No one could have predicted that one day the Prussian monarchs would become the emperors of a new and unified German empire, at last making Germany more than just a name of geographic convenience. The man arguably responsible for putting Prussia on the path to future glory was King Friedrich's son, Friedrich Wilhelm (Frederick William), who bestowed on Prussia an organized army and an efficient government at the heavy cost of giving it the questionable distinction of being possibly the world's first modern police state. In spite of his qualities and his stamp on European, if not world, history, Friedrich Wilhelm was, as the historian Walter Henry Nelson succinctly puts it, a 'sadistic boor'.

Even as a child, Friedrich loudly resented his parents for their spendthrift lifestyles and had a taste for a more Spartan life. Instead of using his allowance on candy and toys, he spent it all on starting up his own regiment of young aristocratic boys whom he drilled personally. At the age of eight, his most cherished possession was an account ledger in which he meticulously kept track of all his earnings and spendings. Another time, when his parents forced him to wear an ornamental, pricey uniform for a ceremony, he threw the whole outfit onto the fire rather than put it on.

Naturally, the relationship between the neurotically frugal Friedrich and his less than restrained parents was anything but a healthy one. But despite the resentment he held for his father, Friedrich did give him the sort of expensive, memorable funeral he would have wanted. When the young Friedrich returned from his father's funeral, though, he ordered that much of the fine furniture and even all of the carpets, which he deemed a silly luxury, be thrown out of the main palace. Jewelry and other finery his father collected over a lifetime were sold to pay off his father's debts and right away Friedrich's new court was ordered to give up their fine French and Viennese fashions in exchange for Prussian military uniforms.

The members of the royal court were far from the only ones who found the minute details of their lives trifled with by the overbearing new king. Driven by his motto, 'Money's the thing!', Friedrich was determined to see Prussia run like a well-oiled machine down to the smallest cog. With his own pen he wrote a manual that detailed the tasks and responsibilities of every government worker. Women who sat at the stalls in the market were not allowed to become idle during slow hours, but had to at least keep busy by knitting. Preachers whose sermons lasted longer than one hour were subject to a fine. Whenever the citizens of Berlin got word that their king was taking one of his regular tours of the city, they quickly made for their homes, because everyone knew that Friedrich was liable to beat with his cane anyone he caught slacking off. On one of these tours Friedrich came across a poor man who suddenly ran off when he caught sight of the king. Friedrich chased after him, calling for him to stop. When the king at last caught up with the man, he gently asked him why he ran.

'I was afraid,' the man stuttered.

'Afraid? Afraid!' Friedrich replied, his temper suddenly bursting forth. 'You are supposed to love me! Love me, scum!' Then the king proceeded to beat the man senseless with his dreaded cane.

Then there were those that Friedrich tormented endlessly. One of the most unlucky victims was Jakob Paul von Gundling, the President of the Academy of Science. Because the king saw all things having to do with art and science as disgustingly frivolous, Gundling not only saw his main duties reduced to just reading newspaper articles to the king in the morning while he ate breakfast, but he literally became the king's main pastime. Gundling was forced to read articles that ruthlessly slandered him: Friedrich had personally had them published, and the king laughed uproariously at the president's grimaces of humiliation.

Then there was an endless series of pranks Friedrich and his drinking buddies inflicted on the poor man on a near daily basis. Once one of the king's guards dunked Gundling in and out of the moat of the castle on a winter morning as the king and others watched from a window above, laughing and pointing each time the terrified Gundling came up for air. Another time, the king forced Gundling to dress in an uncomfortable, puffed-up uniform and then led him to a room where an ape in a cage was dressed in the exact same way. Friedrich then commanded that Gundling acknowledge the ape as his long lost bastard child. One evening Gundling returned home to find that his apartments had been sealed up with brick. The worst of all these pranks was when Friedrich pretended to be furious with Gundling and told him flatly that he had just been sentenced to die. No wonder, in the end, that Gundling died from alcoholism. Even after all that, Friedrich insisted on getting one last good joke at his expense: Friedrich had Gundling solemnly buried in a wine barrel.

Although he was in the habit of treating many people almost as badly as he did Gundling, Friedrich did have two great loves in his life. The first was his wife Sophia Dorothea of Hanover, who actually hated him with every particle of her being, not only because of Friedrich's natural 'charms', but also due to his treatment of Sophia's brother and his own cousin, King George II of Britain, whom Friedrich had bullied and beaten up when they were both children. Regardless, Sophia heroically bore her loathed husband fourteen children and Friedrich was endlessly devoted to her. She was the only person he never dared lay a finger or his cane on and, even though it was highly fashionable at the time, he never kept a mistress.

Friedrich's other love was gigantic soldiers. 'He who sends me tall soldiers,' Friedrich once sheepishly confessed, 'can do with me whatever he likes.' He started to keep a special regiment of men over six feet tall called the Potsdam Giants' Guard. None of them ever saw actual combat, but they were always given fat paychecks. One member of the Giants' Guard was even raised to the aristocracy because he astonished the king by being almost seven feet tall. Friedrich loved to spend hours watching them march in unison and carry out maneuvers. Not only was any Prussian man over six feet tall in danger of being drafted into this regiment, but so was anyone that height who happened to be traveling through the country. Friedrich did not shy away from sending 'scouts' out across Europe to literally kidnap anyone who was Giants' Guard material. Although Friedrich's little hobby of having the citizens of other sovereign nations abducted grated on diplomatic relations at times, foreign governments made a point of occasionally sending him tall men as a sure way to get into the king's – and Prussia's – good graces.

Unfortunately, Friedrich's son and heir of the same name, nicknamed 'Fritz', did not receive a quarter as much loving attention as the Giants' Guard. Fritz, a bright and affectionate child, was attracted to all the things Friedrich despised – art, music, the sciences, and literature. Because Friedrich forbade Fritz to read for pleasure, Fritz had to sneak books into his room that he read only when his father was away or into the midnight hours. He even had to teach himself Latin in secret, since his father had condemned it as a useless language and had forbidden his son's tutors to even discuss it. Fritz's closest ally during his childhood was his sister Wilhelmina, with whom he developed a secret language to use around their father. The codename they used to name dad was 'Stumpy'. Once Fritz was old enough, Friedrich tried to improve his son by drafting him into the army. Just to make sure army life would put some steel into the boy, he also assigned officers the task of watching Fritz's every move.

Unfortunately, Fritz's immersion into army life did nothing to improve Friedrich's near psychotic loathing for his son. Once at a dinner, the king started ranting about Fritz's countless faults and started tapping his fingers on Fritz, who was sitting next to him. Then Friedrich began pulling at his hair and punching him while still raving. When his raving reached a new crescendo, Friedrich then got up and began hurling plates from the table into the wall. A courtier who happened to be eating with them tried to make light of what was happening by joining the king in smashing the plates. Another time Friedrich came very close to strangling Fritz with a rope. Neither was he reluctant to beat Fritz in public, once in front of a regiment of soldiers. After Fritz dared to complain about his father's treatment of him, Friedrich screeched, 'Had I been treated so by my father, I would have put a bullet through my head, but you do not even have the courage to do that!' Despite all this, Fritz was too good-natured to resent his father and tried a number of times to be reconciled with him, but Friedrich always turned a deaf ear.

Fritz found some deeply-needed release in a friendship with an officer near his age named Hans Hermann von Katte. It is possible that the two men were lovers, and in fact, later in Fritz's life his friend and correspondent Voltaire liked to hint at Friedrich's 'unacceptable inclinations'. At any rate, Fritz and Katte were very close, mostly because Katte shared Friedrich's appetite for the arts and learning. When Fritz finally reached breaking point with his father, he plotted to escape to France with Katte during a tour of Europe with his father and the court. All the preparations were made, but then one of Fritz's servants betrayed the plan to Friedrich.

For a while, Friedrich held back his temper, but finally the dam burst. Viciously, Friedrich began smacking and kicking Fritz while bellowing accusations of treason and conspiracy at him. A general present had to step forward and physically restrain the king from killing his son. Friedrich immediately ordered Fritz's imprisonment at Küstrin Castle while Katte was condemned to death.

When Sophia met Friedrich, she anxiously asked him what was Fritz's fate. He coldly replied to her, 'Your worthless son is no more. He is dead!'. Worse, he thought that Wilhelmina was an accomplice in Fritz's plot and became determined to find her out: 'Now I shall have proof about the scoundrel Fritz and the scum Wilhelmina, clear proofs to cut the heads off them!'

Before he was arrested, fortunately, Katte had managed to get hold of some slightly incriminating letters Fritz had written to Queen Sophia and Wilhelmina and burn them, meticulously forging some more innocent replacements.

At the least, Friedrich was determined to have the head of Katte and teach his son a lesson he would never forget. The king personally arranged for Katte's execution to take place directly in front of the window of Fritz's cell. On the morning of November 6, 1730, the time for Katte's execution, Fritz's guards were ordered to awaken him to make sure he 'will have a good view'. Until that morning, Fritz did not even know that Katte was convicted of treason, much less scheduled to die. From his window, Fritz tearfully shouted out a farewell and an apology to Katte, who in return said that he, even then, did not regret ever becoming the prince's friend. After he saw the fatal blow dealt to Katte, Fritz collapsed sobbing and remained in a nearly delirious state the rest of the day.

Eventually, Fritz was freed from his cell, but only because Wilhelmina had agreed to marry her father's choice for her husband without a fuss if he agreed to pardon Fritz. Soon afterwards, Friedrich forced Fritz into a mutually unhappy marriage with Elizabeth Christine of Brunswick-Bevern. Considering Fritz's sexuality, the fact that their marriage stayed cold and celibate certainly comes as no surprise, but it did not help that Elizabeth Christine was as dense and boring as Fritz was gifted and passionate. However, with marriage came his own household, so Fritz was at last liberated from the domestic tyranny of his father, a freedom that was certainly worth the price.

Fritz did not have much longer to suffer, at any rate. Old age, increasing corpulence and possibly even the hereditary illness of porphyria, something he might have shared with his relative King George III, had worn the indomitable Friedrich Wilhelm of Prussia down. He became, at last, willing to treat his son better and even admitted that Fritz would make a good king after him. On the morning of May 30, 1740, Friedrich Wilhelm called for his wheelchair and then gathered his family and household together, stating plainly that today was the day he was going to die. Hours later, he was proven correct. In her memoirs, the future Russian tsarina Catherine the Great, who was an adolescent when Friedrich died and was once taken to his court, wrote: 'Never before, I believe, did a nation show greater rejoicing upon hearing such news: people in the street kissed and congratulated each other on the death of their king, coupling his names with suitable epithets. In short he was loathed equally by the small and the great. He was stern, cruel, miserly and passionate, and though he must have had great qualities as a king, I do not think there was anything lovable in his public or private life.' As for Fritz, when all was said and done, he would become known to history as King Friedrich the Great.

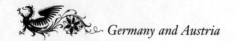

Further Reading

Fischer-Fabian, S. *Prussia's Glory: The Rise of a Military State* (Macmillan, 1981)

Fraser, David *Frederick the Great: King of Prussia* (A. Lane, 2000)

Nelson, Walter Henry *The Soldier Kings: The House of Hohenzollern* (G.P. Putnam's Sons, 1971)

FERDINAND[40]

Reign: *March 12, 1835–December 2, 1848*
Born: *April 19, 1793*
Died: *June 29, 1875*
Buried: *Capuchin Church, Vienna*

Not all monarchs were conditioned by their unusual circumstances into becoming cynical, cruel, tyrannical, vicious, jealous, self-indulged, overbearing, eccentric, power-hungry, arrogant, or imperious. One interesting exception was Emperor Ferdinand, but he had the benefit of being a mental deficient. The fruits of the Habsburg policy of intermarriage found full flower in

[40] After the dissolution of the Holy Roman Empire, the Habsburgs became the Emperors of Austria and so the counting of the Emperors' names started anew. Because of this, Ferdinand is sometimes confused with a Holy Roman Emperor of the 1500s, Ferdinand I.

Ferdinand, who was not only scarred by the infamous drooping Habsburg lip and a misshapen head but was also plagued by epilepsy, and a mind that would never reach full adulthood.

Luckily, Ferdinand's father, the Emperor Franz II, was a kind man who was absolutely devoted to his many children, especially Ferdinand, whose myriad infirmities and child-like nature invoked Franz's sympathy, not scorn. Although Franz was greatly saddened by his son's difficulty in walking, talking and performing everyday tasks, even in lifting a heavy object, the Emperor could be seen playing with Ferdinand. His favorite game with the boy was to push him for a ride in a wheelbarrow inside the palace gardens.

Naturally it was assumed by everyone that Ferdinand would be barred from the succession in favor of his only surviving brother, Franz Karl. To the shock of the family and the country, Franz's determination to stick to the laws of primogeniture led him to formally name his son heir by granting him the titles of King of Hungary and Bohemia. In order to better prepare his son for his future role, even though the doctors had diagnosed Ferdinand as impotent, Franz set about finding him a queen. The perfect victim was found in Maria Anna of Sardinia, a woman too pious and submissive to resent the groom put on her. Nevertheless she could not help but appear terrified as she watched her tottering husband-to-be on the wedding day. When witnessing the tragicomical nuptials, Emperor Franz was heard to whisper, 'May God have mercy.' Actually the marriage, while undoubtedly a celibate one, was not entirely miserable, as Maria Anna became an affectionate friend and nurse to Ferdinand. When for one year his epilepsy became severe and almost claimed his life on occasion, her careful attentions helped him make a full recovery.

Eventually, the inevitable happened and, despite the objections of many, Ferdinand was crowned Emperor of Austria. Austria did not need to be too concerned, since the resourceful minister Klemens Wenzel Nepomuk Lothar von Metternich was essentially placed in charge of the government. In the meantime, Ferdinand exercised his authority selectively. When he was not allowed to eat dumplings because of his weak digestion, he pouted and proclaimed, 'I am Emperor and I want dumplings.' Even with his difficulties, Ferdinand was popular, especially in Bohemia, because of his good nature and his habit of handing anything he had to anyone he ran into during his usual walks around Vienna.

Although Ferdinand was certainly loved, the government he represented was not. The unfolding Industrial Revolution was rapidly bringing with it economic turmoil and social unrest. While the aristocrats continued living exuberantly off the rents from their estates, workers, even young children, labored for twelve-hour days for meager pay under noxious working conditions. Matters finally came to a head when a serious recession struck Austria in the years after 1840. By 1848, the working and middle classes revolted, inspired by similar insurrections rising up across Europe. Once word of what was happening reached him, Ferdinand was shocked and, according to one story, asked quietly, 'Can they do that?'

Despite his inability to grasp the gravity of the situation, Ferdinand did his best to stop the reactionaries at court from arranging a harsh military response to the revolts and actually suggested to his ministers that the rebels should be met halfway. As the flames of unrest ignited in the other imperial lands, Metternich resigned and fled the country while Ferdinand and the rest of the Habsburg clan took refuge outside of Vienna. The situation was steadily getting worse, but, fortunately, the level head of Empress Maria Anna prevailed. With the support of the rest of the family, she managed to convince Ferdinand that the best course of action was abdicating and letting his young nephew, Franz Josef, take the throne. With a little reluctance, Ferdinand did so.

Like the Holy Roman Emperor, Rudolf II, before him, Ferdinand spent his retirement at Hradcany Castle in Prague. There we can imagine that his life with Maria Anna was considerably happier than that of his depressed ancestor. Ferdinand, obviously not missing the imperial throne, spent his life playing music and collecting heraldic symbols[41]. Although his health remained somewhat unsteady, Ferdinand managed to live to the age of eighty-two, due perhaps in no small part to his happy temperament. To sum up what he learned from his old days as Emperor of Austria, Ferdinand in particular had this to say: 'It is easy to govern, but what is difficult is signing one's name.'

Further Reading

Holzer, Hans *The Habsburg Curse* (Bailey and Swinfen, 1974)

Sked, Alan *The Decline and Fall of the Habsburg Empire* (Longman, 1989)

Ward, David *1848: The Fall of Metternich and the Year of Revolution* (Hamilton, 1970)

[41] By the time of his death, Ferdinand owned thousands.

LUDWIG II

Reign: *March 10, 1864–June 8, 1886*
Born: *August 25, 1845*
Died: *June 13, 1886*
Buried: *St. Michael's Church, Munich*

A cross standing in the shallow waters of Lake Starnberg marks where Ludwig II, once King of Bavaria, drowned with his doctor Bernard von Gudden in one of history's most bizarre murder mysteries. Ludwig would probably have found the tragic ending to his life strangely ironic considering how much time he spent trying to bring to reality his private, idealized fantasy world where ancient German legends and the ideals of chivalry were still very much real. To this end, Ludwig II left to the world three exquisite fairy-tale castles, all to provide him an escape from the dreariness of a modern world he loathed, but today serving as places for tourists to marvel at the eccentricity or madness of a dead man.

Young Ludwig was marked for the crown after his uncle, King Ludwig I, abdicated in 1848, in no small part because of his disastrous affair with the dancer Lola Montez. Ludwig's father, Maximilian, came to the throne and raised his sons, Ludwig and Otto, for their destiny by shielding them from the harshness of the world. Unfortunately, Maximilian was much too zealous in this effort. For example, Ludwig, when he was a young man, had to have the meaning of the word 'rape' explained to him. But early on there might have been something more wrong with the young man than simply being out of touch with the world. As one minister of Ludwig would plainly state, 'He was mentally gifted in the highest degree, but the contents of his mind were stored in a very disordered fashion.'

Although Ludwig grew into a very tall, striking man, he was morbidly shy and prone to daydreaming, tendencies no doubt inflated by his isolated childhood. He had a deep-rooted fascination with German folklore, especially the stories of Parzifal and the Holy Grail. So it was inevitable that, after being first introduced to the work of the composer Wagner on June 2, 1861 through the opera *Lohengrin*, Ludwig was entranced with the epic and uniquely German themes Wagner brilliantly brought to life. When Ludwig inherited the throne on the death of his father on March 10, 1864, one of his first acts as the new king was to ask Wagner to come to live in the Bavarian capital of Munich. The king also generously paid off Wagner's rather hefty debts and provided the master composer with whatever he claimed to need, including rare fabrics and expensive furniture imported straight from Vienna for his new home in Munich. Ludwig even planned to provide Wagner with his own music school and opera house. The two then kicked off an extensive correspondence dripping with an almost psychotic mutual devotion. Here is a part of one such letter, written by Ludwig to Wagner:

> [O]nly when I think of my dear one and his work am I truly

> happy . . . How are things with you just now, up there in the joyful wooded heights? Dear One, please grant me a request! I beg of you. Tell me something of your plans for *Die Sieger* and *Parzifal*! I am yearning to hear. Please quench this burning thirst! Oh, how null is the world! How wretched and vulgar so many men! Their lives revolve in the narrow circle of everyday banality. Oh, if only I had the world behind me!

Of course, there has been some suggestion that the relationship between Ludwig and Wagner was homosexual on some level. Deeply passionate as their letters were, Ludwig's melodramatic and burning need for Wagner's music needs to be taken into account as well as Wagner's sexual, but purely heterosexual, nature. Ludwig worshipped Wagner as a genius who could work miracles out of thin air, the only artist who could, if only momentarily, make Ludwig forget what a boring world he was trapped in and instead make him believe he was in the realm of heroic German knights. Wagner could not help but respond appropriately to Ludwig's hero-worship and, since Ludwig was not only Wagner's king but also his patron, it is completely understandable why Wagner laid it on a bit thick. In their letters, Wagner was often addressed as 'Beloved and Only Friend' and 'Holy One', and Ludwig as 'Exalted One'. Wagner also saw that his relationship with Ludwig had practical value, which he showed when he wrote to his mistress, 'A quite incredibly foolish upbringing has made the boy utterly reluctant to take any real interest in state affairs. There is only one way to arouse his active sympathy and that is through my works and my art which he sees as the real world: everything else seems to him sham and ridiculous.'

Ludwig's ministers and the press did not view Ludwig's patronage of Wagner in a similar practical light. Once Ludwig started handing over massive sums from State revenues to his beloved composer, fears that Wagner was another kind of Lola Montez started to emerge. Luckily enough for Bavaria, even the friendship between Wagner and Ludwig was not entirely enduring.

One of the first falling-outs between Wagner and Ludwig happened over Wagner trying to influence Ludwig in political decisions and ended with Wagner being 'asked' to leave Munich in 1865. Ludwig once again gave Wagner the cold shoulder when he found out that Wagner had lied about his longtime affair with a married woman two decades his junior, Cosima von Bürlow, but Ludwig happily gave up his grudge when Cosima's marriage was dissolved and she at last married Wagner on August 25, 1870, a wedding Wagner scheduled to coincide with the king's birthday.

Although his relationship with Wagner was probably free of sexual feeling, Ludwig, who was a bisexual, tried to find intimacy and even romance among both men and women. His lovers almost always included people of lower classes, such as Baron von Varicourt, a cavalry officer, and Alfonso Welcker, a servant. He was also very fond of those in the theatre, including the Polish actress Lila von Bulyowsky and the Austrian actor Josef Kainz. However, all of his attempts at relationships were doomed to failure simply because no one could join Ludwig in the fantastic universe he began to construct in his own mind.

Ludwig did have high hopes for one woman, the Duchess Sophie von Brayen, who won Ludwig's respect and love mostly because she was a fellow Wagner aficionado. She was at least enough of a promising prospect that one evening Ludwig announced to the press that he was engaged to Sophie, but his commitment was made on a whim. Ludwig eventually lost all interest in Sophie and pushed her aside until she finally broke off the engagement, something that, for whatever reason, he could not do himself. When he heard about Sophie's decision, he wrote in his diary: 'Sophie got rid of. The gloomy picture fades. I longed for, am athirst for, freedom. Now I live again after this torturing nightmare.'

Ludwig's rich fantasy life not only interfered with his romantic prospects, but also his responsibilities as king. This became a painful issue after Bavaria joined Austria in an alliance against Prussia as part of the Seven Weeks' War. A Prussian triumph was bound to make it the dominant power in Central Europe but, rather than raising morale by appearing in public or visiting the Bavarian troops at camp, Ludwig busied himself with an upcoming opera about William Tell. He had no liking for modern warfare to begin with, preferring instead to think about the more honorable modes of chivalric combat. Concerning a recently proposed international ban on explosive bullets, Ludwig wrote, '*Cui bono?* If battles are to be fought by machinery, let us all do our worst against each other until we are sick of carnage and then return to the time when nations settled their differences by single combat.' Unfortunately, the events of the twentieth century would go far to prove Ludwig's optimistic theory wrong.

Even more decisive for Prussia, Bavaria and all of Germany was the Franco-Prussian War. It finished with the Prussians gaining a decisive victory against Napoleon III, bringing about the fall of the Second Empire of France. Thanks to Prussian Chancellor Otto von Bismarck's skillful diplomacy, the war also led to King Wilhelm I of Prussia being crowned Emperor, or *Kaiser*, of the Germans at Versailles on January 18, 1871. Ludwig himself had been urged by Bismarck to write the *Kaiserbrief*, the letter inviting Wilhelm to claim the title of Emperor, and to consent to the formation of a unified German nation. Bavaria was still an autonomous kingdom, but it was crippled nonetheless. If Bavaria had a less eccentric and more attentive monarch at this time, would the Prussian monarchy have found a serious roadblock to its elevation? It is difficult to say for sure, but even an exceptional ruler would likely have found a match and more in Bismarck.

As Ludwig grew from an attractive youth to an obese and balding man, his chronic shyness became almost pathological. Although he was always remarkably friendly toward the peasants and laborers he came across in his walks around his estates, he was painfully awkward around his household staff and his own family. To compensate for this, he demanded rigid formality and etiquette from them at all times. One servant was punished because he looked upward too much and another time Ludwig coolly addressed his mother as 'the widow of my predecessor'. Ministers had to communicate with him through shut doors and important documents went unsigned. Ludwig found it increasingly daunting just to appear in public and began preferring instead the comfort and solitude of his residences in the country and on the Alps. When family dinners and state functions demanded his presence, he often skipped them, lamely excusing himself on account of a toothache or a headache. His once regular appearances at the theatres and opera houses in Munich had become a rarity. Instead he started to prefer hosting private performances, even of his favorite Wagnerian operas, in the comfort of his own home.

Not even the 700th anniversary of the rule of his family, the Wittelsbach dynasty, in 1880 was enough to lure Ludwig away from his seclusion. Ludwig finally opened up to a court secretary who had tried to convince the king to make an appearance: 'I can't! I can't! It's dreadful! I can't any longer stand being stared at by thousands of people. I can't stand having to smile and to bow a thousand times, having to ask questions of people who are nothing to me and listen to answers that bore me. No! No! I can't come out of my shell – not ever again!' This secretary, in his memoirs, continues:

> Then, softly and sadly, [Ludwig] added: 'Sometimes when I am tired of reading and everything is silent as the grave, I feel the irresistible need to hear a human voice. So I summon a valet or a postillion and get him to tell me about his home and his family.' And it tore my heart-strings when he concluded by saying, 'If I didn't, I would lose the power of speech.'

In the end, Ludwig determined that he could not get enough of the stories he loved and sought to bring his visions out of his mind and into the world. In 1868, he started construction of the palace that would be named Neuschwanstein. Ludwig was personally involved in the planning and building as far as possible, forcing bizarre and impractical designs on his long-suffering architects. The castle, situated in Upper Bavaria among the Alps, was conceived more as a monument to *Parzival* and the story of the Holy Grail than a royal residence. One hall was heavily adorned with friezes depicting scenes from a medieval version of *Parzival.*

Almost immediately after the plans for Neuschwanstein were set in motion, Ludwig set about his next grand project, Linderhof. Ludwig had always admired the Bourbons of France, particularly King Louis XIV, and wanted to build a palace modeled after Versailles. The interior was unabashedly lavish, filled to the brim with elaborate designs and vibrant sights. The most extravagant feature of the palace was the Grotto of Lindersten, the upkeep of which alone cost a small fortune. Electric lights were installed behind the walls of the grotto in order to make them change color, while a group of workers labored behind the scenes to keep the water's temperature constant. Scenes from Ludwig's favorite operas were sometimes performed here, even with a full orchestra playing in the background. Of the three castles, Linderhof was the only one that was completed in Ludwig's lifetime.

The third palace was Herrenchiemsee, which was built on an island on the middle of Lake Chiemsee. Like Linderhof before it, Herrenchiemsee imitated Versailles in no small degree. It even managed to surpass the original with its own Hall of Mirrors that was ninety feet longer. The rising cost of such toys set the press buzzing and frustrated Ludwig's ministers, but the king himself had a good justification in mind: 'It is essential to create such paradises, such poetical sanctuaries, where one can forget for a while the dreadful age in which we live.'

Unfortunately, Ludwig's palaces could only provide temporary relief from the nightmares the world had to offer. Ludwig's brother, Otto, was diagnosed as incurably insane after he abruptly threw himself on an altar to loudly confess his sins during a solemn ceremony. In 1878, he was confined to the castle of Fürstenried where he would live in incoherent madness for almost four decades. Even more devastating was the death of Wagner on February 13, 1883, which, despite the fact that their relationship had long since declined, left Ludwig heartbroken. Although Ludwig had countless other designs for more palaces, including one for a castle modeled after the Winter Palace in Beijing, the money soon evaporated. The press and the public did not get any enjoyment out of Ludwig's very expensive hobby while Ludwig's government was unable to procure any more funds. In fact, Ludwig's household found itself unable to pay its own gas and water bills. Ludwig sent off agents to see about the likelihood of procuring loans from nations ranging from Brazil to Sweden to the Ottoman Empire. He also thought about hiring men to rob banks for him.

His most outrageous scheme for raising cash was to send his men around the world to find some isolated place not claimed by a sovereign government. After finding such a place and arranging to move there, Ludwig planned to either abdicate or sell off his kingdom and then set up a new state, in this fantasized Eden, one that would be much more absolutist like the government of his idol Louis XIV. Unfortunately, such a place could not be found in the Americas, the Pacific Islands or the Middle East, and eventually his servantsjust started humoring Ludwig's stranger orders and schemes.

Ludwig's hermit-like lifestyle and reckless spending had become an embarrassment to the government, so a plan was devised to have him declared insane and deposed in favor of his 65-year-old uncle Luitpold, who would rule as regent in the name of Ludwig's brother, Otto, still incapacitated by madness. At the request of the government, Dr. Bernard von Gudden, who taught psychiatry at the University of Munich and directed an insane asylum, wrote a report that King Ludwig was clinically mad on June 8, 1886, even though he never saw the royal patient himself and only made his decision through witness testimonies and other second-hand accounts.

The next day, Gudden, a small contingent of the country's

leading men, and a pack of medical orderlies came to Neuschwanstein where the king was currently residing. When they came upon the household's coachman preparing the royal carriage for some trip, they ordered him to stop to prevent a possible getaway. Immediately the coachman ran to the king, to warn him what was going on. Not quite out of his wits, Ludwig had the gates closed and requested that the local police arrest the group. One of the king's friends, the very eccentric Baroness Spera von Truchess (who had also on several occasions been obliged to become a patient at a mental hospital), and his advisors begged Ludwig to go to Munich to rally popular support, but even then the king could not master his chronic terror of crowds. Meanwhile Gudden and his group, after finding that they could not enter the palace, rode back to Hohenschwangau where, to their horror, the police detained them and threw them into prison.

Ludwig wanted to have the men mutilated and starved to death for treason and conspiracy, but the government not only freed Gudden and the others, but officially declared Otto king and Luitpold regent. On June 11, Gudden finally succeeded in subduing the king and transporting him to his palace at Berg, where he was to become a virtual prisoner. 'How can you declare me insane when you have not examined me?' Ludwig rightly asked Gudden. At any rate, a king whose madness was under debate had just been deposed in favor of his brother, who was definitely insane by any definition.

Although Ludwig was humiliated and the ultimate fate of Otto must have weighed heavily on his mind, he was the ideal patient, calmly accepting his captivity and his treatments. Gudden believed in treating his patients with patience and giving them as much dignity and freedom as feasible, so he let Ludwig resume his habit of evening strolls under his personal watch. On the evening of June 12, 1886, at around 6:45p.m., Ludwig went on a walk by the nearby lake personally accompanied as always by Gudden. That night, it started to rain and the two men still had not returned. A search party was then sent out and by ten o'clock they had found the king's coat and umbrella in the shallow end of the lake. Soon after, the bodies of Ludwig and Gudden were found floating nearby. Ludwig's watch had stopped at 6:54, Gudden's at eight. Gudden's friends had always joked about how he constantly forgot to wind his watch.

The mystery of what actually happened to the deposed king and his doctor has gone unsolved, although naturally countless theories have been put forward. One of the most widely accepted explanations is that Ludwig attempted to kill himself by drowning and Gudden struggled with him to try to save him, but was overpowered by the younger man and either drowned with him or suddenly suffered a stroke or heart attack brought on by the stress of the struggle.

However it happened, Ludwig's death and his clearly insane brother Otto's 'ascension' marked the beginning of the end of the Wittelsbach family's 700-year-old reign. In 1913, although Otto was still alive, Ludwig's cousin took over the kingdom and named himself King Ludwig III. The First World War and its aftershocks deprived all German royals, even the *Kaiser* himself, of their ancient crowns and today King Ludwig II's dream castles, once built to help a tortured mind cope with a world it found unbearable, are nothing more than tourist attractions, leaving an eccentric's dream life visible for anyone to see.

Further Reading

Green, Vivian *The Madness of Kings: Personal Trauma and the Fate of Nations* (Sutton, 1993)

McIntosh, Christopher *The Swan King: Ludwig II of Bavaria* (Robin Clark, 1986)

Rall, Hans (trans. Leslie Owen and Anthony Rich) *King Ludwig II: The Reality and the Mystery* (Schnell & Steiner, 1980)

Wahl, Josef *The Dream King: King Ludwig II of Bavaria* (Viking, 1970)

GERMANY AND AUSTRIA IN FILM AND LITERATURE

Frances Sherwood's novel *The Book of Splendour* examines in great detail the court of Rudolf II and the Prague of his reign. Life at his Bohemian court is also detailed in the 1936 French film *Le Golem*.

Der Alte und der junge König or *The Young and the Old King*, a German film of 1935, depicts the 'relationship' between Friedrich Wilhelm I and his son 'Fritz.'

A pseudo-autobiography from Ludwig II has been written, titled *The Royal Recluse* and written by Werner Betram. He has also been the subject of a novel by David Stacton called *Remember Me* and the circumstances around his death were even the premise for a Sherlock Holmes adventure, *The Truth About Ludwig II*. Ludwig's relationship with Josef Kainz has found its way to film with *Ludwig 1881*, but Ludwig himself was the subject of a self-titled 1955 German movie.

ITALY

GIOVANNA I

Reign: *1343–1382*
Born: *August 2, 1327*
Died: *May 22, 1382 (assassinated)*
Buried: *St Chiara's Church, Naples*

There is a saying in Italy, 'To be like Queen Giovanna', that is used for a woman who allegedly has an unrestrained appetite for sex and luxury. This proverb ignores the fact that Giovanna was a renowned patron of artists and writers, as well as a queen who exhibited great strength of will and political ability at a time when female rulers were looked upon with contempt. While more than a few of her decisions may have been self-destructive (but, of course, it is possible she was more the victim of bad luck than bad planning), her crimes were no more shocking than those of many of her male peers. Compared to some, they were even less so.

At the time, the ruling family of Naples and Sicily was a branch of the always robust Anjou clan. Another branch of the family, closely tied to the Angevins of Naples, ruled over Hungary at the time but looked with envy toward the flourishing kingdom of their Italian cousins. To stave off his jealous kin, King Roberto of Naples offered to give up his granddaughter Giovanna, then only seven years old, in marriage to her six-year-old Hungarian cousin Andre.

Although Andre was raised in King Roberto's court alongside Giovanna, this did nothing to engineer a sibling-like or even a friendly relationship between the two. As Giovanna once complained, 'I was sacrificed to a man whom I can never love.' Andre felt he was in no better a position. Their mutual dislike was spurred on when, after the king's death, the Pope crowned the fifteen-year-old Giovanna, the sole living heir to the throne, as queen regnant. Meanwhile Andre, who not only hoped but expected to rule jointly with his wife, was left in the cold with the nice but meaningless title of prince consort. One would think that Andre, a macho braggart, would have been more galled by his wife cuckolding him. The queen's blatant affair with a man named Roberto Cabano was the topic on everyone's mind at court, although it was supposedly to prevent the romance from going public that Giovanna gave in to blackmail threatened by Roberto's mother and made Roberto a count. The relationship ended only when Giovanna moved on to another lover, Bertrand de Artois, a nobleman who was a member of the regency council that would technically be in command of the kingdom until Giovanna reached the majority age of twenty-five.

Giovanna was a strikingly beautiful, dark-haired woman with a vivid intelligence that far surpassed that of her boorish, self-absorbed husband. Nevertheless, a few members of the court, inspired by misogyny or self-interest, began to throw their lot in with Andre. Worse, Giovanna's authority was shaken when Carlo, the Duke of Durazzo and one of the men closest by blood to the throne, kidnapped Giovanna's younger sister, Maria, and married her in secret. Carlo was so powerful that, when word of the marriage leaked out, Giovanna was powerless even to give Carlo a slap on the wrist.

A worse blow was yet to be struck. Andre's mother, Elizabeth of Poland, bribed her way into the Pope's good graces and convinced him to crown Andre as king regnant of Naples, at last giving him power over the kingdom – and his wife. Once word of Andre's promotion reached her, Giovanna allegedly whispered to her lover Artois, 'That decides it. The man must die.' It is more or less assumed that Giovanna actually did hatch a plot against her husband's life, although the verdict made by her contemporaries and by consequent historians may have been shaped by a bad reputation, a case not entirely unlike that of Mary, Queen of Scots, who was also accused of engineering a plot to kill her vapid spouse. But while the hard facts are kinder to Mary, the evidence for Giovanna is less clear-cut.

Whether or not Giovanna was really involved, the attempt on Andre's life was made during a hunting expedition undertaken by the royal court. While stopping for the night at the monastery of San Pietro a Maiella, a party was thrown that went on until the early morning hours. Andre went to bed at dawn drunk and exhausted. Several hours later, he was woken up from his heavy sleep by a loud knock on the door. A group of armed men led by Artois waited outside. As soon as Andre threw open the door, Artois grabbed Andre by his long hair. He attempted to go for his own weapon, but was kept from reaching it. Not quite a weakling, Andre was able to fight off the men with his bare hands and fled down the hall, calling for help that would never arrive. He might have been able to reach safety, but he tripped, giving Artois the chance to catch up and wrestle him to the ground.

One of the conspirators then brought out a rope and used it to hang Andre from a nearby balcony. Andre's fresh corpse was allowed to drop to the gardens below, where it would remain for days. Even though she shared Andre's bedroom that night, Giovanna claimed that she had slept through the entire incident and that the murder was committed by men acting independently, but her own family was skeptical. Giovanna did anything but free herself from suspicion when she became intimate with Ludovico, the Duke of Taranto, right after Andre's death and married him shortly afterwards. An official inquiry into the murder of Andre was made on June 2, 1346 by the Pope, who condemned to death anyone who would be found to have been involved in the conspiracy, but declined to allow the queen or any member of the royal family to become implicated in the murder, save at the Pope's own discretion.

The investigation of Andre's murder was undertaken with brutal efficiency. Authorities at the request of the Pope arrested the two valets that were supposed to have been guarding Andre's chambers that night. They were tortured until they gave out a series of names that were supposed to be a reliable list of the names of the conspirators. Then, after being dragged through the streets of Naples by horses, the helpless valets were lynched in the public square.

Urged on by Andre's elder brother, who happened to be King Lajos (Louis) I of Hungary, the Counts of Terlizzi and Morcone and their wives were next persecuted and publicly executed for the murder. After their tongues were cut out, the men were whipped until their skin was raw and then knives and red-hot pincers were taken to their bodies. The women had parts of their bodies cut off which were then thrown as gifts to the cheering crowds. The few who survived the free-for-all were then taken to the city square and burned alive. Once the flames died down, their bones were gathered as souvenirs by the Neapolitans, who carved them into whistles. Another alleged conspirator, Conrad of Catanzaro, was tortured to death under a wheel of sharp knives. Artois's father, Charles, after starting a plot to get rid of Ludovico and replace him at the queen's side with Artois, was thrown in prison, where he killed himself by chewing through his own wrists. Soon afterward, Artois hanged himself.

In the midst of this massacre, Carlo of Durazzo, never reluctant to take an opportunity for self-aggrandizement, sent a letter to King Lajos asking him to invade the country to avenge his brother's death on those untouched by the papacy's prosecutions. To win back Durazzo, Giovanna played to Durazzo's instinct for power and willingness to stab backs by offering to make him and Maria the heirs apparent if he agreed to support her and Ludovico against Lajos. The stratagem worked, but in the long run it was a useless effort. Giovanna's cause was rapidly abandoned by her soldiers once the leading citizens of Naples handed the keys to the city over to King Lajos to avoid risking the sight of their beloved city being looted. Barely with their hides intact, Giovanna, Maria, her children, and Ludovico fled the country for Avignon, where the papacy was then located, to plead their case.

Durazzo foolishly stayed behind in Naples, hoping to take his chances with his onetime ally. Despite his astonishing betrayal, Durazzo fell perfectly for Lajos's act as the forgiving, merciful conqueror. Unfortunately for him, Lajos suspected – probably rightfully – that he was at least marginally involved in the murder of his brother. Suddenly, after days of being treated with smiles and friendship by Lajos, Durazzo was put under arrest. Then, after he was taken to the balcony where Andre was killed, his throat was cut at the scene of the crime and his lifeless body thrown down into the same garden where Andre's corpse had landed.

For Giovanna and Ludovico, fortune was kinder. Not only did the Pope, after interviewing Giovanna himself, declare that she was innocent of any and all involvement in the crime, but also he confirmed the marriage between Giovanna and Ludovico and crowned Ludovico as King of Naples. For months, Giovanna and Ludovico fought to force Lajos off their hard-won throne. While they failed time and again, the people of Naples took matters into their own hands and drove out the obnoxious Hungarians who had lorded over them for much too long. On May 25, 1351, Lajos was gone and Ludovico was accepted as both Giovanna's consort and Naples' co-ruler.

Giovanna was deprived of her consort and partner on July 5, 1362 when Ludovico suddenly died from malaria. Afterwards, she married

Jaime, king of the small Spanish kingdom of Majorca, whom she had met at Avignon during the long days of exile. He may have been the only one of all her husbands she actually loved. After all, when they met both were political exiles and had many hardships and heartaches in common. If it is true that they were sincere lovers, then it makes it doubly tragic that he died soon after the wedding, either from illness or because he was poisoned at the command of his enemy and former brother-in-law, Pedro the Cruel of Castile.

Misfortune struck again when Giovanna was excommunicated for backing the pope in Avignon when a rival pope had taken charge in Rome. Not only did Giovanna's excommunication mean that her subjects were relieved of their allegiance to her, but the Roman Pope declared Giovanna's nephew, Carlo, to be the legitimate King of Naples. To try to strengthen her position, Giovanna married again, this time to Otto of Brunswick. Unfortunately, Carlo, who decided he had no qualms about waging war against his aunt, asked for and won the support of King Lajos.

Beaten back by the forces gathered by Carlo and Lajos, Otto fled Naples, abandoning his wife to her fate. She was deposed and then imprisoned at the castle of Muro in Calabria. At last, Lajos could satisfy his lust for revenge. Men sent by Lajos entered the queen's chambers and strangled her with a cord, allegedly the same rope used to hang Andre all those years ago. As similar as Giovanna's tragedy and its conclusion was to that of Mary, Queen of Scots, no real effort has been made to ascertain her guilt or innocence.

Further Reading

Croce, Benedetto (trans. Frances Frenaye) *History of the Kingdom of Naples* (University of Chicago Press, 1970)

Steele, Maria Francesca *The Beautiful Queen, Joanna I of Naples* (Hutchinson, 1910)

CESARE BORGIA

Born: *September 1475*
Died: *March 12, 1507*
Buried: *Church of Santa Maria, Viana*

Like his more than appropriate namesake, Cesare (Caesar) was a creature of ambition who happened to have been born with the abilities and the opportunity to achieve his many goals. Unfortunately, also like Julius Caesar, he was also destined for an ugly and abrupt end before he could reach what might have been a pinnacle in his career. However, he lived long enough to make his mark in Chapter VII of Niccoló Machiavelli's

The Prince, serving as a role model to future generations of the ruthlessly ambitious.

Although Cesare was not born to royalty as he may have thought he deserved, he was the son of Rodrigo Borgia, a rapidly ascending star on the scene of the Catholic Church and one of the wealthiest, most well-connected and politically astute cardinals in Rome. The Borgias were originally from Valencia, Spain, where they retained links. Cesare's mother was Rodrigo's favorite mistress, Vannozza dei Cattanei, an independently rich Roman noblewoman whose children by Rodrigo were the only ones he ever loved. However, even Rodrigo could not afford too unfriendly a reputation and, after he became Pope Alexander VI, he issued a bull on September 20, 1493 that declared Cesare to be the legitimate son of Vannozza's husband at the time, Domenico da Rignano. But secretly he wrote another bull, stating Cesare was actually his rightful son.

Even at an early age, Cesare exhibited a number of exceptional qualities. He was famous for his striking features, although in early adulthood syphilis would mar his features, much to his misery. He was also well known for his silver tongue, but many times he was the victim of dark periods of depression and hated being bothered with human company. The few times he agreed to appear in public, he often wore a mask, a habit his more sociable father hated. The only person who could reach him was his sister Lucrezia, who shared a strong bond with him that would last throughout their too-short lives. While the company of others beyond his sister did not entice him, physical activity did, and Cesare would be as celebrated an athlete as he was an adventurer. Almost daily he kept in shape by bullfighting on horseback and was said to be unbeatable.

Despite Cesare's obvious appeal as an heir, Rodrigo's favorite son remained Cesare's younger brother Juan, a spoiled boy who shared Cesare's charisma but lacked any of his real talents. As if knowing Juan was daddy's undeserving favorite was not enough for Cesare to bear, Rodrigo's affections were made all the more blatant when he gave all of his deceased brother Pedro Luis's rich estates to Juan and later made Juan the head of the papal armies, even though Cesare already showed an aptitude toward the military whereas Juan did not.

That is not to say that Cesare got nothing from the nepotism of Rodrigo Borgia. Although he had not taken holy orders, Cesare was named to the lucrative office of Bishop of Pamplona at the age of fifteen. Later on, at seventeen, he was made Archbishop of Valencia, which yielded even more church revenues, but still Cesare was not ordained. At the time, he also proved an excellent student at the University of Pisa and earned a doctorate in law. Eventually, though, Cesare was called upon to fully leave behind the secular life when he was appointed a cardinal at seventeen, but none of this was too unusual. In Cesare's time, it was almost a requisite that all of Italy's great families bestow a cardinal's hat on a young relative, so they could have some say in papal elections as well as that of a future candidate. There was no reason why the popular son of the reigning pope should not get the same opportunity.

Once Rodrigo was elected Pope Alexander VI on August 11, 1492, Cesare's career was about to receive a jump forward. Ludovico Sforza, the Duke of Milan, had fully encouraged King Charles VIII of France to press his own blood claim to the crown of Naples, then in the grasp of Ludovico's arch-enemy, King Ferrante of the House of Aragon. Ludovico either did not know or did not realize that Charles VIII was not a king who would inspire confidence. Besides having a misshapen face and malformed body, it was whispered 'he hardly knew the letters of the alphabet'. Further, Alexander recognized something that Ludovico did not: the interference of a power like France in the combustible political climate in Italy could lead only to catastrophe.

Alexander's anxieties were soon justified once Charles VIII marched into Italy to conquer Naples, planning to force Alexander into handing over his approval. To this end, Charles would have to put military pressure on Rome, since Alexander was staunchly loyal to the House of Aragon. The papal armies were no match for the

French and in too short a time the barbarians were at the gates of Rome. Realizing he had to bide his time, Alexander warmly welcomed Charles into the Holy City. Unfortunately, this did not stop Charles's troops from having their run of the streets and robbing the homes of Rome's leading citizens, including the villa of Cesare's own mother. This was not something Cesare quietly accepted.

Although Charles had the upper hand in almost every way, Alexander still had centuries of tradition behind him as the Vicar of Christ and he knew precisely how to exploit it for all it was worth. Overawing the simple-minded boy-king with the luxurious yet sanctified atmosphere of the Vatican and the countless, detailed rituals of pomp and ceremony surrounding him, Alexander, ever the skillful diplomat, got Charles to agree to advantageous terms – for Alexander. However, even Charles remained wary of the Borgia Pope, who had already cultivated such a bad reputation that Charles kept a food-taster handy to guard him from poison while at the Vatican. Also, despite Alexander's careful diplomatic stratagems, he would not let go of his key demand to be crowned King of Naples by Alexander's own hands.

On January 15, 1495, both king and pope reached a compromise: Alexander would send Cesare with Charles: not only as a hostage, but as an envoy to crown Charles once he arrived in Naples. The night of January 30, when Charles's army stopped at Velletri, Cesare disguised himself as a groom of the royal stables and escaped from the French camp with nineteen mules, each one loaded with valuables stolen from the French coffers. The day after, Charles was heard screaming, 'All Italians are dirty dogs and the Holy Father is as bad as the worst of them!'

This incident, minor as it may seem, marked the point where Charles's Neapolitan dream went bad. A regiment of Charles' Swiss mercenaries in Rome, reportedly the same ones who looted Vannozza's house, were attacked and massacred by Cesare and his men. Meanwhile Alexander engineered an alliance with Venice, Milan, Spain and Austria against France, named the Holy League of Venice. Although Charles accomplished the capture of Naples, he spent most of his time, like a teenager who has finally started to live on his own, gorging himself on the temptations of the city rather than actually doing anything to counter the threat of the Holy League. The French followed their king's example, bringing with them a disease then unknown in Italy, syphilis, which was named in Naples 'the French disease', with good reason. With the Holy League and an enraged Neapolitan populace snipping at his heels, Charles was thrown out of Italy by July.

Without a doubt, Alexander was very pleased with his son's performance, but soon enough a shadow would be cast over their father–son relationship. Juan, who kept his place as his father's favorite, was still head of the papal armies, a position Cesare craved. Cesare quietly nursed his resentment until, on June 14, 1497 Vannozza hosted a banquet in Cesare's honor. An unidentified masked man who had been seen with Juan many times before appeared at the festivities and took a seat next to Juan. As the celebration continued late into the night, Juan left with the masked man and a valet but did not return. It was assumed that Juan and his friend had found some female courtesan or a brothel ready to entertain them for a night.

As the next day came and went, Alexander became deeply worried for his son and opened an investigation into his disappearance. The Pope's agents found a woodcarver named Giorgio Schiavi who said he saw four men throw a body into the Tiber River the night of Juan's disappearance. When asked why he had not reported what he witnessed to the authorities before, Schiavi replied it was because he had seen about a hundred bodies dumped in there that night alone. Juan eventually did turn up on a bank of the river, the wounds on his corpse revealing that he had been stabbed eight times and his throat had been cut.

The Vatican echoed with Alexander's sobs, something commented on by many observers: 'From the Wednesday evening until the following Saturday morning the Pope ate and drank nothing, whilst from Thursday morning to Sunday he was quiet for no moment of any hour.' To a cardinal, Alexander said, 'The blow which has fallen upon us is the heaviest we possibly could have sustained. We loved [Juan] more than anyone else in the world. We would give seven tiaras to be able to recall him to life. God has done this in punishment for our sins, for [he] had done nothing to deserve this mysterious and terrible death.'

Although it is not a stretch to say that a boy like Juan would develop more than a few deadly enemies, there is the tantalizing clue that his death was not so mysterious to Alexander after all and Juan's killer was close to home. Not only did Cesare's jealousy and resentment of Juan give him an adequate motive but after Juan's death the relationship between Alexander and Cesare cooled. Far more tellingly, Alexander halted the investigation twenty days after Juan's disappearance. But even if Cesare were the murderer of his own brother, it did not end in a permanent rupture between father and son. Before too long Cesare would at last be given the position he coveted at the head of the papal armies.

A similar and equally curious incident would occur between Cesare and his favorite sibling Lucrezia. Although Alexander arranged her marriage to Alfonso de Bisceglie solely for political purposes, it was a joyful agreement for both parties. Nevertheless, Alfonso was attacked on the steps of St Peter, by one of Cesare's henchmen, Miguel de Corella. Although Alfonso survived in spite of the knife wounds inflicted on him, days later, while being nursed back to health by Lucrezia and his sister Sancha, Cesare's lackeys burst into his room, forced everyone out, and strangled him. It is unknown what motives Cesare had in mind, but it was reported that he feared that his brother-in-law would try to murder him, which was not unlikely, since Cesare was associated with the pro-French faction while Alfonso was linked by family with Spanish interests. Another, even more dramatic theory, is that Cesare murdered Alfonso out of jealousy for his sister, even if he did not have an incestuous relationship with her like the Roman rumor-mongers claimed. In this case too, the relationship between Cesare and Lucrezia was not permanently marred by this murder, although Lucrezia was so grief-stricken by her husband's violent demise that she retired from Rome for months.

Yearning for a more secular career, Cesare renounced his priestly vows on August 17, 1498 and entered the laity. His father, who may have hoped that his son would one day follow him as Pope just as Alexander had eventually succeeded his uncle who had been Pope Callixtus III, nevertheless did not resist this decision. Instead he worked to help Cesare gain much with this new career: Alexander first made Cesare the governor of Orvieto, where he received invaluable training in politics. After having a short but heated affair with the wife of his youngest brother Jorfe, Sancia of Aragon, Cesare, with Alexander's blessing, went about marriage negotiations for Carlotta of Aragon, the daughter of the new Neapolitan king, Federigo.

The marriage plans won another powerful backer in the new French king Louis XII, who succeeded his cousin Charles VIII after he died from accidentally hitting his head against a stone beam while on his way to watch a tennis match. Louis not only inherited Charles's claim to the crown of Naples, but also had hereditary rights to the duchy of Milan, both of which he was determined to cash in on. Although Alexander knew that the ambitions of France and the other European nations could turn all of Italy into an open battleground (which, incidentally, was exactly what would happen), Alexander made himself friendlier to Louis' demands, knowing Rome did not stand much chance against the military juggernaut of France. Once again, Alexander took the realm of diplomacy as his battlefield. Louis needed a papal annulment for his marriage to the sickly and crippled Jeanne de Valois so he could remarry Charles's widow, Anne of Brittany, whose dowry was the entire duchy of Brittany. With this dispensation as the hook, Alexander lured Louis into making Cesare Duke of Valence and Valentinois and Count of Diois.

Unfortunately, the marriage desired by Cesare, the King of France and the Pope would be stopped cold by the bride herself. Carlotta, who was a ward of Louis, flatly refused again and again to marry Cesare. When Louis sent a message to Federigo asking him to persuade or force his daughter to agree to the match, Federigo's envoys replied coolly, 'To a bastard son of the Pope the king not only would not give his legitimate daughter, but not even a bastard child.' Louis, his queen, and Cesare tried to talk her into changing her mind during a friendly private dinner, but to no avail.

To compensate Cesare and avoid irritating the Pope, Louis dredged up a substitute bride, Charlotte d'Albret, a princess of the small kingdom of Navarre. Alexander, who still wanted Cesare to have a wife from the House of Aragon, was bitterly disappointed, but Cesare, ever slowly ingratiating himself to the French, was happy to accept the solution. However, he felt no obligation to actually love or even care for his wife. Although she was showered with expensive gifts, Cesare all in all treated her more like a piece of furniture than a spouse.

Instead, Cesare was determined to carve out more lands of his own, rather than have more handed to him. The perfect *tabula rasa* was in the Romagna, a profitable but chaotic territory in central Italy that was nominally under the papacy's dominion but was in fact under the control of a pack of unimportant but rapacious lords. Eager to assist his son's plan to carve out a sizeable Italian duchy or even a kingdom from the Romagna, an act that would also rid himself of his bothersome vassals, Alexander issued a bull condemning and deposing many of them, thus giving Cesare's self-serving invasions the weight of legality.

Empowered by his father's act of cleaning house and followed by an army of French mercenaries, Cesare seized by force the territories of the Romagna one by one. One of his greatest and most indomitable adversaries in this venture was Catalina Sforza, a match for Cesare in cunning and ability. A rumor had it that she even attempted to assassinate Alexander by hiding a cloth worn by a man who died from the plague among letters addressed to him. Even such creative strikes were not enough to stop Cesare from capturing the last of Catalina's fortresses, along with the woman herself, and throwing her in prison. It was said that Catalina took Cesare as a lover, which is likely, since both of them were infamous for their libidos. Yet there is some suggestion from contemporary sources that Catalina did not willingly submit to Cesare's advances.

Catalina would be far from Cesare's only victim in his Romagna venture. He also drowned two young heirs of one Romagnol lord he had recently vanquished and tricked a rival, the Duke of Urbino, into letting down his guard, only to suddenly declare that he had found 'evidence' that Urbino was scheming to betray him and use that as a reason for confiscating Urbino's lands. A certain Florentine ambassador, Niccoló Machiavelli, was very much impressed by Cesare's bloody, brilliant accomplishments, especially once his duties led him to meet the master in person.

Although such naked aggression had already made Cesare's name synonymous with notoriety, the long-oppressed people of the Romagna looked at him almost as a savior once he won the right to the title 'Lord of the Romagna' in 1501. According to one admirer, 'He is considered brave, strong and liberal, and it is said that he sets great store by straightforward men. He is hard in revenge, so I have been told by many, a man of soaring spirit, thirsting for greatness and fame, he seems more eager to seize states than to keep and administer them.' Despite the author's last judgment, Cesare was actually a conscientious administrator, who won the confidence of the people with his almost populist attitudes. On a good day he could be caught competing in racing and wrestling matches with young peasants.

Saddled as he may have been with his newfound responsibilities as a ruler in his own right, Cesare was as always the adventurer and the outlaw. When Dorotea Malatesta Caracciolo, 'one of the most beautiful and notable women in Italy', traveled through Cesare's lands to meet her arranged husband, a Neapolitan nobleman in the employ of the Republic of Venice, on February of 1501, ten masked horsemen, all heavily armed, abducted her from her party. Seething, the Republic of Venice sent an ambassador to demand that Cesare, who was naturally the number one suspect, return her to her husband safely. Cesare greeted the ambassador with a casual arrogance but proclaimed his innocence, adding that 'he did not lack for women'. Instead, Cesare blamed one of his Spanish mercenaries, Diego Ramires, for the abduction, hinting all the while that Diego had secretly seduced her before she was ambushed, and promised to bring him to justice, which he never did, arguing that Ramires was completely missing in action. Upon hearing of the incident and Cesare's likely involvement, Alexander commented bluntly and publicly, 'If the Duke has done it, he has lost his mind.' In the meantime, Dorotea was not returned and may have stayed with Cesare secretly, probably against her will.

Although Machiavelli remained impressed with Cesare, his masters' feelings on the subject were not so warm. Cesare bullied the Florentine envoys as much as he charmed them, and even told them flat out: 'Between you and myself there can be no middle way: either you are my friends or my enemies.' However, even with all the threats and promises he could muster, a beneficial alliance remained out of reach, causing Cesare to mutter bitterly, 'These men do not want my friendship or care anything about it.' The truth, Cesare must have realized, was that the fledgling Lord of the Romagna needed the Republic of Florence far more than they needed him.

Undeterred by Florence's rejection, Cesare continued with his newfound passion for governing. In 1502, he hired a brilliant but still unknown young man named Leonardo da Vinci as an architect and engineer for a year. Cesare also introduced a number of reforms to the people of the Romagna, earning him their utmost loyalty. Busy as he was with politics, he still had time for his favorite sister, then the Duchess of Ferrara. When Lucrezia became badly ill after a miscarriage, Cesare visited her on September 7 and tended to her personally, trying to cheer her up to make her more receptive to the painful operations performed on her by her physicians. One doctor wrote, 'Today at the twentieth hour we bled [Lucrezia] on the right foot. Her Majesty spent two hours with the Duke who made her laugh and cheered her greatly.'

Unfortunately, trouble was once again at Cesare's doorstep. Cesare's own captains, all mercenaries or *condottieri*, turned against him, backed by a strong Roman family, the Orsini, who were longtime enemies of the Borgias. Cesare, not at all fooled by their deceptive claims of loyalty, intimidated them into an agreement that put them in a worse position than before.

For the time being, though, it appeared that Cesare would keep the sword of Damocles from falling on the heads of his disloyal men, at least for a while. After they had captured a small town for their master, Cesare invited his *condottieri* to come to his temporary headquarters in the town to discuss further plans, but these were only false pretenses. After Cesare briefly stepped out of the room, claiming to have the need to answer nature's call, soldiers loyal to Cesare burst into the room and arrested the defenseless captains. They were garroted that night.

But even a man as cautious and ruthless as Cesare could not be prepared for every disaster. While meeting his father for dinner on the evening of August 11, 1504 at the home of a humanist scholar, an owl flew into the room where they were dining and fell at Alexander's feet, causing him to scream, 'It's an omen! A bad omen!' That same night, both men became ill with malaria. After days of agony, Pope Alexander VI died, surrounded by stories that a black cat or ape had appeared near his deathbed to claim his soul for the Devil. Cesare made a slow recovery, but found that his inability to do anything right after his powerful father's death would cost him dearly. He later told Machiavelli that he was prepared for any problem that would arise after his father's death except for the possibility that he himself would also be at death's door.

Cesare tried as hard as he could to make up for lost time. As soon as he could stand and think, he ordered his men to barricade the Pope's chambers. One of them threatened to cut the throat of the chamberlain if he did not provide the keys to the Pope's treasures, which Cesare knew could help fund his ventures in the dark times ahead. Although Cesare was genuinely grieved at his father's death, he knew his many enemies would not allow him the luxury of a quiet mourning period.

The worst portent of troubles ahead came from the return of Giuliano della Rovere, an old enemy of Alexander who went into voluntary exile in France during Alexander's time as Pope. The man endorsed by Rovere to fill the papal seat, Francesco Piccolomini, was elected as Pope Pius III on January 22, 1504. One of this new pope's first acts was ordering that Cesare be detained in Rome. Meanwhile back in the Romagna Cesare's men, now without their master's iron fist looming overhead, mutinied and his enemies circled the all but defenseless territories. In time nothing in the Romagna remained in Cesare's possession except two towns and a handful of fortresses.

Matters could only go further downhill. Pius III, riddled with gout and ulcers even before his election, died after a reign that lasted barely a month. Riding a wave of sentiment against the election of non-Italians to the papacy, Rovere was elected on November 1 and named himself Julius II. His victory was so assured that even Cesare found it in his best interests to give him his support, even if it meant placing an implacable enemy of his family on the highest pinnacle possible.

Julius was well known as a vigorous, temperamental man with a mania that bordered on insanity. One cardinal who had to deal with him wrote, 'Anything he has been thinking of overnight has to be carried out immediately the next morning and he insists on doing everything himself. It is almost impossible to describe how strong and violent and difficult to manage he is. In body and soul he is a giant.' This pope was even known to have fought in battles with the bravado of a warlord. During his time as Pope, while personally leading an army against the King of France, Julius is credited with bellowing, 'Let's see who has the bigger balls, the King of France or the Pope!'

Yet Julius was no hysterical fool and knew he had to play Cesare at his own games of deception to beat him. Although Cesare was technically a prisoner of the papacy, Julius treated him like an honored guest, promising that, despite his old bitter rivalry with his father, Julius would help Cesare recover all of the Romagna and once again place him in charge of the papal armies. It seems that Cesare was all too ready to believe Julius's honey-coated promises. The death of his father, his illness, the betrayals of his men and the staggering loss of most of the Romagna had left Cesare drained and anxious, in all likelihood the victim of a nervous breakdown. Desperation crippled him to the point where he was willing to trust even a man who had no reason to give him the time of day.

The axe finally came down when Julius, in order to counter aggression from the Republic of Venice, confiscated Cesare's remaining fortresses in the Romagna for the papal states. When Cesare, who was at the time gathering funds and rallying troops to reclaim his lost power, vehemently protested, Julius threw a tantrum and Cesare found himself a prisoner very much in fact. Gleefully Julius prepared to begin legal proceedings against Cesare where many of his old enemies would be allowed to place huge compensation claims against him. Among them was, of course, the husband of Dorotea Caracciolo, who was at last discovered and rescued.

Cesare was still not entirely bereft of allies, even in a Rome overshadowed by Julius II's demonic personality. Cardinals loyal to the Borgia name talked Julius into agreeing to free Cesare in exchange for his last lands in the Romagna. Cesare reluctantly agreed to this and was taken to Ustia in Italy where he was finally released. Cesare and his party were granted safe conduct through Naples, but the Spanish Viceroy, Gunsalvo de Cordoba, betrayed him and arrested him in the name of Spain. To Queen Isabel and King Ferdinand, the Francophile Cesare was an excellent prize, as well as a trump card to be used against Pope Julius should any unpleasant difficulties arise.

Cesare was kept prisoner at the fortress of Chinchilla, which was ironically located in his father's ancestral home of Valencia. Lucrezia wrote tirelessly to the Spanish court, begging for Cesare's release, but the ink was spent in vain. Her ever resourceful brother, however, was busy effecting his own escape. Making a rope out of his bedsheets, Cesare tried to climb out of a window but fell and broke his shoulder, to be found by the guards and returned to his cell.

He would find better luck after being transported to a new and even more intimidating prison, the castle of La Mota. This time, however, he did not have to make a rope, thanks to a sympathizer who provided him with the genuine article. Successfully escaping the prison and carefully eluding the authorities, Cesare made a harrowing escape from Spain into Navarre, ruled by his brother-in-law, Jean d'Albret.

There Cesare won a new lease of life and began working as a mercenary captain for Navarre. Unfortunately, Navarre would play the setting for the final adventures of the former Lord of the Romagna. On March 12, 1507, while leading an army against a rebellious count, Cesare was killed in the heat of the battle, left naked in the dirt, and was found to have been stabbed twenty-five times. He was only thirty-one at the time of his death, his remarkable life amounting to nothing but a few good stories. A marble tomb was erected in his memory, but it was destroyed about a century later because of a local bishop who could not bear the sight of a grave dedicated to so infamous a man. Fortunately, the words that were written on this tomb have been remembered:

Here in a scant spot of earth
Lies he whom all the earth once feared,
He who in his hand once bore
Mankind's fate of peace or war.
O you that now would wander wide
Seeking things that merit praise,
Here you may your journey stay:
Never farther seek to stray!

Further Reading

Bradford, Sarah *Cesare Borgia, His Life and Times* (Weidenfeld & Nicolson, 1974)

Cloulas, Ivan (trans. Gilda Roberts) *The Borgias* (F. Watts, 1989)

Mallett, Michael Edward *The Borgias: The Rise and Fall of a Renaissance Dynasty* (Bodley Head, 1969)

LUCREZIA BORGIA

Born: *April 18, 1480*
Died: *June 14, 1519*
Buried: *Church of Corpus Domini, Ferrara*

The Renaissance found its embodiment in one family, the Borgias, whose exquisite lifestyles and grandiose ambitions captured the fierce but beautiful spirit of that age. The patriarch of the Borgias, Rodrigo, better known as Pope Alexander VI, became one of the most notoriously worldly popes ever to reign and his son Cesare was one of the topics in Niccoló Machiavelli's *The Prince*. Understandably such colorful and infuriating personalities as the

Borgias harvested bad reputations, originating mostly from half-true stories and blatant propaganda. The saddest victim of the centuries-long slander against the Borgias was Lucrezia, who was in real life probably a very kind, forward-thinking and headstrong woman, but was transformed for future generations into a cold-blooded black widow.

Although Lucrezia and her family would gain their infamy in Italy, their story begins in Spain, specifically the province of Valencia in the kingdom of Aragon. There the Borgias were a minor aristocratic family that became established during the wars against the Iberian Muslims. Rodrigo journeyed to Italy to study law as a young man under the wing of his uncle, Pope Calixtus III. At this time, nepotism was not only tolerated but expected from the papacy, so, after Rodrigo received his doctorate in law from the University of Bologna, he was given a cardinal's hat. Many of Rodrigo's other relatives had much to gain from Calixtus, whose flagrant generosity toward people who happened to share his blood appalled even the cynical Romans.

With his pragmatic mind and undefeatable charisma which could win over almost any enemy, Calixtus eventually made Rodrigo Vice Chancellor, the highest office next to the papal throne itself. After Calixtus died, seemingly breaking the Borgia clan's hold over the Vatican, Rodrigo continued to prosper, having accumulated a vast amount of wealth from his church incomes and possessing an uncanny instinct for knowing which candidate for the papacy to throw his support behind, thus ensuring their support once they were invested in their office.

Rodrigo not only had much of Rome and the popes themselves eating out of his hand, but also the ladies. But even though he had a great number of mistresses, perhaps the only one he ever truly loved was Vannozza Cattanei, a lovely and wealthy Roman woman. She would bear Rodrigo four children: Juan, Cesare, Lucrezia, and Jofre. Although Rodrigo acknowledged and provided for many of his bastards, his four children by Vannozza would receive the lion's share of his love and attention. To protect Vannozza's honor more than his own, however, Rodrigo married her to Domenico da Rignano, a church clerk whose job conveniently took him out of Rome most days.

Lucrezia was born a few days after Domenico's death. She was a well-formed girl who apparently bore a great resemblance to her mother. As one courtier would describe her in her adulthood:

> She is of middle height and graceful of form; her face is rather long, as is her nose; her hair is golden, her eyes gray, her mouth rather large, the teeth brilliantly white, her bosom smooth and white and admirably proportioned. Her whole being exudes good humor and gaiety.

Although Rodrigo was not yet in a position where he could be intimately involved in his children's lives and not suffer the wrath of some prudish individuals who still stayed with the Church, he doted especially on Lucrezia, who spent her childhood under the care of Rodrigo's cousin, Adriana de Mila.

Although the brilliant and cold Cesare would end up being the main instrument for the Borgias' ambitions, Rodrigo harbored dynastic dreams for his golden-haired daughter from her early childhood. On February 26, 1491 he engaged her to marry Juan de Centelles, a Spanish noble. The contract was promptly annulled when in the spring of 1492 a better opportunity presented itself in the form of a more prestigious Spaniard, Gasparo de Procida, heir to the Count of Aversa.

Lucrezia and Procida actually made it far enough along the road to the chapel that according to the customs of the day they were as good as married, but Rodrigo abruptly dissolved the match and engaged Lucrezia to the 28-year-old Giovanni Sforza, the Lord of Pesaro. The Sforzas were one of the great Italian families of the day and had the rich duchy of Milan in their grasp. Such a match could be quite advantageous, especially for a man who had just been elected Pope.

After years of building himself up through bribes and promises, the 53-year-old Rodrigo Borgia at last ascended to the papal seat on August 10, 1492 and proclaimed himself Pope Alexander VI. Although it is hard to argue that Alexander made for a good spiritual leader (as one dissenter put it, 'It is impossible to imagine a more avowed enemy of God than this Pope'), he was a born politician and his bull-headed pragmatism served the papacy well in the turbulent days ahead. Unfortunately, it also meant that despite his overwhelming love for Lucrezia he would continue using her as a pawn to further his own ends, although such a seeming contradiction to us would not have been puzzling to most Renaissance fathers, no matter how devoted.

Lucrezia already bore a stain on her reputation because of her father's plans, since in the eyes of some she had already been married to Gasparo de Procida. She was only thirteen and had already been involved in two failed marriage negotiations. Yet the future must have seemed bright, because with his usual taste for pomp and ceremony Alexander gave the couple a wedding to remember, complete with a rich banquet, scantily-clad Spanish dancers and a theatrical sex comedy from pagan Rome. Such displays were far from uncommon for Renaissance princes, but for a Vicar of Christ it was another matter entirely.

In fact, even though in reality he was a shrewd but warm-hearted and accessible man, Alexander had already done a good job of surrounding himself in scandal. Although in private Alexander's lifestyle was simple and even frugal, when greeting foreign dignitaries and princes he did everything in his power to overawe them with the wealth of the papacy. Furthermore, while Alexander had had to keep his dear bastard children at arm's length while a cardinal, as Pope he now surrounded himself with them. Even though it was Pope Innocent VIII who first openly acknowledged his bastards, rather than tactfully refer to them as his 'nephews' and 'nieces' as previous popes had done, Pope Alexander VI was the first to have his children live near him. He had even insisted Lucrezia and her husband live in a palace situated near the Vatican which they would share with his new mistress, Giuliana Farnese.

The tightly-knit Borgias and their licentious yet holy patriarch inspired some bizarre rumors that proved useful ammunition to the Borgias' ever growing list of rivals. Most persistent were the biting rumors of incest between Lucrezia and both her father and her brother. One story claimed that the Borgias held midnight orgies where the best prostitutes in the city would crawl on their knees to pick up hot chestnuts thrown on the floor by the watching Borgias, followed by an orgy.

If this bizarre gossip of unhealthy family bonding reached the ears of Lucrezia's lawful husband, their marriage was still a comfortable enough business arrangement for both parties. However, factors beyond both Lucrezia and Giovanni's control would destroy it. In 1494 King Charles VIII of France, a young man whose stupidity was said to have been exceeded only by his ugliness, had a falling out with Alexander VI over Charles's ancestral claim to the throne of the kingdom of Naples. Ludovico Sforza, the patriarch of that family, threw his lot in with France, hoping to rid himself of the troublesome King Ferrante, who ruled Naples, and ingratiate himself with the King of France in one swoop. Alexander, on the other hand, felt obligated to the ruling dynasty of Naples, who were linked to his homeland Aragon and the royal family of Spain.

Giovanni was stuck in a dangerous situation, forced to choose between his family and his in-laws. He did agree to lead a Neapolitan regiment against France, but he also leaked battle plans back to Milan, his wife unaware that her husband was stabbing her father in the back. By March Giovanni either could no longer stand the risk or he felt that the ink was drying on his death warrant so he left Rome in the middle of the night. Even if Alexander was not planning on serving up his treacherous son-in-law's head on a silver platter, he was deeply offended and planned to dissolve the marriage, no matter what the consequences.

But, first things first, Alexander had to take care of the young Charles VIII, who did not stand half a chance against the wily pope. Through clever diplomacy and outright treachery, including Alexander's successful plan to put his son Cesare in a position to rob Charles's men blind, Alexander turned the tables on Charles and entered into an anti-French alliance, the Holy League of Venice, with Austria, Spain, Milan and Venice. In the end, Charles was able to claim Naples for a short time only before he was forced to cut his losses and flee Italy.

Now free to focus on his treacherous son-in-law, Alexander dissolved the marriage by papal decree on December 22. The grounds for the annulment were that Giovanni was impotent and unable to consummate the marriage, a little detail Giovanni protested because not only was it a dire affront to his honor, but it was also a massive obstacle to any future marriage negotiations. Even more importantly, he did not want to have to relinquish Lucrezia's dowry to Alexander, which a verdict of impotence would by law require. Although Giovanni went crying to the family patriarch Ludovico, he was unwilling to further aggravate this Pope for the sake of his foolish young, obscure relative's honor and some pocket change. In the end, Giovanni had no choice but to let the issue of his masculinity hang where it did.

For Lucrezia, the matter of her most recent failed marriage was far more devastating. At the age of seventeen, she had seen her first full marriage end with disgrace for both parties, not to mention the path of trashed marriage negotiations that preceded it. She must have also realized that the same father who adored her was also more than willing to use her as his cipher, regardless of the consequences to her own happiness or reputation. It is telling that in the period following the annulment Lucrezia fled to the convent of San Sisto where she stayed for some time in defiance of her father's orders to return to Rome. Lucrezia's action was not at all unusual. Often aristocratic women took sanctuary at convents where they had a safe refuge away from the power of overbearing male relatives.

Still, there is another possible motive given about Lucrezia's brief stay at the convent, although it might have been inspired more by anti-Borgia hysteria than fact. According to the story, Lucrezia had a long-term affair with one of her father's favorite valets, a young and very attractive man named Pedro 'Perotto' Calderon, and became pregnant by him. To hush up any possible scandal, Lucrezia agreed to hide herself away at the convent until she came to term and the baby could be spirited away. What gives this otherwise typical story some weight is the fact that, at about the same period when Lucrezia lived at the convent, Pedro's corpse was found floating in the Tiber River.

If Lucrezia actually bore a bastard Calderon, if they were at least guilty of some serious indiscretion at one point, or if Pedro himself was just the unlucky victim of a timely but random act of violence unrelated at all to the Borgias, we cannot know.

Despite the tale about her unmaidenly behavior and its grisly result, Alexander managed to arrange one more beneficial marriage for Lucrezia. The suitor was Alfonso de Bisceglie, a Neapolitan duke and the acknowledged bastard half-brother of the new king of Naples, Ferrante. Not only was this the most lucrative marital alliance Alexander engineered, but it would give Lucrezia the happiest years of her life. Alfonso was not only, according to observers, 'the handsomest young man ever seen in the imperial city', but also intelligent, generous, and good-natured. Between Lucrezia and Alfonso, who also happened to match each other in age, it was literally love at first sight and, only six days after their very first meeting, they were married on July 21, 1498 in a fairly modest ceremony in the Vatican, modest at least by the dizzyingly high standards set by the Borgias.

For once, Lucrezia was overjoyed with the match her father had made for her. The two newlyweds were completely devoted to each other and proved the perfect couple, both physically and intellectually. To Lucrezia's horror, however, external matters were once again about to work against her happiness.

King Charles VIII, the indirect cause of Lucrezia's trouble the last time, died after accidentally hitting his head against a stone rafter, a poetic end for such a worthless king. His successor was a distant cousin, who became Louis XII, and who had not only inherited Charles's claim to the kingdom of Naples, but also had a blood claim to the duchy of Milan. Realizing that another French invasion of Italy would be inevitable, Alexander did his best to get into the new king's good graces. When Louis wished to divorce his unwanted wife Jeanne de Valois for Charles's widow, Anne of Brittany, who brought with her the duchy of Brittany as a dowry, Alexander signed the papers for an annulment in exchange for Louis' favors.

Reading the writing on the wall, cardinals and nobles who were passionately anti-French fled Rome. Alfonso, who was despite his illegitimacy still a close relative to the King of Naples, was among them and joined his allies at a fortress at Genazzano. He sent a letter to Lucrezia, asking her to join him, but unfortunately her father's agents intercepted it. Understandably this separation wore down the nineteen-year-old Lucrezia. To help keep her mind off things Alexander sent her to the town of Spoleto, where she was appointed governor. This was more than just a coddling gesture from her father, who recognized Lucrezia's talent and intelligence despite the age's popular misconceptions about women. It is also interesting to note that her brother Jofre, who accompanied her to Spoleto and was of age, was given no responsibilities or power. Like her father, Lucrezia was a meticulous and approachable ruler, always appointing at least one day in the week to hear and decide on cases from any citizens who approached her. Word of her political abilities must have pleased her father, because he later made her governor of another town, Nepi.

Once the political atmosphere surrounding them simmered down, Lucrezia and Alfonso finally reunited on September 19, 1498, and returned to live in Rome. A year later, after a previous miscarriage, she gave birth to a son, named Rodrigo after her father. Alfonso was also given a secure and lucrative position as head of the papal army. At last, it seemed to Lucrezia that her troubles were over.

Unfortunately, the happiest period of her life would be abruptly cut short by a tragedy engineered by the brother she loved. During a humid summer night, on July 15, 1500, Alfonso was ambushed and stabbed by five masked men on the steps of St Peter's. A servant managed to carry the severely injured man to the Vatican, where Lucrezia and Alfonso's sister, Sancha, found him and took him to his room to be nursed back to health.

Despite the severity of the wounds, it seemed Alfonso would survive. Keeping a vigil over him, Lucrezia and Sancha made sure he did not spend one minute unattended while they also prepared his food themselves to prevent the possibility of poison. In the end, their efforts were not enough. On August 18, apparently on the verge of a complete recovery, Alfonso either suffered a severe relapse or his killers returned to finish the job. The accounts vary wildly, but the most persistent and interesting version involves Lucrezia, Sancha and all other attendants and doctors being forced out of Alfonso's bedchamber by a gang of killers led by Miguel de Corella, one of Cesare's followers and one of Alfonso's original attackers. As Lucrezia and Sancha ran to get help, Alfonso was strangled. He was only nineteen years old.

Oddly enough, Alfonso's killer was almost assuredly Cesare. No one else would have had such easy access to Alfonso's person. Even though it must have been a drastic step to murder the beloved husband of his sister, Cesare's motives are unclear. One strong possibility is that Cesare, who was strongly identified with the

French cause in Italy, had a justifiable fear that Alfonso was or would be out for his blood. After all, Alfonso had betrayed the Borgias once before – why should he be trusted again? It also seems likely that Alexander might have had some part in the murder himself. What is known is that, perhaps out of guilt for either himself or Cesare, Alexander allowed Lucrezia to leave Rome to temporarily resume her political duties in Nepi. Strangely enough, though, there is little indication that Lucrezia's relationship with either her brother or her father became shattered after the murder, even though it is hard to go through the records with doubts over her passion for Alfonso.

That is not to say Lucrezia had a total amnesia when it came to the circumstances surrounding her husband's death. When she heard that her father had already started thinking about marrying her off to a Roman nobleman, Francesco Orsini, she vowed in front of him that she would never remarry.

When Alexander demanded to know why, she replied, 'Because my husbands have been very unlucky.'

As defiant as Lucrezia was, she could not resist her father for long. On August 4, 1501, a new marriage contract was signed, promising Lucrezia as a bride to the 24-year-old Alfonso d'Este, heir apparent to the Italian Duchy of Ferrara. Where Alfonso de Besciglie had been affable and loving, this new groom was indifferent and misogynistic. He also had an unusual sexual fetish that made him prefer the company of street prostitutes to that of women of his own class. Even worse, Alfonso and his family were conscious of the fact that Lucrezia was merely the bastard daughter of a foreigner pope while Alfonso came from an old lineage that could trace their rule over Ferrara back to the 1200s. Alfonso's father, the reigning Duke of Ferrara, Ercole, was not enthusiastic about the match even though he was the one who agreed to it, and he gave Lucrezia a shoddy allowance for her household. Lucrezia next found a bitter rival in her sister-in-law Isabella, a renowned patroness of the arts and collector of art who never let Lucrezia forget her dark past and less than patrician background.

Although matters between Lucrezia and Alfonso became so tense that she fled to a convent where she stayed for a long time, she at least found advocates among her adopted people. According to one contemporary, 'She pleased the people so greatly that they are perfectly satisfied with her and they look to Her Majesty for protection and good government.' Unfortunately, among her family's enemies, she was still a living *femme fatale*, trained in the arts of intrigue and murder by her lover/brother and armed with an impressive arsenal of deadly weapons, including a ring laced with poison.

Although burdened by a blackened name, Lucrezia even began to win over her in-laws. Ercole, while maybe not becoming a surrogate father for Lucrezia[42], warmed to her. Even the misogynistic Alfonso came to see his wife in a different light. When Lucrezia gave birth to a stillborn girl, one of her physicians wrote that during the difficult labor Alfonso was 'besieging us with questions and encouraging the midwife'. Later in a letter he lamented 'the most terrible grief' Lucrezia would feel when she learned that her child was dead.

Severely weakened by the painful labor from that birth, Lucrezia seemed to be on the point of death. In her feverish delirium, she was heard to murmur, 'Oh good, I'm dead.' Cesare took some time off from his usual exploits to stay by her side. Lucrezia's doctors observed how Cesare tried to make her laugh to make her more receptive to the doctors' blood-letting treatments and how his presence drastically aided her recovery. Lucrezia eventually did fully recover, although more miscarriages would follow. Fortunately, she did have her successful deliveries: Ercole in 1508, Ippolito in 1509, Alessandro in 1514 (tragically, he would die at the age of two),

[42] At any rate, Lucrezia had no need for a father figure. Alexander wrote to Lucrezia on an almost daily basis and would complain if her responses were delayed by just a single day.

Eleonora in 1515, Francesco in 1516 and Isabella-Maria in 1519, but this birth would cost her life.

Although she at last gave birth to more healthy children despite her miscarriages, death remained a persistent companion to Lucrezia. Malaria claimed both her father in 1504, whom gossip claimed was accidentally poisoned, and his namesake, her son by Bisceglie, in 1512, with whom she always kept in close contact. Most devastating of all was Cesare's unexpected death at the age of thirty-one. He had been ousted by the venomously anti-Borgia Pope Julius II and wound up in a Spanish prison. Cesare succeeded in making a daring escape and became a mercenary leader for the King of Navarre, but died in a battle. When Lucrezia learned of her brother's death, she was heard to say, 'The more I try to do God's will the more He visits me with misfortune.' That night, her ladies-in-waiting could hear her endlessly crying out her brother's name.

Lucrezia, weighed down by grief as she was, excelled as the dowager Duchess far beyond her in-laws' expectations. She turned into a popular patron of artists and poets, a few of whom developed chivalrous relationships with her. One such poet was Pietro Bembo, who received from the lady herself a lock of Lucrezia's hair that is today on display at the Galleria Ambrosia in Milan. Another was Ercole Strozzi, who was one day found dead with his body stabbed twenty-two times, his throat cut, and his hair torn out and arranged in tidy piles around his corpse. One rumor claimed that Alfonso ordered his death because Strozzi's friendship – or romance – with Lucrezia became intolerable. Another said that Lucrezia, driven to madness because Strozzi had married a woman named Barbara Torelli, hired the killers. The most likely truth is only a little less colorful: Torelli had been previously married to an Ercole Bentivoglio, an abusive man she left for Strozzi. The Bentivoglio clan wanted revenge and perhaps by killing Strozzi and desecrating his corpse they found it.

While Lucrezia's life remained one of tragedy, it was not without its successes. Given the regency of Ferrara while her husband was away at war, Lucrezia once again became known for her personal touch and her willingness to address grievances brought to her by any citizen, no matter what their rank in society. In an age not well known for equality or tolerance, she stood against anti-Semitism by ordering that the punishment for injuring a Jew should be as severe as the punishment for injuring a Christian.

If Lucrezia could have used her abilities even further, she would not be given that opportunity by history. She died on June 14, 1519 after giving birth to her last child, Isabella-Maria. The husband who once greeted her with disgust wrote in a letter to his nephew, 'It has just pleased the Lord to summon unto Himself the soul of the illustrious lady the duchess, my dearest wife. I cannot write this without tears, knowing myself to be deprived of such a dear and sweet companion. For such her exemplary conduct and the tender love which existed between us made her to me.' Unfortunately, history would not be so kind to Lucrezia's memory, preferring instead the woman who was a scheming murderess to the woman that inspired great artists and was a kinder, more progressive ruler than most of her male peers.

Further Reading

Cloulas, Ivan (trans. Gilda Roberts) *The Borgias* (F. Watts, 1989)
Erlanger, Rachel *Lucrezia Borgia* (Hawthorn Books, 1978)
Mallett, Michael Edward *The Borgias: The Rise and Fall of a Renaissance Dynasty* (Bodley Head, 1969)

COSIMO III

Reign: *May 24, 1670–October 31, 1723*
Born: *August 14, 1642*
Died: *October 31, 1723*
Buried: *Basilica di San Lorenzo, Florence*

The Medici were one of the greatest families ever to dominate Italy: as the Dukes of Florence and later the Grand Dukes of Tuscany, they rivaled the monarchies of Europe in both power and wealth. But by the time of Cosimo III, the once prodigious family was accelerating toward its end. Not only would Cosimo, whose puritanical tendencies contrasted so jarringly with the humanistic heritage of his ancestors, be granted the rare privilege of watching his family come so close to its extinction, he would also unwittingly play an essential role in it.

When Cosimo was born, his father, the Grand Duke Ferdinando II, wanted to give his son and heir the sort of enlightened education worthy of a Medici. Cosimo's pious mother, Vittoria della Rovere, intervened and instead young Cosimo was reared like a priest. The staunchly pious training Cosimo received did nothing to help his natural disposition toward depression. Courtiers noted that even at a very young age he never smiled or danced, and one contemporary wrote that '[h]e is dominated by melancholy beyond all that is usual.' Cosimo was all in all a strangely sensitive child, who preferred to spend hours at prayer and was unable to bear the sight of human or animal suffering. When obliged to go hunting, Cosimo was always seen letting his prey escape.

Although this gloomy and sanctimonious young man might have happily embraced a life of celibacy, like his younger brother Francesco Maria who went on to become a cardinal, his duties as heir demanded that he one day produce legitimate children for the cause of reviving the fading Medici line. For that sacred goal, Ferdinando arranged for Cosimo to marry Marguerite Louise de Orléans, a cousin of the French king Louis XIV.

Although both Ferdinando and Louis XIV thought the match was a perfectly good idea at the time, at least in a political sense, Cosimo and Marguerite Louise would defy the odds by becoming one of the most ill-matched couples in history. While Cosimo was chubby and unattractive, Marguerite Louise was ravishing and athletic. Instead of perusing Scripture as Cosimo did all afternoon, the bride was much more likely to be found going through the latest romance novels. Marguerite Louise was also opinionated, extroverted, proud, and witty, all qualities that would make a husband with Cosimo's sterile outlook cringe.

Even then, no prophetic sense of doom came to warn either Ferdinando II or Louis XIV of the looming marital catastrophe and the two married by proxy on April 17, 1661. Although Cosimo was enthusiastic for married life at first, he eventually became more of a prude than ever. 'He sleeps with his wife but once a week and then under supervision of a doctor who has him taken out of bed lest he should impair his health by staying there overlong', a member of the court wrote. On her part, Marguerite Louise, unsurprisingly bored with her neurotic husband, kept contact with her longtime lover, Charles of Lorraine, and not only exchanged romantic letters with him, but sometimes received him in the flesh as a visitor.

Matters between the couple got to the point where Marguerite Louise, disgusted with the prospect of carrying her unloved husband's child, tried to induce miscarriages whenever pregnant by running races, riding violently on horseback, or even starving herself. Unfortunately for her all this effort went to nothing: she would give birth to Ferdinando on August 9, 1663; Anna Maria Luisa on August 11, 1667; and Gian Gastone on April 24, 1671.

Most of the time, Marguerite Louise did everything in her power to avoid Cosimo, even going so far as staying in separate residences from him. In retaliation, Cosimo wanted to cut off her allowance, but was terrified of offending Louis XIV. He could get away with placing spies in her household staff, who weekly sent Cosimo detailed reports of his wife's extravagant lifestyle, where she threw expensive hunting parties and hosted improper dancing contests for the peasants living around her residences. Because of their reputation, Marguerite Louise was convinced that the Medici would try to poison her and so she always kept a food taster on hand. After Ferdinando II died on May 27, 1670 and Cosimo was named Grand Duke, he decided to keep his wife under lock and key at the castle of Poggio a Caiano indefinitely.

After giving birth to Gian Gastone, Marguerite Louise deemed that she had fulfilled her obligations as a wife by giving the Medici two sons and demanded to be allowed to return to France. Louis XIV refused to consider it, since doing so would have been an admission that he made a rare mistake in setting up the marriage, so instead the king sent bishops and envoys from his court to work as marriage counselors for the two. While Cosimo would certainly have been glad

to be rid of his sybaritic wife, he could not, in his own eyes, end the marriage and still be a good Christian. In response to Cosimo's refusal, Marguerite Louise furiously fired off a letter to him:

> I have done what I could until now to gain your friendship, and I have not succeeded. The more consideration I showed for you, the more contempt you showed me. For a long time I have tried to bear it, but this is beyond my power. So I have made a resolution which will not surprise you, when you reflect on your base usage of me for nearly twelve years. It is, that I declare I can live with you no longer: I am the source of your unhappiness, as you are of mine. I beg you to consent to a separation to set my conscience and yours at rest.

Realizing what she had to do, Marguerite Louise worked hard to convince both Cosimo and Louis XIV that she had a sincere desire to lead a religious life by joining a French convent. The unfortunate marriage was finally dissolved on December 26, 1674 and Marguerite Louise left for France the next year, never to see Tuscany or her loathed husband again.

Living off a fat pension reluctantly given to her by Cosimo, Marguerite Louise kept up her usual lifestyle at the convent, throwing parties, entertaining courtiers, and now enjoying the attentions of lovers. One abbess who was foolish enough to complain about Marguerite Louise's less than saintly way of living found herself pursued through the convent corridors by the lady herself, wielding a pistol in one hand and a hatchet in the other.

Back in Tuscany things were much less festive than in Marguerite Louise's convent. One Tuscan writer succinctly summed up Cosimo's reign with this: 'Theology became a substitute for statesmanship.' Any citizen of Tuscany who failed to kneel whenever an *Ave Maria* was sounded could be sent to prison. Cosimo made a number of draconian laws to try to bridle his subjects' lust, including a law against young men entering any house with at least one unmarried woman in it. He founded a new government department worthy of the McCarthy-era United States, the Office of Public Decency, which placed spies and informers everywhere. One report claims, 'When any persons are informed against, the officers come in the middle of the night and carry them away; and no one of whatever rank dare oppose them.'

The people who suffered most for Cosimo's religious zeal were the Jews of Tuscany. Any interaction between Christians and Jews became risky: a Jew visiting a Christian prostitute, a Christian working for a Jew, and even a Christian woman nursing a Jewish baby without a special license all became serious offenses that could be punished with anything from a lengthy imprisonment to a public lashing.

While once upon a time Florence was a refuge for scholars, writers, and artists hounded by the Church for alleged heretical views, during Cosimo's reign that was no longer the case. Cosimo's predecessors were likely to shield any 'heretics' from the Inquisition; Cosimo was much more liable to hand them over without a second thought. Florence had already seen its own artists and scientists driven to poverty and obscurity by their Grand Duke's refusal to employ them. Instead he preferred to spend his money on procuring relics, bribing hordes of his subjects to be baptized, and hiring men to infiltrate the courts of Protestant dukes and kings and try to convert them to the true faith.

State funds poured toward funding Cosimo's day-to-day habits, which contrasted so glaringly with his otherwise pious thinking. Visitors to Cosimo's court often found themselves literally surrounded with exquisite banquets and costly gifts. For his regular dinners, Cosimo often sent for the rarest ingredients from Persia to China to the Americas. Like many moralists Cosimo was blind to his own hypocrisy and kept being appalled at the reports of Marguerite Louise's excesses over in France.

Cosimo's oldest son and heir, Ferdinando, had the misfortune to take after his detested mother. He inherited none of his father's gloominess, but much of his mother's libido and stubbornness. He would have made a good reigning Medici, but the domineering and bullying attitude his father took with him drove him to greater extremes of recklessness until, finally, he caught syphilis from one of his many one-night stands. The disease would in time drive him mad and then kill him.

Tuscany itself did no better with Cosimo at the helm. When he inherited the country, it was already trying to recover from a bad economy, but Cosimo's squandering of state funds and preference for spiritual matters over temporal made an ugly situation even more hideous. Cosimo's fragile ego did inspire him to take part in one political action, and that was his successful petition to gain the right to be referred to as 'His Royal Highness', a title usually reserved for kings. He also spent a lot of attention and money on being appointed as a canon of St. John Lateran, an office that gave him the dear privilege of holding the handkerchief of St Veronica, a relic which was said to have the features of Jesus Christ imprinted on it. This was the happiest moment in Cosimo's life.

Cosimo found that he would need to concentrate on his family when Ferdinando's illness and demise as well as Gian Gastone's homosexuality forced him to face the cold fact that the Medici were dying out. To try to save Medici blood, Cosimo convinced his brother Francesco to renounce his vows in order for him to marry. Unfortunately, Cosimo ignored the fact that Francesco Maria, who ironically was as suited for the priesthood as Cosimo was for a secular life, was notorious in Florence for keeping a virtual harem of strapping young men at his exquisitely furnished villa to perform gymnastic feats and wrestling matches for his amusement. Although Francesco, no matter what his personal inclinations might have been, readily agreed to a marriage, his chosen bride, the much younger Eleonora Gonzaga, was not as willing. Repulsed by her fat and old groom, she spurred his advances for days after their marriage, claiming she was afraid of 'contracting dreadful diseases'. Eventually, Eleonora did share a bed with her disgusting husband, but it did not lead to a child. She was spared a second try when Francesco died from dropsy on February 3, 1711.

As the Medici lurched toward oblivion, Cosimo himself was nearing death. In his doting old age it was reported that 'he had a machine in his own apartment where on were fix'd little images in silver of every saint in the calendar. The machine was made to turn so as still to present in front the saint of the day, before which he continually performed his offices'.

After remaining painfully ill for almost two months, Cosimo died on October 31, 1723, All Saints' Day. Undoubtedly for him this was the perfect day to die. Cosimo would not have been nearly as pleased, however, to see himself replaced by an heir who was every bit as hedonistic as he himself had been devout.

Further Reading

Acton, Harold Mario Mitchell *The Last Medici* (St. Martin's Press, 1959)

Young, G.F. *The Medici* (Charles Boni, 1930)

GIAN GASTONE

Reign: *October 31, 1723–July 9, 1737*
Born: *May 24, 1671*
Died: *July 9, 1737*
Buried: *Basilica di San Lorenzo, Florence*

It seems that sometimes a strict upbringing at the hands of a pious parent produces a child with a taste for everything their parent hated. One very clear example of this is the youngest son and heir of Grand Duke Cosimo de' Medici III of Tuscany, Gian Gastone, who proved to be almost the exact antithesis of his excessively austere father.

From the start of his life Gian Gastone showed that he had inherited his father's chronic depression. Even at an early age he was shy and quiet, prone to spend hours in his room crying because of some unknown sadness. Perhaps much of young Gian Gastone's misery came not only from his genetics, but also a lonely childhood. His father was anything but affectionate and his mother Marguerite Louise of Orléans, who hated her husband to the point that she detested all her children and had even tried to miscarry them, completely ignored him. Eventually the miserable marriage between Marguerite Louise and Cosimo was dissolved and Marguerite Louise moved to a convent in France, where she rarely bothered keeping in touch with any of her children, especially Gian Gastone. He did not find much sympathy or companionship from his two older siblings, Ferdinando and Anna Maria, both of whom were considerably older. Gian Gastone might as well have been an only child as well as an orphan. As he aged, he learned how to mask his depression behind a wall of wit and sarcasm, just as his father had found his own refuge in religion.

The tragic fact that the Medici family was slowly fading away would force this sad and unwanted son into the spotlight. The question of whether or not there would be yet another generation of Medici rested entirely on the vibrant but self-destructive Ferdinando and on Gian Gastone. Unfortunately, from all indications, Gian Gastone was a homosexual.

If Cosimo was aware of his son's disposition, he gave no sign and put him as a pawn on the European marriage market anyway. Perhaps Cosimo hoped that Gastone could put aside his tastes for the sake of the survival of the Medici bloodline. But Cosimo apparently learned nothing from his own disastrous marriage to Marguerite Louise and engaged the 23-year-old Gian Gastone to Anne Marie Francesca, the daughter of a German duke, a woman who would not prove to be the best choice for Gian Gastone.

Anne Marie, already a wealthy widow thanks to a previous marriage, was proud enough to believe she was fit for a king's bed, not the bed of an heir whose ancestors were merchants and bankers.

She also refused to move from her beloved homeland of Bohemia for Florence and insisted in the marriage negotiations that Gian Gastone instead come to live with her. Unable to resist his father's demands, Gian Gastone set out for Bohemia in order to marry Anne Marie on July 2, 1697 and live by her side in the Bohemian castle of Reichstadt near Prague.

If homosexual royal scions throughout history were always unable to take the plunge and impregnate their brides with heirs or accept the attentions of their grooms, then more dynasties throughout the ages would have gone extinct. The marriage between Gian Gastone and Anne Marie had an added and even more insurmountable disadvantage: the newlyweds were absolutely repulsed by each other. Loathing her shy, studious, but rude husband, Marie Louise bossed him around like a servant while telling everyone willing to listen that her pathetic weakling of a husband was impotent. Gian Gastone in turn hated his wife, whom he described as 'immensely fat'. She also stank of horses, since she was not only an avid rider, but spent hours in the stables having imaginary conversations with her precious steeds. In a letter to his father, Gian Gastone wrote, 'She is haughty and vain enough to trample on everybody and govern everybody, believing that she is the greatest lady in the world, because she owns these clods in Bohemia.' To preserve his sanity, Gian Gastone began to turn to alcohol and gambling for comfort. One person who knew Gian Gastone well noted, 'He wished to drown the thoughts that oppressed his whole being.' He started to rent out a townhouse in Prague to flee to when married life became too unbearable.

The year after the unhappy marriage began Gian Gastonehad finally had enough and fled to France, hoping to find refuge with his distant mother, whom he imagined would be more sympathetic to his plight than his uptight father would ever be. Surely she of all people would know what it was like to be lonely and stressed because of an arranged marriage? He was wrong. Instead, his mother gave him a frigid reception and was more anxious each day to see him off to Italy. Luckily, Gian Gastone found a more polite welcome from his relative, King Louis XIV, at Versailles, where he indulged himself in the glitter of the Sun King's famous court.

All good times have to come to an end and Gian Gastone returned with a heavy heart to his wife in Bohemia, but, emboldened by his successful if temporary vacation, he spent more time roaming Prague and took a lover, Giuliano Dami, who doubled as his pimp: 'There were scores of fresh young students in Prague, smooth-chinned Bohemians and Germans, who were so impecunious they wandered begging from door to door. In this wide preserve Guiliano [Dami] could always hunt for amorous game and introduced some new and comely morsel to the Prince.'

In 1705, Gian Gastone finally gave up the enterprise of bestowing the Medici with fresh blood and left to return to Florence for good. There he lived in isolation, rarely appearing in public, although occasionally he indulged in actions that the public viewed as extraordinarily eccentric. One time he purchased a street vendor's entire stock of brooms and sent them to the offices of the city government. It was a subtle joke to tell them to 'clean up' the bureaucratic corruption in the city.

Meanwhile Cosimo's last hopes for his family's preservation were dashed. Ferdinando, after long years of pain and insanity, died from the syphilis he caught from a one-night adventure. After the death of Cosimo III himself, Tuscany was left to the now fifty-year-old Gian Gastone, the last male Medici. Although he actually did little to govern directly, he had a good eye for ministers who were certain to reform the corrupt government and throw Cosimo III's old stifling laws off the books. Under Gian Gastone's lax but progressive administration, Florence was once again a Mecca of culture and art.

Although he did not squander money on luxury as his pious yet ostentatious father had done, he gradually began to settle into a life of happy hedonism. To the horror of the Florentine elite, he had a tendency to become massively drunk at parties and let fly an endless *blitzkrieg* of lewd jokes and loud swearing. Gian Gastone always came attended by his young male servants, carefully picked because of their looks and brawn, whose chief duty was to make sure their drunken employer would make it home safely after a night of hard drinking. After one gathering he became so drunk he had to be pushed puking into his coach before the horrified eyes of his fellow noblemen.

Guiliano Dami stayed in the new Grand Duke's service and gathered for him young men (and a few women) that would become known as the *ruspanti*, because they were paid up to five ruspi for the time they spent with Gian Gastone. To be eligible for employment, they had to be inspected by the Grand Duke himself, who was particularly on the look out for clean teeth and large genitalia.

One of Gian Gastone's favorite games with the *ruspanti* was to have them pretend to be some of the most important nobles and ministers in Tuscany. Referring to them with the names of the aristocrats they imitated, he would 'introduce' a male *ruspanto* to a female *ruspanta* and say, 'Now Marquis ____, does the Marchioness ____ appeal to you? If so, proceed to business; away and forge ahead.' As the man would caress and kiss the woman, Gian Gastone would urge them on by bellowing, 'Go on! Top her!' One night a handsome Florentine barber was solemnly invited to consummate his new marriage in the Grand Duke's presence.

Not everything in Gian Gastone's orgies was fun and games. He seemed to also enjoy having his *ruspanti* beat and insult him whenever that particular mood struck. One Bohemian *ruspanto*, Michael Henzchemic, who was known for his muscular build, was covered with vomit from a very drunken Gian. Enraged, Michael began to pummel Gian so mercilessly he had to call for help. Even then, Gian Gastone could not bring himself to hold a grudge against the well-built Bohemian.

After spraining his ankle in 1730, Gian Gastone perpetually stayed in his bedroom, surrounded by his servants and *ruspanti*. He ate, signed papers, consulted his ministers and did everything else from the comfort of his mattress. Soon his bedroom became a place not for the weak of heart, as it began to stink horribly of wine, tobacco, vomit, and the dogs Gian Gastone allowed to sleep in his bed. Gian Gastone's own appearance became nothing to be proud of, as he let his hair and nails grow out and used his wig to wipe the tobacco and vomit from his mouth.

Such a lifestyle was obviously not conducive to healthy living and, after a month of illness and near-senility, he died on June 21, 1737 and Tuscany passed on to Francis of Lorraine, husband to Maria Theresa, heir to Austria, so soon Tuscany became a dominion under the Habsburgs. Gastone's sister, Anna Maria, was the last of the Medici and she was allowed to inherit most of the Medici's private possessions. In the spirit of munificence and before her death, perhaps to spite the Habsburgs as well, Anna Maria willed all the art and treasures of the Medici to the people of Florence.

Further Reading

Acton, Harold Mario Mitchell *The Last Medici* (St. Martin's Press, 1959)

Green, Vivian *The Madness of Kings: Personal Trauma and the Fate of Nations* (Sutton, 1993)

Young, G.F. *The Medici* (Charles Boni, 1930)

ITALY IN FILM AND LITERATURE

W. Somerset Maugham's novel *Then and Now* follows a diplomatic mission by Machiavelli to Cesare Borgia. In her book, *Lucrezia Borgia and the Mother of Poisons*, Roberta Gilles gives Lucrezia a sympathetic portrayal and puts her in the unexpected position of having to solve a murder mystery. John Faunce wrote *Lucrezia Borgia*, a pseudo-autobiography by Borgia herself. The entire Borgia clan was the subject of a BBC mini-series, *The Borgias*, in 1981 and were topics in the 1974 French film *Contes Immoraux*. Orson Welles himself played the role of Cesare Borgia in the 1949 film *Prince of Foxes*. Also in 1949, both Cesare and Lucrezia Borgia were central to the film *Bride of Vengeance*, starring Paulette Goddard, which works on the premise that Lucrezia really was a *femme fatale* whose murders carried out her family's agenda. Two Italian films feature Lucrezia Borgia and are titled after her: one made in 1940 and the other in 1990. There is also a 1923 silent film from Britain titled *Lucrezia Borgia, or Plaything of Power*.

HUNGARY AND THE BALKANS

VLAD III 'THE IMPALER'

Reign: *October 1448–November 1448; September 6, 1456–December 6, 1462; November 6, 1476–December 1476*
Born: *1431 (?)*
Died: *December 1476 (killed in battle)*
Buried: *Monastery of Snagov, Romania*

Today Vlad III is known mostly for being a likely inspiration for Bram Stoker's novel *Dracula*, but the historical Vlad III stands well on his own as a figure of interest. Like Peter the Great or Henry VIII, Vlad is remembered as an almost superhuman tyrant and mass murderer, yet in Romania he is also recalled as a ruler who was genuinely interested in the welfare of his people. In the eyes of his own homeland he was a more complex autocrat than any connections to the monster of Dracula would have us believe.

Although Bram Stoker's vampire was most likely the composite of various folktales and legends Stoker had heard and read from the Balkan region, a solid and attractive connection exists between the fictional vampire and the historical tyrant in the very name 'Dracula'. Vlad III's father, Vlad II, was known as 'Dracul', the Romanian for 'dragon', since he was a member of the Order of the Dragon, a knightly society founded by Sigismund, the King of Hungary. Being Vlad II's son, the future Vlad III was sometimes referred to as 'Dracula', son of the dragon. However, in his own country and to his adversaries, he was best known as Vlad *Tepes*, 'the Impaler.'

The land Vlad the Impaler was destined to inherit from his father was Wallachia, a Romanian principality. His father had many illegitimate children from a number of mistresses, but he was legitimately married to Vlad III's mother, a Transylvanian native whose name has been forgotten. From her Vlad also had two brothers, Mircea, Vlad II's eldest son and original heir, and a younger brother, Radu.

Vlad happened to grow up during a bad time for his country and for Europe. The military might of the Ottoman Turks was fast sweeping across Eastern Europe from Asia Minor. The Ottomans would finally put an end to the ancient Byzantine Empire once they conquered Constantinople on May 29, 1453, with total victories over the Balkan kingdoms of Bulgaria and Serbia preceding the invasion of that crumbling empire. Even ten years before Constantinople fell, Vlad's life was affected by the rapidly escalating threat of the Ottomans when Hungary, furious over Vlad II's neutrality in a recent war with the Ottoman Empire, deposed Vlad II in favor of his cousin Basarab.

That spring, Vlad II was restored through the aid of the Ottoman Sultan in exchange for his homage. In order to ensure his loyalty, the Sultan demanded that Vlad II hand over his sons Vlad and Radu as hostages. At the time, Vlad was only barely in his teens and Radu only eight or nine. Although it could not have been the best situation for two royal children to be growing up in the hands of their country's enemies, their captors did give them a good education in both books and swords. However, Radu, knowing nothing but the world of the Ottomans, grew into a puppet of the Sultan, while Vlad, who lived always in resentment of his father, became a hardened and cynical man.

As the young Vlad earned the respect of Sultan Murad II and was even allowed to hone his skills as an officer in the ranks of the Ottoman army, his father had a deadly crisis on his hands. One of his rivals, János Hunyady, the Hungarian Viceroy of Transylvania, raised an army against Wallachia late in 1447 and found support with an influential group of treacherous boyars, or nobles, in the principality. Captured in the middle of the fighting, Mircea was buried alive, while Vlad II himself was struck down while trying to get out of the battlefield. Ignoring Prince Vlad's right to the throne, Hunyady instead installed a puppet prince, Vladislav, another cousin of Vlad II's.

When word of Vlad II's death reached Murad II, Vlad III was released from Ottoman hands, in hopes that he would overthrow the new pro-Hungarian regime in Wallachia. A vivid description of Vlad, who had now reached manhood, is shared:

> He was not very tall, but very stocky and strong, with a cold and terrible appearance, a strong and aquiline nose, swollen nostrils, a thin and reddish face in which the very long eye lashes framed large wide green eyes; the bushy black eyebrows made them appear threatening. His face and chin were shaven, but for a moustache. The swollen temples increased the bulk of his head. A bull's neck connected his head [to his body] from which black curly locks hung on his wide shouldered person.

If this description was at all accurate, and the few portraits of Vlad suggest that it is, then he was not only a prince by blood, but he certainly looked the part as well.

Vlad was able to assume power easily, but briefly, when he simply proclaimed himself the rightful Prince in Wallachia while Vladislav was away leading an army to battle. The situation was still too unfavorable and Vladislav managed to drive Vlad out of the country by the end of the year. After spending some time as an honored guest, not a prisoner this time, of Murad II, Vlad traveled to the court of an old ally of his father, Bogdan II, Prince of the other Romanian principality, Moldavia. Unfortunately, the sudden assassination of Bogdan and the consequent unrest forced Vlad to abandon that refuge as well and, ultimately, Vlad had to seek protection from the man responsible for his father's death, Hunyady. Whether Vlad saw this merely as an act of political expediency or if he still hated his father for using him and his brother as bargaining chips, is impossible to say for certain.

Relations between Hunyady and his former puppet Vladislav were rapidly breaking apart, which was why Hunyady found it useful to have Vladislav's most dangerous enemy at his right hand, but Vlad did not act until after Hunyady died from a plague in August of 1456. With Hungary's backing, he succeeded in overthrowing and killing his cousin on September 4. At last taking his rightful inheritance, one of Prince Vlad III's first acts was to pay homage to both Hungary and the Ottoman Empire.

Vlad III meant to be mindful of his more internal enemies. Aware that his brother Mircea and father were in part the victims of boyar insolence, Vlad III invited some 500 boyars involved in his father's betrayal and their families to an Easter feast, only to have them arrested *en masse* afterwards. The old, the crippled, and the females among them were immediately impaled and left to rot in the open countryside, while the young and middle-aged men and the male children were forced to work on the construction of a castle until they literally dropped dead from exhaustion.

This brutality was only the beginning of a full-on assault on the native aristocracy. For crimes of treason, real or exaggerated, not only were the offending boyars massacred, but so were their families. Vlad then redistributed the lands and titles of the executed boyars to men who had proved their loyalty to him, thus replacing an old self-interested nobility with a new one dependent on their Prince's goodwill.

If the aristocrats suffered from Vlad's cruelty, so did the very poor, at least according to one legend. According to this story, Vlad invited all the poor and the crippled from his capital of Târgoviste to a grand feast in his castle. Late into the night, after the crowd had done with the banquet, Vlad suddenly appeared personally, dressed in his finest robes, and addressed his guests with a broad smile. 'What else do you desire?' Vlad asked. 'Do you want to be without cares, lacking nothing in this world?' When the crowd enthusiastically answered 'Yes', Vlad then left and told his guards that the palace was to be sealed and then set ablaze, orders that they carried out right away. About this ruthless experiment in economics, Vlad later commented, 'I did this in order that they represent no further burden to other men so that no one will be poor in my realm.'

Women were another group that suffered under Vlad's harsh regime. Displaying a curious and deep-rooted misogyny, it was said that Vlad composed laws ordering that women found guilty of adultery should have their genitalia mutilated, followed by being skinned alive. Afterwards the body of the victim was to be exposed in public, with the skin hanging separately from a hook. Another punishment prescribed for adulterous women in Vlad's codes involved having a red-hot iron stitched to the victim's vagina until it pierced her entrails.

Despite what conclusions many people might reach about a man who would commit such meticulous mass murder, Vlad III was a deeply devout member of the Orthodox Church who never failed to give all of his victims a Christian burial and often kept both Orthodox and Catholic monks in his court. One legend, however, states that Vlad impaled one Catholic monk who dared lecture him on the morality of his methods. Yet in some of the old Romanian stories it looks as though Vlad had created a paradise on earth. The Wallachia of Vlad III was remembered as a place where crime was rare, if not non-existent. One story went that a cup made of gold was kept in the Square of Târgoviste for thirsty travelers. As long as Vlad III reigned, the cup was never stolen because, the tale concludes, fear of Vlad's justice reached everywhere in his land.

Even outside the legends, it is clear that Vlad ruled his people with an iron, but supposedly benevolent, fist, but he was little kinder to his former captors, the Ottomans. His brother Radu was still in Istanbul as a powerful rival to the throne, backed by the new Sultan Mahomet II. Vlad was also moving away from his old ties with the Ottomans and was becoming closely aligned with Hungary, something that made the Ottomans uneasy. War between Wallachia and the Ottoman Empire was becoming increasingly inevitable.

For the coming storm, Vlad sought help from Hungary, Poland and the Republic of Venice, only to get back in abundance empty promises. Vlad was simply living in the wrong age, when Europe had long gone past the era of crusading fanaticism and entered a time when pragmatism, not religious sentiment, was far more likely to sway nations. The Christian kingdoms of this new Europe were actually more likely to open trade routes with their Muslim neighbors than wage holy war against them.

In 1462 the Ottomans at last struck Wallachia. Vlad was reduced to using a scorched earth policy and guerilla tactics against the far superior armies of Mahomet II. Vlad's strategy paid off on June 17 when, deep into the night, he led a swift, vicious assault on the Sultan's camp. Although Vlad failed to kill the Sultan himself, many of his retinue were slaughtered, but not without cost to Vlad's own men.

Unfortunately, betrayal would prove Vlad's downfall, just as it had with his father. 'The Romanian boyars,' one report goes, 'realizing that the Turks were stronger, abandoned [Vlad] and associated themselves with his brother who was with the Turkish Sultan.' Given the shocking success of the Ottoman Empire and the loss of liberty and dignity their Balkan neighbors suffered under the Ottoman yoke, one can hardly blame them. It must have seemed that there was no alternative outside of submission or annihilation.

With the support of both Mahomet II and the boyars, Radu gained control of Wallachia and Vlad reluctantly fled to one of his castles in Transylvania. On the night of Vlad's arrival an arrow was shot into the castle with a message attached warning him that the Ottomans were preparing for an assault. Vlad's wife, whose name has been forgotten, got to the message first. Declaring that she would 'rather have her body rot and be eaten by the fish of the [river] than be led into captivity by the Turks' she threw herself from the top of the castle into a river. Although this may only be a story, the river is called *Rîul Doanmei*, which in Romanian means 'the River of the Princess'.

With little time to grieve, Vlad moved quickly to Hungary where he sought sanctuary from the king Matthias. Almost overnight, Vlad went from being a guest of the court to a prisoner of the state, due to what has been termed the 'Rothel letters'. These documents, which may very well have been simply forgeries, were allegedly written by Vlad to the Prince of Moldavia and the Sultan of Turkey asking for support in recovering Wallachia in exchange for a military alliance against Hungary. The possibility that the letters were forged is a strong one, but, given Vlad's knack for expediency, it would not be out of character for him to have betrayed a welcoming ally to a recent enemy if it meant recovering his honor and his land.

Whatever their origins, the letters were seized by Matthias who angrily ordered Vlad's imprisonment in Buda. Eventually Matthias gave Vlad an easy choice: stay a prisoner in Hungary, probably for the rest of his life, or convert to Catholicism, marry a member of the Hungarian royal family and earn Hungarian support for any future bid to reclaim his old throne. Not willing to be a martyr to his native faith when there was a second chance to be gained, Vlad agreed to all the conditions and in 1466 married a Hungarian princess, whose name has also been lost to the ages.

In reward for his wise decision, Vlad was given a position as a captain of the army as well as a house in Pest where he lived a fairly quiet life with his Hungarian wife and, later, the two sons she bore him. Although the period of his life in Pest seems strangely idyllic compared to the rest of his career, one peculiar anecdote comes from this time. One day a thief pursued by local authorities broke into Vlad's house. A captain of the guards followed the thief in without bothering to make Vlad aware of what happened. Vlad ambushed the captain and stabbed him to death. When the authorities complained to the king, Vlad calmly said in his defense, 'I did no evil. The captain is responsible for his own death. Anyone will perish thus who trespasses into the house of a great ruler. If this captain had come to me and introduced himself, I would have found the thief and either surrendered him or spared him from death.'

Outside Hungary events were unfolding that would rescue Vlad from the prospect of too peaceful a life. Radu was deposed by Prince Stephen of Moldavia, who replaced him with Basarab, a rival claimant from another branch of Vlad's unwieldy family. Basarab did not rule long until, allied with Stephen Bathory, Prince of Transylvania, Vuc Brancovic, a Serbian chieftain, and King Matthias, Vlad was finally restored in 1476. Unfortunately, the boyars were less than eager to accept the rule of a man who had murdered countless men among their own ranks and put Wallachian autonomy in jeopardy by reaping the ire of the Ottomans.

His third reign did not even last a year before, besieged by both Ottomans and rebellious boyars, Vlad was killed by a volley of arrows, either by accident or by design. Vlad had become something of a black legend among the Ottomans, a story that inspired nightmares in their most battle-hardened troops, so his head was sent to Istanbul to be put on display as a proud trophy of victory. Although there is still debate over the degree Stoker to which used the stories of Vlad III *Tepes* as the cornerstone to his masterpiece, the life of the historical 'Dracula' needs no embellishment.

Further Reading

Florescu, Radu and McNally, Raymond *Dracula: A Biography of Vlad the Impaler, 1431-1476* (Hawthorn Books, 1973)

Treptow, Kurt *Vlad III Dracula: The Life and Times of the Historical Dracula* (Center of Romanian Studies, 2000)

ELIZABETH BATHORY

Born: *August 7, 1560*
Died: *August 24, 1614*
Buried: *Nyirbator, Hungary (?)*

Although Vlad III the Impaler of Wallachia has become entangled in modern vampire lore, so much so that he may be called the 'historical vampire', maybe that designation more aptly belongs to Elizabeth Bathory, a Hungarian countess born in the sixteenth century who earned her fame by a legend that she bathed in the blood of virgins as a beauty treatment. As gruesome and fascinating as the concept is, this story, which can be traced back only to the eighteenth century, is, after all, only a story. Beyond that, her name also invokes, perhaps more justifiably, images of a sadistic sexual predator, a true vampire.

The time when Elizabeth Bathory was born was an uncertain one for her homeland Hungary. In 1526, King Lajos II of Hungary had died fighting the Ottoman Sultan Süleyman at the Battle of Mohács. Following this crushing defeat, that not only cost Hungary the life of its king but also claimed the lives of much of Hungary's aristocracy, the native royal family died out and the crown of Hungary was claimed by right of blood by the Habsburgs of Austria. However, Austrian authority could not stretch across the kingdom in its entirety and soon Hungary was divided between Austria, Turkey and the semi-autonomous principality of Transylvania.

The Bathorys were the most influential family in Transylvania and a constant thorn in the Habsburgs' side. One Bathory, Stephen, was elected the first Prince of Transylvania in 1571 and was succeeded by his nephew, Christopher, in 1575. Elizabeth's uncle, also named Stephen, was elected the King of Poland in 1574 and went on to become a success in the art of war.

Born and raised at the zenith of the Bathorys' influence, Elizabeth was brought up to be a proud representative of the family and to serve as more than an aristocratic brood mare to her future husband, Ferenc Nádasdy, to whom Elizabeth was already engaged at the age of eleven. Her education was elaborate. At a young age, during a time when many of the noblemen in her homeland were barely literate in their own language, she could read and write in Hungarian, Latin, Greek, and German.

Such a young woman, born to a life of privilege and the daughter of such a prominent family, might also be expected to become a very defiant teenager. One surviving rumor claims that Bathory slept with László Benda, a dashing young man who lived on the Bathory estates. Elizabeth, the story goes, became pregnant by him, but as soon as the baby was born it was spirited away and the Bathorys hushed up the affair. Even if this were true or if this rumor was a contemporary one, the marriage contract with Nádasdy went forward. The two were wed without a hitch on May 8, 1575. The bride was fifteen, the groom twenty-one.

Although the Nádasdys were a bit below the Bathorys' radar as far as blue blood went, the marriage was at least a satisfying one, even if Ferenc and Elizabeth both come across more like business partners than spouses in their surviving correspondence . The only dark spot, Elizabeth's seeming inability to conceive with Nádasdy, was soon cleaned away a decade after the marriage. Past 1585 Elizabeth had three healthy children: Anna, Kate and Paul, as well as two children who died in infancy. In an age when infant mortality was very high, Elizabeth's would have been considered a success story.

Elizabeth rarely saw her husband, who was urgently needed on the frontiers against the Turks. The space between the Ottoman Empire, Hungary and Transylvania was a constant war zone, with boundaries that were in flux with each skirmish. Nádasdy not only excelled in war, he was devoted to it, and earned through hardship and blood the position of Captain of the Field Army in Upper Hungary. He became so notorious among the Turkish armies that the soldiers name for him was the 'Black Bey'. With her husband away on duty so much, Elizabeth was left to utilize her background and intelligence to skillfully manage his estates.

Alone, Elizabeth began to develop a taste for torturing her servants – at first to punish them for various misdemeanors, but increasingly because it simply became a hobby to pass the time. It was in 1595 when two people who would later become suspected of aiding Elizabeth in her crimes, a young man named János 'Ficzko' Újváry and an elderly widow named Anna Darvulia, joined her household staff. Darvulia, who was said to have helped and encouraged Elizabeth in maiming and torturing servants even after she went blind, is thought to have tutored her in the fine art of sadism. But it is also likely that her husband not only gave his blessing to his wife's brutal habit, but shared certain exotic techniques with Elizabeth, learned from a lifetime spent among the horrors of war. An interesting letter written in 1602 by a pastor on Bathory's estates scolds both Elizabeth and her husband for certain unnamed crimes. It obliquely declares its own purpose as 'regarding the admonition of His Excellency (Ferenc) and his wife for their acts of cruelty, and there is a woman about whom everyone knows who the Lady uses as her assistant in that place.' The 'assistant' mentioned is almost certainly Darvulia. The implication is that she proved instrumental in these mysterious 'acts of cruelty.'

Whatever her husband's involvement, he died on January 4, 1604, leaving Elizabeth alone but not defenseless. Both her formidable heritage and her equal partnership with her husband had prepared her for what Ferenc's death had made her: one of the most powerful landowners in Hungary. Far from the helpless widow, Elizabeth did not shrink from her new position, as she made clear to one noble who tried to annex a small portion of her estates. In a forceful letter written to this enemy, Elizabeth haughtily challenged him and told him flatly that he would 'find a man in me'.

Elizabeth was a woman with a strong stomach and, like many nobles at the time, she took a cool view of her servants and the serfs on her estates. As has often been pointed out, the unwashed masses were considered to be almost subhuman by those placed above them by birth in those years, but it seems that even for that era and for a place ravaged by war and hardship Elizabeth's treatment of her female servants was shocking – or at least the rumors about it were, unfounded or not.

With the encouragement of Darvulia and the help of a select few servants, including Ficzko, Dorothea 'Dorko' Szentes, Katalin 'Kata' Benecká, and Helena Jo, Elizabeth often had her servants flagellated as she watched, if she did not beat them herself. Servants who were caught stealing had red-hot coins pressed against their skin.

Personally Elizabeth enjoyed stabbing their skin with needles or burning their genitals with lit candles. Sometimes she would even bite into their bodies, breaking the skin. One girl who infuriated her was dragged to a field and had ice-cold water thrown on her until she died from hypothermia. Another was tied to a tree and smeared with honey, then left to be literally eaten alive by insects. One story alleged that, at a townhouse Elizabeth owned in Vienna, a girl was locked in a cage with spikes built around the edges. The cage was raised above the floor and Darvulia attacked the girl with a spear while Elizabeth shouted sexual obscenities from below. As the girl tried to avoid the spear, she would stab herself on the spikes that surrounded her. It was late at night when this took place and it was said that the monks in a monastery that was adjacent to the townhouse were unable to sleep because of the girl's screams and threw clay pots at the wall in protest.

According to the tale that made Bathory's fame and connected her to the vampire mythology, she took her brutality to one more level. On her fortieth birthday, Elizabeth, depressed about her declining looks, struck a young servant so hard her blood splashed on her hand. Believing that the blood had actually made her skin smoother, Elizabeth got the idea that the blood of virgin girls could rejuvenate her and renew her fading beauty. To test her revolutionary theory on skin treatment, Elizabeth had the same unfortunate servant suspended over her bath, where she slashed open her throat, letting the blood drain into her tub as she bathed. After that, she began to routinely bathe in the blood of virgins sent to work in her household staff, until she became disappointed in the results and concluded that only the blood of noble virgins would be good enough. It was only then, when she began to kill the daughters of the nobility, that her downfall began. It is a colorful legend, but it only dates from a text printed in the eighteenth century.

In Elizabeth's own time, it was definitely alleged that, after 1600, a number of her servants began to die under mysterious circumstances. All of the servants, whose bodies bore strange and noticeable cuts, burns and bruises, were given Christian burials on Elizabeth's estates, with the help of local pastors. But then one day a pastor named János Ponikenusz, who would come to testify against Elizabeth, refused to bury any more on his church's grounds, so Elizabeth's inner circle had to bury them. Another clergyman, Andreas Berthoni, asked Elizabeth why so many girls from her household were dying so suddenly. Testily she replied, 'Do not ask how they died. Just bury them.'

Before 1610, it was thought that Elizabeth began taking in aristocratic girls, and it would not have been unusual for a family, usually of the lower nobility seeking to make connections and improve their social standing, to send a daughter to be educated in the household of a great personage like Elizabeth. As the noble daughters under Elizabeth's watch also began to suffer abrupt deaths, questions began to be asked and the rumors shrouding Elizabeth's activities gained ground.

At Elizabeth's main residence at Cachtice in modern-day Slovakia, around the evening of December 10, 1610 at seven o'clock, a squad of armed men, led by the imperial governor of Hungary, Count George Thurzó, entered the estate and arrested the fifty-year-old Elizabeth Bathory and a number of her confidants and servants. According to the popular story, a naked and blood-soaked Elizabeth was caught in the very act of murder with the bruised and bleeding naked corpse of a young woman at her feet.

The reason given for Elizabeth's fall is that a pastor from one of her estates stepped forward with evidence of her crimes that, compounded with the number of noble girls who had disappeared or died during their service under Elizabeth, brought about her arrest. However, the politics that may have been behind the arrest of Elizabeth are too enticing to ignore. She had financially supported her cousin Gabor's bid to become Prince of Transylvania in 1608 and Gabor was a staunch supporter of greater autonomy for Transylvania from Austria. The very man who arrested Elizabeth, Thurzó, backed Habsburg interests and resented the strength and wealth the Bathorys held.

The question remains, was Elizabeth a true serial killer, the victim of an elaborate power play, or both? Whatever the truth, and we will never have the privilege of knowing it for certain, it would be Elizabeth's alleged accomplices that paid the full price. Darvulia had died long ago, but Dorko, Kata, Helena, and Ficzko were taken to trial at the town of Bytca. Ficzko, still a young man at the time, told authorities in detail that he and the others had been involved in various atrocities under the direction of the countess. According to court documents, hundreds of witnesses were called over time to give colorful and incriminating testimonies against Elizabeth and her inner circle, but the exact number of girls allegedly killed by Elizabeth was never pinned down, although estimates varied between forty and 600.

Elizabeth's helpers were all condemned to die except for Kata, who was spared even imprisonment due to lack of evidence. Dorko and Helena were sentenced to have their fingers torn off with red-hot pincers and then be burned at the stake. Ficzko, slightly excused because of his young age, was simply beheaded, but to keep up good form his corpse was burned alongside a very much alive Helena and Dorko.

Meanwhile Elizabeth was tried and condemned *in absentia*, despite her own angry protests. Because of her respectable lineage, or perhaps because it was feared even by the pro-Habsburg Thurzó that a death sentence would lead to her substantial lands being confiscated by the Habsburgs, it was decided that her punishment should be a kind of lifelong house arrest. In a small room in her own castle at Cachtice she was locked away with just a few narrow slits in the walls for air and a slot in the door to pass food through. No one was allowed to see her, although she continued to write and receive letters to and from the outside world.

A second trial for Elizabeth was considered, but the Bathorys themselves resisted it to save face. Elizabeth's own son-in-law, Count Miklos Zrinyi, wrote to the Austrian Emperor Matthias concerning the prospect of a further trial, 'For your Highness can, without a doubt, envisage the extent of the disgrace and the magnitude of the harm that would befall all of us.'

One hot summer night, three years after her lonely imprisonment began, Elizabeth approached her guards and held out her hands through the slot where the food was passed in. 'See my hands, how cold they are,' she said.

The guard replied, 'It is nothing, my Lady. Will you not now retire for the night?'

When the guards returned the next day – August 25, 1614 – they found her dead. If the stories of her trying to maintain her beauty by bathing in the easily obtained blood of the poor have no foundation in fact, her reputation as a serial killer, a sexual monster, who took the concept of a class predator beyond metaphor has a more solid basis, although there have been many arguments that Elizabeth was the victim of politics, not her own crimes. It is easy enough to doubt the motives behind Elizabeth's trial, but the vividness of the contemporary accounts and the number of willing witnesses suggest that, at the very least, Elizabeth was a nightmare employer.

Further Reading

McNally, Raymond *Dracula Was A Woman: In Search of the Blood Countess of Transylvania* (McGraw-Hill, 1987)

Penrose, Valentine (trans. Alexander Trocchi) *The Bloody Countess* (Creation Books, 1970)

Thorne, Tony *Countess Dracula* (Bloomsbury, 1997)

GABOR BATHORY

Reign: *November 11, 1608–October 1613*
Born: *1589*
Died: *October 1613*

Like all highly successful families, the Bathorys, who turned into the most influential family in the unstable principality of Transylvania, became viewed as more than mortal beings who somehow experienced emotions and lusts beyond the scope of lesser mortals. This perception was almost certainly true in the case of Gabor Bathory, the cousin of the notorious Elizabeth Bathory and the elected Prince of Transylvania, who came to rule after an illustrious line of reigning Bathorys. Gabor, superhuman or not, was not as successful as his more well remembered ancestors in the realm of politics, but he did prove to be a Genghis Khan in the bedroom.

After the death of Sigismund Rákóczy, who kept the title of Prince of Transylvania away from the Bathorys, Gabor was elected in his place at the age of just seventeen, obviously riding his family's reputation rather than his own. As his minister, Gabor Bethlen, dealt with the affairs of the State, Gabor devoted himself fully to the life of a hedonist and became notorious for his romantic conquests. Even when on serious business, such as leading a campaign against the Romanian principality of Wallachia, it was said that, at a party, Gabor placed beside him a teenaged boy, Pal Szilaszy, and at his other side a pretty young Romanian noblewoman. He encouraged Szilaszy to kiss the woman and then '[h]e embraced them both, and now he kissed and fondled the boy, then the girl.' Not even the wives and daughters of his ministers and courtiers were safe from his overfriendly attentions. To keep them from becoming too annoyed, Gabor was known to have bribed them while he seduced and played with their spouses in public. So excessive were Gabor's yearnings and his willingness to act upon them that he had the nickname 'Crazy Gabor'.

Although at first few were willing to protest even when he became too friendly toward their wives, one nobleman, Balthazar Kornis, who found himself cuckolded numerous times by the Prince, joined Stephen Kendy, one of Gabor's ministers, in plotting an assassination in 1610. The assassin chosen for the deed made it so far that he was able to break into Gabor's bedroom while he slept, but on the sacred sight of royalty he found himself unable to stab Gabor and instead woke him up and confessed everything. The conspirators were punished with the necessary bloodshed, but since Kornis was a Catholic the plot was given a religious flavor. Gabor then began to persecute Transylvanian Catholics and passed a law forbidding any of the aristocracy to convert to Catholicism.

This would not be the only significant challenge to Gabor's half-hearted rule. His own most trusted and crucial minister, Bethlen, became sick of having his policies dismissed and tried asserting himself over Gabor. One day, though, he went too far with his nagging and Gabor became so enraged by Bethlen's insolence that he threatened him with a sword and set his beard on fire with a candle. Bethlen was then exiled from court on September 12, 1612, but came back as a rival candidate for Prince of Transylvania, backed by the Ottoman Empire and the wealthy Saxon merchants of Transylvania.

Gabor's past recklessness caught up with him as he found himself quickly deserted on all sides. He attempted to escape to wait for a better day, but ended up being betrayed by his own friend, Andre Ghyczy, and was handed over to die at the hands of the Hajdùks, an independent and brutal Hungarian military order whose leader was at one time persecuted and executed at Gabor's personal order. Apparently Gabor was made to be a gigolo, not the ruler of a turbulent land.

Further Reading

Barta, Gabor (trans. Adrienne Chambers-Makkai et al.) *The History of Transylvania* (Akadémiai Kiadó, 1994)

ALEXANDER OBRENOVIC V

Reign: *March 6, 1889–June 11, 1903*
Born: *August 2, 1876*
Died: *June 11, 1903 (assassinated)*
Buried: *St Mark's Church, Belgrade*

Exactly seven years after Serbia was declared a kingdom, following centuries of domination by the Ottoman Empire, on March 6, 1889, King Milan Obrenovic of Serbia abdicated and left the throne to his son Alexander, who was only thirteen years old. Like many monarchs who are crowned at a very early age, Alexander would become too obsessed with his own power. However, he also had the misfortune to be born at a time when his kind of autocracy was out of fashion in Europe.

Alexander's own father and predecessor never served as a model for good leadership. A man who devoted himself to impressing European high society rather than winning over his subjects, King Milan was talked about as a 'Parisian vagabond' by his own people. Milan had a turbulent and always unhappy relationship with his wife, Alexander's mother, Natalie, which eventually ended in a divorce. One of the sticking points between the two was that Natalie, the daughter of a Russian general, wanted Alexander to have a traditional Russian education. When Milan refused, Natalie went as far as kidnapping the young Alexander and shipping him off to Russia, although, much to Natalie's frustration, the prince was rescued soon afterwards.

Both Milan and Natalie were both widely despised by their own subjects for their penchant for immodest living. Milan in the long run had little choice but to abdicate. To seal the deal, the Serbian government even bribed him to renounce his Serbian citizenship and leave the country. If the government officials wanted to mold more of a puppet king and less of an embarrassment with Milan's son, they were sorely out of luck. Three years after becoming king, at the age of sixteen, Alexander calmly announced to his ministers and officials that he had commanded the army to secure important areas in the capital of Belgrade. Then he suddenly ordered that everyone in the room be arrested. In a matter of moments, Alexander had made himself an absolute monarch.

In 1894, Alexander's parents remarried and returned to Serbia, hoping to have a say in how Serbia was being run. They returned to find that Alexander had abolished the country's more democratic constitution, created in 1888; stripped the press of its freedoms; robbed the Parliament of anything but the illusion of power; and all but banned political parties. Enslaving the country was bad enough, but what would really make his parents wash their hands of him, however, was the fact that Alexander soon fell in love with a servant of Natalie's, Draga Mashin, who happened to be twelve years his senior. Milan and Natalie threatened Alexander, who had already put in motion plans to marry Draga and crown her his queen, but he was not about to back down.

'If this decision of yours is irrevocable, as you say, then there is nothing left for me but to pray for the Fatherland,' Milan said to his son. 'After this impulsive act, I will be the first to greet the cabinet which would overthrow you.'

Milan's prediction was not a hasty one. Alexander and Draga had surpassed even Natalie and Milan in sheer unpopularity. If the playboy lifestyles of his parents were grating, his cold, dictatorial ways and his wife's tough, arrogant personality were infuriating. Although Alexander tried to cobble together a liberal constitution at one point, he could not dredge up any love from his people. Finally, on June 11, 1903, the king and queen were shot dead by military officers, prompted to assassination by rumors that Alexander was planning to declare his brother-in-law heir to the throne. The royal corpses were unceremoniously thrown into a palace garden: there was no regret for his brutal murder.

Further Reading

Pavlowitch, Stevan *Serbia: The History Behind The Name* (C. Hurst, 2002)

HUNGARY AND THE BALKANS IN FILM AND LITERATURE

There is still an unsettled debate over how much the legends around Vlad III inspired Bram Stoker's novel *Dracula*, but it is generally accepted that Vlad was at least one of the main sources. It would be beyond the scope of this project to provide a filmography of all the many Dracula films made since Tod Browning's *Dracula* in 1931. It should be mentioned, though, that few Dracula films have capitalized on the connection between Vlad III and the fictional monster (including Francis Ford Coppola's 1992 production of *Dracula* and the 1993 B-movie *Dracula Rising*) and only one, to date, has attempted to depict the historical Prince Vlad with no supernatural overtones: a TV movie titled *Dark Prince: The True Story of Dracula*.

Elizabeth Bathory herself was the topic of 1970's *Countess Dracula*, a Hammer Studios production that, while not following the real-life biography of Elizabeth Bathory closely, was directly based on the story of her bathing in blood. There is also the 1974 film *Contes Immoraux*, which has Elizabeth Bathory played by Pablo Picasso's daughter, Paloma. Two novels have been written about Bathory: Andrei Codrescu's *Blood Countess*, where Elizabeth Bathory haunts a present-day descendant, and Frances Gordon's *Blood Ritual*, also about the bloodthirsty descendants of Elizabeth Bathory.

THE BYZANTINE AND OTTOMAN EMPIRES

PHOKAS

Reign: *November 23, 599–October 609*
Died: *October 609*

Even after the year 476, when the last Emperor in Rome, the adolescent Romulus Augustulus, was forced into a very early retirement by the German chieftain Odoacer, the Roman Empire lived on in the East, centered around the magnificent city of Constantinople. The western and eastern halves of the Roman Empire had been divided between two emperors since 395, but while the Western Empire slowly died, the Eastern flourished and retained a unique Greek culture and identity although it remained Latin in name. In recent centuries, the Eastern Roman Empire, better known today as the Byzantine Empire, acquired the reputation of being opulent yet barbaric. The Byzantines never did lack cruel men like Phokas, but neither did the more kindly remembered Romans of the West.

Phokas, completely devoid of blue blood as he was, clawed his way to power from the ranks of the military. The way was paved by Emperor Maurice, a neurotic cheapskate who turned his own armies against him when he refused to spend the money needed to bring home one regiment for the winter from the Balkans. Disgusted to have an Emperor who refused to open his pockets for a simple favor, the regiment revolted and proclaimed Phokas, one of their centurions, as the new emperor. Once the rebellion gained speed, Maurice and his family fled Constantinople disguised as civilians and set out for Persia, whose king, Chosroes, was a personal friend of Maurice's. Unfortunately, Maurice's gout and some bad weather stranded the imperial family at the Bay of Nikomedia, just as Phokas was crowned the new Emperor of the Romans.

One of the new Emperor's first acts was to secure his future by sending a troop of soldiers to kill his predecessor and his family. During the flight, Maurice suffered a breakdown and when his killers found him he greeted them with a smile. Right before his eyes he saw the troops butcher his sons. Quietly Maurice mumbled, 'Thou art just, O Lord, and just are thy judgments', over and over again until the assassins finally came for him. The Empress Constantina and Maurice's daughters were at first spared and exiled to a convent, but later even they were put to death for being suspected of having secret communications with Germanos, a rival of Phokas.

Although such casual violence had been an ugly side-effect of the imperial office for centuries, historians are unanimous in claiming that this sort of thing was second nature to Phokas. Even his appearance seemed a reflection of his brutish personality: he had blazing red hair, thick eyebrows resting above glaring eyes, and a scar

spanning his face that turned red whenever he was angry. Phokas was also known to have been an alcoholic, and an angry drunk at that, as well as a sadist, whose favorite pastime was watching prisoners being tortured on the rack.

Although he was both by career and nature a military man, Phokas tarnished his reputation as Emperor by some disastrous decisions with the army. The nomadic Slavs and the Avars were flooding across Byzantine provinces in the Balkans, but Phokas showed himself inept at turning the tide. Using his friend Maurice's murder as an excuse, in 603 King Chosroes of Persia declared war on the Byzantine Empire, pinning Phokas between the threats of Persia in the East and the nomads in the West. The one man who might have made a difference, the vastly talented general Narses, was burned alive because he was involved in a minor and all too brief revolt against Phokas. Instead of selecting a soldier with skills matching those of Narses to command the armies, Phokas bowed to nepotism and chose his incompetent nephew, Domentziolos.

As for Phokas himself, he was much too busy to cope with the enemies chipping away at his empire from every side. The one concern that stayed fresh in his mind was to keep up the persecution of his Jewish subjects. The anger caused by Phokas's oppression became so intense that the Jewish citizens of Antioch rioted, massacring their Christian neighbors and even going so far as abducting that city's patriarch, Anastasios, and killing him in a way so ghoulish that several chroniclers of the period refuse to describe what really happened to the holy man in any detail.

It became only a matter of time until someone would muster enough popular support to rid Constantinople of Phokas. That someone was Heraklios, the son of a renowned general from Carthage, who traveled to Constantinople in 609 at the head of an army to have himself proclaimed Emperor. Phokas had succeeded in alienating so many of his citizens that Heraklios found almost no swords raised against him at the gates of Constantinople. The now ex-Emperor suddenly found himself dragged to the new Emperor's presence and thrown down to his knees.

'Is it thus that you have governed the Empire?' Heraklios is said to have asked his crushed predecessor.

Phokas answered, 'Will you govern it any better?'

Heraklios's response to this challenge has not been recorded. He might have had Phokas literally cut into pieces or thrown to a furious mob, but the accounts vary. It is also unknown if Heraklios ever really worried that he might end up like Phokas, who had himself ended up like his predecessor Maurice. Luckily, Heraklios was both a capable and a beloved Emperor, who would go on to establish a dynasty, yet the old cycle of violence would repeat itself with his descendant, Emperor Justinian II.

Further Reading

Norwich, John Julius *Byzantium: The Early Centuries* (Alfred A. Knopf, 1989)

Olster, David Michael *The Politics of Usurpation in the Seventh Century: Rhetoric and Revolution in Byzantium* (A.M. Hakkert, 1993)

JUSTINIAN II

Born: *669*
Reign: *685–695 (deposed); 705–November 4 (?), 711*
Died: *November 4 (?), 711*

In Byzantine culture, it was thought that a serious physical deformity was an insurmountable bar for anyone seeking the imperial office. For that reason, it was actually considered a merciful alternative to the penalty of death for an emperor to blind or mutilate a dangerous rival. One favorite 'act of mercy' of the Byzantine emperors for their rivals was *rhinokopia*, a practice that called for cutting the victim's nose off. This happened to the deposed emperor Justinian II, but it did not keep him from claiming the Empire. It only succeeded in one respect: it helped him become a bitter and vindictive tyrant.

Justinian II was raised to the purple after the death of his father, Constantine IV, from dysentery at the age of thirty-three. To ensure that his son would succeed unhindered, Constantine IV subjected his brothers, Heraklios and Tiberius, to *rhinokopia*. Yet even in the dangerous gilded world of the Byzantine imperial court Justinian II seemed to have a bright future. He was the latest member of an esteemed dynasty and named after one of the most renowned and effective emperors ever to reign in Constantinople, which alone seemed a good mark in his favor.

Unfortunately, the prospects for the Byzantine Empire itself did not seem so rosy. Constantinople was endlessly besieged by the Arabs from the East and the Slavs from the West. To try to solve one problem with the other, Justinian relocated a number of Slavs to a colony east of Constantinople, hoping that they would indirectly serve the Empire by defending their land against the Arabs. The policy backfired horrifically when instead most of the Slavic warriors in the colony defected to the enemy. Justinian, who always seemed to have a vindictive temperament, ordered that the families of those who had betrayed the Empire be massacred – or so the legend says. Evidence has been put forward that the massacre was either not as extensive as the chroniclers claim or that the incident may not have happened at all. Still, the account is not at all inconsistent with the sort of ruler Justinian seems to have been.

In the first years of his reign, Justinian had little more luck with the Church. In his time, the Great Schism between the Catholic and Eastern Orthodox Churches had not yet happened, so when Justinian held a church council to institute some new clerical laws and condemn certain heretical sects, the Pope in Rome had every right to have his say on the matter. Especially unhappy with a clause giving priests in the Byzantine churches freedom to marry, Pope Sergius I angrily proclaimed with regard to the entire declarations of the council, 'I would rather be dead than consent to the new errors they contain.' Justinian was happy to oblige him.

When threats and pleas did not work to get the Pope's consent to the council's decisions, Justinian arrested two important papal officials in Constantinople, John and Boniface. He threatened to do worse and even arrest the Pope himself. This was not without precedent: both Justinian and Sergius were well aware that Justinian's grandfather, Emperor Constans, had Pope Martin I imprisoned and probably starved to death in a jail cell for his defiance. With this legacy in mind, Justinian sent an imperial officer, Zechariah, to oversee the arrest of the Vicar of Christ, but things had changed in Rome since the time of Constans and Martin. The papacy was on a firmer footing than it was in Martin's day, and, worse, the people of Rome cherished Sergius like a saint.

As soon as Zechariah stepped into the great city, an angry mob shouting their support for Sergius attacked him, forcing him to run into the papal palace for his own safety. He fell to his knees before the man he was ordered to arrest, 'asking tearfully that the Pope have mercy on him'. Sergius turned to the crowds outside the palace, chanting for Zechariah's blood, and asked them to spare the Emperor's lackey. Thanks to Sergius's intervention, Zechariah was able to make it out of Rome with his life, but not his pride and certainly not with a pope in chains.

Justinian's troubles were only beginning. An influential general named Leontios began to rebel: he had once been thrown into prison for some unknown offense against the Emperor but was later pardoned and made *strategos*, military governor, of a province in central Greece. His treasonous designs were inspired by two monks, Gregory and Paul, who claimed that they had cast his horoscope and learned he was destined to become the next Emperor, but only by the sword. The Patriarch of Constantinople, Kalinikos, apparently had faith in the two monks' predictions too. He proclaimed Leontios Emperor at the Hagia Sophia to a crowd of hundreds chanting, 'Let Justinian's bones be dug up!' the ultimate Byzantine insult for the living as much as the dead. At the age of just twenty-six, after nearly a decade of ruling, Justinian was deposed. The new Emperor ordered that not only should he endure *rhinokopia* like his uncles, but also *glossotomia*, mutilation of the tongue.

Apparently the latter operation was poorly done and Justinian's tongue healed completely, because his ability to speak was never hindered (in fact, Justinian was actually said to have been a chatterbox until the end of his life). Unfortunately, Justinian's nose was not as lucky. Posterity would give Justinian the not so flattering nickname of *Rhinokopimenos*, 'the man with the cut-off nose'. But even though serious facial disfigurement theoretically made him incapable of becoming Emperor once more, Justinian was then banished to Cherson, a desolate city on the Black Sea at the farthest reaches of the Empire. Quite literally, Justinian was shipped off to the edge of the world.

However, the power of prophecy was not enough to keep Leontios safe. His tenure as Emperor did not last long before Arabs took the crucial city of Carthage in North Africa. This loss was so staggering that another rebellion broke out behind a naval officer, a German named Apsimar who later adopted the more Roman name Tiberius. The stars apparently did not warn Leontios that Tiberius's rebellion would succeed and that he too would be forced to undergo the same punishment he had inflicted on Justinian.

Meanwhile at Cherson, Justinian became a celebrity to the poor, bored young men of the city. Even disgraced and disfigured, Justinian's imperial heritage drew the attentions of Cherson's dissatisfied youth and, in hopes of leaving their sinkhole of a city behind, they started talking loudly about the rewards an exiled emperor would give to the people responsible for putting him back on his rightful throne. Local authorities were not deaf to the chatter surrounding Justinian, idle as it may have been, nor were they unaware of the news of unrest from Constantinople. No longer welcome, Justinian escaped the city with a handful of followers in 704 and sought protection from Ibouzeros Gliabanos, the Khan of the Khazars. At the Khan's court, Justinian married the Khan's sister, renamed Theodora upon being baptized into the Church, possibly after the wife of the first Emperor Justinian. It was the first time a Byzantine emperor had married a woman born and raised outside the Empire's borders. Indeed, they must have seemed an unlikely couple: the Emperor with the mutilated nose and the princess of nomadic 'barbarians'. It seems from the records that their marriage was more than a way for Justinian to set up a firm alliance with his wife's brother. The two, from all indications, actually did deeply love each other.

It did not appear that their mutual devotion, as strong as it might have been, led to good in-law relations. The Emperor Tiberius II[43] bribed Gliabanos into planning Justinian's death, when it became clear that one day soon Justinian would want to return to Constantinople to reclaim his throne. To that end, Gliabanos sent a 'bodyguard' of two men to protect Justinian, but in reality they were two loyal agents of the Khan under orders to kill Justinian when a signal was given. Theodora heard about the plan and warned Justinian in time. Able to overpower his 'bodyguard', Justinian strangled the two would-be assassins with a cord held in his own two hands.

Now Justinian could no longer trust his brother-in-law and he knew he had to make a move right away, but he was loath to leave his wife behind, who was pregnant and thus could not travel easily with him. Despite the Medea-like betrayal of her family and homeland, she reluctantly returned to her brother's court while Justinian made his way to Constantinople in a tiny fishing boat with a small but loyal band of supporters. After stopping back at Cherson to gather more followers, a rough storm broke out and threatened to destroy the boat and everyone on it. One of Justinian's men, Myakes, is said to have exclaimed, 'Behold, master, we are dying. Make a compact with God concerning your safety, that if God restore your sovereignty,

[43] Also sometimes referred to as Tiberius III, depending on whether or not one includes the first-century Emperor of the Western Roman Empire.

you will take vengeance on none of your enemies.'

Justinian replied, 'If I spare any one of them, may God drown me here!'

God did not accept the challenge. Justinian and his men arrived safely at their next destination, the land of the Bulgar people, unharmed. The Khan of the Bulgars, Tervel, welcomed them warmly and promised to lend Justinian military aid. In 705, Justinian was leading a sizeable force, consisting of many well-armed Bulgars, toward Constantinople. Justinian brought his army to an old aqueduct that led past the walls into the city, guaranteeing him a swift and easy victory over Tiberius II. After years of a bitter exile and adventures among barbarians, Justinian was once again Emperor of the Eastern Roman Empire.

It is hard to fault Justinian, then, for the perverse glee he took in his triumph. On February 15, the two former Emperors were led in chains to the Hippodrome, the same place where Justinian was officially deposed and once had his nose cut off. Before a great throng of people, Justinian forced the two usurpers to crouch down. Then, as if they were human footstools, Justinian planted a foot on each of their necks. After the crowd was satisfied by the display, the two men were dragged out of sight and decapitated. Justinian would not take any chances by showing mercy with them. He himself was now living proof that the age-old practice of *rhinokopia* was no longer good enough to get rid of a would-be Emperor. If Justinian was terrible to his enemies, he could also be generous to his allies, as he demonstrated to the Bulgars. Not only did he grant those people lands, but he also proclaimed Tervel *Caesar* or 'tsar', in effect making him a trusted vassal to the Emperor.

Sweetening Justinian's victory was the long anticipated coming of Theodora to Constantinople with a baby boy and heir, oddly enough named Tiberius like Justinian's rival. Maybe the boy was named after Justinian's ill-fated uncle, since it is very unlikely that Tiberius was named for the detested Roman Emperor from the first century AD.

At any rate, Justinian was so pleased at being presented with a son and heir that he made Tiberius his co-emperor, even though he was not long past infancy.

Justinian's second tenure as Emperor went better than his first, at least to start with. He was even able to reconcile himself with the papacy, albeit with a new pope in Rome, Constantine. However, his natural thirst for revenge once again spoiled his reputation. When his treacherous brother-in-law took over Cherson with the backing of the authorities there, Justinian saw the opportunity to settle two old scores, one with Gliabanos and the other with the local government at Cherson. After the Byzantine forces successfully took over Cherson, the top citizens of the city were massacred and a number of the Khazar youths that were captured in the fighting were marked to be sold into slavery. This annoyed Justinian who angrily ordered that the young Khazars instead be sent to Constantinople with the Byzantine fleet. However, on the journey home a storm came up and sank the fleet, costing, according to an exaggerated legend, 73,000 lives.

By then the situation in Cherson was beyond repair. The Byzantine troops trapped in Cherson revolted against Justinian, unhappy that he cheated them out of the profits that would have been earned if they were allowed to sell the Khazars into slavery. Even worse, the rebels put forward one of Justinian's own generals as a rival Emperor, an Armenian named Vardan who took the Greek name Philippikos. Frightened of Justinian's violent cruelty against those who betrayed him before and satisfied by a general amnesty offered by Philippikos's agents, army officers and others flocked from Justinian's side. Justinian tried to recover his standing by facing Philippikos in battle, but he was decapitated in the fighting. His severed head was sent to Constantinople as a trophy and his body was tossed unceremoniously into the ocean.

Justinian's mother Anastasia, after hearing news of Justinian's death, took the boy Tiberius, then six years old, with her to a cathedral to seek sanctuary. Two men sent by Philippikos, Maurice and John, found Tiberius clutching the altar with one hand, fragments of what was believed to have been the cross on which Jesus Christ was crucified in the other and wearing a container of holy relics from the imperial treasury around his neck. Although his grandmother hoped that dressing Tiberius in such sanctity would deter any assassins, it only stopped Maurice. John, unfortunately, was made of sterner stuff and dragged Tiberius from the altar after patiently stripping him of the sacred objects his grandmother had placed on him. Ignoring both the scene and Anastasia's desperate pleas, John carried the boy outside and killed him on the steps of the cathedral. Anastasia was apparently spared and, as the wife and mother of emperors, spent the rest of her days treated with dignity. Concerning the final fate of Theodora, the woman who had saved Justinian's life only to see him destroyed by the very goal he pursued, there is no account.

Further Reading

Head, Constance *Justinian II of Byzantium* (University of Wisconsin Press, 1972)

Norwich, John Julius *Byzantium: The Early Centuries* (Alfred A. Knopf, 1989)

IRENE

Born: *750 (?)*
Reign: *September 8, 780–August 15, 797 (as regent)*
–October 31, 802 (as Empress)
Died: *Athens; August 9, 803*
Buried: *Prinkipo Monastery, Athens*

One of the most notorious crimes in antiquity was the murder of Agrippina by her own son, the universally reviled Emperor Nero. Not nearly as well known, but perhaps even more shocking, is that almost the reverse happened over seven centuries later in Constantinople. In order to have claim to the title of empress-regnant, something completely unprecedented in the long history of the Roman Empire, Western or Eastern, Irene had the eyes of her own son gouged out with a dagger.

Although not much is known about Irene's background, it is thought that she came from a poor Greek family, the Sarandapechys. Irene was orphaned when she was very young and raised by relatives in Athens. How and when she came to the attention of the imperial family in Constantinople is not at all certain, especially if the reports of her humble origins are true, but she did have enough qualities, physical or otherwise, to ensure that she was married to Leo, the son of the Emperor Constantine V.

Constantine V was the latest ruler in the dynasty established by Leo III, who started life as nothing more illustrious than a shepherd. Leo was a bright young Syrian, fluent in both Greek and Arabic, who caught the attention of Emperor Justinian II during a campaign and was soon made into a court official. After Justinian II was killed in battle, Leo fought to keep in the good graces of the succeeding emperors until, finally, he cobbled together enough of a following to take the imperial office for himself in 717.

Leo III and his successors endorsed one of the most destructive policies ever to come out of the marriage of church and state: iconoclasm. According to the iconoclast ideas circulating in Constantinople at the time, the veneration of images of Jesus Christ, the Virgin Mary and the saints, if not the very existence of such images, was blasphemy. Unfortunately, Constantinople was filled to the brim with countless religious icons and art. Zealous to atone for their countrymen's idolatry, the iconoclasts, armed with the blessing of the Emperor himself, stripped the cathedrals of sacred art and icons, burning and smashing them in the streets. Priests, nuns, and any other so-called 'iconodoles' who refused to recant their heresy were either punished under the law or beaten and murdered in public by godly-minded citizens.

After Constantine V's son claimed the throne as Leo IV, the iconoclasm movement cooled and the new Emperor declared that the mere ownership of icons was no longer tantamount to sacrilege, although the reverence of icons was still a crime and authorities with iconoclast sympathies still controlled nearly every level of government. It is hard to tell if Leo IV's decision to abandon the hard line against iconodoles was influenced by his bride, who probably secretly held her own iconodole beliefs, but the legends hint that even Irene, the wife of the Emperor, had to keep her beliefs

completely to herself.

At least she did not have to keep her opinions hidden for long. Leo IV died from leukemia on September 8, 780 after only five years of ruling, leaving behind his only son by Irene, the eleven-year-old Constantine. Despite opposition from her brothers-in-law, all of whom she immediately placed in the priesthood[44], Irene arranged to have herself proclaimed regent on September 4 for her young son, whom no one would argue was old enough to head the bothersome Empire. People did grumble about certain undue displays of superiority made by Irene , such as the fact that, on coins minted in the Emperor Constantine VI's name, her face appeared on the front while the face of the Emperor himself appeared on the reverse, the unimportant, side: but no one stood in the way of Irene's right to a regency.

Irene's iconolatry came to a head when she appointed an iconodole Patriarch of Constantinople, Tarasios, who in 785 decided to hold a council in Constantinople condemning iconoclastic views as 'contrary to all truth and piety, audaciously and temerariously subversive of the traditional law of the Church by the insults that it hurled and the contempt that it showed towards the holy and venerable images.' Unfortunately, even with the full weight of the imperial office behind such a council, it was much easier said than done. Officers from the armies, urged on by diehard iconoclastic bishops, threatened to butcher delegates if they dared attend, causing the entire council to reach a definite impasse. Outraged, Irene carefully purged the imperial armies of dissidents, replacing them with men she could rely on for support, even a number of her own court eunuchs. Another try at a council officially blessing iconolatry was made, this time successfully, in May of 787. That time, Irene had

[44] Members of the imperial family who were consecrated as priests were barred from the throne, so the forceful tonsure of unwanted relatives was a common practice in the Byzantine Empire.

the foresight to arrange to hold this council well outside the walls of Constantinople itself and beyond the army's easy reach.

Besides the business of re-establishing proper respect for sacred icons, Irene also busied herself with the business of finding a suitable bride for her son, who was now old enough to have a bride whose duty would be to provide sons for the dynasty. At first she was determined to marry the Emperor to Rotrund, the daughter of Charlemagne, King of the Franks. The court's disgust at the very idea of marrying a reigning emperor to the daughter of a 'barbarian' got in the way, as probably did Constantine's own revulsion at the thought. Instead Constantine wanted to marry Maria of Amnia, who was selected by Constantine himself from a 'bride-show', where dozens of women from across the Empire were herded in front of Irene, Constantine, and the imperial court and looked over like cattle. If Constantine's wife was really selected mainly on the merits of her physical qualities, then it is not too surprising that Constantine came to hate her and instead preferred the company of a mistress, Theodota, one of his mother's handmaidens. As mother and regent Irene disapproved, and voiced her opinion on her son's love life very loudly.

Even more galling to Irene was the fact that Constantine was not at all reluctant to become a rallying point against the lackeys Irene placed throughout the army and government to support her policies. Whenever it seemed Constantine was getting too troublesome, she always tried to give him an unmistakable warning. Once she went as far as having some of Constantine's sycophants, including his childhood tutor John, arrested, tortured and then either tonsured or exiled. In one episode when he was seventeen, Constantine was flogged and then locked up for days in his apartments.

The stricter the mother became, the more defiant the son grew. While this was at its core a family problem, it involved the Byzantine Emperor and his mother, the regent, so an entire empire was in the crossfire. The stalemate between the two was finally ended when the army, sick of being lorded over by Irene's eunuchs and servants,

mutinied in the fall of 790. At their hands Constantine was installed as the sole ruler. Irene, in the meantime, was imprisoned at a palace she had recently had built.

Unfortunately, disastrous campaigns against both the Bulgars and the Arabs disillusioned the soldiers with their choice of Emperor. Although Constantine was kept on the throne, Irene was released from prison and allowed to resume a place by her son's side – and behind his throne. Naturally, relations between the two only worsened and complete control of the empire became a tug-of-war between mother and son. One chronicler succinctly summed up the times, 'They went for each other, hit and hit back, in turn, and now Irene exercised absolute power, now Constantine took possession of the palace alone, again the mother, again the son, until their conflict resulted in a disaster for both.'

Eventually, Constantine's popularity started to leak away. He won no fans when he had his uncle Nikephoros blinded on suspicion of treason and had the tongues of his other uncles cut out. A bigger blow to his reputation came when he had the popular general Alexius Mousele, actually always a loyal supporter of Constantine, blinded and imprisoned on a weak charge of conspiracy. Against the Orthodox Church, Constantine committed a worse transgression: he divorced his wife Maria and sent her packing to a convent so he could marry his mistress Theodota in September of 795. She gave birth to a son named Leo, but the child was born prematurely and died shortly after. To the faithful, here was the proof that Constantine had angered God with his sacrilegious marriage.

Constantine tried once again to recover his standing by going on campaign, but to no avail. Using bribes and promises, Irene managed to draw many disgruntled army officials back into her camp. Warned that his mother was ready to make a move against him, Constantine tried escaping from Constantinople but supporters of his mother caught him and had him arrested. Dragged back to the city and imprisoned in a palace, Constantine just waited for the blow to come.

He did not have to wait too long. On August 19, 797, in the very same chamber where his mother had given birth to him, Constantine was blinded with a dagger. The operation amazingly did not kill him and, in fact, he was destined to live longer than his mother. But now, according to custom, he could never again be Emperor.

With her son now deposed and believed dead by many, Irene claimed the title of *basileus*, the Greek word for king, that had been used by the Byzantine sovereigns as their chief title since the Emperor Heraklios. Tellingly, Irene applied to herself the masculine form of the word, not *basilessa*, which would have been a closer approximation for 'empress'. This careful wordplay did not lessen the impact of what Irene had done: she was the first woman to claim the imperial office not as a regent or as a power behind the scenes, but in her own right.

Unfortunately, Pope Leo III in Rome was not fooled by the niceties of language. As far as he and much of Western Europe was concerned, the throne of the ancient Roman Empire was vacant, because it was impossible that it could be occupied by a woman. On Christmas Day of 800, the Pope crowned Charlemagne, who had become not only the King of the Franks, but also the King of the Saxons and Bavarians in Germany, the Avars in Hungary and the Lombards in Italy, as 'Emperor of the Romans', not only robbing Irene of the importance of her title, but also the old claim of the Emperors in Constantinople to be the sole successors to the Roman Empire. The thought that this barbarian upstart Charlemagne, who was even rumored to be illiterate, would dare claim to be an Emperor was outrageous enough to the blue bloods in the Byzantine court, but Irene poured salt on the wounds when she proposed that she herself should marry Charlemagne to settle the matter. Perhaps she saw it as a way to protect herself from further rebellion or to save Constantinople from a potential invasion by Charlemagne to settle the problem of two Emperors in Christendom. Maybe she even believed that marriage between the

two 'Emperors' would actually reunite East and West and resurrect the Roman Empire to its former glory.

The idea that an ancient empire would, at least superficially, be reborn through one marriage is an interesting one. It is also impossible to imagine what kind of spouses Irene and Charlemagne, the revolutionary empress and the superhuman warrior-emperor, would have been to each other. Unfortunately for all medieval historians, such a scenario remained fictional, because Irene in the end could not stay in power long enough to begin to put the marriage plans in motion, if she seriously entertained them. Even someone of Irene's ability and ruthlessness, male or female, could suddenly lose everything to the capriciousness of imperial politics.

Irene's own finance minister, Nikephoros, began to become the focal point for a rebellion, possibly spurred on by the mere prospect of Irene marrying a 'barbarian'. Irene was thrown out of power on October 31, 802, but she was luckier than many of her predecessors. At first she was banished to the island of Prinkipo, but because of lingering support for her in Constantinople she was later sent to the island of Lesbos and then exiled to spend her last years in Athens, the same place she had left long before to become the bride of a future emperor. More than one historian claims that Irene also came full circle in another way: she became so poor in exile that she was reduced to sewing to make a living. Despite this final disgrace and her atrocious crime against her own son, for her efforts in the name of iconolatry, she was declared a saint by the Eastern Orthodox Church.

Further Reading

Arvites, James *Irene, Woman Emperor of Constantinople: Her Life and Times* (1979)

Herrin, Judith *Women in Purple: Rulers of Medieval Byzantium* (Princeton University Press, 2001)

CONSTANTINE VIII

Reign: *December 15, 1025–November 11, 1028*
Born: *ca. 960*
Died: *November 11, 1028*
Buried: *Mausoleum of Constantine, Istanbul*

For all the wealth and prestige the Byzantine emperors had at their fingertips, it was not an easy life for even the best of them. It rarely took long for a military revolt or a rival to seize control and leave the unfortunate ex-emperor facing exile, mutilation or death. In this light, one wonders if any of the Byzantine emperors could ever really enjoy the delights that came attached to the danger. One emperor, Constantine VIII, spent every day enjoying himself to the fullest, yet remained terrified of the chasm that threatened to split open under him.

Although Constantine was past his prime when he was dragged to the top, he had been a very important person since he was a boy, when his father, Emperor Romanos II, had died. At the time Constantine was only three and his brother Basil six, but their father had given them the pretty if meaningless designations of co-emperors. Realizing the vulnerabilities of her two little imperial sons and not willing or able to become regent, Constantine's mother, Theophano, married a general named Nikephoros, decades older than her, but powerful enough to keep her sons safe.

Although Nikephoros was a practical choice, he was not a personally satisfying one. The general was not only very old, but also very boring. A much more attractive alternative arrived in the form of John Tzimisces, a well-built young man with reddish-blonde hair, a handsome face and a brilliant mind. After a brief and unremarkable reign, Nikephoros either died a natural death or was helped along to the grave by John himself. Either way, his wife's lover effortlessly took Nikephoros's place as Emperor.

After John's reign, Basil, who was then eighteen years old, at last succeeded his father in full, although he always remained a co-emperor. Constantine was also still co-emperor, but while Basil went on to become one of the best Byzantine emperors, Constantine left all problems of policy and war to his brother while he went about the important business of attending banquets and orgies. He seems to have enjoyed the *dolce vita* enough for both himself and his brother. In complete contrast to his hedonist brother, Basil led a simple, austere private life that perhaps helped him live and reign for sixty-five years.

When Basil died without naming an heir, Constantine was declared the new Emperor. He did have some talent for politics, even if he did not use it while Basil was still alive. Although his education was rather shoddy compared to Basil's, he knew how to negotiate with, and how to impress, foreign dignitaries. He was also no sloppy thinker: once he was emperor Constantine talked so fast about imperial business that his secretaries had to develop their own system of shorthand to keep up with him.

Most of the time, though, Constantine could not give up his old ways and was more likely to gamble all night or watch pornographic plays in his private theatre than revise the laws or lead an army into battle. Unfortunately for his subjects, Constantine was only politically vigorous when it came to acting on his paranoia. John Julius Norwich, in his history of the Byzantine Empire, wrote, 'He believed every rumor and, lacking the courage for trials and confrontations, ordered the execution or mutilation of hundreds of innocent men.' Utterly unable to trust anyone but his own inner circle of eunuchs and attendants, Constantine appointed them to the highest positions in his government. He even gave his own valet the most important office in the army.

As many precautions as Constantine took to avoid the threat of conspiracy, he could do nothing to change the obvious fact that he did not have much time left and urgently needed an heir. Constantine did have two daughters, Zoë and Theodora, but in spite of, or perhaps because of, the Empress Irene's career two centuries previously, leaving the empire to either of them was inconceivable. Because of the importance of their blood, Zoë and Theodora had been kept in the chambers known as the *gynaeceum*, the place that awaited aristocratic women who were neither married nor encloistered. Men could only visit the *gynaeceum* under strict conditions, while the women there were expected only to while away their days in sterile spinsterhood. That was the life the two women had been resigned to until Constantine, under pressure from his advisors and the shadow of death to finally select an heir, decided that his daughters could pass the empire to a candidate as a dowry.

By that time both of his daughters were middle-aged and Zoë in particular was very eager to put an end to her intolerable isolation. Constantine arranged for Zoë to marry the candidate he preferred the most, a distinguished senator and a distant relative to the dynasty named Romanos Argyros, who not only seemed to have the ability to head the Empire, but was trustworthy enough not to try to help Constantine on his way to the tomb. The one small flaw in Constantine's plan was that Romanos was already married to a woman he loved dearly.

Of course, to an emperor, no obstacle is insurmountable. In an audience with Constantine himself, Romanos was politely informed that he had a very reasonable choice: divorce his wife and gain both Zoë and the Empire, or be blinded and gain nothing. It might have been a bluff on Constantine's part, but given the Emperor's less than savoury reputation, Romanos took this threat seriously. After learning what her husband was faced with, Romanos's wife sheared her hair, a traditional act for a woman who chose the religious life, and entered a convent, bringing an end to their marriage. The choice was made. Romanos and Zoë married on November 10, 1028 and, as if on cue, Constantine died from his illness five days later. It goes without saying that the marriage was an unhappy one and it was thought that Romanos was in the end poisoned by Zoë so she could make her chamberlain and lover, Michael, the next Emperor.

Further Reading

Norwich, John Julius *Byzantium: The Decline and Fall* (Alfred A. Knopf, 1989)

MUSTAFA I

Born: *1591*
Reign: *November 22, 1617–February 26, 1618;*
May 1622–August 1623
Died: *January 20, 1639*
Buried: *Hagia Sophia, Istanbul*

The nearly 1,000-year-old Byzantine Empire, the last fragment of the Roman Empire, came to a violent end on May 29, 1453 after a two-year siege of Constantinople by Mehmet II, Sultan of the Ottoman Turks. Constantinople became Istanbul, the heart of a new empire that would reign over most of Eastern Europe, hold six of the seven ancient wonders of the world within its borders, and boast twenty languages spoken among its subjects. At least at the beginning, the Ottoman Sultans proved themselves worthy of such an immense and fantastic empire. Not only did they work as leaders and generals, but they also excelled in literature, architecture and history.

Yet even though the early Sultans were all remarkable people, there was a very dark side to the private realm of the Sultan. It was a horrible thing to be born a brother to the Sultan or to the imperial heir, since even a son fathered on a harem girl by the Sultan was an eligible candidate for the throne. It was expected that, if he wanted to reign untroubled, any Sultan would have to arrange for the deaths of his brothers. With quite a bit of reluctance, Sultan Mahomet III bowed to this tradition and ordered his nineteen half-brothers, the eldest of whom was just eleven, to be strangled with a bowstring.

By 1603 a more humane alternative to this custom of fratricide had been dreamed up. It was the *Kafes*, or 'the Cage', a two-story building in the palace of the Sultans, the Grand Seraglio, that was secluded away from the rest of the building by a high wall. On the surface it looked like a typical royal residence, with beautiful gardens surrounding it and art decorating the walls, but one odd feature an observer could notice right away was that there were no windows on the ground floor. Rather than being killed outright, it was decided that it was kinder that the brothers of a newly ascended Sultan, no matter how young, should be incarcerated in this 'Cage', with only a few servants and concubines for company.

Sultan Ahmed I established the Cage for his eleven-year-old brother Mustafa, who would remain there until Ahmed's death a decade later. Mustafa was utterly neurotic and bereft of any social skills, probably as a result of being trapped in a small space for so long, but he was still chosen to be the next Sultan through the intervention of Ahmed's favorite mistress, Kiusem, who was afraid that Osman, Ahmed's eldest son, would put to death her own two sons by Ahmed.

Mustafa's subjects were not exactly confident in their new ruler, a trembling young man with a tendency to hallucinations and incapable of even the most simple human interaction. This new Sultan was also utterly whimsical. When a peasant farmer gave him a drink of water during a hunting expedition, Mustafa rewarded the man by making him a high-ranking official. Unwilling to saddle the empire with a madman, in 1618 Mustafa's own officials arranged a five-day hunting trip for him away from Istanbul, giving them the breathing space they needed to depose him. When Mustafa returned he found himself suddenly dragged back to his lonely incarceration in the Cage. Now Kiusem was unable to stop Mustafa's nephew from becoming Sultan Osman II.

Court officials were not pleased to discover that Osman, although a boisterous and powerfully built man, was not in a much better state of mind than his deranged uncle. Only two things occupied Osman's mind: his archery skills, which he liked to practice with his own pages and prisoners of war as targets, and his religion, which made him feel compelled to try to reform the Janissaries, the elite corps of the Ottoman Empire. The Janissaries were composed of exceptionally well-trained men, skilled not only in armed and hand-to-hand combat, but also in administration. Their numbers were supplied with boys taken from Balkan villages, who were from the start trained and conditioned to absolute obedience to the Sultan. Initially the Janissaries were expected to remain chaste and observe Islamic law with more rigidity than even the citizens of the nation they were raised to serve, but over the generations their once legendary discipline slackened. Osman blamed a failed campaign against Poland on this lack of good, traditional morals and talked openly of forcing the Janissaries to reform under his boot.

Unfortunately, he did not understand just how powerful and audacious the Janissaries had become. When Osman started to plan a pilgrimage to Mecca, the Janissaries presumed that he was really going to hide in some safe corner of the Empire from where he could order their murderous reformation. When it came, their strike was quick and deadly. The Janissaries, effortlessly overcoming the meager resistance they were offered, discovered Osman cowering in his harem and threw him in prison. Soon afterwards a number of Janissaries came to rid themselves of the former Sultan for good, but Osman was not going to die without a fight and was able to kill six of his assassins with his bare hands before he was wrestled down to the floor and strangled.

The Janissaries found Mustafa in the Cage sitting next to his two concubines and 'grinning vacantly', but weakened with hunger since no one had bothered to feed him in days. Terrified that the Janissaries were now coming to kill him at Osman's orders, Mustafa refused to come out through the now open door, so the Janissaries were obliged to tie him to a rope and drag him through a hole in the roof.

In the long run, the second reign of Mustafa was more of a disaster than his first. Mustafa constantly dismissed his highest officials, making the central government so unstable that the provincial governors refused to send their tax revenues to Istanbul. Although one of his first acts was to have everyone involved in the imprisonment and murder of Osman II executed, he could be heard calling out to his dead nephew, begging him to come back so he could retire and give up the burden of being the Sultan. With the blessing of the Grand Mufti, the highest religious authority in the empire, the Janissaries once again deposed Mustafa and threw him back in the Cage, where he would remain for the rest of his life. Unfortunately, Mustafa would not be the last Sultan scarred beyond repair by a childhood in the Cage.

Further Reading

Freely, John *Inside the Seraglio: Private Lives of the Sultans in Istanbul* (Penguin, 2000)

Turnball, Stephen *The Ottoman Empire, 1326-1699* (Routledge, 2003)

MURAD IV

Born: *July 27, 1612*
Reign: *September 10, 1623–February 8, 1640*
Died: *February 8, 1640*
Buried: *The Blue Mosque, Istanbul*

A nephew of the insane Sultan Mustafa, Murad was only twelve years old when he was chosen to be the next Sultan after his uncle was dragged back to the Cage once and for all. His mother Kiusem, who was his father Sultan Ahmed I's favorite lover from the harem, ruled in Istanbul unofficially while her son was young. As Murad matured, he showed the early promise of a strong ruler, but in his adolescence he witnessed the humiliation of the empire at the hands of the Persians, who conquered the territory of modern day Iraq from the once seemingly invincible Ottoman armies, and the treachery of the Janissaries, supposedly the right hand of the Sultan, as they revolted and murdered the Grand Vizier, the Grand Mufti, a number of other high officials and a servant Murad had befriended. As Murad's actions as an adult and a Sultan would reveal, these incidents did not fail to leave scars on him.

It was rumored that Kiusem, afraid that her son would fall in love with some harem girl who would usurp her place at Murad's side, had raised her son to dislike women and prefer the company of men. Kiusem did not succeed in making her son a homosexual, if that was her goal, but she did make him into a vicious misogynist. A typical example of the adult Murad's attitude toward females was the occasion when a boat rowed by a few women came too close to Murad's palace: he opened fire on them with a cannon. On another occasion a group of women were drowned for waking Murad up with their singing.

It would be the women in his harem that would suffer even more than his other female subjects. Murad enjoyed firing pellets at them after stripping them naked. He would also force them to stand in a pool so filled with water that they would have to jump up and down in it to catch a breath. Although he never stopped burdening his harem girls with contempt, he was fiercely protective of them. When he heard that a man named Zanetti, who owned a large house near his palace, had built an extra room at the top of the building, he thought it was made for the purpose of spying over the palace walls into the harem. Zanetti was immediately put to death, the fate shared by any man unlucky enough to get too close to the walls around the harem.

For all his disgust for women, Murad was not really confident in his masculinity and tried to compensate by honing his skills in athletics and war. Rumors said that he was so strong he liked challenging men to try to open his clenched fist, but no one ever succeeded in doing it. He was also an expert soldier, willing to lead his soldiers into battle and share in their dangers and hardships.

Unfortunately, the memory of him as a would-be moralist was enough to eclipse his solid reputation as a general. Described by one historian as a 'gloomy despot', Murad tried to dispense personal justice by riding through the streets of Istanbul with a professional executioner, trying, sentencing, and executing anyone caught in some petty offense on the spot. Drinking coffee or alcohol, smoking tobacco or opium, and performing Persian music were all capital offenses, yet Murad himself was addicted to coffee, alcohol, tobacco, and opium and some of his favorite court musicians were Persians. Chroniclers claim that, through his strong yet hypocritical zeal for moral perfection, Murad killed thousands of his own people.

Under the strain of ruling the vast Ottoman Empire, Murad became an alcoholic and an opium-addict, which worsened his already precarious mental state. Whereas before he often had an excuse for killing his subjects, no matter how phony or ridiculous, towards the end of his reign he would come out of his palace late at night with a sword and kill anyone on the streets who came within sight. If Murad's mind was truly disintegrating, his body fell apart first, and he lost his life at the age of only twenty-seven. The cause of death for the great moralist of the Ottoman Empire was cirrhosis of the liver.

Further Reading

Freely, John *Inside the Seraglio: Private Lives of the Sultans in Istanbul* (Penguin, 2000)

Turnball, Stephen *The Ottoman Empire, 1326-1699* (Routledge, 2003)

IBRAHIM

Born: *November 4, 1615*
Reign: *February 8, 1640–August 18, 1648*
Died: *August 12, 1648*
Buried: *Hagia Sophia, Istanbul*

From the age of only two, Ibrahim had been kept in the Cage during the reigns of his brothers Osman II and Murad IV. As if this were not enough to ensure a miserable childhood, Ibrahim was well aware that, one by one, his other brothers were being killed by his reigning siblings. By adulthood the lack of any social contact and living under the threat of death had taken their toll on Ibrahim's mind, so much so that Murad IV considered having him killed – not because he feared that Ibrahim would usurp him, but because Murad thought it better that the dynasty should die with him rather than continue with a bloodline 'contaminated' by madness. Yet his life was spared, thanks to the timely intervention of his mother, the ubiquitious Kiusem.

After Murad breathed his last, officials came to take their new Sultan, the now twenty-four year old Ibrahim, from the Cage. Thinking that the men were coming to murder him at Murad's orders, Ibrahim and the concubines that lived with him barricaded the door with the furniture. The men pounded on the door, pleading with the newly appointed Sultan to come out, but Ibrahim believed it was all a trick. Finally, Kiusem was brought out to reassure Ibrahim everything was safe while the Grand Vizier brought down Murad's corpse for him to view. At first Ibrahim was unwilling to believe what had happened even then, but finally he left the Cage convinced and danced around the palace, screaming, 'The butcher of the Empire is dead at last!'

The new Sultan wasted no time in reclaiming his lost years. His favorite pastime by far was enjoying the fruits of the harem, especially fat concubines, in spite of the fact that he was plagued with impotence. He fought this affliction with a steady stream of aphrodisiacs provided by his mother and by treatments given by a magician named Cinci Huseyin, whose brand of quackery was apparently successful since Ibrahim went on to have ten children. But the real cause of Ibrahim's impotence might have been psychological from the beginning, since he often found himself passionately attracted to the women outside his harem, the ones whom he could not have and were in a position to tell him no.

Once he fell madly in love with probably the most inaccessible woman in Istanbul, the daughter of the Grand Mufti, whom he abruptly asked to be his wife. Knowing full well about the Sultan's reputation, the Grand Mufti delicately claimed that, although such a marriage would be to his honor, it would be sacrilegious for him to 'impose upon the affections of his child' and so it was up to his

daughter, who politely but firmly refused. Ibrahim's favorite – and most overweight – harem girl, who went by the name of Sachir Para or 'Lump of Sugar', was sent to talk some sense into the woman at the public baths, but she still refused. Insulted and enraged, the Sultan had the Grand Mufti's daughter brought to the palace against her will, where he raped her and kept her captive for days before he sent her home to her father. Ibrahim had just made a powerful, relentless enemy out of the highest religious authority in the Empire.

However, such practical concerns did not bother him for an instant. While Kiusem, as she had done so often before, attended to the troublesome business of government, Ibrahim busied himself with hours of debauchery. He developed an obsession for fur: he had all his furniture and walls covered in it and enjoyed having sex on it. He covered his body in the most expensive perfumes to be found from across Asia and Europe. The Sultan probably also had the most exhaustive collection of pornography and sexual manuals in Turkey and it was even rumored that he had invented one or two new techniques himself. His favorite game with the girls in his harem was to pretend he was a stallion while he chased his 'ponies' around the room.

When Sachir Para, probably seeking to further her own place in the Sultan's eyes, told Ibrahim that there was a rumor one of the girls in the harem was having an affair, but there was neither proof nor details, he nevertheless went wild with rage. He ordered the Kislar Aga, the chief eunuch in charge of the harem, to brutally interrogate the entire harem, but even the most painful tortures could not shake loose a confession. Ibrahim's son, Mahomet, made a joke in front of his father about what happened and Ibrahim slashed him across the face with a knife, leaving him scarred for life. Impatient with the hopeless investigation, he commanded that all 280 girls in the harem, with the exception of his beloved Sachir Para, be tied into sacks and drowned in a river. One of the sacks was poorly tied and the girl inside managed to escape to the surface, where she was rescued by

French sailors on a passing merchant vessel. The others were not so fortunate.

If Sachir Para had lied about the scandal in the harem, then what became of her could be thought of as retribution. Kiusem, who started her career as a harem girl herself, was always afraid that some new mistress would win the Sultan's undying love and use it to jockey for her position, with possibly fatal consequences for Kiusem. Deciding that Sachir Para had finally become an intolerable threat, Kiusem invited the unsuspecting woman to a private dinner one evening. Sachir Para wound up being strangled with a bowstring by a servant loyal to Kiusem. That night the mother warmly comforted her grief-stricken son, telling him that Sachir Para had died from a sudden illness.

The death of his favorite concubine soon became the least of Ibrahim's troubles. The Grand Mufti took advantage of discontent in the government and engineered a coup against the Sultan. The Grand Vizier was assassinated and, with the Grand Mufti, a number of officials drew up a declaration demanding Ibrahim's deposition. Most damning was the fact that Kiusem, realizing either the hopelessness of her son's chances or his insanity, threw her support behind the declaration as well.

Surprisingly enough, Ibrahim took the news well. He had become bored of the hassles of ruling an empire anyway and was actually happy to go back to the familiar, sweet seclusion of the Cage. Unfortunately for him, the Grand Mufti was not about to allow the madman who had brutalized his daughter a peaceful retirement. With his approval, if not his encouragement, assassins burst into the Cage a week after Ibrahim was deposed, holding a bowstring, the traditional tool used by the Ottomans for strangling royals whose existences were no longer convenient. Ibrahim greeted them warmly, thinking they had come to ask him to take up the mantle of Sultan again, but their real intentions quickly became quite clear.

Ibrahim grabbed a copy of the Koran and held it in front of him,

declaring, 'Behold, God's book! By what writ will you murder me?'

When appealing to God did not stop the killers from advancing on him, Ibrahim shouted for help, 'These cruel men have come to kill me!'

There was no mercy to be found, however. The same death that he always feared would come from his brother had finally arrived, a number of years later than he had expected.

Further Reading

Freely, John *Inside the Seraglio: Private Lives of the Sultans in Istanbul* (Penguin, 2000)

Turnball, Stephen *The Ottoman Empire, 1326-1699* (Routledge, 2003)

ABDUL AZIZ

Born: *February 9, 1830*
Reign: *June 25, 1861–May 30, 1876*
Died: *June 4, 1876 (suicide)*
Buried: *Mausoleum of Mahmud II, Istanbul*

By the nineteenth century, the Ottoman Empire, once the terror of Christendom, had been dubbed 'the sick man of Europe'. Beginning with Greece, many of the Ottomans' former provinces in the Balkans strove for independence, escalating an already dire economic situation caused by the government's outdated financial systems. Turkey's military was not as advanced as those of the major European powers, so when Russia staked its claim to swathes of the vanishing Ottoman territory, and even to Istanbul itself, the once formidable empire was now helpless. Eventually Russia's attempts to carve up the dying empire led to the Crimean War in which Britain, France and Sardinia effectively fought the dying empire's battles for it. The only thing keeping the Ottoman Empire alive at this point was the simple fact that no European power was prepared to sit back and watch any of the others benefit from the Ottomans' death.

It was this fading star that Abdul Aziz inherited from his brother, Abdul Mejid. With his massive frame and regal bearing, Abdul Aziz certainly looked the part of a Sultan, but he was weighed down by an almost childish personality that did not lend itself well to being an absolute sovereign. Even as an adult he liked playing soldiers – but with real soldiers, in mock battles that sometimes ended in very real deaths. Another pastime of his was to chase a chicken or two around the rooms of his palace and award the one he caught with a medal of bravery around its neck. Deathly terrified of being burned alive, he read at night by a candle kept floating in the middle of a bucket of water. One day he believed a rumor that someone in the court was trying to poison him, so for weeks he lived only on hard-boiled eggs personally prepared by his mother.

Even a Sultan with a more sober personality would have had a hard time facing down the problems Aziz became heir to. Abdul Mejid had tried to prop up the country's collapsing economy by relying on loans from foreign bankers, but had only succeeded in getting the government trapped in debt. Besides shoddy finances, Aziz was also forced to cope with the flames of revolution. Along with much of Europe, Turkey was hearing a deafening demand for reform. One powerful advocate was the 'Society of New Ottomans', a liberal organization that strove for the modernization of the government, including the placement of constitutional limits on the absolutist Sultanate. Aziz tried to have the group proscribed by the government, but it continued to attract members at an accelerating rate, even members of the Sultan's family.

Although he was not quite willing to go so far as to actually entertain the demands of the radicals, Aziz decided the best course of action was to cultivate at least the image of an enlightened autocrat and to give his subjects the impression that Turkey and Europe were now one. To that end, he declared that he would take a tour of Europe, something not even conceived of by any of his predecessors. The highlights of this ambitious trip included the famous courts of Napoleon III and Queen Victoria. The former tried to impress his guest by turning the Elysée Palace in Paris into a stage set of *The Arabian Nights*; the latter only reluctantly came out of mourning for her cherished late husband, Prince Albert, to greet the exotic visitor.

Even if Victoria was not exactly thrilled by the prospect of meeting the Sultan, Aziz was overwhelmed by the welcomes he had received. As soon as he was back in Istanbul, the only thing on Aziz's mind was to find ways to imitate the models of Western European industry and luxury he had been shown. Despite his lousy finances, he purchased many trains, although Turkey had few tracks. Inspired by a palace he saw in Paris, he had the walls of one of his own residences paneled with mother-of-pearl. The European experience also bestowed a love of pianos on Aziz, who purchased dozens of them, but he was disappointed when he discovered that it was impractical to strap a piano on a man's back and have someone play it while the piano-bearer walked next to the Sultan during his usual stroll in the gardens.

What the expedition through Britain and France did not give Aziz was a greater tolerance for radicalism. Once Aziz realized that his jaunt had done little to make his reign seem more progressive to the public, his fear of a revolt escalated into a mania. He personally edited out all references to the French Revolution and any other anti-monarchist movement from Turkish schoolbooks. Aziz became driven to act more and more like a despot, as if he wanted to force a battle with the revolutionaries he dreaded. On a bizarre whim, he ordered all of his subjects named 'Aziz' to change their names. He also began to insist that all of his ministers and courtiers greet him by falling to their knees and kissing his feet.

His tyranny, however it manifested itself, did not excite much attention, especially outside the Empire, until 1876 when, for one of the first times, a tragedy that would have once been considered just another regional incident excited international anger. That year the Bulgarians, who had been subjects of the Ottoman Empire since 1396, rebelled, seeking their independence. The response from Istanbul was harsh, reaching a crescendo when Ottoman troops obliterated the Bulgarian town of Batak. An American journalist and correspondent for the *Daily News* in London, J.A. MacGahan, was present in Batak and claimed that he saw the remains of 12,000 people who had been burned alive. MacGahan wrote:

> On every side were skulls and skeletons charred among the ruins, or lying entire where they fell in their clothing. There were skeletons of girls and women with long brown hair hanging to their skulls. We approached the church. There these remains were more frequent, until the ground was literally covered with skeletons, skulls and putrefying bodies in clothing . . . The man who did all this, Achmed Aga, has been promoted and is still governor of this district.

Nearly seventy Bulgarian villages suffered a similar fate to Batak. After the entire world was appalled by graphic reports of what had happened in Batak, Walter Baring, from the British Embassy in Istanbul, described it as 'perhaps the most heinous crime that has stained the history of the present century.'

This may have directly prompted the coup that Abdul Aziz feared so much; or perhaps Aziz's fall, given his unsteady mind and the condition of the Empire, was inevitable no matter what happened or what was exposed. At any rate, the coup was brought on by Hussein Avni, the Minister of War, and Midhat Pasha, a celebrated liberal associated with the Society of New Ottomans and a former Grand Vizier. On May 29, Avni and Pasha confronted Aziz in the harem while he stood silently with his beloved and visibly pregnant mistress Mihri Hanoum sobbing on one arm and a sword in his other hand. The two men announced that Aziz was deposed and his young nephew, Murad, was now Sultan. In an eloquent response, Aziz's mother downed Avni with a well-placed kick to the stomach. Aziz, on the other hand, had no fighting spirit. Faced with his worst nightmare come to fruition, he simply locked himself in a room and slit his wrists with a pair of scissors two weeks after his deposition.

Further Reading

Freely, John *Inside the Seraglio: Private Lives of the Sultans in Istanbul* (Penguin, 2000)

Palmer, Alan *The Decline and Fall of the Ottoman Empire* (Barnes & Noble, 1992)

THE BYZANTINE AND OTTOMAN EMPIRES IN FILM AND LITERATURE

H.N. Turtletaub wrote a narrative about the adventurous life of Justinian II, titled simply *Justinian*, published in 1998.

The life of Empress Irene has also been fictionalized in Gabriella Kara Kolias's novel *Irene, King and Autocrat*.

A 1981 Turkish TV mini-series was made on Murad IV, *IV. Murad.*

RUSSIA

SVIATOPOLK 'THE ACCURSED'

Reign: *July 1015–1019*
Died: *1019*

Before Moscow rose to prominence as the capital and figurehead for the vast land of Russia, Kiev was the political and cultural center for the evolving nation, a position it held until civil war forced Kiev to wane in the twelfth century, a decline that would be complete once Mongol invaders swept across Russia in 1223. Reigning from the Kievan state was the house of Rurik, believed to have been established by a Scandinavian adventurer, which reached its peak in a man called Vladimir. While Vladimir ruled Kiev as its Grand Prince, apparently libido ruled Vladimir, who fathered twelve sons on different wives and mistresses. Vladimir's famous conversion to Christianity later in adulthood was apparently sincere, since from all accounts he gave up his playboy lifestyle. Unfortunately, the damage was already done. His sons, each of whom was given their own little slice of territory, all vied with each other for power and the eldest of them, Sviatopolk, would emerge from this sibling conflict as one of the most notorious villains in Russian history.

Whatever peace Vladimir's newfound religion brought him, his sons were sure to have disrupted his spiritual tranquility. In fact, it was while traveling with an army to 'chastise' his son Yaroslav in July 1015 that Vladimir became ill and died. Although Sviatopolk had a strong claim to succeed Vladimir as the eldest son, his brother Boris was chosen, probably because his mother was a Byzantine heiress. Boris declined to accept the throne, but that did not stop Sviatopolk from sending assassins after him. According to legend, Boris was at prayer when the assassins discovered him ten days after his father's death. Boris, the legend goes, had sent his bodyguards away earlier, saying, 'It is better for me to die alone than be the occasion of death for many.' When the killers arrived, he calmly asked them to spare him because of his young age, but they did not. Another brother, Gleb, was murdered at Smolensk on September 8, tricked into believing that Sviatopolk had nothing but good intentions toward him. These crimes earned Sviatopolk's place in infamy, while the victims, Boris and Gleb, were made into the first saints of the Russian Orthodox Church and are still said to receive the prayers of those who have suffered undue persecution.

Unfortunately, Sviatopolk did not remove all threats to his rule. His brother Yaroslav was able to seize Kiev with his own private army in 1016. Sviatopolk escaped to Poland and enlisted the aid of Boleslaus, the King of Poland, who happened to be his father-in-law.

Sviatopolk made an awful mistake, though, when he underestimated anti-Polish feeling in Kiev. While the Polish soldiers who helped in Sviatopolk's restoration were quartered in Kievan homes, at night the citizens massacred the troops in their sleep. The surviving soldiers were naturally no longer inclined to serve Sviatopolk and once again he had to abandon his cause.

In 1019, he next tried to set up an alliance with the Pechenegs, a nomadic people who had long been a thorn in the side of Kiev, but his trust was misplaced. Seduced by the possibility of ingratiating themselves with Yaroslav's regime, they handed Sviatopolk over to his brother's supporters, who butchered him on the spot. Not long after Sviatopolk's death, the days of Kiev's supremacy were numbered, but the house of Rurik would outlast even Kiev's domination of Russia and would survive to produce the first, and perhaps the most well-known, of Russia's tsars.

Further Reading

Duffy, James and Ricci, Vincent *Tsars: Russia's Rulers For More Than One Thousand Years* (Barnes & Noble, 1995)

Paszkiewicz, Henryk *The Origin of Russia* (George Allen & Unwin, 1954)

IVAN IV 'THE TERRIBLE'

Born: *August 25, 1530*
Reign: *December 3, 1533–January 16, 1547 (crowned tsar)–December 3, 1564 (abdicated); February 1565 (returned)–August 1575 (abdicated again); September 1, 1576 (returned)–March 18, 1584*
Died: *March 18, 1584*
Buried: *Cathedral of the Archangel Michael, The Kremlin*

In English Ivan's sobriquet is usually translated as 'the Terrible', but the original Russian word, *grozny*, is better rendered as something along the lines of 'Awe-Inspiring'. This seeming contradiction between the original word and its English counterpart is a perfect reflection of the complex image Ivan left behind. He was Russia's first tsar, who strengthened a country that was still reeling from the catastrophes of the Mongol invasion and started Russia on its first crucial steps out of a long isolation: in particular by opening trade relations with distant England. But if Ivan was the medicine Russia needed to swallow at the time, he had a very bitter taste.

Ivan was born the heir of Vasily III, Grand Prince of Muscovy, yet his childhood was a nightmare, one he would often talk about in adulthood with bitterness and anger. His father died from a sudden illness on December 3, 1533, leaving the three-year-old Ivan alone with his mother Elena Glinskaya, a Lithuanian with royal Mongolian ancestry, and his younger brother Yury, born a deaf-mute. While Vasily's body was still warm, Ivan's uncle Yury made a bid for the regency, but he was soon locked out of power by Elena and a boyar, Ivan Ovchina-Telepnev-Obolensky, who took the role of the comforting lover with the grieving widow. Uncle Yury, as punishment for his ambition, was locked in a dungeon in the Kremlin and left to starve. Another uncle of Ivan's, Andrey, was also put to death, just out of suspicion.

Only five years after his father's death, Ivan lost his mother, allegedly poisoned by one of her many enemies. Deprived of his guardian, Ivan Ovchina was immediately arrested and thrown in a tiny, out-of-the-way cell. Without a head, the government became the rope in a tug-of-war between the two most powerful families in Russia, the Shuiskys and the Belskys. This family feud at the top did nothing to help the government run smoothly. 'The boyars do as they please, behave unconscionably, and are at each other's throats. There is no order in the land. The State barely exists,' wrote one dissatisfied chronicler. Actually, the State did indeed very much exist, but the only way it could respond to the growing anarchy was by nurturing a legion of informers across the country, whose accusations almost always led to arrest, and arrest almost always led to death.

Even little Ivan, who despite his age was still Grand Prince of

Muscovy, suffered in this less than ideal environment. For the rest of his life Ivan would remember how the boyars and representatives from both the contending families ransacked his parents' belongings after his mother's death and how one boyar impudently slung his dirty boots on his father's favorite chair. Nor did Ivan forget how he and his brother Yury were treated by the boyars who made themselves the boys' caretakers. Later in life, Ivan said, 'As for my brother Yury and me, they treated us like foreigners or beggars. What privations did we not endure, lacking both food and clothing . . . We were not brought up as children should be.' One of the worst events Ivan recalled was when, late one night, he woke up to see the Metropolitan of Moscow, Joseph, standing in his room, shaking with fear and stuttering that he was hiding from men sent to kill him by the Shiuskys. Suddenly, armed men threw open the door before Ivan's frightened eyes and, completely ignoring the sight of their Grand Prince trembling in his bed, grabbed the screaming priest and dragged him out of the room. He was not killed, but exiled to a faraway monastery, yet the sight of the midnight abduction left a dark impression on young Ivan.

Despite the apathetic approach of the boyars to his education, Ivan grew into a bookworm. Voraciously he read whatever he could get his hands on, especially history and theology, and developed strong skills in writing, oratory and music. If he was not born a tsar, Ivan probably would have made a good scholar and historian. But he was scarred by the humiliations and traumas he had suffered. From an early age, Ivan showed the world his pain by dropping dogs from the heights of the Kremlin and watching them die on the ground. After he entered his teenaged years, he and his friends roamed through Moscow at night beating up and robbing anyone unlucky enough to run into them.

Ivan would not be satisfied with avenging the wrongs he had endured on animals and his subjects forever. At sixteen, a tall and gray-eyed young man, he watched helplessly as Andrey Shuisky, head of the Shuisky clan, viciously pummeled his confidant, Fyodor Vorontsov, with his fists. The same year, on December 29, 1543, Ivan finally made a bid for the authority that had been denied him for so long by having Andrey Shuisky thrown to a pack of hungry dogs. A decade after he was crowned, Ivan at last came into his own.

One of the first steps Ivan took in cementing his own God-given power was also a dramatic moment in Russian history. On January 16, 1547, a solemn coronation was held in Moscow to declare Ivan Tsar of Russia. The title was a Slavicized version of 'Caesar', a title once used by the Byzantine emperors until the Greek word for king, *basileus*, became their prominent title. 'Tsar' was still the word Russian writers used to name the Emperors of Byzantium until their ancient empire finally fell to the Ottoman Turks almost a century before Ivan's birth. Because of this, Ivan's adoption of the title 'Tsar' was much more than a self-ordained promotion. Ivan was naming himself heir to the long line of Roman Emperors and declaring Moscow to be the 'Third Rome' after Constantinople. This lofty assumption was not something that Ivan invented out of thin air. There was a long established legend, which Ivan had no doubt been familiar with since an early age, that claimed that Ivan's dynasty, the house of Rurik, was descended directly from a long-lost brother of the Emperor Augustus.

Despite a severe fire that broke out in Moscow and the death of his unpopular uncle Yury Glinksy at the hands of a rioting mob, the start of Ivan's career as unchallenged ruler was promising. The same year of his coronation, on February 3, he married the love of his life, Anastasia Romanova Zakharina, whose intimacy with Ivan was said to have soothed his more savage tendencies. She was described as 'benign and bearing no malice toward anyone' and Ivan affectionately called her his 'little heifer'.

Meanwhile, on the political front, Ivan managed to impose successful reforms on the law code and the church as well as curb the long unchecked power of the boyars. In time, Ivan would add the khanates of Astrakhan and Kazan, among the last remnants of Mongol power in Russia, to his empire.

Then suddenly, after showing so much promise, it seemed that the young tsar's rule would come to an abrupt stop in the spring of 1553. Ivan was bedridden with a severe fever and his prospects for survival seemed grim. Recently Ivan had a son by Anastasia, Dmitry, whom he declared his heir. But Dmitry was little more than an infant and it seemed that the events surrounding Ivan's father's death would repeat themselves. Even as the boyars came to Ivan's room to give their condolences, they scrambled to see who was most likely to steal the crown from Dmitry and how much they should do to ingratiate themselves to that person while Ivan was still in the realm of the living. The most promising candidate seemed Ivan's cousin, Vladimir Stanitsky, who did nothing to distance himself from all the greedy attention being thrown his way. Ivan, however, was more than aware of what was happening and ordered the most influential boyars and his advisors to come to his sickbed and swear their loyalty to the Tsarevitch Dmitry. Many of them flat-out refused to do so, including Ivan's two most trusted advisors, the priest Sylvester and Alexei Adashev. Still fighting for his life, Ivan had Vladimir dragged to his bedside and told him, 'I don't know what will become of you. And I'm not interested.' Using the sheer force of his personality from his sickbed, Ivan made Vladimir sign an oath of loyalty to his infant son. Although he managed to make this show of strength, Ivan bitterly commented once he made his recovery at the start of the next year, 'In word I was sovereign, but in fact I ruled nothing.' Against all odds Ivan did make a full recovery, but the fickleness of the men he relied on the most taught the tsar a very valuable – and dangerous – lesson.

While Ivan deeply felt his loss of trust in his own subjects, personal tragedy would sharpen the blow. His infant heir Dmitry, whose rights he fought to preserve, was dropped into the water and drowned when his nurse tripped while boarding a ship. Although Anastasia bore Ivan six children, only two others, Ivan and Fyodor, would survive past the age of two. In the summer of 1560, the unthinkable then happened: Anastasia became dangerously sick. When the priest Sylvester had the audacity to suggest that Anastasia's illness was God's punishment for an unpopular and dragged-out war against Poland and Lithuania in Livonia, Ivan in turn accused Sylvester of being involved in a plot to poison Anastasia and forced him to move to a distant monastery. Even with the alleged murderer gone, Anastasia succumbed to her sickness on August 7 of that year.

There is reason to think that Anastasia's death shattered something deep in Ivan's mind, but the heartsick tsar tried numerous times to fill the void she left, racking up a marital reputation to beat even that of Henry VIII of England. Ivan next married Maria Temrivkovna, who was said to have been stunningly beautiful, but was also stunningly uncouth, although she was always an angel in Ivan's eyes. Unfortunately, she was a devil to the court. She was so venomously hated in Russia's upper circles that, when she died on September 1, 1569, the rumors of a poisoning were numerous and loud. Two years later, Ivan married Martha Sobakina, the daughter of a merchant, who was apparently ill even on her wedding bed because she died only months after the marriage. Ivan would be forced to argue that the marriage was never official since Martha died before it could be consummated.

A widower once more, Ivan then married Anna Alexeevna, but he packed her off to a convent when he started regretting this newest choice. Defying the laws of the Eastern Orthodox Church, which dictated that a man could only have three marriages at most, he married again, this time to Anna Vassilchikura, who lived only two years after the marriage. Next on the list was Vassilissa Melentievna who recklessly had an affair with a boyar, Ivan Devtelev. The affair was soon discovered, and Devtelev was impaled, while Vassilissa was sentenced to while away her days at a convent. Ivan's last wife was Maria Nagaya, who was the only one of his wives to bear him another child, named Dmitry after the son he lost long ago. According to other accounts, he still kept a steady stream of lovers outside the marriage bed, both women and, a few claim, men.

Ivan's unusual marriage record was just one aspect of his intense lifestyle. The tsar was a man who liked to live in extremes. He and his chosen confidants spent many a night in drunken parties and orgies. Once he got his royal council drunk on vodka but kept a few secretaries on hand to record all the obscene jokes and dirty songs the ministers came up with as the night went on. The next morning, Ivan greeted his hungover officials with the notes and a grin. Behind this happy, mad drunk, the scholar in Ivan was still alive. One treacherous general who dared criticize Ivan (from the safety of Poland) was sent a brilliant 28,000-word rebuttal from the pen of the Tsar himself, who supported his divine right to rule with examples culled from sources ranging from the Old Testament to Roman history. Ivan was extremely well read and was still, in his own way, as religiously devout as he was hopelessly decadent. When he was not drinking the nights away, he could be found on his knees at prayer, bashing his head against stone to accentuate his humility before God.

One day Ivan did the truly unexpected and announced that he would abdicate from the throne. With hundreds of sleds loaded up with Moscow's treasures and various holy relics and a train of courtiers and priests, Ivan left the capital for the small village of Kolomenskoe at the end of the year 1564. He renounced his crown, but named no one to follow him. Matters were made worse when Ivan sent a letter to both the Metropolitan of Moscow and the Duma, or Council of State, accusing the entire Russian establishment of treason against the Tsar. 'Wherefore the Tsar and Grand Prince, not wishing to endure these many acts of treachery, has abandoned the Tsardom with a heavy heart and now travels wheresoever God may lead him,' Ivan wrote. At the same time, Ivan had written another letter that was read at his command to the working classes in Kremlin Square, stating that his abrupt abdication was not a strike against them and claiming that he understood that they were all victims of rapacious boyars. It was all an act, and it worked perfectly. The Archbishop of Novgorod was sent to beg Ivan to reclaim his throne for the sake of the Russian people. 'We are now without a shepherd,' the Archbishop said to an undoubtedly amused Ivan. 'And the wolves, our enemies, surround us.' Ivan agreed to play the shepherd again – for a price. Claiming that the reason he abdicated was because the boyars who tormented him in his childhood were still running and exploiting the government, Ivan insisted that, if he return, he must be given full authority. He would choose his own advisors and ministers, all of Russia would be considered his private property, and he would have the power of life and death over even his mightiest subjects. All of Ivan's demands were granted without debate.

By this time, Ivan was entering middle age and the long, stressful years had taken their toll on him. Increasingly paranoid, Ivan decided the best way to capitalize on his newly gained power was to establish the *oprichnina*, an organization not unlike the secret police of recent times. Dressed entirely in black and riding black horses, the men of the *oprichnina*, called the *oprichniki*, hunted down and slaughtered anyone the Tsar suspected of disloyalty. Entire families died under the swords of the *oprichniki*, who were above the law at all times. Anyone, peasant or boyar, could join their ranks, but many of their members were simply criminals who just wanted a fun way to put their bloodlust to productive use. Eventually, as the tsar's dependence on them grew, the *oprichnina* became a sort of a state within a state, with its own court and bureaucracy operating entirely free of the government in Moscow.

The *oprichniki* even had its own religious order. Inspired by their master's dual nature, the *oprichniki* at times pretended to be 'monks' while Ivan himself was the 'abbot'. After listening to their master read verses of Scripture to them over dinner, they would then start the drinking and begin a mock religious ceremony, with mass orgies or the jovial torturing of prisoners mixed with sacrilegious prayers and drunken hymns. Then suddenly a sense of the sacred would overcome Ivan once more and he would smash his head against the floor in repentance, with his 'monks' following suit.

With the *oprichniki* behind him, Ivan's rule became a true reign of terror. When the popular Metropolitan Philip attacked Ivan for his bad habits and worse politics, Ivan started a campaign of harassment against the priest, culminating in his sending Philip's cousin's head to the priest in a leather bag. The harsh harassment finally ended with Philip being stripped of his powers in public and then sent to a monastery, where he was later strangled by a man loyal to Ivan. One boyar, knowing he was accused of treason and would be struck down by the *oprichniki* any day, tried to save himself by becoming a monk. This only infuriated his assassins, who drove needles under his fingernails and then roasted him alive. Two of Ivan's own ministers, his treasurer Nikita Funikov and an advisor Ivan Viskovaty, were both murdered by *oprichniki* at Ivan's command in front of a large crowd in Moscow. The former was boiled alive in a giant pot, the latter was hanged while the *oprichniki* made a game of hacking pieces of his body off.

An entire city provided the victims for Ivan and the *oprichniki*'s most atrocious crime. After the authorities of the city of Novgorod were falsely accused of aiding Ivan's enemy, the King of Poland, Ivan struck hard: 400 of the city's leading citizens were tortured and killed. Everything from the city's palaces to the cathedrals were looted of anything of value. Men, women, and children were tied to sleds and pushed down into an icy river, where *oprichniki* stabbed and hacked away at anyone they saw coming up for air. Leaving this city in a bloody ruin, it was said Ivan had also set his eyes on the neighboring city of Pshov. He went as far as having some of the officials in that city executed until a hermit named Niholay told Ivan that he would be struck down by God if he laid a finger on the city. As soon as Niholay spoke, Ivan could hear rumbling thunder in the distance. Ivan heeded the divine warning. While this story could be dismissed as a mere legend, it is not inconsistent with Ivan's monstrous yet pious character.

By the time of the Novgorod massacres, Ivan was getting quite old. He was balding, his youthful stamina was starting to desert him, and the years had taken their toll on him. An observer who met Ivan in these years wrote: 'He has large eyes which are perpetually darting about, observing everything thoroughly . . . They say that when he is in the grip of anger he foams at the mouth like a stallion, appears close to madness and rages against everyone he meets.' It might have been this sense of exhaustion and emotional weakness, and not a cynical political ploy like his first abdication, that led Ivan once again to abdicate in August of 1575. This time, he did pick a man to take his place, Simeon Bakbulatovich, a relative of Ivan by marriage and a direct descendant of Genghis Khan. Whatever the point behind this drastic move, it was only a year before Ivan reassumed the throne. It was as if the brief reign of Simeon had not happened at all.

Whether or not Ivan ever really intended to stay a private citizen, he soon had cause to regret his decision. The last years of his reign would stack up badly compared to the years of his youth. The Livonian War, never the best of his endeavors, ended in disgrace and disaster. Poland came under the rule of the talented Stephen Bathory and under his brilliant direction Polish soldiers threatened the territories of Russia itself. An even bigger pain for Ivan to deal with was his son, the Tsarevitch Ivan, who squabbled with his father endlessly on matters of policy. Ivan also loathed his daughter-in-law, Elena Sheremetova, whom Ivan saw as encouraging his son's insolence.

On November 14, 1581, Ivan accused Elena, who was pregnant at the time, of being 'immodestly attired'. Elena started arguing back at Ivan, who became so enraged he struck Elena with the metal-tipped staff he always carried with him. The blow was so hard that Elena fell to the floor and later miscarried. The Tsarevitch leaped to his wife's defense and started wrestling with his father. Ivan viciously struck at him, driving the tip of the staff into his son's head. The wound soon became infected and the bedridden Tsarevitch died five days later at the age of twenty-seven. Ivan, grieved to the point of insanity, never left his son's bedside. At the Tsarevitch's funeral, Ivan banged his head against his son's coffin in repentance and begged two renowned monks to remember his son in their prayers for the rest of their lives.

After his son's death, Ivan continued to decline. His health was bad, but was made even worse by the daily doses of mercury he took to treat his arthritis. Eventually his condition deteriorated to the point that he could barely get anywhere without being transported in a sedan chair. On the morning of March 18, 1584, Ivan woke up feeling unusually invigorated and began setting up a chess board next to his bed for a few games, when he suddenly collapsed and died.

Like all of Russia's great tsars, Ivan had a severe personality. His emotions and the ways he expressed them seem beyond the scope of most people and even most monarchs. Yet there is something strangely childlike in the way Ivan so casually made drastic decisions, such as his two abdication attempts, or even in the way he could throw away human lives without a second thought. No wonder his biographer, Benson Bobrick, wrote, 'To the end, some part of Ivan would remain the hysterical child.'

Further Reading

Bobrick, Benson *Fearful Majesty: The Life and Reign of Ivan the Terrible* (G.P. Putnam's Sons, 1987)

Carr, Francis *Ivan the Terrible* (Barnes & Noble, 1981)

Duffy, James and Ricci, Vincent *Tsars: Russia's Rulers For More Than One Thousand Years* (Barnes & Noble, 1995)

Hingley, Ronald *The Tsars, 1533-1917* (Macmillan, 1968)

FYODOR I 'THE SANCTIFIED TSAR'

Reign: *March 18, 1584–January 8, 1598*
Born: *May 31, 1557*
Died: *January 8, 1598*
Buried: *Cathedral of the Archangel Michael, The Kremlin*

The accidental death of the Tsarevitch Ivan at the hands of his own father, Ivan the Terrible, left the first of the Russian tsars with two less than suitable heirs. There was Fyodor, a son of the tsar's first marriage to Anastasia Romanova Zakharina, and then there was Dmitry, Ivan's son by his last marriage to Maria Nagaya. Since the Orthodox Church forbade a man to marry more than three times and Maria was either Ivan's sixth or seventh wife, Dmitry was, in the eyes of the Church, a bastard. Unfortunately, Fyodor was not a perfect alternative. He was sickly, frail and stuck with a childish mind. In other words, he was the antithesis of his infamous father.

Ivan was not oblivious to his son's weaknesses and so he laid the foundations for a five-member regency council to head the government once Fyodor ascended the throne. The council was to be headed by two of Ivan's most trusted and influential boyars, Nikita Romanov and Boris Godunov. After Ivan the Terrible died, Godunov was suspected of aiming for the throne itself, suspicions that gained speed after Godunov's only serious rival, Nikita Romanov, died. Godunov did have the credentials to become the next tsar. He was, through his sister Irina, brother-in-law to Fyodor and had long enjoyed the support of even Fyodor's pathologically suspicious father. The only thing holding Godunov back was the simple fact that he lacked the blue blood many of his peers shared. In fact, by the standards of the time, he was probably considered 'new money'. Even with this handicap, Godunov managed to successfully grab the position of sole regent after the death of Romanov in 1588.

As Godunov accumulated power, Fyodor busied himself with prayers and visits to famous monasteries. He delighted in ringing church bells, hence the nickname 'Bell-Ringer', and handling holy relics. In Russia at the time, people who were not mentally gifted were considered 'holy fools', to have a special connection with the divine, so Fyodor came to be considered a living saint by his own subjects. To them, he was 'the Sanctified Tsar'.

Unfortunately, a family tragedy would spoil an otherwise uneventful reign. Godunov had demonstrated to all of Russia his determination to stay in power when, after the Shuisky family tried to dislodge him from power by encouraging Fyodor to divorce Irina because of her barrenness, he put to death a number of that family's leading members. On May 15, 1591, Boris became the chief suspect when Dmitry, who had been living with his mother in exile in Ugliach, was found dead from a knife wound to the throat. The official word was that the boy was playing with a knife and accidentally cut himself when he had an epileptic seizure. Everyone realized that Godunov had much to gain from the death of the boy who was Fyodor's most likely heir, bastard or not, but Fyodor refused to even consider that Godunov was guilty of any wrong-doing.

So complete was Fyodor's trust in Godunov that, after Fyodor died peacefully in his sleep on January 8, 1598, Boris Godunov was immediately proclaimed tsar. Fyodor had been the last of the Rurik dynasty, which had been in power for 400 years and twenty-one generations. Godunov and the dynasty he tried to establish would not be nearly as successful. Rival claimants and imposters claiming to be the dead heir Dmitry would rise up, bringing about an ugly period still known in Russian history as the 'Time of Troubles'. This anarchy would last until a new dynasty, the Romanovs, emerged to fill the void.

Further Reading

Duffy, James and Ricci, Vincent *Tsars: Russia's Rulers For More Than One Thousand Years* (Barnes & Noble, 1995)

Hingley, Ronald *The Tsars, 1533-1917* (Macmillan, 1968)

PETER I 'THE GREAT'

Reign: *May 7, 1682-February 8, 1725*
Born: *June 9, 1672*
Died: *February 8, 1725*
Buried: *Peter and Paul Cathedral, St Petersburg*

It is not much of an exaggeration to call Peter, the first tsar to also declare himself Emperor of Russia, the father of modern Russia and the man who bound the country to Europe. As one Russian writer put it, 'Peter the Great found only a blank sheet of paper and he wrote on it "Europe and the West", since when we have belonged to Europe and the West.' Unusually tall even by today's standards at six feet and seven inches, dashing with dark features, and displaying a physical and intellectual energy that bordered on the manic throughout his life, Peter's very bearing merited his complex reputation: it reflected a man who, almost paradoxically, was both a great reformer and a brutal totalitarian.

The crown that Peter inherited was not just handed over to him. He was the son of the second Romanov tsar, Alexis, through his second wife, Natalia Naryshkin. By his first wife, Maria Miloslavsky, Alexis had two other sons, the eldest of whom inherited the crown as Tsar Fyodor III. His reign would not last long since Fyodor was never a healthy child and had trouble just standing. His frailty finally overcame him on April 27, 1682 when he died from scurvy. While Fyodor's death was expected, he had died without naming an heir. Fyodor's sixteen-year-old younger brother Ivan was both mildly retarded and half-blind, while Peter was only nine years old at the time. To the Russian boyars, however, the choice between a healthy child and a mentally weak adult was not an impossible one. Even though by the right of primogeniture Ivan should have inherited the throne, Peter was quickly proclaimed tsar by a council of nobles.

Unfortunately for Peter, it is tricky to assert the authority of a child king even in the best of times. Soon the family of Maria Miloslavsky, rightfully afraid of being shifted out of power by the mother of the new tsar, spread a rumor that Tsarevitch Ivan had been brutally murdered by assassins sent by Natalia Naryshkin. Since the Naryshkin family was never the object of adoration in the first place, the rumor was taken as an excuse for the soldiers to revolt in the guise of demanding justice for Ivan's 'killers'. Even after Peter and Ivan were both shown alive and well, if terrified out of their minds, they still demanded Naryshkin blood. The soldiers were only appeased once they got their hands on Peter's uncle, Ivan Naryshkin, who was tortured and then impaled on a pike as Peter watched by his mother's side in the Kremlin. For the rest of his life Peter would always hate Moscow, so much so he would one day simply build his own capital.

After three days of anarchy, a wary compromise was reached. Both Ivan and Peter would rule as co-tsars, with Ivan's older sister, Sophia, becoming regent. In reality, Sophia had the seat of power in Moscow, while Peter was sent to live quietly with his mother in the town of Preobrazhenskoye. Although Peter was living in a sort of exile, and the threat of what would happen if his half-sister found his existence a nuisance loomed over his head, his childhood in that town was far from miserable. Even at a young age Peter proved a precocious learner: determined to discover why everything worked, he mastered all the trades and skills he could. Peter was given his own little army of local boys and aristocratic sons, whom he trained and marched like a real regiment and who were loaned real weapons from the Moscow armory. On his own, Peter spent days with the Dutch and German craftsmen in the German Suburb, a Moscow neighborhood where foreign nationals were quartered, learning first-hand trades like carpentry, masonry and printing.

His characteristic craving for knowledge and experience was strong even then, and he was more than eager to apply what he learned. One episode that would become the stuff of national legend was when he discovered an abandoned, broken boat washed up on the shore of the nearby lake. Using what carpentry skills he had learned, and with the aid of a Dutchman he befriended, Peter was able to repair the boat and used it to sail around the lake nearly every day. Peter went on to try his hand at helping make new boats, but he never forgot the little ship he rescued, especially after he went on to focus his fascination with shipbuilding by creating a navy for Russia. Calling this groundbreaking ship 'The Grandfather of the Russian Navy' with little exaggeration, Peter kept it well preserved and today it is still proudly exhibited at the Central Navy Museum in St Petersburg.

Peter's adventurous childhood, like any golden age, could not last long. He was quickly growing to manhood and, in 1689, was saddled with a wife he would come to detest, Eudoxia Lopukhin.

Furthermore, the boyars and officials who were tired of their invalid tsar and his haughty sister started putting their hopes behind the young, brilliant man kept miles away from the government. Sophia was afraid of Peter, but Peter, who still remembered the violent death that took his uncle, was absolutely terrified at the possibility that, under Sophia's command, soldiers could attack his home in the middle of the night and kill him. Even after Peter began to rule as Tsar in his right, this old terror from his childhood never left him. He could not bear to spend a single night in bed alone and, if his mistress and future wife Catherine or one of his other mistresses was not at hand, he insisted that a valet sleep beside him. The left side of Peter's face was also at times distorted by a nervous twitch, a deformity that was said to have started after one special night.

Frightened by spreading rumors that Sophia was gearing up to take the throne for herself and believing that he was on the verge of assassination, Peter fled his home in his nightclothes on horseback late in the night to the heavily fortified Monastery of the Trinity, where the monks were eager to give shelter to their frightened, nearly exhausted tsar. As stories about Peter's flight reached Moscow, the boyars, one by one, began to travel to the monastery to show Peter their undying loyalty. Even when Sophia began to threaten them, they stayed at Peter's side, eventually forming a rival court to the one in Moscow. With horror and frustration, Sophia watched helplessly as men who once pledged their eternal loyalty to her and Ivan drifted away to her brother's hands. With very few alternatives, Sophia gave up the regency and agreed to a comfortable imprisonment at a convent in Moscow. Meanwhile Ivan, who was only ever really a pawn wheeled out for ceremonies, was allowed to keep his title until he finally died in 1696. But now Peter ruled Russia alone.

This tall, active young tsar did not disappoint. Peter worked hard to tame the two great rivals of the Russian monarchy, the aristocracy and the church. The first Russian newspapers would appear during

Peter's reign and even the Russian alphabet was simplified under Peter's specifications. The hopelessly cumbersome Russian bureaucracy was reformed according to modern Western standards and Peter's own ideas. Russia's military also benefited from Peter, who brought contemporary tactics to the once archaic Russian army and became famous as a tsar who would courageously fight the enemy himself on the front lines. And it was Peter who channeled his passion for the sea and shipbuilding into his efforts to give Russia a fully functioning navy.

Peter's most daring deed was the building of his own capital. At the start of his reign, Russia had only one major port city, Archangel, located on the Northern Dvina River near the White Sea. Because Russia still did not have any link to the strategically important Baltic Sea, Archangel was the country's only gateway to the ocean, a very problematic situation since the waters around Archangel tended to freeze over during the winter. In order to provide the much needed Baltic port and thereby create a path to the West, the Tsar decided to construct a new city on Livonian land that had been reconquered from Sweden in the course of the Great Northern War. The land was dangerously swampy and the lives of countless workers were claimed during construction, but the city, immodestly christened St Petersburg, was finally completed on May 27, 1703. Still haunted by memories of what happened at Moscow, Peter declared that this new city would become the capital of Russia, in spite of the fact that it was precariously close to the western border. Even with its strategic failings, St Petersburg would remain Russia's capital until 1918 when the First World War would force the Russian government to relocate to the safer ground of Moscow.

St Petersburg was not only meant to serve as a new home for Peter and a new seat for the government: it was also a doorway between Russia and Europe. In fact, if Peter's reign had a single theme, 'Westernization' was very much it. Painfully conscious of Russia's reputation as a mysterious, barbaric country, Peter started personally cutting off the beards of his own courtiers. Beards were very important to Russians, especially since the Russian Orthodox Church considered it a sacrilege for a man to shave off his beard, so Peter's actions, harmless as they might seem today, were more or less blasphemous. Peter did not care though: he went ahead with passing a tax on beards, with the only people exempted being peasants or priests. But even people who paid their tax had to be wary if they were ever in their Tsar's presence, since he was likely to playfully, but painfully, pull at the beard, if not take a razor to it on the spot.

Peter's obsession with the West culminated in his decision to tour Europe in 1698 and 1699. Everywhere Peter went, he tried to consume as much knowledge as his mind could digest, whether it was carpentry, cobbling, anatomy or dentistry. In Holland he was taught the newest shipbuilding techniques and with his own two hands assisted in building and repair work, knowledge he eagerly brought back to Russia and taught to his men himself. He also visited Poland, Germany and England while trying to travel in cognito, but even the Tsar and Emperor of Russia could do nothing to stop his cover from being blown: he was assailed by crowds of gawkers. After all, it was hard for a man who was nearly seven feet tall to travel anonymously.

Naturally, a tsar could not be expected to travel alone and Peter brought along a number of courtiers, but it is very unlikely they enjoyed the trip as much as Peter did. Once when Peter and his courtiers were present for an anatomy lesson, a few of them groaned at the sight of a corpse being cut wide open. Angered at this – to him – cowardly reaction, Peter ordered the unlucky men to get over their squeamishness by leaning down and taking a bite out of the body. Peter became so excited by the lessons in dentistry he received that, after he returned to Russia, it became dangerous to complain about a toothache when Peter was within hearing distance: he was likely to pull out his own pair of pliers and rip the tooth out of the victim's mouth right away as a favor.

The people who provided Peter with lodgings throughout his British adventure would likewise be inconvenienced. John Evelyn, Peter's kind host in Britain, returned to find that Peter and his court had left his house in a shambles. The bed linen was ripped to shreds, the floors were covered in grease, portraits had been used for target practice with pistols, windows were broken, and many of his chairs had been used as firewood. Worst of all, Evelyn found that his prize-winning garden had been completely obliterated. His neighbors later told him that one night Peter's drunken men had pushed an equally intoxicated Tsar around the garden in a wheelbarrow, an unknown contraption in Russia at the time. Luckily, Evelyn received some compensation from the deeply apologetic Russian government, but not quite enough to make up for all the damage.

If these were the types of parties Peter enjoyed at the homes of foreign hosts, one can only imagine what an average evening at his court in St Petersburg was like. Peter always kept a large collection of dwarves and other physically deformed figures around for his own and the court's amusement. It was a special day for Peter's court when the tsar would announce that two of his dwarves were to marry and a celebration was to be held. Peter himself would always volunteer to give away the bride. When his niece Anna married the Duke of Courland, Peter threw a grand party whose centerpiece was a massive pie with dozens of dwarves hiding inside who ran out after the pie was cut open.

Imitating the blasphemous ceremonies held by Ivan the Terrible, Peter, even though he was a deeply religious man, set up the 'Synod of Most Drunken Fools and Jesters'. Peter was a deacon for the synod, while traditional Orthodox rites mixed with orgies and drinking, with vodka substituted for holy water, were presided over by a patriarch. The Synod's first commandment was to 'get drunk every day and never go to bed sober'. During Lent, Peter and the rest of the synod rode through St Petersburg on donkeys or sleighs drawn by bears, pigs or goats. Another special festival was held for the Greek god of wine, Dionysus, where the patriarch blessed attendants with a cross made from two tobacco pipes. To staunchly traditional observers, this was especially blasphemous, since the Russian Orthodox Church had for a long time condemned smoking tobacco.

When a new patriarch was elected in 1721, the 'cardinals' of the synod celebrated by sitting in boxes built for the occasion where they were obliged to drink a spoonful of vodka every fifteen minutes throughout the night. After hearing about the legend of Pope Joan, a woman who supposedly passed herself off as male and became Pope, Peter thought it would be a hilarious idea to have the patriarch-to-be, Ivan Buturlin, and his wife sit in chairs with special holes constructed in them, through which Peter and the synod could examine their genitalia to 'determine' their true sexes. There Peter groped Buturlin's testicles, shouting, 'He has an opening!' At dawn the next day the groggy and hung-over synod were greeted by the 'princess-abbess', a topless young woman carrying a basket of eggs. After kissing the woman's breasts, each cardinal took one of the eggs, which were then used to cast the vote for Buturlin.

All this jolly drunkenness could have been a mask for some deeply rooted problems in Peter's mind. Besides the lifelong nervous twitch in his face, Peter also suffered from constant seizures. 'He has convulsions, sometimes of the eyes, sometimes in his arms and sometimes in his whole body,' a contemporary wrote. 'At times he rolls his eyes so much only the whites can be seen.' One historian has theorized that Peter was enduring the debilitating effects of syphilis. Epilepsy was also a possibility. In this state Peter could be soothed only by his favorite mistress, and the wife he would secretly marry, Catherine Skavronskaya, a Lithuanian peasant who met and fell in love with Peter because she was the servant of one of Russia's premier boyars. When Peter felt an 'attack' coming on, Catherine would place Peter's head on her lap and whisper soothing words to him, gently stroking his head all the while. Eventually Peter would fall asleep and, hours later, wake up feeling completely refreshed.

Still afraid of losing his life and throne, even after the specter of his sister Sophia had long been vanquished, Peter had no mercy for his enemies. When a conspiracy involving the Miloslavskys was uncovered in 1687, Peter did not let the fact that the hated Ivan Miloslavsky was dead stop him from revenge. Instead he dug up Miloslavsky's corpse and placed it under the scaffold: as the limbs of the living conspirators were hacked off, the blood was allowed to drop on the body, which was later destroyed. After another group of rebels were arrested, Peter beheaded them with his own hands gripping the axe.

The most pathetic victim of Peter's demonic tendencies was his own son and heir, the Tsarevitch Alexis. Not only was Alexis the son of Peter's first wife, whom he came to detest and eventually banished to a convent, but he also seemed to lack his father's old drive and ambition. Of course, few human beings could hope to emulate Peter's jack-of-all-trades life, but Alexis, a quiet and pious man completely uninterested in his heritage, seemed Peter's living antithesis. Throughout his life, Alexis was a poor student in academics, politics, and war, arousing Peter's antipathy, then disgust, and finally rage.

Viewing his son as lazy and irresolute, Peter hoped that a tour of Europe and marriage to a German heiress, Charlotte of Brunswick-Wolfenbüttel, would shape up the young man. While Peter expected Alexis to pick up all the skills he did, Alexis instead spent all his energies toward being entertained by the courts of Europe and taking more than his fill of parties and plays. Once Alexis arrived back in Russia, Peter exclaimed that he would test his heir himself to see how much he had actually learned from his European journey. Alexis was so terrified by the prospect of an exam that he tried to get out of it by 'accidentally' shooting his hand.

Unfortunately, he botched even that job. The bullet missed its mark and his hand suffered only a powder burn.

This was about the last straw for Peter. He gave his son a stern lecture, telling him that he had to prove himself worthy to be tsar or give up his inheritance. Peter hoped that the threat of losing his place in the line of succession would spur Alexis on to more serious things, but, sadly, this little father-to-son talk only backfired. Alexis astonished his father by saying he never wanted the Russian throne and would not mind being disinherited. Recovering from his shock, Peter added that, in order for Alexis not to prove a threat to whomever would take the crown in his place, he would have to become a monk to completely remove himself from his place in the succession. While Alexis was not studious, he was devout, so he happily agreed to that too.

Peter was not about to let his son off the hook so easily. During a military campaign, Peter, who was in Copenhagen, sent a letter to Alexis, commanding him to join him and be prepared to fight. Alexis wrote back that he would travel to meet his father in Denmark right away, but in reality he made preparations to travel to Vienna where he hoped to be the long-term guest of the Holy Roman Emperor, Charles VI. The wayward prince hoped this ploy would coax his father into accepting his wish to retire to private life. What Alexis did not consider was that Charlotte had recently given birth to a boy named Peter – a new heir. Alexis was now expendable.

When word of what his son had done reached Peter, his anger burst like a volcano. Peter's first reaction was to arrange to have Alexis kidnapped from the Austrian court, but, once his mind cooled and he saw in a clearer light the potential political problems that would come with such a rash act, he realized that it was better to trap his son with sugar than with vinegar. In Naples, Alexis met Peter Tolstoy, a Russian diplomat, who told Alexis that Peter was willing to pardon his crimes, which could include treason, and would consider allowing him to renounce his claim to Russia if he returned willingly. In a letter Peter wrote and sent with Tolstoy, he declared, 'If you are afraid of me, I assure you and I promise to God and His judgment that I will not punish you. If you submit to my will by obeying me and if you return, I will love you better than ever.' To make it appear that there was little alternative outside of seeking his father's forgiveness, Tolstoy also told Alexis that his welcome was wearing out. Not only would the Austrians separate Alexis from his mistress, a Finnish peasant named Euphrosyne, but he could at any moment be sent back to Peter against his will. These were all lies, but Tolstoy bribed several Austrian officials into giving them substance.

Taking the bait Tolstoy worked hard to lay out, Alexis returned to Russia in January of 1718, believing with naïve confidence that his father would not only forgive him, but would also let him become a private citizen and marry Euphrosyne. Perhaps Peter did intend at some point to show his son some degree of leniency, but there were certain questions that were still rooted in his mind. What if his son actually left Russia to join a conspiracy to depose or kill him and place himself on the throne? If not that, were Alexiss' actions clear proof that he would be willing to betray his father in the future? Rather than the warm fatherly welcome he expected, Alexis found himself quickly arrested as soon as he passed the Russian border and put on trial for conspiracy and treason. Peter assured Alexis that no harm would come to him if he gave up the names of his 'accomplices'. Meekly Alexis turned over the names of the friends and servants who helped him in fleeing Russia. Many of them went under the axe, but even this betrayal would not save him. After being thoroughly bribed and tortured, Euphrosyne gave a highly damaging testimony against her lover, 'proving' that Alexis had in fact intended to steal his father's throne from the very beginning. Alexis was tied up and given forty lashes on the back with a thick whip, the knout. He did not survive. The government spread word that the Tsarevitch had died unexpectedly of natural causes. The day after his son's death, June 26, Peter went ahead with plans for an annual celebration in St Petersburg without any hesitation.

If the persecution and death of his son ever weakened Peter's resolve, he gave no sign. Even into old age, he remained as active as ever, and in 1722 dived into freezing, turbulent waters to help rescue the crew of a capsized boat. Soon after this episode, though, Peter became seriously ill. In the morning of January 28, 1725 he was carried off by a severe bladder infection and, to no one's great surprise, cirrhosis of the liver. Catherine stayed by her husband's bedside until the very end. Her loyalty was well rewarded – after Peter's death, she succeeded her husband as the first tsarina and Empress of Russia, despite having been a peasant, a foreigner and a servant.

Further Reading

Cracraft, James *The Revolution of Peter the Great* (Harvard University Press, 2003)

Duffy, James and Ricci, Vincent *Tsars: Russia's Rulers For More Than One Thousand Years* (Barnes & Noble, 1995)

Hingley, Ronald *The Tsars, 1533–1917* (Macmillan, 1968)

Massie, Robert *Peter the Great: His Life and World* (Ballantine Books, 1980)

ANNA

Born: *February 7, 1693*
Reign: *February 1730–October 28, 1740*
Died: *October 28, 1740*
Buried: *Cathedral of Peter and Paul, St. Petersburg*

At some point it must have seemed to Anna that her life would be a wasted one. Her father was an anointed tsar, Ivan V, but he was also a crippled, quiet man and a cipher in the hands of his sister, Sophia. Eventually her uncle, Ivan's half-brother, Peter, who 'shared' the title of tsar but grew up in virtual exile, took power in Moscow. Although Ivan was allowed to remain 'co-tsar', it was blindingly obvious that Peter, and by extension, his part of the family, was now in the ascendant. Nonetheless, circumstances

would not only lead Anna to claim her uncle's throne against all odds, but it would also help her preserve the autocracy of the Russian tsars.

Anna was married off on October 31, 1710 to Frederick William, the duke of the Polish province of Courland[45]. Since Anna was always a favorite niece of Peter's, the celebration was lavish even by his standards: the wine and vodka flowed like rivers and the main attraction was a giant pie filled with dwarves who rushed out of it once it was cut open. Unfortunately, all this Russian hospitality was too much for Frederick, who suddenly became sick and died before the marriage could even be consummated. Brief as the marriage was, Anna still inherited her husband's duchy, and there she was obligated to stay, seemingly for the rest of her life.

Bored with running her dead husband's small land, Anna amused herself by racking up debts and starting a series of affairs with her own ministers, many of whom were Germans. Short and heavyset with dark features, Anna was considered at least reasonably attractive by her contemporaries, and she was able to inspire strong loyalty in quite a few of her lovers. The one bad episode in her romantic history was with Maurice de Saxe, a handsome adventurer and the bastard son of Augustus I, the King of Poland. Although Anna was smitten with him for some time, she eventually realized he was only after her money and influence when she caught him carrying a laughing lady-in-waiting on his shoulders in the courtyard.

As Anna languished in Courland, dynastic events in Russia were slowly unfolding in her favor. Peter's throne was given to his second wife, Catherine, who reigned for only two years before she too died. Next was Peter's grandson and namesake who became tsar at only the age of twelve. Tsar Peter II lost his life to smallpox at the ripe age of fifteen and, despite efforts to force his wife to conceive a child with him by forcibly pushing her into his sickbed, he left no direct heirs. The privy council of the Russian court were then left with only a few

[45] Today the land is part of the country of Latvia.

feasible options. There was Peter's daughter by Catherine, Elizabeth, but in the eyes of the Russian Orthodox Church she was a bastard since she was born before her father and mother had properly married. Then there was Anna's older sister, also named Catherine, but she was married to a detested German duke, Karl Leopold of Brunswick-Wolfenbüttel. There were others too, but most were too young or had obnoxious foreign ties. Anna, free of both legitimacy concerns and hated husbands, seemed the obvious choice.

The council had some hope that Anna, the helpless widow trapped for years in a tiny, out-of-the-way duchy, would agree to become a cipher. Confident they had nothing to fear from the plump, 37-year-old woman who seemed more concerned with getting the money needed to untangle herself from a mountain of debt than with Russian politics, the privy council drew up a detailed set of agreements Anna had to accept if she were to take the crown of Russia. Among the conditions, Anna was required not to marry or appoint an heir, to relinquish her power to declare war, make peace, grant lands, access state revenues, create new taxes or condemn people of noble blood without trial. For a Russia that had only recently experienced the very personal autocracy of Peter the Great these demands were quite revolutionary and in fact laid the certain if unsteady foundations for a constitutional monarchy. To everyone's surprise, Anna was perfectly happy to sign the document and so she was crowned Tsarina and Empress in St Petersburg on February 10, 1730 without a fuss.

It all seemed too easy and, actually, it was. Fifteen days after she ascended the throne, a small crowd of Russia's best presented Anna with a petition against the new restrictions signed by a large number of military officials, nobles, and other dignitaries. Anna was told about the petition beforehand and everything that followed was carefully rehearsed, but Anna went about the charade like an experienced actress.

After she finished skimming the petition she took from the crowd, she looked up with feigned surprise and exclaimed in an

outraged tone, 'What! Do you mean to tell me that the Articles I signed in Mitau were not approved by all my people?'

'No, they were not, Your Sovereign Majesty,' the crowd answered.

Perhaps acting on impulse and not by the script, Anna gripped the documents she had signed and ripped them to pieces with her own hands. Had these provisions remained in place, the tsars would no longer have been autocrats and Russian – and world – history might have been drastically altered. As it was, the one chance to create a limited monarchy in Russia was gone in an instant, reduced to nothing more than shreds of paper on the floor.

All things considered, the privy council should have expected as much. Anna was in every way the niece of Peter the Great. She shared his desire to see Russia move forward in the European arena and, in fact, Russian culture began once again to flourish under Anna's reign, with the first Russian opera being performed while Anna ruled. At the same time, Empress Anna was no elitist. She never stopped appalling the aristocrats with her own passion for folk dancing and peasant ballads.

The new tsarina shared more than a small part of her uncle's eccentricity and taste for wild fun. Anna kept loaded pistols around every room of the palace, so there would always be guns at hand for when birds flew past a window. The Empress expected her ladies-in-waiting to grab a pistol and try to join in the fun as well. Peter's lifelong fascination with dwarves and the physically deformed had also been passed on to Anna, who always kept a large retinue of such figures at hand.

The dark parts of Peter's personality – his quick, nasty temper and his petty vindictiveness – were also aspects of the Empress Anna's rough-and-tumble personality, but fortunately she combined her appetite for revenge with a crude sense of humor. People who annoyed her were not put to death or banished, but forced to become court jesters and perform games with Anna's dwarves. Some days they were forced to ride the dwarves like horses in front of the court, which sometimes led to violent fights when the men toppled over the dwarves, much to Anne's hysterical delight. One courtier who really infuriated Anna, Prince Mikhail Golitsyn, was stripped of his title, reduced to a page and on pain of death forced to strut and cluck like a hen, sitting over a large basket stuffed with straw, before the eyes of all the court.

Her most elaborate prank by far was played on the same unlucky man. After Golistyn's wife died, Anna decided to arrange for him a new marriage to a woman reported to be the ugliest in all of Russia. During the wedding party, the lucky couple were pulled in a cage, led by a team of hogs, behind a parade of freaks and dwarves and drunks. Their destination was the bank of the icy Neva River, where Anna had an intricate palace of ice constructed. At the entrance were 80-foot-long, 30-foot-tall statues of dolphins and a sculpture of an elephant, ridden by a fully dressed Persian, all in ice. There were even carved ice trees with detailed ice birds perched on the branches. Six cannons made of ice, that were even capable of firing, served as sentinels at the strange little fortress. Inside, too, all the furniture, even the wedding bed the new couple was forced to consumate their marriage on, was made entirely of ice. Astonishingly pneumonia did not visit them after their wedding night and, despite the circumstances, it was reported they went on to become a happy couple.

Since special projects like this ice palace were Anna's main concern, the everyday business of the government fell in the hands of her favorite lover, Ernst Johann von Biron, who was created Duke of Courland after Anna became Empress. Biron's influence was seen as so prevalent that Anna's reign is sometimes referred to as the *Bironovshckina* or 'the Age of the German Yoke'. Anna was blissfully oblivious to the growing anti-German sentiments being nourished inside and outside the Russian court, so without much hesitation she adopted her nephew, the newborn Ivan, the son of a very unpopular German duke, as her heir.

Brought low by kidney problems and gout, Anna, now forty-six, found herself dying. Naming Biron as the regent for her nephew, she died on October 17, 1740: her last words were 'Farewell, all!' She died without realizing that by giving the universally loathed Biron full charge of the realm, she had effectively sealed the fate of her branch of the Romanov clan. It took only a year before Peter the Great's daughter Elizabeth, riding the anti-German sentiment Biron's corruption and incompetence inspired, pulled off a successful *coup d'état*. Tsar Ivan VI, before he could even speak, was deposed and condemned to a lifetime in a prison cell.

Further Reading

Curtiss, Mina *A Forgotten Empress: Anna Ivanovna and Her Era* (Frederick Ungar, 1974)

Duffy, James and Ricci, Vincent *Tsars: Russia's Rulers For More Than One Thousand Years* (Barnes & Noble, 1995)

Hingley, Ronald *The Tsars, 1533-1917* (Macmillan, 1968)

PETER III

Born: *February 21, 1728*
Reign: *January 5, 1762–June 9, 1762*
Died: *July 18, 1762*
Buried: *Cathedral of Peter and Paul, St Petersburg*

Tsarina Catherine the Great not only represented the Enlightenment, to many people she *was* the Enlightenment in the flesh. She took a long series of masculine, witty lovers with a frankness and a freedom simply unavailable to most women at the time. She kept lengthy correspondences with the revolutionary philosopher Voltaire and other liberal scholars and thinkers from the era and went on to become one of the most celebrated rulers in the history of Russia, if not in all of Europe. Yet the story of how she gained her power is not as glamorous as the image her name provokes. Her accession sprang from one of the most disastrous and bizarre marriages in royal – or any – history, her own marriage to Peter III, a man she, perhaps inadvertently, condemned to death in order to earn her place in the world.

After his aunt Elizabeth usurped the throne of Russia from Ivan VI, the infant son of her cousin Catherine, Peter was summoned to Russia from his homeland of Holstein to take his place as Elizabeth's adopted son and heir. Peter loved Holstein, a German duchy he inherited from his father, with a patriotic fervor and would later say to anyone who had to listen that the Holstein capital of Kiel alone had more merit than all of Russia put together. After a childhood spent ignored by his mother and abused by his father, Peter came to Russia, a land he knew nothing about, emotionally stunted, clinging to memories of his homeland and to his Lutheranism. Although it was Elizabeth's decision to make him her heir, later on she would write, 'My nephew, Devil take him, is a monster.'

Hoping to provide an heir for her nephew, and also to give him a stabilizing influence, Elizabeth arranged for Peter to marry Sophia von Anhalt-Zerbst, the daughter of a poor German duke and a relative of the Swedish royal family. Renamed Catherine after she was baptized into the Russian Orthodox Church (something Peter never did), she married Peter on August 21, 1745. Catherine recorded her first impressions of the young prince in her memoirs: 'He was sixteen, quite good looking before [he later caught smallpox], but small and infantile, talking of nothing but soldiers and toys. I listened politely and often yawned . . .' The perceptive Catherine also hit upon what made Peter so distasteful to his aunt and others, '[T]he trouble was that his entourage tried to make this child behave as an adult and forced him to a strict discipline, thus developing in him deceitfulness and hypocrisy.'

Peter's problems extended to the bedroom and, according to both Catherine's memoirs and other first hand sources, the young couple never consummated their marriage. One theory is that Peter had a deformity of the penis called phimosis that made erections excruciating, although it could have been easily cured by circumcision. Since Peter did have his own mistresses, many of whom were servants, it is more likely that he suffered some strange psychological terror of sleeping with a woman who was his equal in social standing. Even stranger, Peter seemed to find some kind of release in telling Catherine in detail about all his sexual encounters, and later on in their marriage Catherine would even agree to start arranging Peter's liaisons for him.

In the meantime, on their first wedding night, Catherine lay in bed anxiously waiting for her husband who was out drinking with his friends and servants. She was nervous and terrified as she had been taught very little about sex by her cold, domineering mother. When Peter did appear in their bedroom, he managed only to laugh and say, 'It would amuse the servants to see us in bed together,' before he passed out.

On other nights Peter would bring all his toy soldiers to the bed and force Catherine to play war games with him. Some nights Catherine was forced to share the bed with Peter's hunting dogs. Another time Catherine returned to their chamber to find that Peter, busy at his usual games, had lynched a large, fat rat. When Catherine asked why he did it, Peter replied that he had found the rat guilty of treason. In the daytime, Peter tormented Catherine with his terrible, screeching violin playing.

Things were made much worse when Elizabeth tried to fix the problem of the celibate marriage by keeping Catherine and Peter literally locked in their apartments for days on end. The living situation with her increasingly erratic husband drove Catherine to thoughts of suicide, according to her memoirs. But as Catherine's naïvety vanished in the often rowdy, sometimes treacherous atmosphere of the Empress Elizabeth's court, she began to find a release in literature and philosophy. She also carefully started to set up alliances with the courtiers as well as earn the support and sympathy of Elizabeth herself. Peter, who was not so out of touch with reality that he did not notice the growing intelligence and influence of his wife, began to yell at Catherine for convenient reasons each day. His favorite excuse to lecture her became the very fact that she had turned her back on her native religion by giving up her Lutheranism to convert to Orthodox Christianity. But Catherine wrote that Peter was not as religious as he might have thought: 'In actual fact, he was attached to no creed and had no idea of the dogmas and principles of the Christian religion. I have never seen a more perfect atheist in practice than this man who, nevertheless, was often scared either by the devil or by God, but more often despised both, depending on the occasion or what whim of the moment possessed him.'

As the marriage dragged on and Peter's attitude toward his wife changed from apathy to hatred, it seemed likely that Catherine would remain barren: but suddenly, she became pregnant. After two miscarriages, she finally gave birth to the long-anticipated heir, who was christened Paul, on September 20, 1754. How did this happen? According to one source, it was a mystery even to the 'father'.

'Heaven alone knows how it is that my wife becomes pregnant,' Peter allegedly said. 'I have no idea whether this child is mine and whether I ought to recognize it as such.'

Catherine's own memoirs offer an interesting clue, which could also explain why these memoirs were not published until 1859, and even then this one passage was edited out of the authorized editions for decades:

> Mme. Choglokov [Catherine's chief attendant], who never abandoned her favorite occupation of watching over the succession, took me aside one day and said: 'Listen to me, I

> must really talk to you about this quite frankly.' I was naturally all ears and eyes. She started in her usual way with a long dissertation on her affection for her husband, on her wisdom, on what had or had not to be done to secure love and facilitate conjugal relations, and then suddenly declared that there were certain situations of major importance which formed exceptions to the rule. I let her say all she had to say without interrupting, unaware of what she was aiming at, slightly surprised and wondering if she was setting a trap for me or whether she was sincere. While I was deliberating this, she added: 'You will see how much I love my country and how frank I can be: I have no doubt that in your heart you have a certain preference for one man over the other; I leave you to choose between Serge Saltikov and Leon Naryshkin, and if I am not mistaken it is the latter.' To this I cried out: 'No, no, not at all!' And she went on: 'Well, if it's not him, it can only be the other.' I remained silent and she added: 'You will see that I shall not be the one to create any obstacles for you.

Saltikov and Naryshkin were both celebrated members of Elizabeth's court, with ancient lineage, who had each caught Catherine's eye with their easy manner and handsome faces. This passage, combined with what else is known about Catherine the Great, is a good clue that the heir Paul was not the son of Peter Romanov, but of Serge Saltikov, meaning that the last generations of Romanovs after Catherine were not Romanovs after all. What Catherine does leave unclear is the question of whether or not Choglokov was acting on her own or under explicit instructions from the Empress herself. Elizabeth was definitely the sort of person who would apply such an unorthodox yet simple solution to the problem of the succession. Either way, Saltikov was conveniently sent off on a diplomatic mission around the time that Paul was born.

Her appetites at last awakened by her encounter with the

strapping Saltikov, Catherine began to take more lovers under Peter's nose and, we may suppose, with Elizabeth's blessing. Eventually, though, even Peter took a hearty attitude toward his wife's indiscretions. Once, Catherine's latest lover, a Polish man named Stanislas Poniatowski[46], was slipping out of Catherine's bedroom at dawn when suddenly he was caught by Peter's guards and brought before the heir himself. Terrified of exposing himself and Catherine to her husband, Stanislas refused to explain why he was there, even after Peter asked him point-blank if he was his wife's lover. Peter, who suspected the truth from the beginning, led Stanislas to believe that he thought he was an assassin or a spy. Afraid for Stanislas's life, Catherine asked Peter's current mistress to explain the situation to him in private. She did so and a jubilant Peter met Stanislas in his quarters and said, 'Aren't you a great fool not to have let me in on the secret in time! If you had, there wouldn't have been any of this row!'

Then Peter exclaimed, 'Since we are good friends now, there's one person missing here!' Next he ordered that Catherine, who was asleep, be woken up and brought into the room to join her husband and her lover. Pointing to Stanislas, Peter said to Catherine, 'Well, there he is! I hope everyone is pleased with me!' Later on, the two couples, spouses and lovers, allegedly had a friendly dinner that lasted well into the night.

Meanwhile Elizabeth began to view her nephew's upcoming ascension with apprehension, if not alarm. At the time Russia was at war with Prussia, but Peter's love for his homeland, linked politically and culturally to Prussia, made him uncomfortably sympathetic toward the enemy. It was even whispered around St Petersburg that Peter sent detailed Russian battle plans to the Prussian king.

'My nephew is hated precisely because of his open aversion to

[46] As Tsarina, Catherine would one day make Stanislas King of Poland. He was destined to be the last.

Russian customs,' Elizabeth said of Peter. 'Once I am dead, he can leave the country and spend his time playing chess with the King of Prussia.'

This was not an empty threat. There was a strong possibility that Elizabeth would by-pass Peter in the succession and make Paul Tsar, with Catherine his regent. After all, the succession laws set by Peter the Great dictated that tsars could choose their own successor, as long as they were a Romanov by blood or marriage. Unfortunately, Elizabeth was either unable to make the move, found it impractical for some reason or died before she could institute it. The despised nephew became Tsar Peter III at the end of 1761.

By the time Peter succeeded his aunt, Russia and Prussia were fighting the Seven Years' War. One of the new Tsar's first acts was to draw a close to hostilities, even though the war was going so much in Russia's favor that the complete invasion of Prussia was on the horizon. Horrifying the nation, Peter gave back all the land Russian soldiers had died to conquer to King Friedrich the Great of Prussia and refused to accept the concessions Friedrich was willing to give Russia. Instead, Peter set up a friendly alliance with Prussia, the country that had been Russia's bitter enemy for years. Later Peter started a war with Denmark for no better reason than to regain some land Denmark had annexed from Holstein. It was a war that was clearly waged for the benefit of Peter's homeland, but he had no qualms about sending Russian men to die for the cause.

Insult was quickly added to injury when Peter ordered that soldiers in the army wear Prussian military outfits and start employing Prussian tactics. Although Peter, at least for the time being, did not try to change the state religion, he ordered that all Russian Orthodox priests start adapting the costumes of Lutheran pastors. Then this once child-like adult became increasingly violent and temperamental as the pressures of ruling began to warp him. After Catherine gave birth to another bastard child, Anna, on April 11, Peter screamed at Catherine and called her a fool in front of a room filled with dignitaries and diplomats. One ambassador

muttered to a Russian next to him, 'Do you know that your Emperor must be mad as a hatter? No man could behave the way he does otherwise.'

Peter's reign was a bleak time for all concerned, but it was destined to last only six months. Motivated by rumors that Peter had plans either to send her to a convent or have her killed so that he could marry his favorite mistress, Elizabeth Worontsov, Catherine decided to take the offensive. 'It was a matter of either perishing with (or because of) him, or else of saving myself, the children and perhaps the state from the carnage to which the moral and physical qualities of this Prince were leading us,' Catherine wrote.

Catherine's newest lover was Gregory Orlov, one of four brothers who were all members of the imperial guard. With the help of the Orlovs, Catherine encouraged a conspiracy against Peter, designed to depose him and put her or Paul on the throne. Unfortunately, while the plotters felt they needed more time to undermine the new tsar, their hands were forced when one of the conspirators, in a haze of intoxication, railed against Peter in public, leading to his arrest.

Protected by one of Gregory's brothers, Alexis, and knowing that the other conspirators, including herself, would be next, Catherine appeared before the guards' camps in the middle of the night and said, confident in her popularity, 'I have come to you for protection. The Emperor has given orders to arrest me. I fear he intends to kill me.'

Given the Emperor's instability and deep-rooted loathing for his wife, this was no exaggeration. Instantly rallying behind this brave, determined woman, the Guards cheered her on, their acclamations seconded by an ever-growing crowd. Soon, with the backing of the Metropolitan of St Petersburg, Catherine was declared Tsarina of Russia in Kazan Cathedral.

Meanwhile Peter, hearing the news of his wife's activities with increasing anxiety, fled with his mistress Elizabeth to try to rally some support. Unfortunately, on one naval ship he approached, he was told coolly that Russia no longer had an Emperor, but an Empress. Turning back, Peter collapsed sobbing into the arms of his mistress Elizabeth.

Eventually captured, Peter was forced to abdicate and was then made a prisoner at Schlüsselburg Fortress. His chief guard was Alexis Orlov, who could not have been kind to the disgraced tsar. Not denied all his dignity, Peter was allowed to write increasingly desperate letters to the new tsarina, in which he used a slavishly submissive tone to the wife he once humiliated in public. In one letter, he made one simple request to his estranged wife: that she provide him with his favorite dog, his fiddle, and his dear mistress. Only the first two requests were fulfilled.

Although his very existence was a danger to Catherine, it seemed that she was content to let her husband spent the rest of his life a prisoner. But on July 5, 1762, Alexis Orlov became so drunk he started an argument with Peter and, when it escalated, he apparently lost control and killed him. As soon as he came to his senses, Alexis sent a letter to Catherine, telling her what happened and begging her for forgiveness. The note was handed to Catherine just before she left to attend a state function. It was said that Catherine calmly read the letter, went about her schedule for the evening, and only when she returned to her private apartments did she give herself over to her grief. To one of her confidants, she admitted, 'My horror at this death is inexpressible.'

Peter would come to haunt Catherine, but not only as a ghost of her past. He would also return in the form of her son Paul who, even though he very likely did not belong to Peter in blood, would become obsessed with his father's memory and would seek to finish what his father had started.

Further Reading

Catherine the Great (trans. Lowell Bair) *The Memoirs of Catherine the Great* (Bantam Books, 1957)

Duffy, James and Ricci, Vincent *Tsars: Russia's Rulers For More Than One Thousand Years* (Barnes & Noble, 2002)

Hingley, Ronald *The Tsars, 1533-1917* (Macmillan, 1968)

Leonard, Carol *Reform and Regicide: The Reign of Peter III of Russia* (Indiana University Press, 1993)

PAUL

Reign: *November 17, 1796–March 23, 1801*
Born: *October 1, 1754*
Died: *March 23, 1801 (assassinated)*
Buried: *Cathedral of Peter and Paul, St Petersburg*

Not even Peter the Great or Friedrich Wilhelm of Prussia dreamed of controlling their subjects' lives to the level that Tsar Paul strove for. Long before the growth of technology provided the means for a more complete totalitarianism, Paul was Orwellian: both in his ideas toward government and in what he dreamed of doing. Despite being her son, Paul's regime was a far cry from that of his mother and predecessor, Catherine the Great, who, at least on the surface, was an avid promoter of the Enlightenment.

The Tsarina Elizabeth arranged for Paul's mother, the daughter of a German duke who would be baptized Catherine in the Russian Orthodox Church, to marry her nephew and heir, the future tsar Peter III. The marriage was unhappy and possibly even celibate, for Peter was a very troubled man. Catherine's only duty was to provide an heir to the dynasty, something she finally did on September 20, 1754 by giving birth to a son, Paul. The boy was very likely the son of Catherine's first lover, Serge Saltikov, but Paul would not only grow up believing that he was a Romanov and the son of Peter III, but would mythologize the fact.

As soon as Paul was brought into the world, he was separated from his mother, who was not even allowed to name him. Paul was taken straight to Elizabeth, who kept the new prince in a room adjacent to her bedroom and wrapped him in hot, suffocating clothes. Every time he cried out in the night or was too quiet, Elizabeth herself rushed into the room in her nightclothes to check on the infant. As Paul became older, he was handed over to a series of nurses and tutors. He did not even meet his mother for the first time until he was six years old, and even after that he saw her only once a week under supervision. Although Catherine tried being loving to her son, she was never anything but a stranger to him. Oddly enough, the one parent he would love, Peter, was not exactly a firm presence in Paul's life either, taking time out from his schedule only to make brief weekly visits to congratulate his son on how well his studies were going or check on his progress.

Paul was from the start always eager to please the adults in his life, and became a studious and polite adolescent. His mother's affection was always returned with cold courtesy. The only unsettling thing Paul's carekeepers noticed about him was that he seemed to succumb quite often to periods of hysteria, and would be visited nearly every night by violent nightmares of his own death that would haunt him for the rest of his life. In one of these dreams, one that would prove prophetic, he imagined that he was about to be lynched by a mob.

Whatever caused Paul's night terrors, his father's fate would soon give Paul a good justification for them. After Elizabeth died, Peter inherited the throne but could hold on to it for just six months before a conspiracy involving his wife Catherine placed her in power. Peter was imprisoned and apparently Catherine hoped to keep him that way in spite of the danger his life posed, but it was not long before Peter's jailer killed him while in a drunken rage. Paul was told simply that his father had died from a 'severe internal disorder'.

Unfortunately, Paul was not so isolated from the rest of the world that he did not hear the stories and the rumors surrounding his father's death. Paul wondered aloud why he was not Tsar and why his mother sat on the throne instead. 'A few days ago, he was asking why they had killed his father and why they had given his mother the throne that rightfully belonged to him,' a diplomat at the Russian court wrote. 'He added that when he grew up, he would get to the bottom of all that.' Paul became convinced that Peter III was only misunderstood. He had just been too lenient to an ungrateful people who ended up deserting him for the promises of a scheming, vicious wife.

As Paul grew older, he started emulating the martyred father who was probably not even his. Like Peter did, Paul started worshipping Friedrich the Great of Prussia and came to deeply admire the Spartan culture of that nation. When his tutor described a theoretical country like Prussia where all the citizens would be trained to be soldiers, Paul exclaimed, 'Why, that would be paradise!' Paul's favorite pastime was playing elaborate war games, where he always acted out the life of a great conqueror and pretended he was marching armies into Paris, North America or China. Yet this

gung-ho attitude toward war did not sit well with Paul's deep terror of death, so he preferred to leave combat as a little fantasy and when he became older he actually disapproved of Catherine's expansionist policy against Turkey and Persia. In one of his many criticisms of his mother's policy, this would-be general said, 'Surely, the Empire is big enough as it is. We don't need any further conquests.' But it was his paranoia that also kept Paul in check, even though he fervently believed that his mother stole the crown from him. He was not only well aware of what had happened to his father, but also the fate of the former Ivan VI, who had been deposed by Paul's great-aunt Elizabeth and then locked in a cell for the rest of his life. When there was a failed attempt to free Ivan and promote him as the rightful Tsar, he was put to death under Elizabeth's instructions. Paul believed, even though Catherine made every effort to bridge the gap between herself and her son, that his mother would not hesitate to do the same to him, so he honestly and bluntly promised her that he would do nothing to try to depose her.

None of this stopped Paul from denouncing his mother's politics at every step. Paul even wrote a lengthy, rambling tract for his mother in 1774 which set forward a system of government that can only be described as a prototype for fascism. 'The whole Empire should have its towns and villages on a military footing . . . Thought, initiative, all independence and private enterprise should be done away with,' Paul wrote in his manifesto. Catherine patiently read through Paul's program and could only shake her head sadly. Instead of writing a rebuttal, she would say only that her sense of humor must be failing in her old age if she could not laugh at such a piece of concentrated lunacy.

History was rapidly beginning to repeat itself. Like Elizabeth, Catherine was faced with the unpleasant prospect of an heir who was sure to bring disaster on himself and the country. The fact that the tyrant to be was her own son made the pill all the more bitter. Fortunately, although Paul's first wife died giving birth to a stillborn child, Paul's second bride, Marie von Würtemberg, gave birth on December 23, 1777 to a son Alexander, followed by another son Constantine in 1779. Although Catherine, remembering her own experience with Paul, did not take her grandchildren away from their mother and father, she did make sure she spent ample time with them and that they were educated by progressive, open-minded tutors approved by her. Catherine had decided early on that Alexander, not Paul, would succeed her, and she would do everything in her power to properly groom him for the role.

While Paul probably did not suspect that his mother would disinherit him, he knew Catherine was trying to influence his sons and was not about to take it lying down, but he did not help matters by being a distant figure to Alexander and Constantine. He also alienated their mother by always snubbing her for his mistress, Catherine Nelidowa. He did try to set up a sort of rival court, but it was only the antithesis of the intellectual Mecca that was his mother's court, presided over by a figure who became increasingly shrill and unpredictable. For instance, one night at his 'court' Paul overheard a young woman make a comment about how a recent snowstorm had been the worst one in Russian history.

All smiles, Paul turned to her and said, 'Tell me again, please.'

The woman did not even remember what she had said, but patiently Paul added, 'It was something about the weather, wasn't it?'

The woman answered, 'Yes, Monseigneur, I believe I said there had never been such a snowstorm before.'

'And how old are you?' Paul asked, in a tone that was still warm.

'Twenty, Monseigneur.'

Suddenly, as though he were a storm himself, Paul's cheeks reddened and his voice rose to almost a bellow. 'Twenty? And what could you know of a storm fifty, thirty, fifteen years ago? How could you say there had never been one like the last? Lying! Lying! Lying – just like the rest of you. Out of my sight!'

At his palace Paul liked to keep up his own regiment of soldiers, whose marches he spent his afternoons watching. His troops were his pride and joy, but one visitor at his court wrote, 'All the soldiers are dressed in the obsolete Prussian fashion . . . They look ugly and miserable.' To Paul, however, he was only preparing for his reign, where he could finally undo his mother's seemingly radical policies and make Russia into a perfect imitation of Prussia's military state.

By 1796, it seemed that Paul would not have much longer to wait. Catherine had barely survived a minor stroke. Realizing there was not much time, Catherine met with Alexander privately, possibly to inform him of her plans to make him the next Tsar, but the words shared at that meeting were never made known. According to speculation, the plan was that Catherine would publish a proclamation disinheriting Paul and naming Alexander the heir on January 1, 1797.

As strong as Catherine's will undoubtedly was, she could not make that deadline. Even as his mother lay dying in the winter of 1796, Paul, or so the story goes, ransacked her study, found all the papers pertaining to naming Alexander heir, and burned them. If Catherine had actually told Alexander she had picked him to steer Russia in the future, he decided not to act on her instructions, at least for the time being. Paul became Tsar and Emperor of Russia unopposed. Either wanting revenge on the mother he detested or acting out the frustration of a child whose parents were always estranged, one of Paul's first acts was to have the remains of Peter III dug up and placed next to the coffin of his mother. Paul was determined that his parents, who hated each other in life, would finally lie side by side for eternity. For good measure, Paul also had the corpse of Gregory Potemkin, Catherine's most closely cherished lover, torn out of his grave and reburied at an unmarked site.

With these family matters taken care of, Paul turned at last to the task of creating a Russia he could take pride in. Paul worked tirelessly to write out a series of decrees that were to reshape Russia down to the smallest detail. The State would now take an interest in the citizens' clothing and hairstyles. Low collars and round hats were banned and in public one's hair was expected always to be brushed away from the forehead. Paul even established a special police force, a real life 'fashion police', to fine or even arrest anyone who failed to meet his specifications. Proper procedures were written down for citizens' conduct at weddings, funerals, holidays and Sundays. If anyone wished to hold a party or a celebration, they were required to inform the local police, who would send an officer to watch the festivities in case any violations of Paul's new laws took place. All foreign literature was banned and most printing presses were shut down for failing to comply with the harsh censorship Paul demanded and had enforced. Even traveling abroad became impossible for most Russians, because of the endless permits that were required.

Paul respected the traditions of the country he now ruled only a little more than he respected the rights of his subjects. Seasoned generals were forced to take basic lessons on Prussian tactics if they wanted to retain their posts. Paul also sent an envoy to the Pope in the winter of 1800 to open discussions about uniting the Russian Orthodox Church with the Catholic Church.

Exasperated at what his father was doing, Alexander said, 'My father has declared war on common sense with the firm resolve of never concluding a truce.' The son had every right to be worried by his father's strange tyrannical behavior. When Paul found out that Alexander owned a copy of Voltaire's pro-republican play *Brutus* he sent his son a biography of Peter the Great: the passage describing the episode where Peter put his own son Alexis on trial for treason and had him killed was underlined. Even though Paul overturned a succession law established by Peter the Great that dictated that a tsar could elect his own heir, as long as that heir was linked by marriage or blood to the Romanovs, in favor of a law that the tsar must always be succeeded by his eldest son or closest male relative, he planned to disinherit both of his sons in favor of his brother-in-law, Eugene von Württemberg.

Like that of his supposed father, though, Paul's tyranny was not destined to last long. History had not yet finished repeating. Alexander reluctantly gave his consent to a conspiracy involving the leading men of the nation after he got them to promise to spare his father's life. On March 11, 1801, the conspirators burst into Paul's private rooms, declaring that he was under arrest in the name of Tsar Alexander.

Faced with what he knew was his worst nightmare, Paul timidly asked, 'But why? What have I done?'

One of the conspirators, Count Platon Zubov, a former lover of Paul's mother, answered, 'Why? Haven't you tortured the whole country ever since you took the throne?'

Paul tried to make a run for it, causing a scuffle to break out. In the confusion, he was knocked to the floor and cried out, 'Gentlemen, in heaven's name, spare me. Give me time to say my prayers.' But then, one of the conspirators, possibly drunk, strangled him with one of his own silk scarves.

Although Paul's death was not part of the original plan, Alexander never absolved himself from his father's murder. Like his grandmother Catherine after the unexpected murder of Peter III, Alexander could never let himself forget what he had done. Although he proved a far more able and fair ruler than his father had been, he was tormented by the memory of how he came to power.

Further Reading

Almedingen, E.M. *So Dark A Stream: A Study of the Emperor Paul I of Russia 1754-1801* (Hutchinson, 1959)

Duffy, James and Ricci, Vincent *Tsars: Russia's Rulers For More Than One Thousand Years* (Barnes & Noble, 1995)

Hingley, Ronald *The Tsars, 1533-1917* (Macmillan, 1968)

NICHOLAS II

Born: *May 18, 1868*
Reign: *November 1, 1894–March 15, 1917*
Died: *July 17, 1918*
Buried: *Cathedral of Peter and Paul, St Petersburg*

Nicholas II was the last of Russia's reigning tsars since Ivan IV the Terrible made the title for himself in 1547. Strangely enough, the last true tsar of Russia was the polar opposite of the ruthless Ivan: a quiet family man who wished no one any ill. Yet it was Nicholas who would be called 'the Blood Drinker', be villainized in Europe and the United States and become best known for the brutal murders of himself and his family as an act of political expediency.

The future Tsar Nicholas II grew up in awe of his father, Alexander III, a grim bear of a man who tightly held his own family in an iron fist. The children, even at an early age, were expected to adhere to a rigid schedule and an even more rigid system of etiquette at all times. Their meals were little more than porridge and water and they all slept on the same simple, hard cots that the average Russian soldier used. Alexander's grip on his country was even tighter. When he was young, he was traumatized by his father Tsar Alexander II's ugly death at the hands of an assassin. Alexander II was a progressive ruler who brought a number of important reforms to every aspect of Russia, especially his historic liberation of the Russian serfs, who still lived with few real legal rights centuries after serfdom had died out elsewhere in Europe and whose situation was rightfully compared to the condition of the slaves in the southern United States.

For bringing an end to serfdom, Alexander became loved as the Tsar-Liberator, but that did not spare him from becoming the target of a series of assassination attempts by radicals. Luck kept saving Alexander's life until, finally, on March 1, 1881, he was in a carriage driving through St. Petersburg when an assassin hurled a bomb at the vehicle, wounding a few of his escorts. Alexander crawled out of the carriage to check one of the wounded men when another unseen assassin hurled a bomb directly at the Tsar's legs. The sight of his father, ironically dying in excruciating pain from an extremist's bomb only hours after he signed a new representative body in the government into existence, taught the new Tsar a hard lesson. He swore on his accession that, unlike his father, he would rule 'with faith in the power and right of autocracy'. Alexander III would imprint this valuable lesson on his own heir, Nicholas, as well.

But as a young man, Nicholas did not spend much time thinking about the theory of absolutism or the political turmoil that was sweeping Europe. His father, judging that Nicholas was capable of 'only infantile judgments', did not bother training him in politics, but left him to spend his days attending parties and plays and traveling to foreign nations to represent his father. During this time as a playboy, Nicholas, at the age of seventeen, fell in love with the 21-year-old Alix of Hesse-Darmstadt, a German granddaughter of Queen Victoria of Britain and the younger sister of his uncle Serge's wife Ella. In return Alix was smitten with this shy, tall young Russian and cared nothing about the fact that he stood to inherit one of the world's vastest empires. It is worth pointing out that Alix had previously turned down a proposal from her cousin, the man who stood to become King George V of Great Britain, because she did not return his love.

At first Nicholas's parents were against the match because of hurt national feelings toward Germany, but they soon warmed to their son's gentle, intelligent girlfriend. At the wedding of Alix's brother Ernst in 1894, which was attended by Queen Victoria, her son the future King Edward VII and Kaiser Wilhelm II of the German Empire, Nicholas proposed to Alix and she tearfully, happily accepted. The couple who would warmly refer to each other as 'Nicky' and 'Sunny' for the rest of their lives were united and, at the time, it seemed they would enter old age side by side. Like any woman who married into the Russian royal family, Alix had to be baptized into the Russian Orthodox Church, something she did with no complaints. At baptism she adopted the name Alexandra.

Despite appearances, Nicholas would not be given long to enjoy a trouble-free life with his dear 'Sunny'. An increasingly ill Alexander III died on March 1 shortly after the engagement. The 26-year-old Nicholas, who had every reason to expect his father to outlast him, said in desperation, 'I am not prepared to be a tsar. I never wanted to become one. I know nothing of the business of ruling. I have no idea of even how to talk to the ministers.' Nicholas and Alexandra were wed just one week after Alexander's funeral, which did not spell out a happy honeymoon.

Although Nicholas called the business of ruling an 'awful job', he did not feel he had anything particular to fear from the great empire he had inherited. Vicious political extremists were still a problem, but the wave of assassinations that marked grandfather Alexander's reign were a thing of the past. Russian culture and literature were at a peak, so much so that the period is sometimes called Russia's intellectual 'Silver Age'. The country was at peace with the rest of the world, something that did not seem likely to change any time soon. Just underneath the surface, however, there was turmoil boiling. Although Alexander II had freed the serfs, he had done little to improve their lives, and many were in heavy, inescapable debt to the country's landowners. The factory workers were scarcely better off and made ready converts to the extremist socialist groups, including the Bolsheviks, that prospered in the crowded, impoverished cities.

Nicholas's uncles, who all frightened him as much as his father did, bullied him into making many of his early decisions, including a reckless and unneeded policy of Asian expansion. But even to the timid Nicholas Asia seemed an open buffet since the vast, ancient Empire of China was falling apart at the seams. Russian troops were sent to occupy Manchuria while Russia also pressured China into allowing them to take a ninety-nine year lease on Port Arthur (modern Lüshunkou), a warm water port city on the Pacific that Russia sorely needed. Japan, which had overnight become a great industrialized power, had its own plans for China and was less than happy to see Russia help itself to slices of Asia, but did not yet feel up to a serious confrontation with a major European power.

Then Russia pushed its luck to the breaking point. Again under pressure from his uncles as well as the bombastic Kaiser Wilhelm II, who saw all of Asia as nothing more than territory set aside for European conquest, Russia set its sights on Korea, a land Japan had already claimed for itself. Some Russian businessmen had the idea of shipping troops into Korea disguised as workmen under the employment of a front company called the Yar Timber Company. Nicholas hoped that, if worse came to worst, the Russian government could simply disavow all knowledge of what happened, but if things turned out well, Russia would have dibs on the Korean peninsula without having to go to war.

Unfortunately, Japan was being deeply underestimated. Nicholas let matters decay between Japan and Russia until, finally, on February 6, 1904, a Japanese ship torpedoed Russian ships at Port Arthur without warning. Nicholas did not want war, but he accepted the reality well enough. How could a distant foreign nation that had only recently emerged from its own feudal past stand half a chance against a solidly established naval power like Russia? With this heroic optimism, Nicholas traveled to his soldiers' camps to give the men the blessing of their 'little father', the Tsar. Alexandra, who always embraced any reason for charitable work, turned the palace ballrooms into workshops, where women of all classes, including herself, made clothing for the soldiers.

As devoted as the Tsar and Tsarina were to the cause, the wartime enthusiasm was not shared by the people. At first the shock of being attacked by an upstart Asian country rallied the Russians, but soon enough, as the more advanced and efficient Japanese forces first humiliated and then virtually annihilated the once famed Russian navy, the people, especially workers and students, where the seeds of revolutionary ideas found the most light, recognized the war for what it was: an unnecessary struggle for unnecessary expansion. In the end, Russia was forced to concede that a newly-emergent Asian state had beaten to the ground one of Europe's strongest nations. Mediated by US President Theodore Roosevelt, an act for which he would later win the 1906 Nobel Peace Prize, the two sides agreed to sign the Treaty of Portsmouth. Manchuria was returned to China and Russia abandoned Korea to the growing empire of Japan. Worst of all for Russia, Port Arthur and the peninsula surrounding it were ceded by the treaty.

Although Japan had actually been unable to pursue the war much further because of severe economic strain at home, the war and its end seemed to act as a catalyst for the tension in Russia. Workers' discontent reached a new high, something recognized by a young St Petersburg priest with police connections named George Gapon. A man with socialist sympathies but also a conservative supporter of the monarchy, Gapon thought that the only way to restore the workers' confidence in their Tsar was to engineer a historic meeting between monarch and people, where the workers could present the Tsar personally with a petition that would ensure their rights. Without his corrupt ministers around to hide him from the truth of his people's suffering, Gapon reasoned, the Tsar would be moved to compassion and then to action by his people's humble devotion and need. The petition's demands were somewhat radical at the time, yet would be considered more than reasonable today: an eight-hour workday, a minimum wage, an income tax, and universal suffrage were among the top demands. But despite his noble intentions, Gapon was only setting the stage for a historic tragedy: 'Bloody Sunday'.

On the appointed day, January 22, 1905, Gapon had gathered over 100,000 workers and their wives and children, all carrying flags, crucifixes, images of saints, and, most of all, miniature portraits of Nicholas II. As one mass they marched toward the Winter Palace where they thought Nicholas would personally receive them, but the Tsar and his family were not even there. However, the armed imperial guards were. At 2P.M., the soldiers became nervous and saw an uprising in the making, instead of a peaceful march. As the crowds walked on, the order to fire was given and the soldiers rained bullets on the men and their families. It was a historic moment as Gapon hoped, but not at all in the way he intended. Nicholas was deeply horrified by the news of what had happened, but, true to his personality, he refused to put the bulk of the blame on the shoulders of his officers.

Other tragedies closer to home were already starting to wear the tsar down. After giving birth to four daughters – Olga, Tatiana, Marie, and Anastasia – Alexandra bore Nicholas a son named Alexis on August 12, 1904. At first the boy seemed healthy and normal, but in only a few weeks' time it was noticed that, when he fell and bumped himself, his bruises did not heal, but became worse and his blood was very slow to clot. Alexis, the infant heir to the Russian throne, had haemophilia, a hereditary disease that slows the clotting of the blood. Only men are affected by the defective genes that carry haemophilia, but a woman can carry the defective gene that causes it and pass it on to her own children. Queen Victoria herself, the matriarch of so many European royals, passed the disease on to her son Leopold. Two of her daughters, including Alexandra's mother Alice, were also carriers, and through them the haemophilia gene was introduced into the Spanish royal family as well as the Russian. Burdened with the knowledge that any fall or any cut could actually kill her son, Alexandra spent all of her energy protecting him and had two sailors hover over Alexis at all times. Exhausted by this anxiety and the knowledge that she had given Alexis the disease that could claim his life at any time, Alexandra threw herself even more into charity. She wanted to spend herself on giving others the aid and comfort she could not really give to her own son. She also turned toward God for comfort, familiarizing herself with all the Orthodox rituals and saints, and spent hours praying in her private chapel for deliverance.

Matters beyond their son's horrible illness would soon demand their attention. Nicholas's uncle, the Grand Duke Serge, who liked to brag about how much he was hated by radicals, was killed by a bomb that was flung at his car. In the meantime, the Russo-Japanese War shook loose whatever stability remained. In 1905, riots erupted across the cities, strikes in factories and transportation services paralyzed the entire country, and mobs of peasants butchered rich landowners and looted their mansions. Although Nicholas resisted it as much as he could, he gave in to his ministers' advice that he make the government more democratic, which was once unthinkable in Russia. Undoubtedly Nicholas could feel his father's resentment from beyond the grave. Nicholas and the reactionaries still had something to be thankful for, however. The Russian monarch was not as restrained as the British monarch, but still had power over war and foreign affairs. Now, however, the Duma at last had more say in politics and the events that led to their empowerment were called the Revolution of 1905.

For Nicholas, it may have seemed that the worst had passed and the remaining years of his reign could hopefully be somewhat peaceful. He did not know that his son's disease would open the way for one man to enter the Tsar's life and single-handedly undermine the entire monarchy. This man was a seemingly superhuman monk named Grigory Rasputin. In late 1912, the family was on vacation in Poland when Alexis got a severe hemorrhage in his thigh. Rushing him home, Alexandra and Nicholas took turns at his bedside and tried in vain to comfort his intense pain. In one rare moment of peace, Alexis was heard to whisper to his mother, 'When I am dead, it will not hurt any more, will it, Mama?' Devastatingly, it seemed to Alexandra that God was not answering her prayers for her son's relief. Although Nicholas had managed to keep the public from learning the truth about Alexis's illness, word leaked that the heir to the throne was mortally ill.

When it seemed that Alexis's death was only a matter of time, Alexandra remembered a strange Siberian holy man she had seen named Rasputin. Immediately she had a friend who knew Rasputin telegraph him. Right away he sent a reply: 'God has seen your tears and heard your prayers. Do not grieve. The Little One will not die. Do not allow the doctors to bother him too much.' Within days, Alexis was miraculously on the long but sure road to recovery.

This odd miracle worker, Father Grigory Rasputin, was an

imposing, bulky man in his mid-thirties who still dressed like the Siberian peasant he once was. His most striking feature was his eyes, which were said among many who met him to have had a hypnotic power. Because of his humble origins, Rasputin was said to have been a *starets*, a holy man who resisted worldliness through a life of poverty and solitude. Rasputin was fond of bragging that he had once traveled to Greece on foot to visit a holy site. In his home village, Rasputin was remembered as a drunkard who picked fights whenever he was not seducing women, but when he traveled to St Petersburg he attracted the attention of even the elite through his vivid claims that he could hear instructions from the Virgin Mary. Through cleverness, charisma or perhaps hypnotism, the uncouth Siberian scaled his way into high society. Now his apparent success with saving the life of the heir to the throne gave him access to the royal family and overnight made him into a celebrity.

From the start there were persistent murmurs and snickers behind Rasputin's back. Although some of St Petersburg's top clergy accepted Rasputin as a living prophet, others angrily denounced him as a fraud and a heretic. Stories from back home in Siberia chased him, such as how he conducted weddings for villagers in exchange for the first night with the bride. In his apartment in St Petersburg, where he lived with his daughter Maria, Rasputin was visited by anyone seeking his blessing, a healing or a favor with the Tsarina. Women, enchanted by the monk's crude mystique, also came to Rasputin for more 'private blessings' and received a private audience in his bedroom, jokingly called 'the Holy of Holies'. Rasputin liked to preach a unique theology, that one must first become familiar with sin before one can have a chance in overcoming it.

As Rasputin became more famous and infamous, he dragged the reputation of the Tsarina and her family down with him. Besides spending time 'healing' Alexis and occasionally telling Nicholas's daughters exciting tales from Russian folklore, Rasputin actually did not spend much time in the presence of the Tsar's family, but Alexandra did write to him extensively and became more and more receptive to the advice from the man she called 'our Friend'. Believing that Rasputin was the sole reason her son was still alive, Alexandra also believed that God spoke through Rasputin. Any stories about his reputation, whether they came from her friends or from state ministers, she dismissed or ignored. Even after Alexandra was told by the director of the national police that a drunk Rasputin exposed himself at a popular Moscow restaurant and bragged to the crowd that Nicholas let him top his wife whenever he wanted, she blamed it on malicious gossip. 'Saints are always calumniated,' she once wrote. 'He is hated because we love him.' Nicholas was not nearly as blind, but even he felt powerless to do anything about the man who seemingly saved his only son's life. One minister of Nicholas's wrote, 'He did not like to send [Rasputin] away, for if Alexis died, in the eyes of the mother, he would have been the murderer of his own son.'

Pamphlets were circulated, showing drawings of a monstrous Rasputin in compromising positions with the Tsarina. While the stories that Alexandra let Rasputin even touch her were only propaganda of the ugliest kind, the widespread allegations that Rasputin had influence over Alexandra had more weight. On politics and even war, Alexandra began to drown Nicholas with her own and Rasputin's shared advice. She was convinced that Rasputin had a sixth sense when it came to determining the character of politicians. Any minister who did not like Rasputin would suddenly find that the Tsarina no longer trusted him and neither would the Tsar. Even Prime Ministers found their careers derailed because they neglected to earn Rasputin's approval.

In spite of Rasputin's place like a cancer at the heart of the monarchy, and the escalating tensions between Tsar and Duma, the horizon was clear in the spring of 1913, when Russia celebrated the 300th anniversary of the day the Romanov dynasty came to power.

Few would have guessed that, in only five years, there would not only no longer be a Romanov dynasty in power, but there would also no longer be a tsar.

The tidal wave that would sweep not only the Romanovs, but also the ancient ruling dynasties of Germany and Austria, from their thrones was about to break. It began with nothing more than gunshots fired by a nineteen-year-old Serb named Gabriel Princip, a possible member of a terrorist organization called the Black Hand. Based in Serbia, the Black Hand yearned to free the Serbs that lived under the government of Austria–Hungary and bring them into the Kingdom of Serbia. Ethnic tensions were not only high with the Serbs in Austria-Hungary, but with the Austrians, Hungarians, Poles, Romanians, Croats, Slovenes, Ukrainians and Slovaks who all lived and worked within the nation's borders, so to help foster a sense of unity Archduke Franz Ferdinand, heir to the throne, took a tour of the nation. As he was driven through the streets of Sarajevo on June 28, 1914, Princip rushed up to his car and fired, killing him and his wife Sophie.

The government of Austria–Hungary had for a long time accused the Kingdom of Serbia of spreading discontent among the Empire's Serb citizens in order to have an excuse to annex some territory. Declaring that Princip must have been armed and smuggled into Austria–Hungary by agents of the Serbian government, Austria–Hungary threatened to declare war on Serbia unless Serbia agreed within forty-eight hours to a set of humiliating conditions issued by Austrian ministers. No one, not even Austria-Hungary, suspected Serbia would actually agree to the ultimatum, but they did agree to all but one of the provisions, and in the most self-degrading language possible. Austria–Hungary, however, craved war and any excuse to cripple or even wipe Serbia off the map of Europe, so a declaration of war was issued on July 28 anyway.

The uneasy, mobilized European powers were now ready to fall like dominos. Russia, which had strong ethnic and political ties with Serbia, mobilized its forces along the border it shared with Austria–Hungary. Enraged that Russia was mobilizing against his own staunch ally, Kaiser Wilhelm II, who always kept a correspondence with his cousin Nicholas, sent Nicholas shrill telegrams telling him not to come to Serbia's defense, but Nicholas had almost no room to maneuver. Despite his bluster, Wilhelm did not want a war on his hands and neither did Nicholas. However, the chain reaction was well beyond anyone's control now. Germany soon declared war on Russia.

After Germany turned on Russia, crowds poured onto Russian streets, singing patriotic songs and shouting praises of the heroic Tsar. This was not some pointless war of expansion, this was a defensive war fought by a brotherhood of Slavs against the arrogant, bellicose Germans. Grudges as old as European civilization were brought back to life. The fact that Great Britain and France were soon drawn into the conflict on Russia's side served to raise national hopes that the war would come to a swift end with Germany and Austria–Hungary being humbled. Unfortunately, the early signs were not promising to those willing to look at the reality. Although the size of Russia's army was legendary, it was hopelessly behind that of Germany in technology. Another disadvantage that invited catastrophe was that the number of Russian factories were few compared even to Great Britain while Germany's railways seriously outnumbered Russia's.

No amount of patriotism could save Russia from these terrible shortcomings. Ammunition eventually became scarce, so scarce that a soldier could be court-martialed for wasting it. Unable to match their enemies' mastery of chemical and technological warfare, 1,700,000 Russian soldiers would die before the war ended. As the Great War dragged on and the people's hopes quickly evaporated, Nicholas wanted to revive the ancient role of the warrior-tsar and take command of the army. At first Nicholas's ministers and relatives dissuaded him from this foolish idea, but by the summer of 1915

Nicholas had his way and left St Petersburg[47] to take command, leaving Alexandra behind to assume many of his political duties.

Although Alexandra saw herself as Russian through and through, her country of birth became a serious liability. Anti-German sentiment had hit a fever pitch and Alexandra was an easy target, even when she and her daughters did what they could for the war effort by serving as nurses for soldiers wounded in the battlefield and doing their best to comfort them. Alexandra was even trained by the Red Cross and earned the diploma of a certified battlefield nurse. For her tasks as Nicholas's regent, Alexandra was not nearly as successful. She could only bring herself to rely on ministers that Rasputin claimed were 'honest'. Often she urged Nicholas to follow Rasputin's advice, especially in topics concerning the war. To Alexandra's mind, Rasputin was indispensable. Not only was he her son's healer, but to her he had become the voice of both God and the unseen Russian people. Outside, though, propaganda was spread that Rasputin was really a German spy or in some kind of treasonous collaboration with Alexandra. In fear of both Rasputin's influence and the effect he was having on the public perception of the monarchy, a young wealthy nobleman and a cousin of Nicholas's, Felix Yussoupov, decided to kill Rasputin for the wellbeing of the nation.

After Rasputin's death, a letter he had allegedly completed weeks before in December 1916, came to light: written in his own rushed, unpolished style, it was a message of warning to Nicholas:

> I write and leave behind me this letter at St Petersburg. I feel that I shall leave life before January 1. I wish to make known to the Russian people, to Papa, to the Russian Mother and to the Children, to the land of Russia, what they must

[47] In the course of the First World War, St. Petersburg was renamed Petrograd to remove any German connotations.

> understand. If I am killed by common assassins, and especially by my brothers the Russian peasants, you, Tsar of Russia, have nothing to fear, remain on your throne and govern, and you, Russian Tsar, will have nothing to fear for your children, they will reign for hundreds of years in Russia. But if I am murdered by boyars, nobles, and if they shed my blood, their hands will remain soiled with my blood, for twenty-five years they will not wash their hands of my blood. They will leave Russia. Brothers will kill brothers, and they will kill each other and hate each other, and for twenty-five years there will be no nobles in the country. Tsar of the land of Russia, if you hear the sound of the bell which will tell you that Gregory has been killed, you must know this: if it was your relations who have wrought my death then no one of your family, that is to say, none of your children or relations will remain alive for more than two years. They will be killed by the Russian people . . . I shall be killed. I am no longer among the living. Pray, pray, be strong, think of your blessed family. Gregory

Yussoupov did not have far to look for willing accomplices in the murder. To all of them, killing Rasputin would be a great patriotic act, saving not only the royal family, but also the nation, from disaster. Yussoupov gradually put himself into Rasputin's good graces and then invited him to come to his residence, Moika Palace in St Petersburg, to attend to his wife, Irina, who suffered from bad headaches. Rasputin was intrigued: after all, Irina was said to be one of the most beautiful women in the city.

On the night of December 31, Rasputin arrived at Moika Palace to tend to Irina. When he arrived, Yussoupov told him that Irina was on the top floor having a small party with some friends and would be down later in the night. In fact, Yussoupov's fellow conspirators were hiding upstairs, playing music for 'Irina's party'. In the meantime,

Yussoupov acted the role of gracious host and offered Rasputin some cakes and wine, all poisoned with cyanide. At first Rasputin refused, giving Yussoupov cause for concern, but then he changed his mind and gulped down two cakes and two glasses of wine. Later he only became a little bit sleepy. Yussoupov was horrified at the sight of a poisoned yet still healthy Rasputin, but kept up the facade. He even agreed to play a guitar for Rasputin after he asked. Two and a half hours of entertaining the intended victim later, Rasputin dozed off and Yussoupov rushed upstairs where he and the other would-be killers whispered to each other, trying desperately to decide what to do. One of the men handed Yussoupov a revolver and sent him back downstairs. Hearing Yussoupov's footsteps, Rasputin opened his eyes and suggested that, since Irina was obviously too busy with her guests to come down, they should go out into the city and find some gypsies to entertain them for the night. Rasputin then winked at him and said, 'With God in thought, but mankind in the flesh.'

Hiding the pistol from Rasputin's view, Yussoupov asked Rasputin to follow him to a room and showed him a cabinet holding a beautiful ornate crucifix. Yussoupov told Rasputin to look at the cross and pray. Rasputin began to turn his head toward Yussoupov, who immediately fired the revolver. The other plotters rushed down, hearing the gunshot, and one of the conspirators, who happened to be a doctor, examined Rasputin and pronounced him dead. Briefly Yussoupov was left alone with the 'corpse', but the eyes of the 'corpse' suddenly opened and Rasputin leaped up, grabbing Yussoupov by the throat. Knocking him down, Rasputin managed to escape the house and ran toward the street, shouting, 'Felix! Felix! I will tell everything to the Empress!'

One of the men fired again at Rasputin and at first missed, but soon two more shots hit him as he rushed across the courtyard, felling him. Catching up with the holy man, Yussoupov breathlessly battered Rasputin with a club. Believing that he was at last dead, they threw him into the frozen Neva River. When his body was later discovered, it was learned that Rasputin, having been poisoned, shot, beaten and thrown into ice-cold water, had really died from drowning. As for Rasputin's chief killers, one was pardoned and allowed to go free, but Yussoupov and another were exiled, which ironically spared them from the holocaust that was to come. So Rasputin's prophecy came true for at least two of his murderers. In time, Rasputin's prophecies would also seem to be true for his patroness and her husband.

It became clear with every grueling year that the war would not soon end, especially not without massive costs to Russia. Exhausted in every sense and ridden with guilt, Nicholas temporarily gave up command of the army and retired to his family's favorite residence, Tsarskoe Selo or 'the Royal Village', for the winter of 1916–17. He may even have suffered a minor nervous breakdown that made this vacation necessary. Outside the isolated little world of Tsarskoe Selo, the people wept for the thousands dead and went about their lives without work or food. Germany struck Russia another blow: on a train passing into the borders of Russia, the German government had secretly placed a number of leading Russian Bolsheviks who had been exiled, among them a man named Vladimir Ilich Ulyanov, who had taken the name Lenin.

Although Lenin did his best to rally support, he could not anticipate what happened on March 12, 1917, when a revolution was born, not made. That day, bread riots suddenly broke out across St Petersburg. Workers went on strike and harassed, sometimes violently, those that continued to work. When military force was authorized in an attempt to restore order, more than a few soldiers refused to fire on their own countrymen and one soldier ended up shooting his own commander when he ordered him to fire into a mob. In the end, the army rallied for the Duma, which suddenly found itself in charge of a new democratic government.

The most powerful politician in this Duma was Alexander Kerensky, the son of a school principal. A passionate orator with strong liberal principles, Kerensky became an opposition leader and, months after the rise of the Duma, was destined to become the Prime Minister. Alongside the Duma emerged a rival body, the Petrograd Soviet, but, as a sort of compromise, the two bodies agreed to share power until nationwide elections could be organized. Kerensky, at heart an idealist, refused to execute anyone from what was now the old regime, bring the Tsar to trial or even raise a fist toward the Soviet. For the time being, Nicholas was still technically the Tsar of Russia.

As soon as it was known that what was happening in St Petersburg was much more than just a disturbance, Nicholas rushed to reach the capital from the army headquarters by train. On the way, he was politely but firmly informed that rebels armed with guns were blocking the tracks and that it would be safer if Nicholas went to Pskov instead. There his generals told him that he had no choice but to abdicate the throne if he wished to preserve the monarchy and save his family. Nicholas grimly accepted the news and was at first willing to abdicate in favor of Alexis, but, taking his son's youth and haemophilia into careful consideration, he instead signed to have the crown handed to his 39-year-old brother, Michael, on March 15. With the stroke of a pen, Michael became Tsar Michael II.

The reign of Tsar Michael II would barely last a day. After considering it, Michael asked plainly if his safety could be guaranteed if he remained as tsar. He was honestly told that it could not and that he would be better off as a political nobody. So, on the same day he learned that his brother had given him his crown, Michael II publicly refused to remain on the throne, leaving it behind for no one. Just as Michael I was the first Romanov to become ruler of Russia, Michael II would be the last. The Russian monarchy died without a bang and with hardly even a whimper.

After a tearful meeting with his mother Marie, who would soon escape to her homeland Denmark, Nicholas was put into the custody of the Provisional Government. Alexandra and the family also came under custody and all were sentenced to a sort of house arrest at Tsarskoe Selo. There the royal family and their attendants and servants lived hour by hour under the strict watch of guards. Some afternoons crowds gathered to stare at Nicholas as he took his daily walks around the estates. Sometimes the people stopped to jeer and shout threats at him. Nicholas tried to ignore them.

What was to be done with the Romanovs? It was assumed by everyone, expatriate Romanovs and members of the Duma, that they would be sent to live in exile in Britain, where Nicholas's cousin was King George V. The Soviet, who wanted the Tsar's head, bitterly fought any move to take him out of Russia, while Britain slowly cooled on the idea as well. Nicholas was viewed on the international scene as an archaic tyrant who was nothing but an embarrassment to his allies from the start: those nations, Great Britain, France and the United States wanted to be seen as the noble champions of democracy and modernization. The idea that Britain would offer bread and shelter to the deposed tyrant and his family was thought to be sheer hypocrisy, never mind that it was Nicholas who had once personally led his men to fight and die alongside Britain in the war.

Although the war, and the horrors it threw on the lap of the Russian people, was a major factor in the collapse of the Tsarist regime, the Provisional Government could not give the people the peace they needed so badly. The United States, Great Britain and France forced Kerensky to choose between funds they could provide, which the new government sorely needed, and complete withdrawal from the war. By choosing the former, Kerensky played right into the hands of the Bolsheviks, who promised the Russian peasant and worker 'bread, peace, and land'. As war weariness reached new levels, so did the Bolsheviks' popularity and the power of the Petrograd Soviet. Although an early uprising on July 16 failed, ending with Lenin being forced to flee to Finland, Kerensky soon realized that power was slipping through the Duma's fingers.

Kerensky knew that, for their own safety, it was imperative to get the Romanovs as far away as possible. Thinking that getting the Romanovs out of the country would not only be unlikely now, but increasingly risky, Kerensky instead selected a small Siberian town, Tobolsk. After generations of political prisoners had been sent into exile in Siberia in the name of the Romanovs, this generation of Romanovs had to flee to Siberia as a last hope. Despite the cruel irony, Tobolsk was actually an ideal choice for Kerensky. It was a small and quiet town, very far from St Petersburg, and a conservative refuge unspoiled by the spread of Marxism and anti-monarchism. Here Nicholas and his family lived an idyllic life considering their circumstances. The children still received lessons from their instructor Pierre Gilliard, Nicholas struck up warm friendships with his more sympathetic guards, and Alexandra continued to watch over Alexis, who tried to live a normal boy's life despite all the forces against him.

It was a strange and uneasy paradise, one not meant to last. In November, the Bolsheviks, after firing only a few shots, took control of the State and Kerensky was driven into exile. Lenin was now in charge, at least in a sense. There were still large parts of Russia that were not quite under the Soviet's control and there was also the matter of fulfilling the promise of peace. Germany would only agree peace with Russia on the harshest terms, and Lenin had to hand over Poland, Finland, the Ukraine, the Crimea and some Baltic territories – one-third of the nation's population – before he could end the war.

It was not long before the change in government affected even distant Tobolsk. Guards who were friendly to the Romanovs were replaced by younger men weaned on revolutionary ideas. These new guards harassed the family, making pornographic pictures on the walls for Nicholas's daughters to see. The family was put on a meager household budget, so much so they soon came to rely on gifts of eggs, butter and other foods and essentials from the local townspeople. Alexandra was fond of calling these presents 'gifts from Heaven'. There were a few plans to rescue the Romanovs and get them out of Russia, but none even came close to fruition.

The family was about to be relocated again, this time by hands that were much less benevolent than Kerensky's. The Soviet of the Ural Region asked the central Soviet, which was relocated to Moscow because of the war, to send the Romanovs to Ekaterinburg, an industrial city with a long history of bitter unrest. The government in Moscow attempted to remove the family to the capital, but officials from Ekaterinburg intervened and, separating the family from the always loyal Gilliard, brought them to their city where they were placed in a simple two-story house on April 30, 1918.

Here the Romanovs enjoyed much less freedom than they had at Tobolsk. No one, not even the children, was let out of the guards' sight and Nicholas was addressed coldly as 'Nicholas the Blood-Drinker'. All the family's movements, even those of the daughters, were severely restricted and their privacy was almost non-existent. That July, when news spread that a pro-monarchist rebel faction called the White Army was quickly approaching Ekaterinburg, intent on liberating Nicholas, simple orders from Moscow were given: the Romanovs, Nicholas and his entire family, had to die.

On July 16, the Romanovs and their captors followed their usual routines. Then, suddenly, at midnight, the family was awakened and told to dress quickly and come down the stairs. The White Army was coming (which was true), their captors told them, so they had to be quickly relocated to another town. Moments later the former imperial family came down the stairs: Anastasia with her pet spaniel, Nicholas carrying Alexis, whose condition had worsened since the last days at Tobolsk, in his arms. They were accompanied by their maid, a cook, a valet and a doctor. All of them were led to a small, unfurnished room on the ground floor where they were told to wait until a car arrived. Noticing there was nowhere for him or Alexandra to sit, Nicholas asked for and received three chairs from the guards. Minutes later, a squad of soldiers, each man armed with a revolver, entered the room. Their leader casually pronounced, 'Your relations have tried to save you. They have failed and we must now shoot you.' Nicholas rose from his chair and only had time to utter, 'What . . . ?' before he was shot in the head. The rest of the squad followed with a hail of bullets. Alexandra died trying to make the sign of the cross. Olga and Tatiana were instantly killed. The maid, Demidova, survived the round of gunfire and made a futile effort to escape before the soldiers stabbed her with bayonets. The room was then silent until a groan from Alexis, who still lay in his dead father's arms, was heard. He was kicked savagely and shot twice in the head. Then Anastasia, who was also unhurt by the opening salvo and had only passed out, woke up and screamed. Right away she was silenced by bayonets and rifle butts.

The grisly work was not yet finished. Unsure of how the international community would respond to the execution of the Romanovs, the government ordered that the evidence be covered up as much as possible. Under strict instructions, the executioners spent the night hacking up the bodies, burning the remains, and dissolving the larger bones in sulfuric acid. What was left was thrown down a mine shaft. At first this was the family's resting place, but when rumors started to spread that the Romanovs had been killed, the remains were hidden in a concealed pit. Other Romanovs not lucky enough to have fled Russia suffered similar ends. The man who, in another world, would have ruled as Michael II was also arrested and executed.

Despite the Soviet government's extreme precautions, the truth came out in a matter of months. Yet the mysterious circumstances surrounding the deaths were enough to give rise to some romantic legends. One claimed that Nicholas was alive and a prisoner at a Siberian labor camp. The most famous claim of all came from the woman who named herself 'Anna Anderson', who claimed to her dying day that she was Anastasia, rescued from Ekaterinburg by a Polish soldier. Even though Anastasia's aunt Olga met with her in Berlin and later said 'she is not who she believes she is' and other surviving Romanovs also denounced her claim, Anderson's story continued to attract speculation and publicity over the decades. Eventually she married one of her own supporters, John Manahan, and settled down in Charlottesville, Virginia. After her death in 1984, a series of DNA tests were taken and the results all indicated that Anna Anderson was not at all related to the Romanovs. Nevertheless, there are to date those who will still defend her claim.

On the eightieth anniversary of their murders, the story of Nicholas II, Alexandra and their children was given something of a happy ending. In 1998, Boris Yeltsin, President of the Russian Federation, presided over a ceremony where the remains of the family were gathered and interred in the Romanov family crypt at Peter and Paul Cathedral in St Petersburg. The long, strange and tragic history of Nicholas II, the harmless man who met an ugly end, at last found a satisfying ending.

Further Reading

Duffy, James and Ricci, Vincent *Tsars: Russia's Rulers For More Than One Thousand Years* (Barnes & Noble, 1995)

Fitzpatrick, Sheila *The Russian Revolution* (Oxford University Press, 1994)

Hingley, Ronald *The Tsars, 1533-1917* (Macmillan, 1968)

Massey, Robert *Nicholas and Alexandra* (Atheneum, 1967)

Warth, Robert *Nicholas II: The Life and Reign of Russia's Last Monarch* (Praeger, 1997)

RUSSIA IN FILM AND LITERATURE

A fictionalized account of Ivan the Terrible's life is provided in Larry Townsend's novel *Tsar!* Count Alexei Konstantinovich Tolstoy, distant relative of the classic Russian writer Leo Tolstoy, dabbled twice in Ivan the Terrible's life: once with the historical novel *Prince Serebryani*, another with the play *The Death of Ivan The Terrible*. Celebrated Soviet film-maker Sergei Eisenstein directed 1945's *Ivan The Terrible Parts 1 and 2*, films which are considered as being among his best work (Eisenstein died before Part 3 could be completed).

Alexei Tolstoy also wrote a drama about Fyodor I, as part of a trilogy that includes *The Death of Ivan the Terrible*.

Peter the Great was the subject of a 1986 BBC mini-series. The ugly relationship between Peter and his son Alexis became the topic for *Antikhrist*, a novel by Dmitry Merezhkovsky whose English title is *Peter and Alexis*.

Peter III was portrayed by Sam Jaffe in 1934's *The Scarlet Empress* alongside Marlene Dietrich's Catherine the Great. The early life of Catherine the Great, beginning with Peter's engagement to her and ending with the coup that led to the death of Peter, is shown in a

1991 television film, *Young Catherine*.

A 1971 film, *Nicholas and Alexandra*, begins with the birth of Alexis and ends with the Romanov family's brutal assassination. Robert Alexander's novel, *Kitchen Boy*, describes the last days of the Romanov family through the eyes of their young servant Leonka. Nicholas II's story also features in a 1974 BBC mini-series, *A Fall of Eagles*, which describes the falls of the Romanovs, the Hohenzollerns, and the Habsburgs. Rasputin himself was the star of a Hammer Studios horror film, *Rasputin: The Mad Monk*, as well as a television movie made in 1996 titled *Rasputin: Dark Servant of Destiny*. Meanwhile the persistent hope that Anastasia survived the murders is addressed in 1953's *Anastasia*, starring Ingrid Bergman, and in a 1997 animated film, also titled *Anastasia*.

INDEX

Abdul Aziz, Ottoman sultan 508–12
Abdul Mejid, Ottoman sultan 509
Abukir Bay, battle of 202
Afonso VI, king of Portugal 119–20
Agincourt, battle of 154
Agreda, Sister Mary de 123
Agrippa, Vispania 11
Agrippina the Elder 25, 41
  banishment of 19, 21, 42
  feud with Tiberius 16–17, 18, 21–2, 27–8
  death of 29, 30–1
Agrippina the Younger 35–6, 41–2, 43
  murdered by Nero 46–7, 485
  poisons Claudius 44
Ahenobarbus, Gnaeus Domitius 41–2
Ahmed I, Ottoman sultan 497, 500
Albuquerque, João Afonso de 90, 91, 92
Alençon, duke of 166, 168, 169–71
Alexander I, tsar of Russia 212, 216, 217, 219, 563–7
Alexander II, tsar of Russia 569, 571
Alexander III, tsar of Russia 568–70
Alexander VI, pope *see* Borgia, Rodrigo
Alexander the Great 67–8
Alexander Obrenovic V, king of Serbia 467–9
Alexandra, tsarina of Nicholas II 569–70, 572–9, 584–8
Alexis, tsar of Russia 533
Alexis (Romanov), tsarevitch 574–7, 584, 586–8
Alexis (son of Peter I), tsarevitch 540–2
Alfhere 229
Alfonso IV, king of Aragon 86
Alfonso XI, king of Castile 89
America 181–2, 211, 319, 323–4
Anastasia, grand duchess of Russia 573, 587–9
Anastasia Romanova, tsarina of Ivan IV 521, 522–3, 529
Andre, king of Naples 401–3
Anicetus 47
Annabella, queen of Scotland 259
Anna, empress of Russia 545–50
Anne of Bohemia, queen of England 263
Anne Boleyn, queen of England 289, 290–5, 303–5, 312, 331
Anne of Brittany, queen of France 99, 412, 428
Anne of Cleves, queen of England 298
Anne Marie Francesca, grand duchess of Tuscany 442–3
Anne Neville, queen of Richard III 278, 281, 284
Antoine de Bourbon, duc de Vendôme 163–4
Antonia (daughter of Claudius) 50
Antonia (mother of Livilla) 20, 21, 25, 28–9, 31–2
Antony, Mark 9, 25, 41
Arthur, duke of Brittany 244, 245, 247, 330
Arthur, prince 287, 289, 290, 293
Aske, Robert 296
Audovera, Frankish queen 144–5
Augusta of Saxe-Coburg 320
Augustus, Octavianus, emperor of Rome 6–7, 9–14, 15, 25, 37, 41
Avni, Hussein 511–12

Bannockburn, battle of 255
Barbara de Braganza, queen of Spain 136
Barras, Paul François de 198, 204
Basil II, emperor of Rome 493
Bathory, Christopher, prince of Transylvania 458
Bathory, Elizabeth 457–64, 471
Bathory, Gabor, prince of Transylvania 465–70
Bathory, Stephen, prince of Transylvania 456, 458, 527
Beaufort, Henry, cardinal 268, 269, 270
Beauharnais, Eugène 198, 199
Beauharnais, Hortense 209, 220
Beauharnais, Joséphine de 198–211, 215, 219
Becket, Thomas 296
Bedford, John, duke of 268
Biron, Ernst Johann von 547–8
Bisceglie, Alfonso de 411–12, 427, 428–30
Bismarck, Otto von 391
Blanche de Bourbon, queen of Castile 90, 91, 92
Blois, Stephen de 238
Bogdan II, prince of Moldavia 452
Boleslaus, king of Poland 516
Bonaparte family 206–10, 214, 216, 218–19
Bonaparte, Caroline 206, 209–10, 214, 218, 219
Bonaparte, Charles Louis 209
Bonaparte, Elisa 206
Bonaparte, Jerome 206–7, 210, 214, 218
Bonaparte, Joseph 196, 199, 200–1, 202, 203, 206–8, 214, 216, 218–19
Bonaparte, Letizia 195, 196, 199, 206, 209
Bonaparte, Louis 206, 209, 216, 218
Bonaparte, Lucien 197, 204–5, 206, 208–9, 214
Bonaparte, Napoleon *see* Napoleon I
Bonaparte, Napoleon François 216
Bonaparte, Napoleon Louis Charles 207, 209, 215
Bonaparte, Pauline 206
Borgia, Cesare 406–20, 422, 423, 425–7, 429–30, 431–2, 447
Borgia, Jofre 422, 428
Borgia, Juan 407, 410–11, 422
Borgia, Lucrezia 407, 411–12, 415–16, 419, 421–33, 447
Borgia, Rodrigo 406–13, 415, 416–17, 421–30, 431
Bosworth, battle of 284

Boudicca 47
Bouillé, Marquis de 188
Brancovic, Vuc 456
Britannicus, Tiberius Claudius Caesar 42, 43, 44, 46
Brunhilde, queen of Austrasia 145–7, 149
Brutus, Lucius Junius 6
Buckingham, Henry Stafford, duke of 281, 283
Burrus (Praetorian prefect) 45

Caesar, Germanicus 15–17, 22, 25–7, 30
Caesar, Julius 8–9, 25, 37
Caesonia, Milonia 35, 38
Caligula, emperor of Rome 20, 22, 23, 24–6, 28–38, 41, 42, 73–4
Calixtus III, pope 412, 422
Canute, king of England 231
Caracalla, emperor of Rome 66–8, 69
Carlo, king of Naples 405
Carlos II, king of Spain 107, 122–8, 129–30, 142
Carlos III, king of Spain 134, 135–6
Carlos IV, king of Spain 208, 213
Caroline of Ansbach, queen of Great Britain 320
Caroline of Brunswick, queen of Great Britain 325
Caroline Matilda, queen of Denmark 323, 327, 353–5, 356–61, 363
Castelo Melhor, count of 119–20
Catalina, queen of Portugal 105, 106, 109
Catherine of Aragon, queen of England 287–91, 292, 293, 303–5
Catherine de' Medici, queen of France 156–72, 173–4, 175, 222
Catherine de Valois, queen of England 155
Catherine the Great, tsarina of Russia 381–2, 550, 551–8, 559–64
Catherine Skavronskaya, empress of Russia 535, 539, 543, 545
Charlemagne, king of the Franks 161, 491–2
Charles, duke of Guise 171–2, 175–6
Charles, Hippolyte 200, 201, 202
Charles IV, Holy Roman emperor 367
Charles V, Holy Roman emperor 289, 300, 308–9, 313, 317, 342, 345
  appearance 109
  appointed emperor 104–6
  retirement 107
Charles V, king of France 87–8
Charles VI, king of France 150–5, 222, 267
Charles VII, king of France 154, 268–9, 272
Charles VIII, king of France 408–10, 412, 425–6, 428
Charles IX, king of France 162, 163, 166, 168, 170, 174
Charles X, king of France 184
Charlotte d'Albret, princess of Navarre 413
Charlotte Sophia, queen of Great Britain 321–2, 326, 328

Childebert II, king of Austrasia 146, 148, 149
Chilperic, king of Neustria 144–8
Chosroes, king of Persia 474, 475
Christian II, king of Denmark and Norway 341–6
Christian VII, king of Denmark 323, 352–62
Clarence, George, duke of 278–9
Claudius, emperor of Rome 38–9, 42, 44, 73
Clement VI, pope 403, 404
Clement VII, pope 157, 158, 289, 291, 297
Cleves, Marie de 174–5
Clovis, Frankish king 144
Coligny, Admiral de 166, 167
Collatinus, Lucius 5
Commodus 60–5, 74
Condé, Louis I de Bourbon, prince de 162, 163, 167–8
Constance of Brittany 245, 247
Constans, Byzantine emperor 478
Constantine IV, Byzantine emperor 476
Constantine V, Byzantine emperor 485
Constantine VI, Byzantine emperor 486–9
Constantine VIII, Byzantine emperor 491–4
Cosimo III *see* Medici, Cosimo III de'
Cranmer, Thomas, archbishop of Canterbury 291, 295
Crispus, Gaius 42
Cromwell, Thomas 290, 291, 292, 294, 296, 298–9
Culpeper, Thomas 299–300

Darvulia, Anna 459–60, 461, 463
David II, king of Scotland 258
Despenser, Hugh (father and son) 255, 256
d'Este, Alfonso 429–30, 432
Dmitry, tsarevitch 522, 529, 530
Domitia Longina 57–8, 74
Domitian, emperor of Rome 54–9, 74
Don Carlos, prince of the Asturias 114–18, 141–2
Drusilla (daughter of Caligula) 35, 38
Drusilla (sister of Caligula) 29, 34, 35
Drusus, Nero Claudius 9–10, 11
Drusus (son of Germanicus) 18, 19, 22, 28, 29, 31
Drusus (son of Tiberius) 9–10, 17–18, 21
Duncan, king of Scotland 232
Durazzo, Carlo, duke of 401, 403–4

Eadred, English king 335, 336
Edgar, English king 229
Edward I, king of England 252, 253–4
Edward II, king of England 252–7, 330–1
Edward III, king of England 150, 154, 256, 257, 261
Edward IV, king of England 272, 273–6, 277–9, 280–1
Edward V, king of England 279, 280–2, 283

Edward VI, king of England 297, 301, 306, 307, 309
Edward, St, king of England 229
Edward the Confessor, king of England 231, 232
Edward the Black Prince 94, 261
Egica, Visigoth king 76–8
Elagabalus, emperor of Rome 66, 69–72, 74
Eleanor of Aquitaine, queen of England 243, 244, 247, 330
Elfrida (mother of Ethelred II) 229
Elizabeth Christine, queen of Prussia 381
Elizabeth de Valois, queen of Spain 116, 160, 164
Elizabeth Farnese of Parma, queen of Spain 131–2, 133–4, 135
Elizabeth I, queen of England 113, 292
  accession of 162
  declared a bastard 295, 309
  as heir to throne 293, 303–5, 316, 317–18
  life under Mary 312–16
  suitors of 166, 168, 348–9
  supports Huguenots 163
Elizabeth Mure, queen of Scotland 259
Elizabeth Petrovna, tsarina of Russia 549, 551, 552, 555–6, 559–60
Elizabeth of Poland 401–2
Elizabeth (sister of Louis XVI) 187, 192, 193
Elizabeth Woodville, queen of Edward IV 275, 278–81, 283–4
Emma of Normandy, queen of Canute 231
Enrique II, king of Castile 87, 89, 92, 93–4
Epaphroditus (slave) 52, 58
Erik XIV, king of Sweden 347–51, 363
Erik Bloodaxe, king of Norway 334–6, 363
Ernest Augustus, king of Hanover 322
Erwig, Visigoth king 76, 77
Ethelred II ('the Unready'), king of England 228–31
Euphemia of Ross, queen of Scotland 259
Evelyn, John 537–8
Eystein II, king of Norway 339

Fadrique, prince of Castile 89, 92, 93
Farsen, Hans Axel von 188, 189, 191, 192, 193, 223
Federigo, king of Naples 412, 413
Ferdinand, emperor of Austria 383–6
Ferdinand V, king of Aragon 94, 96–7, 99, 102–4, 419
Fernandino II, grand duke of Tuscany 434–6
Fernando VI, king of Spain 134, 135–6
Fernando VII, king of Spain 213, 218
Fernando, prince of Aragon 86–7
Ferrante, king of Naples 408, 425
Fonseca, bishop 100
Fourès, Pauline 203
Fra Diego 115–16
François I, king of France 158, 159
François II, king of France 158, 159, 161, 162
Franz Josef I, emperor of Austria 215, 219, 385
Franz II, emperor of Austria 383–4
Franz Ferdinand, archduke 578
Fredegund, Frankish queen 144–9
Frederick I, king of Denmark 345, 346
Frederick V, king of Denmark 352
Frederick VI, king of Denmark 354, 357, 361–2
Frederick, prince of Wales 319–20
French Revolution 186–94, 197–8, 204
Friedland, battle of 212
Friedrich I, king of Prussia 375–6
Friedrich II ('the Great'), king of Prussia 379–82, 397, 556
Friedrich Wilhelm I, king of Prussia 375–82, 397
Friedrich Wilhelm III, king of Prussia 211
Fyodor I, tsar of Russia 522, 529–30
Fyodor III, tsar of Russia 533

Gaius (son of Julia) 11, 12, 13
Galba, emperor of Rome 51, 52, 55
Galswinth, Frankish queen 145
Gapon, George 572–3
Gaveston, Piers 253–5, 330
Geoffrey, count of Anjou 238
Geoffrey, duke of Brittany 243, 244
George II, king of Great Britain 320–1, 378
George III, king of Great Britain 319–28, 331, 356, 361
  loss of America 319, 323–4
  madness of 139, 325–8
George IV, king of Great Britain 322, 325, 326–7, 328
George V, king of Great Britain 585
Germaine de Foix, queen of Aragon 104
Geta, emperor of Rome 67–8
Gian Gastone *see* Medici, Gian Gastone de'
Giovanna I, queen of Naples 400–5
Gliabanos, khan of the Khazars 480–1, 483
Gloucester, Humphrey, duke of 268, 269–70
Godunov, Boris, tsar of Russia 530–1
Gordon, George 324
Grey, Lady Jane 309, 310, 311
Gruffydd, Rhys ap 257
Gudden, Bernard von 387, 394–6
Guesclin, Bertrand du 94
Gundling, Jakob Paul von 377–8
Gustav I Vasa, king of Sweden 343, 344, 345, 347–8
Gustavus III, king of Sweden 188
Guzman, Leonor de 89, 90

Haäkon, king of Norway 335
Habsburg family 107, 108–9, 114–15, 122–3, 370, 383
al-Hajjaj, Ibrahim ben 80–1
al-Hakim, Ibn 83
Harald 'Fair-Hair', king of Norway 334, 335

Harald IV ('Gilchrist'), king of Norway 337–9
Heinrich V, Holy Roman emperor 238
Heinrich VI, Holy Roman emperor 245
Henri II, king of France 158–61
Henri III, king of France 166, 168–9, 171–2, 173–6, 222
Henri IV, king of France 164–6, 167–72
Henri, duke of Guise 163–4, 167
Henrique, king of Portugal 109, 111, 112
Henry I, king of England 235, 236, 238
Henry II, king of England 239, 240, 242, 243–4, 330
Henry III, king of England 251
Henry IV, king of England 260, 263, 264–6, 267, 331
Henry V, king of England 154, 267–8
Henry VI, king of England 155, 267–76, 278
Henry VII, king of England 282–4, 287, 288, 289
Henry VIII, king of England 286–301, 303–6, 331
  break with Rome 291–2
  dissolution of monasteries 296
  excommunication 297–8
  death 307
Henry 'the Young King' 243, 244
Heraklios, emperor of Rome 475–6
Herod Agrippa, king of Judea 37
Huguenots 161–4, 166–8, 170–1
Hundred Years' War 88, 150, 154, 261, 263, 272
Hunyady, János 451, 452
Hussite Revolution 366, 368–9

Ibn al-Hakim 83
Ibn Muhammad, Abdallah 79–81
Ibrahim, Ottoman sultan 503–7
Inge Crookback, king of Norway 339
Innocent III, pope 248–9, 250–1
Irene, St, Byzantine empress 485–91, 513
Irina Romanov, tsarina of Fyodor I 530
Isabeau of Bavaria, queen of France 151–5
Isabel of Angoulême, queen of England 246
Isabel of Castile, queen of Christian II 342, 345
Isabella I, queen of Castile 94, 96–7, 99–100, 101–2, 418
Isabelle of France, queen of England 254, 256, 257
Isabelle of Gloucester, queen of England 246
Ivan IV ('the Terrible'), tsar of Russia 518–28, 529–30, 538, 567
  character 520, 523–4, 527
  marriages 521, 522–3
  oprichniki of 525–6
  retirements 524–5, 527
Ivan V, tsar of Russia 533, 535, 544
Ivan VI, tsar of Russia 548–9, 551, 562
Ivan, tsarevitch 522, 527–8, 529

Jaime III, king of Majorca 86
Jaime IV, king of Majorca 404–5
Jaime, prince of Aragon 86
James I, king of Scotland 260
James II (VII of Scotland), king of England 323
James IV, king of Scotland 288
Jane Seymour, queen of England 293, 295, 297, 301, 306
Jean the Fearless, duke of Burgundy 154
Jeanne de Valois, queen of France 412, 428
Jeanne of Navarre 164–5
Jena, battle of 211
Joan of Arc 268
Joan of Kent, queen of England 261
Johan III, king of Sweden 349, 351
John, king of England 241–51, 253, 330
John IV, duke of Brittany 151
João III, king of Portugal 108, 109
João IV, king of Portugal 119
João VI, king of Portugal 139
José I, king of Portugal 138–9
Joseph II, Holy Roman emperor 179
Joséphine, empress of Napoleon I *see* Beauharnais, Joséphine de
Jourdan, Nicholas 186
Juana de Castro 92
Juana 'the Mad', queen of Castile 95–107, 109, 123, 141
Julia (daughter of Augustus) 11, 12–13, 25
Julia Domna 66, 69
Julia Drusilla (sister of Caligula) 29, 34, 35–6, 37
Julia Livilla Minor (sister of Caligula) 35–6
Julia Maesa 69–70, 71
Juliana of Brunswick, queen of Denmark 353, 359–61
Julius II, pope 417–19, 432
Junia (wife of Caligula) 29
Junot, Jean-Andoche 213
Justinian II, emperor of Rome 476, 477–84, 486, 513

Karin Månsdotter, queen of Erik XIV 349, 351
Katherine Howard, queen of England 298, 299–300
Katherine Parr, queen of England 300–1, 306
Katte, Hans Hermann von 380–1
Kerensky, Alexander 583–6
Kiusem, Ottoman regent 497–8, 500–1, 503–6
Krumau, Julius Caesar, duke of 372–4

Laetus 64
Lajos I, king of Hungary 403–4, 405
Lajos II, king of Hungary 457–8
La Motte, countess de 185, 223
Lancaster, John of Gaunt, duke of 263, 264
Landeric (Mayor) 148
Langton, Stephen, archbishop of Canterbury 248

le Brun, Hugh 246–7
Leipzig, battle of 218
Lenin, Vladimir Ilich 583, 585, 586
Leo III, emperor of Rome 486
Leo IV, emperor of Rome 486–7
Leo III, pope 490
Leonor, queen of Aragon 86
Leontios, emperor of Rome 479–80
Lepida, Domitia 42, 44
Lepidus, Marcus Aemilius 35
Leuben, Treaty of 201
Livia, Drusilla 8, 9, 10–11, 13, 15, 16, 19, 28
Livilla (sister of Caligula) 35–6
Livilla (wife of Drusus) 17, 18, 21
Longchamp, Hugh, bishop of Ely 244
Lothair II, king of Austrasia 148, 149
Louis VIII, king of France 251
Louis XII, king of France 99, 412, 428
Louis XIV, king of France 125, 126, 130, 178, 436, 443
Louis XV, king of France 133, 178, 180, 356
Louis XVI, king of France 177–93, 197, 223, 324
'Louis XVII' (Louis Charles) 179–80, 187, 192–4
Louis XVIII, king of France 218, 219, 220
Louis, dauphin of France 178
Louis, duke of Orléans 151, 152, 154
Louisa of Hanover, queen of Denmark 352–3
Louise de Vaudemont, queen of France 175
Louise Elizabeth, queen of Spain 132–3
Lucilla (sister of Commodus) 62
Lucius (son of Julia) 11, 12, 13
Lucius III, pope 243
Lucretia: Sextus's rape of 5–6
Ludovico, king of Naples 402–3, 404
Ludwig I, king of Bavaria 387–8
Ludwig II, king of Bavaria 387–96, 397
  love of Wagner 388–91, 392
  palaces of 392–4, 396
'Ludwig III', king of Bavaria 396
Luis I, king of Spain 132–3
Luisa de Guzman, queen of Portugal 119
Luther, Martin 345

Macbeth, king of Scotland 232–3, 330
Macrinus, emperor of Rome 68, 69, 70
Macro (Praetorian prefect) 22, 30, 33
Maelgwyn, king of Gwynedd 226–7
Magna Carta 242, 250–1
Magnus III ('Barefoot'), king of Norway 337, 338
Magnus IV ('the Blind'), king of Norway 338, 339
Mahomet II, Ottoman sultan 454
Mahomet III, Ottoman sultan 497
Malcolm I, king of Scotland 336
Malcolm III, king of Scotland 232–3
Maldon, battle of 229
el-Malek, 'Abd 111–12
Marcus Aurelius 60, 61, 67
Margaret of Anjou, queen of England 269–76
Margeurite de Valois, queen of France 164–6
Marguerite Louise, grand duchess of Tuscany 435–7, 438, 442
Maria I, queen of Portugal 138–40
Maria Anna, empress of Austria 384, 385
Maria Ann of Neuburg, queen of Spain 126–7
Maria Miloslavsky, tsarina of Peter I 533
Maria Nagaya, tsarina of Ivan IV 529
Maria of Portugal, queen of Castile 89, 90, 91–3
Maria of Portugal, queen of Spain 114
Maria of Savoy, queen of Portugal 120
Maria Theresa, empress of Austria 178
Mariana, queen of Spain 123, 124–7
Marie Antoinette, queen of France 177, 178–80, 185–93, 223
Marie de Guise, queen of Scotland 161, 274
Marie, grand duchess of Russia 573
Marie Joseph of Saxe 178
Marie Louise, empress of France 215–16, 219
Marie Louise, queen of Spain 125–6
Marie Louise of Savoy, queen of Spain 130–1
Marie-Thérèse (daughter of Louis XVI) 179, 194
Marie, tsarina of Paul I 564
Marshal, William 239–40, 250, 251
Martin I, pope 479
Mary I, Tudor, queen of England 162, 288, 293, 302–18, 331
  becomes queen 309–10
  declared a bastard 293, 303–5, 307
  marriage 116, 311–13, 314–17
  death 116, 162, 317–18
Mary II, queen of Great Britain 323
Mary Stewart, queen of France 159, 161
Matilda, empress of Heinrich V 238, 239
Matilda, queen of Stephen 239
Matthias, king of Hungary 455, 456
Maurice, Byzantine emperor 474–6
Maximilian I, Holy Roman emperor 96, 97, 388
Maximilian II, Holy Roman emperor 370–1
Medici, Anna Maria de' 436, 446
Medici, Cosimo III de', grand duke of Tuscany 434–40, 442, 444
Medici, Gian Gastone de', grand duke of Tuscany 436, 441–6
Mehmet II, Ottoman sultan 496
Merovec, Frankish prince 146–7
Messalina (wife of Claudius) 42–3
Michael II, tsar of Russia 584, 588
Michael IV, emperor of Rome 495
Milan, Ludovico Sforza, duke of 408, 425, 426
Milan Obrenovic, king of Serbia 468–9
Montholon, Gharreu Tristan de 221
More, Sir Thomas 292, 331
Mortimer, Edmund, 5th earl of March 265
Mortimer, Roger, 1st earl of March 256, 257,

271
Mowbray, Thomas, duke of Norfolk 264
Muhammad II, emir of Granada 82
Muhammad III, emir of Granada 82–3
Muhammad V, emir of Granada 83
Muhammad, Abdallah Ibn 79–81
Muhammad, Mulai 111, 112
al-Mundhir 79–80
Murad II, Ottoman sultan 451, 503
Murad IV, Ottoman sultan 500–2, 513
Murad V, Ottoman sultan 511
Mustafa I, Ottoman sultan 496–9
al-Mutarrif 80

Nádasdy, Ferenc 458–60
Napoleon I, emperor of France 140, 195–221, 223
  abdications 218–19, 220–1
  conquest of Egypt 201–3
  coronation of 206
  'Hundred Days' 219–20
  Russian campaign 216–17
Napoleon III, emperor of France 391, 511
Natalia Naryshkin, tsarina of Peter I 533
Nemours, Treaty of 171
Nero, emperor of Rome 40–53, 74
  kills Poppaea 48
  murders mother 46–7, 485
  overthrown 51–2
Nero (son of Germanicus) 18, 19, 28
Nerva, emperor of Rome 59
Nicholas II, tsar of Russia 568–89
North, Lord 323–4
Northumberland, John Dudley, duke of 308, 309–10
Nymphidius (Praetorian prefect) 51

Octavia (wife of Nero) 46, 47
Odoacer, German chieftain 473
Olga, grand duchess of Russia 573, 588
Orestilla, Livia 35
Orlov, Alexis 557–8, 561
Osman II, Ottoman sultan 497, 498–9, 503
Otho, emperor of Rome 55
Otto IV, Holy Roman emperor 250
Otto, king of Bavaria 388, 395–6

Padilla, Maria de 90–1, 92
Paoli, Pasquale 197
Pasha, Midhat 511
Paulia, Lollia 35
Paul I, tsar of Russia 553, 558, 559–66
Pedro I, 'the Cruel', king of Castile 87, 88, 89–94, 141
Pedro II, king of Spain 120
Pedro III, king of Portugal 139
Pedro IV ('the Ceremonious'), king of Aragon 85–8, 93–4
Perennis (Praetorian prefect) 61–2
Persson, Jöran 350–1
Pertinax, emperor of Rome 64
Peter I ('the Great'), tsar of Russia 532–43, 544–5, 565
Peter II, tsar of Russia 545
Peter III, tsar of Russia 550–8, 559–61
Philip I, king of Castile 96–104
Philip II, king of Spain 109, 110, 112–13, 114–18, 160, 303, 311–17, 371
Philip IV, king of Spain 123, 124
Philip V, king of Spain 127, 129–34, 135
Philippe II, king of France 244, 245, 246–7, 249, 250
Philippikos, emperor of Rome 483
Phokas, emperor of the Romans 473–6
Pilgrimage of Grace 296
Piso, Gnaeus 16, 17, 26, 27, 49–50
Pius III, pope 417
Pius IV, pope 201
Pius VII, pope 206
Plancina (wife of Gnaeus Piso) 16, 27
Plautianus (Praetorian prefect) 66–7
Plessen, Madame von 354–5
Poitiers, Diane de 158, 159–60, 161, 222
Pombal, marquis of 138–9
Pompeianus, Claudius 62
Pompilius, Sextus 9
Poppaea Sabina, empress of Rome 46, 47, 48, 74
Portsmouth, Treaty of 572
Postumus, Agrippa 13, 14
Princip, Gabriel 578

Radu, prince of Wallachia 450, 454, 456
al-Rahman, 'Abd 79
Rasputin, Grigory 575–7, 580–2
Richard I, king of England 242, 243–5
Richard II, king of England 261–6, 331
Richard III, king of England 277–85, 331
  as princes' custodian 280
  princes' murder 281–2, 283
  death at Bosworth 284
Richmond, Henry Fitzroy, duke of 288, 295
Robert, duke of Albany 258, 259–60
Robert II, king of Scotland 258
Robert III, king of Scotland 258–60
Robert Bruce, king of Scots 255
Robert Curthose, duke of Normandy 234, 235
Robert de Vere, earl of Oxford 263
Robert, earl of Gloucester 238–9
Roberto, king of Naples 401
Robespierre, Augustine 198
Robespierre, Maximilien 190, 194, 198
Roger-Ducos, Pierre 205
Rohan, Cardinal de 185
Romanos II, Byzantine emperor 492–3
Romanos III, Byzantine emperor 495
Romanov family 573–4, 584–9

Romanov, Nikita 530
Romulus Augustulus, emperor of Rome 473
Roosevelt, Theodore 572
Roses, Wars of the 273–6, 278
Rovere, Giuliano della *see* Julius II
Rovere, Vittoria della 433–4
Rudolf II, Holy Roman emperor 370–4, 397
Ruprecht III, Holy Roman emperor 368
Russian Revolution 575, 583–9
Russo-Japanese War 571–2, 574

Sachir Para (harem girl) 506–7
St Bartholomew's Day Massacre 167
Saturninus, Antoninus 58
Sebastian, king of Portugal 108–13, 141
Sejanus 17–18, 19, 20–1, 28–9
Seneca 43–4, 45, 49–50
Sergius I, pope 478–9
Servius Tullius, king of Rome 3, 4
Severus, emperor of Rome 66
Sextus V, pope 171
Sforza, Giovanni 423, 424, 425–6
Sheremetova, Elena 527
Sieyès, Emmanuele 204, 205
Sigibert, king of Austrasia 145, 146
Sigismund, king of Hungary 367, 451
Sigurd I, king of Norway 338
Sigurd II, king of Norway 339
Sigurd Slembediakn 338–9
Silius, Gaius 43
Simeon Bakbulatovich, 'tsar' of Russia 527
Simon of Sudbury, archbishop of Canterbury 262
Somerset, Edmund Beaufort, duke of 272, 273
Somerset, Edward Seymour, duke of 307, 308
Sophia Dorothea, queen of Prussia 378, 380
Spanish Succession, War of the 128, 131, 132
Stephen, king of England 237–40
Stephen, king of Poland 458
Stephen, prince of Moldavia 456
Stockholm Massacre 343–5
Struensee, Johann Friedrich 323, 355, 356–62, 363
Sture, Sten 343, 344
Süleyman, Ottoman sultan 458
Sven I, king of Denmark 230–1
Sviatopolk, grand prince of Kiev 515–17

Talleyrand-Périgord, Maurice de 211, 213, 215, 218, 221
Tarquin, Lucius ('the Proud') 2–7
Tarquin, Sextus 4–6
Tatiana, grand duchess 573, 588
Tello, prince of Castile 90, 92
Thomas of Lancaster 254, 255
Thomas of Woodstock, duke of Gloucester 263, 264
Three Henris, War of the 171–2
Three Kings, battle of the 111–12
Tiberius, emperor of Rome 8–23, 26–30, 31, 54–5, 73
Tiberius II, emperor of Rome 480, 482
Tiberius, Gemellus 17, 22, 30, 32
Titus, emperor of Rome 55
Tours, Treaty of 155
Trolle, Gustav, archbishop 343–4
Tryggvason, Olaf 229–30
Tullia (daughter of Servius) 3–4, 5, 6
Tyler, Wat 262

Újváry, János 459, 460, 463
Utrecht, Treaty of 131, 134

Vasily III, grand prince of Moscovy 519
Vespasian, emperor of Rome 52, 55
Victoria, queen of Great Britain 103, 511, 570, 574
Vindex, General 51
Visigoths 76–8
Vitellius, emperor of Rome 55
Vlad II ('Dracul') 450, 451
Vlad III ('the Impaler') 449–56, 471
Vladimir, grand prince of Kiev 515–16

Wagner, Richard 388–90, 393–4
Walter of Coutances, archbishop of Rouen 244
Warwick, Richard Neville, earl of 274, 275, 278
Waterloo, Battle of 220
Wellington, Arthur Wellesley, 1st duke of 220
Wenceslas IV, Holy Roman emperor 153–4, 366–9
Wilhelm I, king of Prussia 391
Wilhelm II, German emperor 570, 571, 578–9
Wilhelmina, princess of Prussia 379–81
William de Briouze 250
William I ('the Conqueror'), king of England 234–5
William II ('Rufus'), king of England 234–6
William III, king of Great Britain 127, 130, 131, 323
Willis, Dr Francis 139, 327
Wolsey, Cardinal 288–90
Woodville family 278–9, 284
Woodville, Elizabeth, princess 282, 283, 284
Wulfstan, archbishop of York 335–6
Wyatt, Sir Thomas 313–14

Xavier, Louis Stanislas *see* Louis XVIII

Yaroslav, grand prince of Kiev 516, 517
'Year of the Four Emperors' 52, 55
Yeltsin, Boris 589
York, Richard, duke of (d.1460) 271–2, 273–4
York, Richard, duke of 279–82, 283
Yussoupov, Felix 580, 581–2